COMPUTER BOOK SERIES FROM IDG

Setting Up An Internet Site For Dummies®, 2nd Edition

Cheat Sheet

W9-BZT-203

Site Information

Write the URL or service address in the second column for each service your Internet site offers.

Service	Address
Home Page URL	
POP Server Address	
List Server Address	
FTP Server URL	
IRC Server Address	
E-Mail Information Server	
Internet BBS Address	
NNTP Server URL	
Gopher URL	

Emergency Contact Information

Type	Contact Name	URL
Police	CERT: Computer Emergency Response Team	http://www.cert.org/
Fire	U.S. Fire Administration	http://www.usfa.fema.gov/
Medical	McAfee Anti-Virus	http://www.mcafee.com/
Network	Access Provider	
Network	Service Provider	
Network	Service Provider	
Family	Mom and Dad	

Useful Keywords for Internet Queries

Use the following terms in searching the Internet for more information:

- ✔ Setting Up an Internet Site
- ✔ Creating an Internet Site
- ✔ Setting Up Shop on the Internet
- ✔ Internet Publishing
- ✔ Providing Information on the Internet
- ✔ Internet Programming
- ✔ WinSock
- ✔ MacTCP
- ✔ Internet Commerce
- ✔ Internet Security
- ✔ Internet Servers
- ✔ Server Software
- ✔ Internet Advertising
- ✔ Internet Presence

...For Dummies: #1 Computer Book Series for Beginners

Setting Up An Internet Site For Dummies®, 2nd Edition

Cheat Sheet

Domain Information

Write the indicated reference information for your Internet domain in the second column.

Domain Name _____

IP Address _____

Primary DNS Server _____

Secondary DNS Server _____

Technical Contact Name _____

Technical Contact E-Mail Address _____

Technical Contact NIC Handle _____

Administrative Contact Name _____

Administrative Contact E-Mail Address _____

Administrative Contact NIC Handle _____

Billing Contact Name _____

Billing Contact E-Mail Address _____

Billing Contact NIC Handle _____

SMTP Relay Host _____

Default Internet Gateway _____

Resources for Site Developers

Resource	URL
SCIENCE.ORG Setting Up An Internet Site page	http://computers.science.org/internet/site/setup/
Web66 Internet Server Cookbook	http://web66.coled.umn.edu/Cookbook/
Apple and the Internet	http://applenet.apple.com/
Building Internet Servers	http://www.cybergroup.com/html/servers.html
WinHTTPd/WebSite Central	http://website.ora.com/
MacHTTP Home Page	http://www.starnine.com/software/
WinSMTP Home Page	http://www.seattlelab.com/
Internet Servers via MacOS	http://www.pism.com/
The InterNIC	http://www.internic.net/

...For Dummies: #1 Computer Book Series for Beginners

COMPUTER BOOK SERIES FROM IDG

References for the Rest of Us!®

Are you intimidated and confused by computers? Do you find that traditional manuals are overloaded with technical details you'll never use? Do your friends and family always call you to fix simple problems on their PCs? Then the ...*For Dummies*® computer book series from IDG Books Worldwide is for you.

...*For Dummies* books are written for those frustrated computer users who know they aren't really dumb but find that PC hardware, software, and indeed the unique vocabulary of computing make them feel helpless. ...*For Dummies* books use a lighthearted approach, a down-to-earth style, and even cartoons and humorous icons to diffuse computer novices' fears and build their confidence. Lighthearted but not lightweight, these books are a perfect survival guide for anyone forced to use a computer.

> *"I like my copy so much I told friends; now they bought copies."*
> **Irene C., Orwell, Ohio**

> *"Quick, concise, nontechnical, and humorous."*
> **Jay A., Elburn, Illinois**

> *"Thanks, I needed this book. Now I can sleep at night."*
> **Robin F., British Columbia, Canada**

Already, hundreds of thousands of satisfied readers agree. They have made ...*For Dummies* books the #1 introductory level computer book series and have written asking for more. So, if you're looking for the most fun and easy way to learn about computers, look to ...*For Dummies* books to give you a helping hand.

SETTING UP AN INTERNET SITE FOR DUMMIES®

2ND EDITION

by Jason Coombs and Ted Coombs

IDG Books Worldwide, Inc.
An International Data Group Company

Foster City, CA ♦ Chicago, IL ♦ Indianapolis, IN ♦ Southlake, TX

Setting Up An Internet Site For Dummies®, 2nd Edition

Published by
IDG Books Worldwide, Inc.
An International Data Group Company
919 E. Hillsdale Blvd.
Suite 400
Foster City, CA 94404
http://www.idgbooks.com (IDG Books Worldwide Web site)
http://www.dummies.com (Dummies Press Web site)

Library of Congress Catalog Card No.: 97-70366

ISBN: 0-7645-0115-1

Printed in the United States of America

10 9 8 7 6 5 4 3 2 1

1O/RV/QV/ZX/IN

Distributed in the United States by IDG Books Worldwide, Inc.

Distributed by Macmillan Canada for Canada; by Transworld Publishers Limited in the United Kingdom and Europe; by WoodsLane Pty. Ltd. for Australia; by WoodsLane Enterprises Ltd. for New Zealand; by Longman Singapore Publishers Ltd. for Singapore, Malaysia, Thailand, and Indonesia; by Simron Pty. Ltd. for South Africa; by Toppan Company Ltd. for Japan; by Distribuidora Cuspide for Argentina; by Livraria Cultura for Brazil; by Ediciencia S.A. for Ecuador; by Addison-Wesley Publishing Company for Korea; by Ediciones ZETA S.C.R. Ltda. for Peru; by WS Computer Publishing Company, Inc., for the Philippines; by Unalis Corporation for Taiwan; by Contemporanea de Ediciones for Venezuela. Authorized Sales Agent: Anthony Rudkin Associates for the Middle East and North Africa.

For general information on IDG Books Worldwide's books in the U.S., please call our Consumer Customer Service department at 800-762-2974. For reseller information, including discounts and premium sales, please call our Reseller Customer Service department at 800-434-3422.

For information on where to purchase IDG Books Worldwide's books outside the U.S., please contact our International Sales department at 415-655-3023 or fax 415-655-3299.

For information on foreign language translations, please contact our Foreign & Subsidiary Rights department at 415-655-3021 or fax 415-655-3281.

For sales inquiries and special prices for bulk quantities, please contact our Sales department at 415-655-3200 or write to the address above.

For information on using IDG Books Worldwide's books in the classroom or for ordering examination copies, please contact our Educational Sales department at 800-434-2086 or fax 817-251-8174.

For press review copies, author interviews, or other publicity information, please contact our Public Relations department at 415-655-3000 or fax 415-655-3299.

For authorization to photocopy items for corporate, personal, or educational use, please contact Copyright Clearance Center, 222 Rosewood Drive, Danvers, MA 01923, or fax 508-750-4470.

 is a trademark under exclusive license to IDG Books Worldwide, Inc., from International Data Group, Inc.

About the Authors

Jason Coombs (jasonc@science.org) and **Ted Coombs** (tedc@science.org) lead an independent research and development laboratory called science.org (located on the World Wide Web at http://www.science.org/). Together, they've cowritten six books about computer technology, including three in the ...*For Dummies* series published by IDG Books Worldwide, Inc. (http://www.dummies.com/) and numerous magazine articles. When not writing, Ted and Jason relentlessly pursue scientific and technical innovation and attend college to work toward their doctorates. They live and work near the Pacific Ocean in Encinitas, California, where they surf, scuba dive, and ocean kayak with the local dolphins.

Visit the Web home page of Jason Coombs at the following URL:

http://www.science.org/jasonc/

Visit the Web home page of Ted Coombs at the following address:

http://www.science.org/tedc/

(And, yes, in case you're wondering, they're father and son. Ted Coombs is the father, and Jason Coombs is the son. Jason is the first author of this book because he was ranting and raving about writing it way back in 1993, when he was a volunteer at *Wired Magazine*. Working with your father/son is rewarding, the Coombs believe, but is also more challenging than working with other people. Not being able to fire each other creates a certain strength of purpose and dedication to your mission. The alternative to success is less acceptable if your business partner is a cherished family member.)

ABOUT IDG BOOKS WORLDWIDE

Welcome to the world of IDG Books Worldwide.

IDG Books Worldwide, Inc., is a subsidiary of International Data Group, the world's largest publisher of computer-related information and the leading global provider of information services on information technology. IDG was founded more than 25 years ago and now employs more than 8,500 people worldwide. IDG publishes more than 275 computer publications in over 75 countries (see listing below). More than 60 million people read one or more IDG publications each month.

Launched in 1990, IDG Books Worldwide is today the #1 publisher of best-selling computer books in the United States. We are proud to have received eight awards from the Computer Press Association in recognition of editorial excellence and three from *Computer Currents'* First Annual Readers' Choice Awards. Our best-selling *...For Dummies*® series has more than 30 million copies in print with translations in 30 languages. IDG Books Worldwide, through a joint venture with IDG's Hi-Tech Beijing, became the first U.S. publisher to publish a computer book in the People's Republic of China. In record time, IDG Books Worldwide has become the first choice for millions of readers around the world who want to learn how to better manage their businesses.

Our mission is simple: Every one of our books is designed to bring extra value and skill-building instructions to the reader. Our books are written by experts who understand and care about our readers. The knowledge base of our editorial staff comes from years of experience in publishing, education, and journalism — experience we use to produce books for the '90s. In short, we care about books, so we attract the best people. We devote special attention to details such as audience, interior design, use of icons, and illustrations. And because we use an efficient process of authoring, editing, and desktop publishing our books electronically, we can spend more time ensuring superior content and spend less time on the technicalities of making books.

You can count on our commitment to deliver high-quality books at competitive prices on topics you want to read about. At IDG Books Worldwide, we continue in the IDG tradition of delivering quality for more than 25 years. You'll find no better book on a subject than one from IDG Books Worldwide.

John Kilcullen
CEO
IDG Books Worldwide, Inc.

Steven Berkowitz
President and Publisher
IDG Books Worldwide, Inc.

Eighth Annual Computer Press Awards ≥ 1992

Ninth Annual Computer Press Awards ≥ 1993

Tenth Annual Computer Press Awards ≥ 1994

Eleventh Annual Computer Press Awards ≥ 1995

IDG Books Worldwide, Inc., is a subsidiary of International Data Group, the world's largest publisher of computer-related information and the leading global provider of information services on information technology. International Data Group publishes over 275 computer publications in over 75 countries. Sixty million people read one or more International Data Group publications each month. International Data Group's publications include: **ARGENTINA:** Buyer's Guide, Computerworld Argentina, PC World Argentina; **AUSTRALIA:** Australian Macworld, Australian PC World, Australian Reseller News, Computerworld, IT Casebook, Network World, Publish, Webmaster; **AUSTRIA:** Computerwelt Österreich, Networks Austria, PC Tip Austria; **BANGLADESH:** PC World Bangladesh; **BELARUS:** PC World Belarus; **BELGIUM:** Data News; **BRAZIL:** Annuário de Informática, Computerworld, Connections, Macworld, PC Player, PC World, Publish, Reseller News, Supergamepower; **BULGARIA:** Computerworld Bulgaria, Network World Bulgaria, PC & MacWorld Bulgaria; **CANADA:** CIO Canada, Client/Server World, ComputerWorld Canada, InfoWorld Canada, NetworkWorld Canada, WebWorld; **CHILE:** Computerworld Chile, PC World Chile; **COLOMBIA:** Computerworld Colombia, PC World Colombia; **COSTA RICA:** PC World Centro America; **THE CZECH AND SLOVAK REPUBLICS:** Computerworld Czechoslovakia, Macworld Czech Republic, PC World Czechoslovakia; **DENMARK:** Communications World Danmark, Computerworld Danmark, Macworld Danmark, PC World Danmark, Techworld Denmark; **DOMINICAN REPUBLIC:** PC World Republica Dominicana; **ECUADOR:** PC World Ecuador; **EGYPT:** Computerworld Middle East, PC World Middle East; **EL SALVADOR:** PC World Centro America; **FINLAND:** MikroPC, Tietoverkko, Tietoviikko; **FRANCE:** Distributique, Hebdo, Info PC, Le Monde Informatique, Macworld, Reseaux & Telecoms, WebMaster France; **GERMANY:** Computer Partner, Computerwoche, Computerwoche Extra, Computerwoche FOCUS, Global Online, Macwelt, PC Welt; **GREECE:** Amiga Computing, GamePro Greece, Multimedia World; **GUATEMALA:** PC World Centro America; **HONDURAS:** PC World Centro America; **HONG KONG:** Computerworld Hong Kong, PC World Hong Kong, Publish in Asia; **HUNGARY:** ABCD CD-ROM, Computerworld Szamitastechnika, Internetto online Magazine, PC World Hungary, PC-X Magazin Hungary; **ICELAND:** Tolvuheimur PC World Island; **INDIA:** Information Communications World, Information Systems Computerworld, PC World India, Publish in Asia; **INDONESIA:** InfoKomputer PC World, Komputek Computerworld, Publish in Asia; **IRELAND:** ComputerScope, PC Live!; **ISRAEL:** Macworld Israel, People & Computers/Computerworld; **ITALY:** Computerworld Italia, Macworld Italia, Networking Italia, PC World Italia; **JAPAN:** DTP World, Macworld Japan, Nikkei Personal Computing, OS/2 World Japan, SunWorld Japan, Windows NT World, Windows World Japan; **KENYA:** PC World East African; **KOREA:** Hi-Tech Information, Macworld Korea, PC World Korea; **MACEDONIA:** PC World Macedonia; **MALAYSIA:** Computerworld Malaysia, PC World Malaysia, Publish in Asia; **MALTA:** PC World Malta; **MEXICO:** Computerworld Mexico, PC World Mexico; **MYANMAR:** PC World Myanmar; **NETHERLANDS:** Computer! Totaal, LAN Internetworking Magazine, LAN World Buyers Guide, Macworld Netherlands, Net, WebWereld; **NEW ZEALAND:** Absolute Beginners Guide and Plain & Simple Series, Computer Buyer, Computer Industry Directory, Computerworld New Zealand, MTB, Network World, PC World New Zealand; **NICARAGUA:** PC World Centro America; **NORWAY:** Computerworld Norge, CW Rapport, Datamagasinet, Financial Rapport, Kursguide Norge, Macworld Norge, Multimediaworld Norge, PC World Ekspress Norge, PC World Nettverk, PC World Norge, PC World ProduktGuide Norge; **PAKISTAN:** Computerworld Pakistan; **PANAMA:** PC World Panama; **PEOPLE'S REPUBLIC OF CHINA:** China Computer Users, China Computerworld, China InfoWorld, China Telecom World Weekly, Computer & Communication, Electronic Design China, Electronics Today, Electronics Weekly, Game Software, PC World China, Popular Computer Week, Software Weekly, Software World, Telecom World; **PERU:** Computerworld Peru, PC World Profesional Peru, PC World SoHo Peru; **PHILIPPINES:** Click!, Computerworld Philippines, PC World Philippines, Publish in Asia; **POLAND:** Computerworld Poland, Computerworld Special Report Poland, Cyber, Macworld Poland, Networld Poland, PC World Komputer; **PORTUGAL:** Cerebro/PC World, Computerworld/Correio Informático, Dealer World Portugal, Mac*In/PC*In Portugal, Multimedia World; **PUERTO RICO:** PC World Puerto Rico; **ROMANIA:** Computerworld Romania, PC World Romania, Telecom Romania; **RUSSIA:** Computerworld Russia, Mir PK, Publish, Seti; **SINGAPORE:** Computerworld Singapore, PC World Singapore, Publish in Asia; **SLOVENIA:** Monitor; **SOUTH AFRICA:** Computing SA, Network World SA, Software World SA; **SPAIN:** Communicaciones World España, Computerworld España, Dealer World España, Macworld España, PC World España; **SRI LANKA:** Infolink PC World; **SWEDEN:** CAP&Design, Computer Sweden, Corporate Computing Sweden, Internetworld Sweden, it.branschen, Macworld Sweden, MaxiData Sweden, MikroDatorn, Nätverk & Kommunikation, PC World Sweden, PCaktiv, Windows World Sweden; **SWITZERLAND:** Computerworld Schweiz, Macworld Schweiz, PCtip; **TAIWAN:** Computerworld Taiwan, Macworld Taiwan, NEW ViSION/Publish, PC World Taiwan, Windows World Taiwan; **THAILAND:** Publish in Asia, Thai Computerworld; **TURKEY:** Computerworld Turkiye, Macworld Turkiye, Network World Turkiye, PC World Turkiye; **UKRAINE:** Computerworld Kiev, Multimedia World Ukraine, PC World Ukraine; **UNITED KINGDOM:** Acorn User UK, Amiga Action UK, Amiga Computing UK, Apple Talk UK, Computing, Macworld, Parents and Computers UK, PC Advisor, PC Home, PSX Pro, The WEB; **UNITED STATES:** Cable in the Classroom, CIO Magazine, Computerworld, DOS World, Federal Computer Week, GamePro Magazine, InfoWorld, I-Way, Macworld, Network World, PC Games, PC World, Publish, Video Event, THE WEB Magazine, and WebMaster; online webzines: JavaWorld, NetscapeWorld, and SunWorld Online; **URUGUAY:** InfoWorld Uruguay; **VENEZUELA:** Computerworld Venezuela, PC World Venezuela; and **VIETNAM:** PC World Vietnam.
3/24/97

Authors' Acknowledgments

We want to thank John Hovis and Margaret Delaney for their help in getting this book completed. We also want to thank Kelly Ewing for her tireless enthusiasm for this project, as well as the entire IDG Books editing team. Special thanks to Matt Wagner at Waterside for his excellent representation and the folks at IDG for believing in this book. Thanks, Joyce Pepple, for putting the CD-ROM together. Most important, we'd like to thank the companies that created the excellent products that this book discusses and for making them available on the CD-ROM. Thanks go to Mike Kelly for his enthusiasm for the book's completion. Lastly, we'd like to thank our dog, Flipper, for tearing us away from the computer at dinner time.

Publisher's Acknowledgments

We're proud of this book; please send us your comments about it by using the Reader Response Card at the back of the book or by e-mailing us at feedback/dummies@idgbooks.com. Some of the people who helped bring this book to market include the following:

Acquisitions, Development, and Editorial

Project Editors: Kelly Ewing, Kathy Simpson

Acquisitions Editor: Michael Kelly, Quality Control Manager

Media Development Manager: Joyce Pepple

Associate Permissions Editor: Heather H. Dismore

Copy Editor: William A. Barton

Technical Editor: Mike Lerch

Editorial Manager: Seta K. Frantz

Editorial Assistant: Chris H. Collins

Production

Project Coordinator: Regina Snyder

Layout and Graphics: Linda M. Boyer, J. Tyler Connor, Dominique DeFelice, Brent Savage

Proofreaders: Melissa D. Buddendeck, Ethel Winslow, Rachel Garvey, Nancy Price, Robert Springer

Indexer: Sharon Hilgenberg

Special Help

Colleen Rainsberger; Publication Services, Inc.

General and Administrative

IDG Books Worldwide, Inc.: John Kilcullen, CEO; Steven Berkowitz, President and Publisher

IDG Books Technology Publishing: Brenda McLaughlin, Senior Vice President and Group Publisher

Dummies Technology Press and Dummies Editorial: Diane Graves Steele, Vice President and Associate Publisher; Judith A. Taylor, Brand Manager; Kristin A. Cocks, Editorial Director

Dummies Trade Press: Kathleen A. Welton, Vice President and Publisher; Stacy S. Collins, Brand Manager

IDG Books Production for Dummies Press: Beth Jenkins, Production Director; Cindy L. Phipps, Supervisor of Project Coordination, Production Proofreading, and Indexing; Kathie S. Schutte, Supervisor of Page Layout; Shelley Lea, Supervisor of Graphics and Design; Debbie J. Gates, Production Systems Specialist; Tony Augsburger, Supervisor of Reprints and Bluelines; Leslie Popplewell, Media Archive Coordinator

Dummies Packaging and Book Design: Patti Sandez, Packaging Specialist; Lance Kayser, Packaging Assistant; Kavish + Kavish, Cover Design

◆

The publisher would like to give special thanks to Patrick J. McGovern, without whom this book would not have been possible.

◆

Contents at a Glance

Table of Contents

Introduction

●●

*T*his book — and its associated Internet site at the `science.org` Computer Lab (`http://computers.science.org/`) — shows you everything that you need to know to set up your own Internet site. We believe that you and other site builders are the future of electronic commerce and the Internet. Our mission is to provide the knowledge and skills that you need to build an Internet site and to turn that site into a mission-critical tool for your business.

The best part is that you don't need to learn complex programming languages, spend hours struggling with a technical manual, or even leave the comfortable and familiar environment of your personal computer.

Should You Read This Internet Book?

Setting Up An Internet Site For Dummies, 2nd Edition, is the ideal book for anyone who wants to create a permanent Internet presence for personal or business purposes. Whether you're an experienced (or travel-weary) Internet navigator or just beginning to explore what the Internet can do for you, this book can serve as a valuable guide.

(If you're interested only in creating Web pages, this book is not for you. Instead, purchase *Creating Web Pages For Dummies,* 2nd Edition, by Bud Smith and Arthur Bebak [IDG Books Worldwide, Inc.], or another book that concentrates only on publishing via the World Wide Web. Return to this book after you reach the limits of the Web and need to do more than just publish Web pages.)

Above all, this book is for people who believe that providing interactive resources and doing business on the Internet should be simple, effective, and fun — not technical, time-consuming, and dull. Buy this book if you want to do something with the Internet. (Take a cruise to a tropical island if you're just looking for entertainment.) We designed this book to meet the needs of the following three types of readers:

- ✔ People who already use the Internet and want to turn it into a more useful tool.
- ✔ Anyone who wants to provide information on the Internet for a business or for personal goals.
- ✔ Experienced Web publishers who realize the limitations of the World Wide Web and need to take their Internet sites to the next level.

This book assumes that you're a relatively experienced computer user. We make no attempt to explain files, icons, mouse actions, or any other basic computer concept. If you're new to computers, you need to pick up some basic training before this book makes much sense to you. For that basic training, check out one of the *Windows For Dummies* books by Andy Rathbone or *The Internet For Dummies,* 4th Edition, by John Levine, Carol Baroudi, and Margaret Levine Young (both by IDG Books Worldwide, Inc.).

Organization of This Book

We did organize this book — we promise. In fact, we organized the book well enough to divide its text into parts, chapters, sections, and paragraphs . . . just to keep everything from spilling out all over the place. The following sections describe the five parts that you find in this book.

Part I: Laying the Foundation of an Internet Site

Anyone who builds a physical structure knows that it needs a solid foundation. Setting up an Internet site is no different. The better your foundation, the more effective your site is. Part I guides you away from weak materials and toward those that make your Internet site strong and vibrant.

This part also presents the basic concepts that you need to understand as you prepare to follow the instructions in this book. As a provider of Internet resources, you need to know some things that the average Internet user doesn't. This part also walks you through the first steps that everyone needs to take in setting up an Internet site: getting a domain name and establishing a dedicated connection to the Internet.

Part II: Publishing Information on the Internet

The World Wide Web has become a popular electronic-publishing medium. Web publishing is no longer difficult or mysterious; anyone can publish information on the Web just by using a favorite word processor or simple graphical Web-page editor. Chapters 5 and 6 give you the lowdown on Web publishing. The Internet offers many other efficient and useful means of providing information, such as electronic mailing lists and Internet News. Chapters 7 and 8 cover what you need to publish information by using these particular tools — everything from setting up the software to marketing your service after you set it up.

Part III: Setting Up Basic Internet Services

This part shows you how to set up the most important enabling resources. As you discover throughout this book, good software tools turn your Internet site into something special. The tools that this part covers include File Transfer Protocol (FTP), e-mail service, and Internet BBS and groupware solutions.

Part IV: Site Builder Skills for Today and Tomorrow

Life on the Internet is what you make of it. This part gives you the basic skills that everyone who runs an Internet site needs. Every site developer should know how to obtain publicity for an Internet site and create a secure environment in which to conduct electronic commerce. This part also reveals the important changes shaping the future of the Internet and shows you how to prepare for these changes today.

Part V: The Part of Tens

The Internet is a happenin' place; its software and sites change rapidly and dramatically. This part presents ten important topics that serve as launching pads into other related subjects, plus our ten favorite Internet add-ons and ten things that your Web site can't live without.

Icons Used in This Book

This book has icons in the margins, but don't worry — they're not infectious. Pay attention to these icons, however, because they guide you to specific points that can make your Internet site work, make your work fly, or keep everything from sinking.

If you see this icon, you find in the accompanying text information about the software or hardware that you need to accomplish the tasks that we describe in this book. If you've got the "Right Stuff," you face no limits to what you can accomplish.

This icon suggests ways in which you can use the technology described in this book to start an Internet business. The Internet is an evolving landscape of opportunity. New products and services are always emerging that use Internet technology or that help other users. Many such businesses exist only on the Internet, having no real-world business location.

This icon points out the hidden wisdom of Internet veterans. Next to this icon, you find insights and war stories from the electronic frontier so that you can benefit from the experience of others.

Watch out — the Information Superhighway is still under construction, and it has a few potholes. This icon points them out to help you avoid trouble.

Sometimes we forget things, so we use this icon to point out important things that you want to remember. You probably don't forget things, but humor us if you see this icon.

Most of the technical stuff in this book appears in simple, readable, entertaining format right in the main text. This icon points out *really* technical things that require a college education to even think about. You can read this stuff, or you can skip it — without hurting our feelings.

We use this icon to mark items contained on the book's CD-ROM.

About the CD-ROM

We put together a CD-ROM full of the software programs that you need to set up and maintain an Internet site. Some of the programs included on the CD-ROM are shareware, so after you set up your site and start using the software, you need to send license fees to the authors of the software that you use. Other programs included on the CD-ROM are demo versions of software that we find useful. Try these programs to determine which ones give you the options that you need to create a compelling, useful Internet site. If you find that some of the demos are just what you need, contact the creators of the software to discover how you can purchase production versions of the software.

Part I

Laying the Foundation of an Internet Site

The 5th Wave   By Rich Tennant

"Hold your horses. It takes time to build a home page for someone your size."

In this part . . .

This part introduces you to the basics of setting up an Internet site. Chapters 1–3 prepare you for action by covering key concepts and introducing the Internet strategy featured throughout this book. Chapter 4 shows you how to begin creating your site by registering a new domain name and setting up a Web site. You are about to discover the new world of Internet technology. Get ready to change forever the way that you think about and use the Internet.

Chapter 1

Anatomy of an Internet Site

● ●

In This Chapter

▶ Understanding what Internet sites are made of

▶ Creating a site with sugar, spice, and everything nice

▶ Avoiding snails and puppy dogs' tails

▶ Viewing the Internet from a site developer's perspective

● ●

*E*very computer that communicates on the Internet is part of some Internet site. An *Internet site* is a collection of computers that are all permanently connected to the Internet and that appear to the outside world to be related to one another. Your personal computer becomes a temporary part of somebody else's Internet site if you connect to an Internet Service Provider by using a modem. Every Web page lives on a computer that is part of somebody's Internet site. Every piece of e-mail that is sent to you moves through the network and hops from one Internet site to another until it ends up on your computer for you to read. Everything that happens on the Internet begins with the construction of an Internet site.

Some Internet sites are built by large companies, government agencies, military installations, schools, and power companies; others are built by small companies, families, individuals, and even Internet-book authors. All Internet sites need electricity and a permanent connection to the Internet, but beyond these two things, every Internet site is different. The needs and preferences of the site builder determine the exact nature of a particular Internet site. Some sites, such as those built by Internet Service Providers, have a way to give customers access to the Internet in exchange for a monthly service fee. Other sites don't provide services to customers but do provide information in the form of Web pages, for example. You are free to do whatever you want or need to do with your Internet site, and this simple fact is what has caused the Internet to grow.

Before you can make the switch from Net surfer to site builder, you must acquire a deeper understanding of the Internet's anatomy. If you surf the Net, the nuances that make up the various parts of the Internet make little difference to your overall experience. If you build an Internet site, however, understanding those nuances can make the difference between a useful and appealing site and a mediocre one. This chapter dissects the Internet to show what makes it work from a site developer's perspective.

Copper Wire, Fiber Optics, and Elbow Grease

The Internet is more than just a bunch of computers tied together; it is a living and breathing organism. Instead of oxygen, the Internet breathes information, and in place of blood, electrons and photons flow through the Internet's veins and arteries, carrying information to each of its many parts. The Internet even has a network heartbeat; if you press this book up against your ear, you just may hear its steady mechanical thump.

The word *Internet* is short for *internetwork,* which means to link many networks. The Internet was created — and continues to grow — by linking computer networks so that they can all communicate with one another. The computers attached to one computer network can communicate with the computers that are attached to another computer network if both computer networks are part of the global Internet. Figure 1-1 depicts the essential structure of the Internet.

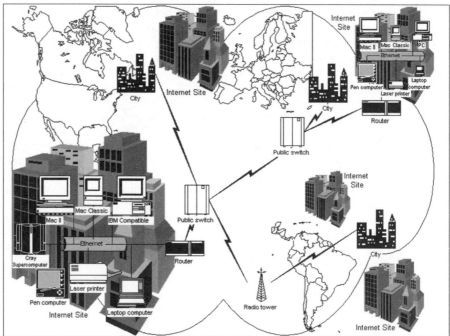

Figure 1-1: The Internet: a very large network that links together smaller networks.

A laptop computer located in North America, connected to a computer network that is also located in North America, can communicate with a Macintosh computer that is connected to a computer network in Europe, provided that both computer networks are connected to the Internet. What being connected to the Internet means may be different for a computer network located in one part of the world than it is for a network located in another part. A computer network in South America may be connected to the Internet through a wireless communications link, for example, whereas a computer in North America may be connected through copper wire. The wireless communications link in South America may be owned and operated by a local government, whereas the copper wire in North America may be part of the Public Switched Telephone Network (PSTN).

Notice that Figure 1-1 depicts entire cities as well as public switches and three continents. No single government or company owns the Internet. Instead, the Internet exists because individual governments and the owners of Internet sites have agreed to link their computers. If a country in Asia decides to terminate its link to the global network, that part of the Internet dies, but the rest of the Internet continues, because people and governments in other parts of the world still want to communicate with one another.

Figure 1-1 is intentionally vague about how an Internet site, city, or country links to the common communications infrastructure, and the figure shows the generic public-switch icon for two reasons:

- ✔ First, a variety of configurations is possible, ranging from using a conventional Internet Service Provider to sharing the Internet link of a university to establishing a dedicated satellite link between two nations. The lightning-bolt connections drawn between elements of Figure 1-1 can represent any of these possibilities. The result is the same; any information that needs to move from one point to another on the global public network is capable of doing so.

- ✔ The second reason for being vague in Figure 1-1 about the type of communications link used in each part of the Internet is that how the link works in your part of the world isn't terribly important — just as long as it *does* work. Whether a site or a continent connects to the Internet by using wireless technology, copper wire and a public telephone network, fiber optic lines, a cable television network, or tin cans and string makes no difference; the end-result is that communication is possible between each site on the network. You see in detail how to connect your Internet site to the Internet in Chapter 3.

The one thing about the Internet's anatomy that you, as a site builder, don't really need to be concerned with is exactly how electrons, photons, or carrier modulation move through wires, cables, or three-dimensional space and time to travel from one Internet site to another or from one computer to another. Unless you go on to become a full-fledged network engineer, knowing in detail the internal structure of Ethernet frames, ATM cells, or error-correcting algorithms that enable a computer to use an unreliable wireless radio link doesn't help you at all. Understanding that an amazing world of physics and telecommunications theory is at work to convert noisy modem sounds, bright laser light, and invisible radio signals into something that makes sense to a computer and that enables the computer to make sense to you is all you need. The Internet's global communications infrastructure varies greatly for each region of the world and it changes a great deal over time, but you need to concern yourself only with how to accomplish Internet access economically in your part of the world today.

Connected to the Internet's communications infrastructure are computers — large computers, small computers, business computers, personal computers, government computers, military computers, computers in the classroom, computers in the space shuttle, computers that power video-game systems, and computers that power the power company. Any computer at all can be connected to the Internet.

One computer, two computer, three computer, four

Linking computers is what the Internet is all about. But what is a computer, really? The massive mainframe computers that are larger than your house hardly resemble the personal computer that sits on your desk, yet both machines are called computers. New gadgets such as WebTV are sometimes called *network computers* or *information appliances,* yet they do the same thing that a computer does to communicate on the Internet.

Other types of Internet data-communications equipment don't easily fit into the computer category, including routers, which move data between locations on the network. Instead of calling every device that is connected to the Internet a computer, the devices are commonly called *network nodes.* Every computer on the Internet is a network node, but not every network node on the Internet is a conventional computer.

Diversity is the language of the Internet

Information moves across the Internet in small units called *packets.* Packets are like little envelopes sent by traditional mail. Each packet contains an address, just as any paper envelope does, and some amount of information. Although a packet really is just a series of ones and zeroes transmitted across wires, fiber-optic cables, or radio waves, thinking of a packet as being a tangible package full of information is helpful.

Here's a story that may help you understand how packets work. When a small community in the western United States decided to purchase the London Bridge, it didn't rent the *Queen Elizabeth II* to ship it over. Instead, the community had the bridge disassembled, stone by stone. Each stone was marked so that the bridge could be reassembled in its new desert home. Then the stones were packaged, so many in each box, and the boxes were sent to their destination.

Packets are kind of like the boxes that were used to transport the stones of the London Bridge. As information (such as a Web page) is sent across the Internet, it is chopped into many bite-sized pieces called *bytes*. These pieces are arranged into packets, and the packets are sent to their destination. It doesn't matter whether the packets follow the same route as they travel through the network — and often, they don't. What is important is that, after all the packets arrive, they are reassembled into their original form. This disassembly and reassembly process is a little like the transporter used in the "Star Trek" series to beam people and physical items from one place to another, although physical items can't be sent through the Internet just yet.

All devices on the Internet rely on a common protocol, called *TCP/IP* (Transmission Control Protocol/Internet Protocol), to communicate with one another. TCP/IP, which determines how packets are sent between network nodes, is the standard way for data to be relayed around the world on the Internet. Many, but not all, computers on the Internet speak TCP/IP directly. Other computers speak a different networking language and rely on translation equipment to convert between TCP/IP and their native network language. Global technical and social diversity make the Internet possible and define its character, but without a standard communications protocol such as TCP/IP, diversity would be a barrier to communications instead of being what it is on the Internet: a reason to communicate.

The cybersphere's connected to the biosphere

The global sphere of life in which we all live and compute (called Earth's *biosphere*) is also a part of the Internet. At every network node on the Internet, you find people. Computer technicians, technical support staff, infrastructure engineers, and Internet-book authors are just some of the people who sit all day long at a particular network node, keeping everything running. These people make the Internet possible. Every site builder should remember that people are also "connected" to the Internet, not just computers. The lifeforms that interact over the network are the Internet's most valuable resource.

People such as you who set up Internet sites make the Internet worthwhile for users, and accomplished site builders are almost always willing to share their experiences with you if you just ask. Unlike the treatment that some

Internet newcomers receive as they stumble around, asking stupid questions and annoying other people, people who build Internet sites are friendly and willing to help their fellow site builders. Ask for help online as you discover how to set up your own Internet site — and make sure that you return the favor later by answering the questions of other newcomers.

Can't we all just get along?

The Internet works — and all its nodes get along with one another — because of worldwide agreements about how Internet technology should function. One such agreement is the TCP/IP protocol described earlier in this chapter, which defines the way in which data moves through the network. These agreements are called *Internet Standards*.

Internet Standards exist to make sure that the technology used on the Internet works for everybody in consistent ways. Imagine how frustrating it would be for everyone if Web pages looked different in different Web browsers or if some Web browsers supported features such as frames and others didn't.

Wait a minute — Web browsers *do* have these differences and many others! Unfortunately, the talented engineers who work as part of the Internet Engineering Task Force (see sidebar) haven't been able to design an engineering process that eliminates politics, minimizes delays, and compels the compliance of everyone, everywhere. So if the standards-development process moves too slowly or fails to achieve perfection, technology developers tend to ignore the standards and do something else.

The World Wide Web is an excellent example of Internet standards gone awry. The incompatibilities between browsers and other Web software almost make the Web unusable for anything more complex than publishing text with pictures. The Web has been such a big letdown for developers of interactive technology that it has splintered into several competing technologies offered by computer superpowers such as Microsoft, Netscape, and Sun Microsystems. In their battle over the Web, these and other companies seem to be on the verge of destroying it.

But never fear — many other technologies are waiting to take the place of the World Wide Web, including the popular push technology, which delivers information and software that users need when they need it, automatically, without browsing. If you intend to move beyond the Web to keep up with the demands and interests of Internet users, you need to understand the material presented in this book and become a proficient site builder.

Domain Names and IP Addresses

The TCP/IP standard enables you to move packets around the Internet, in part because it defines the way in which unique addresses are assigned to each network node. Rather than label each node with a street address, city, state, country, and Zip code, as the U.S. Postal Service does, TCP/IP uses unique network numbers called *IP addresses*.

An IP address is a little like a phone number. A telephone must have a unique phone number so that any other telephone in the world can call it. IP addresses are like phone numbers for network nodes. An IP address is a set of four numbers separated by periods, or dots (also called a *dotted quad*). An IP address looks as follows:

```
207.92.75.100
```

IP addresses aren't user-friendly. An easier way of referring to a computer without having to memorize confusing numbers is to give the computer a name. A standard called the *Domain Name System* (DNS) enables computers on the Internet to have names that are easier for people to remember. The names assigned to computers through DNS are called *domain names*. DNS is discussed in detail in Chapter 4, but the most important part of DNS for you to understand now is the fact that the term *domain name* means two different things, depending on the context in which the term is used.

A domain name such as `science.org` refers to the Internet site run by a particular organization, whereas a domain name such as `titanium.science.org` refers to a particular network node within the `science.org` domain. The longer domain name is sometimes referred to as the network node's *fully qualified domain name* to differentiate it from the larger domain, but the term usually is shortened to *domain name*. Therefore, both `titanium.science.org` and `science.org` are domain names. The former, however, refers to a particular computer named `titanium` that exists within the `science.org` domain; the latter refers generally to a group of related computers that belong to a single organization.

Creating Internet standards

A group known as the Internet Engineering Task Force (IETF) is responsible for keeping track of existing Internet Standards and helping create new ones.

Anyone can join the IETF for free and participate directly in the creation of new Internet Standards. Visit the following Web site for more information.

`www.ietf.org`

The subtle difference between a domain name and a fully qualified domain name becomes clearer later in this book, as you see the difference in action. Just remember that people often use the term *domain name* when they should be using the term *fully qualified domain name*. In some cases, a direct correlation exists between an Internet site and a domain name, meaning that a single Internet site is known by a single domain name. As you discover in Chapter 4, however, a single Internet site can have many domain names.

Whether your Internet site has one or many domain names, a domain name is an indication of identity and ownership on the network. Every computer that shares a common domain name appears to be owned or controlled by the same organization. A domain can be a single computer or a network of computers, which is like saying, "I live at 1515 Elm Street." This address could be a private house or a huge apartment complex.

Standards for information services

Information services on the Internet also have standards that are designed and approved by the IETF. Throughout this book, we introduce the odd abbreviations and cryptic code names by which these standards are known, so that you know what it means when somebody says, "HTTP is less versatile than FTP for transferring files, but it is simpler than SMTP, POP, and IMAP; maybe it should be used to send and receive e-mail." Unfortunately, after you finally do understand statements such as these, you're often just tempted to argue more frequently with people who say such silly things about the Internet. Go easy on them.

To differentiate one information service from another, TCP/IP provides an additional addressing scheme to augment the IP address: *port numbers*. Port numbers are unique for a particular IP address, meaning that two information services can't both use port 80 on network node 207.92.75.100. But port numbers are not unique globally. The network node at IP address 207.92.75.100 can provide an information service by using port 80, and at the same time, IP address 207.92.75.101 can provide a service by using port 80.

Together, an IP address and a port number identify a unique network node and a unique information service on the network node, respectively. To help prevent conflicts between information services that may otherwise use the same port number on a single network node, the Internet Assigned Numbers Authority (IANA) makes port-number assignments on a first-come, first-served basis. Only developers of network software need to worry about having a port number reserved for their software, but the IANA Web site is an important place for you to visit anyway, to understand more about how Internet software works. The address is as follows:

```
http://www.iana.org/iana/
```

To help clarify what port numbers do, here's a real-world analogy. If you say you're going to your garage and your friend says that she's going to her garage, you and your friend know that you're each going to a different garage, because you live in different houses with different addresses. If you lived in a garage, and your friend lived in a garage, you wouldn't even need to tell each other that you'd be in your respective garages because that would be assumed. If you have multiple rooms in each of your houses, however, you can be specific about where each of you is going to be in your homes only if you add the name of the room to which you're going. Port numbers enable you to be just as specific about where to go on a particular network node. You may, for example, say that you're going to contact a Web server on port number 80, and your friend may say that she's going to contact an FTP server on port 21. You're both going to contact the same computer, but you're going to be "in" different electronic "rooms."

Some people look better in Uniform Resource Locators

You can't go anywhere on the Internet without knowing what a URL is. *URL* stands for *Uniform Resource Locator*. Sounds more like something that you'd use to find your laundry at the dry cleaner's than it does a computer term, doesn't it? The comparison isn't too far off. If you think of everything on the Internet as needing intensive dry-cleaning before it is fit for human use, a URL *does* help you locate laundry on the network.

The URL is the key to uniquely identifying your site and the information stored there. A URL is much more than just a name, however. Simply giving each resource on the Internet a name isn't good enough, because names are not always unique. (The authors just discovered, for example, that the world has other people named Jason and Ted Coombs.)

For Net surfers, URLs may seem to have little reasoning behind them. But for site developers, understanding the makeup of URLs is critical. Each bit of information on the Internet is known as a *resource,* and resources are stored in many formats. Some of the information is stored in files used on the World Wide Web, called *HTML files*. Other information is stored in documents on special servers, such as Gopher or FTP servers. The list of file types is large; so is the number of ways in which file types can be served.

Resource URLs

Files that contain information are not the only resource on the Internet. Resources also include interactive programs, searchable databases, games, and other types of software. Each resource on the Internet can be identified uniquely by a URL, which specifies the following information:

> ✔ The type of resource (the protocol and server used to provide it)
>
> ✔ The computer on which the resource is located
>
> ✔ The name of the resource

By using a resource's type, location, and name, people can create a unique address for every resource on the Internet. Essentially, the URL goes one step beyond IP addresses and port numbers. The URL adds a specific resource name, such as a filename, to the IP address and port-number combination. Instead of just telling somebody to communicate with port 80 on network node 207.92.75.100, a URL enables you to tell somebody to look at the file called index.html, which is located on network node 207.92.75.100 and accessible through port 80. Every URL says something equally complicated and makes the complete address of any resource barely understandable to Internet users. Each chapter of this book explains the anatomy of the URL used to locate the specific type of resource discussed in that chapter.

You may have heard that URLs identify resources on the World Wide Web. You see URLs all over the place, on billboards and in newspaper ads and magazines, and you hear them in radio announcements. More than simply being a way to identify Web resources, however, URLs are a shorthand way to identify every bit of information on the Internet. Including URLs in your advertising or on your business cards to identify your important Internet resources is more than just a great idea; it's also the only way to tell people how to find your resources on the network.

The parts of a URL

As an information provider and a site builder, you must understand the different parts of a URL. The first part, or *prefix,* of a URL describes the type of software that is used to handle the resource. A URL prefix is short enough not to get in the way and always appears right before a colon (:). The pair of forward slashes (//) that appears after the colon in a URL is dumb. But these slashes are a fact of life on the Internet for most URL types except those for e-mail addresses, as you see in Table 1-1.

Table 1-1	URL Prefixes for Some Information Services	
Prefix	*Information Service*	*Example URL*
http://	World Wide Web	http://www.science.org/
ftp://	File Transfer Protocol	ftp://ftp.science.org/
gopher://	Gopher	gopher://science.org/
mailto:	E-mail address	mailto:info@science.org

Each type of URL can have slight variations in structure, but most types follow the convention `http://` (for the Web) or `ftp://` (for File Transfer Protocol).

Now look at a URL for an FTP site, and check out the naming convention:

```
ftp://ftp.science.org/pub/win31/gatt_1.zip
```

This URL tells you where you can go to download the text of GATT (Global Agreement on Tariffs and Trade) for Microsoft Windows. Without getting into the political side of the Internet, the following paragraphs examine the URL of this site to show what you can determine from its address.

The first part of the URL, `ftp://`, tells you that the resource is an FTP site. The next part, `ftp.science.org`, is the fully qualified domain name of the computer that's running the FTP server. Next comes the directory path, where the information is stored. For this example, the directory path `/pub/win31/` is where you can find the file `gatt_1.zip`.

Want to know more about GATT? Follow these steps to download the document from this site:

1. **Open your Web browser, and locate the dialog box that enables you to enter a URL.**
2. **Type the URL as follows:**
   ```
   ftp://ftp.science.org/pub/win31/gatt_1.zip
   ```
3. **Tell the computer where you want to store the file on your machine.**
4. **Sit back and watch those bytes fly down your phone line.**

URLs are fairly simple to understand; they provide the surfer and site developer a great deal of information about the resources that are being delivered on the Internet. In this book, we help you gain a better understanding of URLs and show you how to best use their syntax to maximize your site's effectiveness.

Clients, Servers, and a Capitalist Paradise

Everyone on the Internet is a client. Only those people who have an Internet site are servers. If you're reading this book, you already know that, without a program such as a Web browser, you can't view pages on the World Wide Web. A Web browser program turns a computer into a client, meaning that it can use the services provided by network servers. This book focuses on showing you how to set up network servers so that any client on the Internet can use the services that you provide through an Internet site of your own.

The Internet must always have fewer servers than clients, just as the world must always have fewer companies than customers. This situation is the nature of electronic capitalism. Simple logic suggests that business opportunities must exist somewhere on the Internet if you have your own Internet site. With the knowledge presented in this book and some perseverance, you can find the opportunity that you're looking for and make something great out of it.

Chapter 2

Preparing a Personal Computer for the Internet

● ●

In This Chapter

▶ Choosing a data-communications device

▶ Installing TCP/IP on your Macintosh or Windows PC

▶ Deciding whether to build your own computer network

● ●

*Y*ou have two different ways to connect your personal computer to the Internet. You can either use a modem to connect your computer to an Internet Access Provider through a telephone line or you can use a network card to connect directly to your own private computer network, called a *LAN* (*Local Area Network*), and then connect your LAN to the Internet. Remember that the Internet is just a very large network of smaller computer networks. If you build your own computer network, you can make your network a part of the Internet so that each of the computers on your network can communicate with every other computer on the Internet. This process is how the Internet grows in size. Figure 2-1 compares a network connection to the Internet with a modem connection.

Remember, too, that every telephone or ISDN modem connection requires a separate phone line, which isn't free, and you may need to pay usage fees to the phone company for each minute of time that each of your computers is connected through a telephone line to the Internet. We highly recommend that you build your own computer network instead and connect it to the Internet so that you pay one fixed monthly fee for unlimited Internet access, regardless of the number of computers in use at your site. We understand, however, that not everyone who wants to set up an Internet site has more than one computer or can afford the additional expense associated with connecting a LAN to the Internet. This chapter, therefore, shows you how to prepare a personal computer to connect to the Internet by using either a modem or your own LAN. Chapter 3 shows you how to link computers

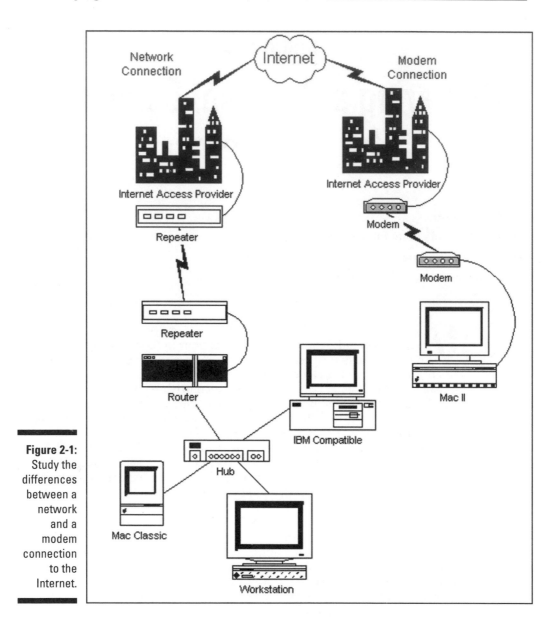

Figure 2-1:
Study the differences between a network and a modem connection to the Internet.

together to form a LAN and then connect your LAN to the Internet. Chapter 3 also shows you how to connect a single computer to the Internet over a dedicated link so that you can avoid the higher costs associated with connecting an entire LAN to the Internet.

Installing Data-Communications Hardware

For the most part throughout this book, we assume that you know how to install hardware and software in your computer. In the past, hardware installation could prove so difficult and complicated if you used an IBM-compatible PC that trying to explain how to do it in a book such as this one would have been almost pointless. Today, however, installing new hardware can be so simple that nothing's left for us to write about. Therefore, we just present the most critical, if somewhat obvious, points about the hardware installation necessary to prepare your personal computer for the Internet.

For your computer to communicate with other computers, your computer must have a way to transmit data to and receive data from other computers. The two most common technologies that enable computer data communications are the *modem,* which is short for *modulator-demodulator,* and the *network adapter.* A modem modulates and demodulates a signal carried by wire or by radio wave so that you can encode, transmit, receive, and decode information without using a purely digital optical or electronic communications network. A network adapter, on the other hand, transmits and receives electrical or optical pulses over a digital computer network. A network adapter doesn't need to modulate or demodulate a carrier signal, and, therefore, it can operate at much higher speeds and with much greater reliability.

Installing a modem or a network adapter

Modems come in three types: *internal modems,* which you must plug into an expansion slot inside your computer; *external modems,* which you must plug into one of the communication ports on the outside of your computer; and credit-card-sized *PC card modems* (PC/MCIA), which you usually use with a notebook computer, that plug into a PC/MCIA card slot the way that a floppy disk fits into your disk drive.

 A fourth kind of modem also exists that's really neat: a *network modem.* Network modems don't plug into your computer at all. Instead, they plug into your computer network and communicate with your computer digitally over the network. Because of special software device drivers provided for use with the network modem, your computer doesn't know the difference between a network modem and a modem that's physically connected to a communication port. Network printers, network fax machines, and network scanners work the same way — by communicating digitally with your computer over a data network. You enjoy many advantages in using network devices such as these, but the most pronounced advantage is that any computer on the network can use the network device, thereby saving unnecessary expense for additional peripheral devices for each computer.

Network adapters are generally internal, meaning that you must open up your computer and plug the adapter into an available expansion port. The big difference between network adapters is in the network cabling and communications standard that they use. One network adapter may use twisted-pair cable and a communications standard known as *Ethernet* to interface to the network, while another may use fiber-optic cable and a communications standard known as *Asynchronous Transfer Mode* (ATM). The two most common cabling types for computer networks are *twisted-pair* and *coaxial cable*. If you have lots of extra money sitting around that you'd like to use for something worthwhile, spend it buying network adapters and cabling that use fiber-optic technology and the ATM communications standard. Otherwise, do as most new site builders do and purchase Ethernet network adapters that use twisted-pair cable. See Chapter 3 for a more in-depth understanding of how to use network cable to connect all the computers in your network.

Using Windows 95 Plug and Play to install hardware

If you use Windows 95's Plug and Play feature, installing a new modem or network adapter is a snap. Literally. Just snap the modem or network adapter into an expansion slot or plug the modem into a communications port and then turn on your computer. Windows 95 automatically detects and configures the new hardware for you. Figure 2-2 shows the New Hardware Found window that Windows 95 displays after it finds new hardware such as a network adapter or a modem connected to your computer.

Figure 2-2:
Use Plug and Play so that installing new hardware is a snap.

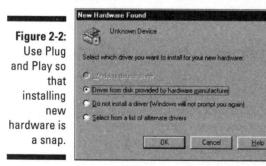

For Plug and Play to work correctly on your Windows 95 computer, you need to be aware of two things. First, not all hardware supports Plug and Play. If you have an old modem or network adapter that doesn't support Plug and Play, Windows 95 may not be capable of configuring the device automatically. Second, not all IBM-compatible PC motherboards support Plug and Play either. If you own an old 386 or 486 computer that doesn't support Plug and Play, Windows 95 may not be capable of configuring your modem or network adapter for you even if the device does support Plug and Play. (The moral of this story is to sell your old computer equipment and buy hardware that supports Plug and Play.)

As you can see in Figure 2-2, Windows 95 gives you several options for locating a software device driver for your new hardware. If Windows 95 already has a default driver available for the hardware that you're adding, the first item in the bullet list is available. Otherwise, you must use a software driver disk provided by the manufacturer of your hardware. Click the Driver from disk provided by hardware manufacturer radio button and then click OK.

The window shown in Figure 2-3 appears on-screen, prompting you to insert the disk containing the software driver provided by your hardware manufacturer. After the disk is in the drive that the Copy manufacturer's files from list box indicates, click OK.

Figure 2-3:
Insert the
disk that
contains
the
software
driver for
your new
hardware.

Install From Disk

Insert the manufacturer's installation disk into
the drive selected, and then click OK.

OK

Cancel

Copy manufacturer's files from:

A:\

Browse...

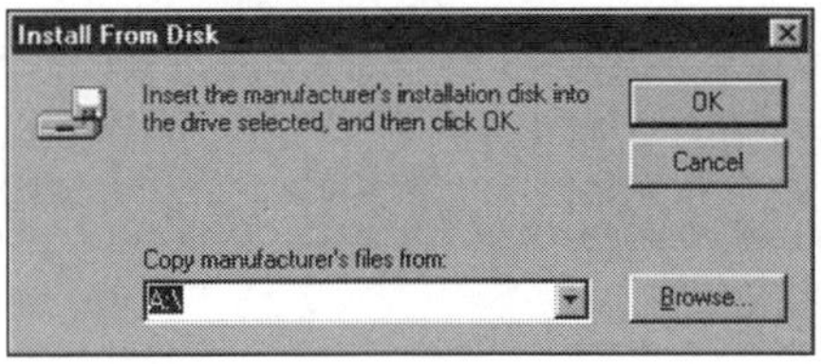

In addition to copying the software driver for your new hardware from the disk that your hardware manufacturer provides, Windows 95 may need to copy files from the Windows 95 CD-ROM or floppy disks. A prompt may appear on-screen if Windows 95 needs to copy additional files from a Windows 95 disk. Insert the disk indicated or insert the Windows 95 CD-ROM and then click OK.

If Windows 95 needs help locating the files that it needs to copy, a window similar to the one shown in Figure 2-4 appears. Specify drive and/or directory location of the Windows 95 system files and then click OK to continue copying files.

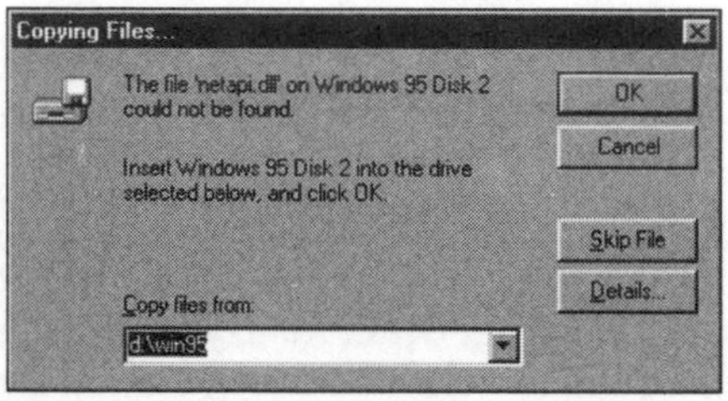

Figure 2-4:
Use this window to help Windows 95 locate the system files it needs if it gets lost.

As Windows 95 copies files, it displays a status window. If any problems arise during file copying, Windows 95 stops and asks you for help. (For being so expensive and powerful, computers sure need a lot of help from a human to do simple things correctly.) One common problem occurs if Windows 95 tries to copy a file from the system disks that already exists on your computer. Sometimes, the file on your computer is newer than the file on the Windows 95 disks.

Figure 2-5 shows what happens if Windows 95 discovers a file on your computer that's newer than a file it's trying to copy. To avoid any problems, you should always keep the newer file. Click the Yes button to keep the newer copy of the file and prevent Windows 95 from copying the older file.

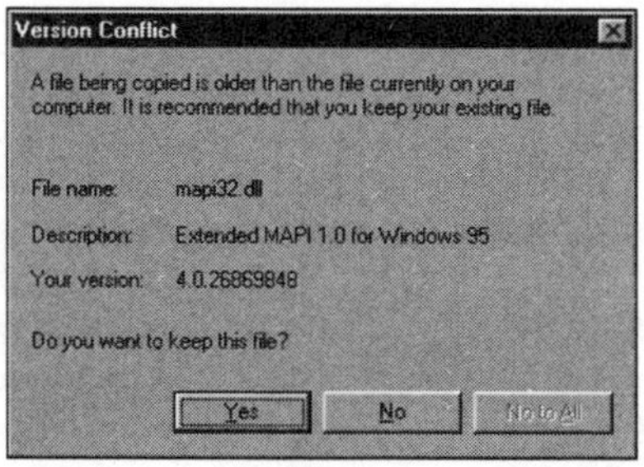

Figure 2-5:
Keep newer files that are already on your computer.

After Windows 95 finishes copying files and asking you questions, you need to reboot your computer so that the changes made to your system can take effect. The window that appears enables you to reboot immediately by clicking the Yes button.

After your computer reboots, you can verify that your modem or network adapter was installed correctly by using the Control Panel. In the Control Panel, you find an icon labeled Modems and one labeled Network. Double-click the Modems icon in the Control Panel to open the Modems Properties window, as shown in Figure 2-6. The modem that you just installed should be listed. If it isn't shown in the Modems Properties window, Windows 95 didn't successfully install and configure your modem. Try removing the device physically from your computer and rebooting your computer. Then shut down your computer again and restart the hardware installation from scratch.

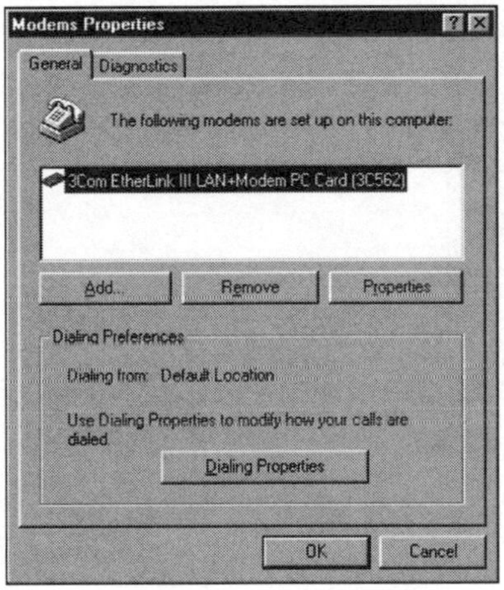

Figure 2-6:
Verify the configuration of your modem by checking the Modems Properties window.

If you have trouble installing your modem or want to view more detailed information about what Windows 95 did as it installed and configured your modem, click the Diagnostics tab in the Modems Properties window. The Diagnostics tab shows you which device is presently configured to use which COM port and enables you to obtain additional information about the hardware configuration, such as the device drivers installed.

If you're installing a network adapter, double-click the Network icon in the Control Panel window. Figure 2-7 shows the Network window, which displays network configuration information for your Windows 95 computer. You should see at least one entry in the Configuration tab's list box for your network adapter if Windows 95 Plug and Play succeeded in installing and configuring your hardware. You may also see an entry for Dial-Up Adapter, as shown in Figure 2-7. Windows 95 installs the Dial-Up Adapter automatically if you install a modem for use with dial-up networking. In the figure, the entry for a 3Com EtherLink III modem/network adapter combination PC card appears above the Dial-Up Adapter entry. If you don't see an entry for your network adapter in the Network window, Windows 95 Plug and Play didn't successfully install and configure your adapter.

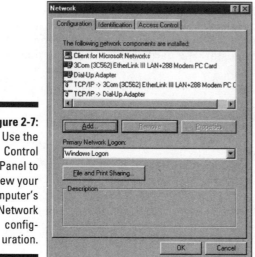

Figure 2-7:
Use the
Control
Panel to
view your
computer's
Network
config-
uration.

If things don't go smoothly with your hardware installation, get help from a computer technician. On Windows-based IBM-compatible PCs, hardware installation is either Plug and Play or it's frustrating, time-consuming, unpleasant, costly, and overly complicated. If you stick with brand-name hardware products and replace all your older hardware with equipment manufactured after 1996, you should have no trouble installing the hardware yourself, and by doing so, you save hundreds of dollars in payments to a computer technician over the life of your computer.

Installing hardware on a Macintosh

Nothing in the computer world is simpler than installing hardware on a Macintosh computer: Turn off your Macintosh, plug the hardware into the right connector in your computer, and then turn on your computer again. The Macintosh Operating System automatically detects and configures your new hardware. That's all you need to do. You can buy either an internal or an external modem or an internal network adapter. (Remember that you must plug internal devices into an expansion port inside your computer, while external devices connect to one of the ports on the outside of your computer.) If you experience trouble installing hardware in your Macintosh, you can use the only thing in the computer world that's as simple as install- ing hardware on a Macintosh: the Apple support line, at 1-800-SOS-APPL.

Configuring TCP/IP on Your Computer

All computers on the Internet rely on a common protocol, called *TCP/IP* (*T*ransmission *C*ontrol *P*rotocol/*I*nternet *P*rotocol), to exchange information packets. TCP/IP is the standard way to relay data around the world on the Internet, but not all computers on the Internet speak TCP/IP directly. Some computers speak a different language that you must translate into TCP/IP before the data can travel across the Internet. Actually for two computers that don't speak TCP/IP to communicate with each other over the Internet is quite common; the two machines rely on translators at either end to convert the conversation to and from TCP/IP. To construct new Internet sites using anything other than TCP/IP, however, is most uncommon, so we do in this section what most people do these days: try to forget that anything other than TCP/IP exists on the Internet.

The technology that enables a Macintosh or an IBM-compatible PC com- puter to speak TCP/IP is now commonplace and easy to configure. Windows 95 and the new versions of MacOS (such as System 7.5.5 and later) come with TCP/IP ready for configuring, so you don't need to worry about getting additional software. You have only a few steps to follow to set up the TCP/IP networking software for Windows 95 or MacOS, and the following sections show you what you need to know to configure both.

Your computer can either speak TCP/IP through a modem or it can speak TCP/IP through a network adapter. If your computer speaks TCP/IP through a network adapter, information packets are "carried" on top of another networking protocol such as *Ethernet.* If your computer speaks TCP/IP through a modem, however, information packets are "carried" on top of a networking protocol designed to work with modems, such as *Point to Point Protocol,* or PPP. Keep in mind as you read the following instructions that two different ways exist for your computer to speak TCP/IP, and the method that your computer uses depends on whether you install a modem or a network adapter.

Macintosh Open Transport TCP/IP

You have two ways to set up TCP/IP on a Macintosh computer: the old way and the new way. The old way was to install MacTCP, a Control Panel component that would add TCP/IP communications capability to MacOS versions such as System 7. The new way, using MacOS versions such as

System 7.5 and on all Power Macs, is to use a technology called *Open Transport*. MacOS System 7.5.5 and later versions include Open Transport 1.1.1 built in. A few Open Transport upgrades are available from Apple on the Internet (at http://www.apple.com/) that work with versions of MacOS prior to System 7.5.5, but the best way to install Open Transport on your Mac is to upgrade your operating system to System 7.5.5 or later. You can also find Open Transport 1.1.1 on Apple sites within America Online (keyword: APPLECOMPUTER) and CompuServe (shortcut: GO APLSUP).

After you upgrade your operating system to System 7.5.5 or later, configuring TCP/IP on your Macintosh is very simple. Start by choosing Apple⇨ TCP/IP Control Panel from the menu bar. If this time is your first in opening the TCP/IP Control Panel, a window appears on-screen alerting you to the fact that TCP/IP is currently inactive. Click the Yes button so that TCP/IP becomes active after you finish with the TCP/IP Control Panel.

The next window that appears on-screen is shown in Figure 2-8. This window, entitled TCP/IP, is where you configure TCP/IP settings for your Macintosh. Select your network adapter from the Connect via drop-down list box. Also select Manually from the Configure drop-down list box so that your TCP/IP window looks something like the one shown in Figure 2-8. Now enter your computer's IP address, subnet mask, the address of the network router to use, the addresses of name servers to use, and the domain of which your computer is a part.

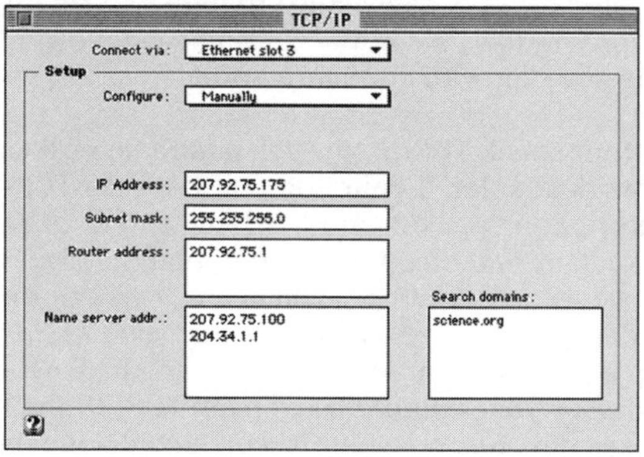

Figure 2-8: Configure TCP/IP settings for your network adapter.

TCP/IP	
Connect via:	Ethernet slot 3
Setup	
Configure:	Manually
IP Address:	207.92.75.175
Subnet mask:	255.255.255.0
Router address:	207.92.75.1
Name server addr.:	207.92.75.100 / 204.34.1.1
Search domains:	science.org

Your Internet Access Provider supplies all this information after you sign up for service. If you're building your own computer network for your Internet site, your Internet Access Provider gives you a range of IP addresses to use for the computers in your network. Pick an unused IP address from the ones supplied by your IAP and enter that address in the IP Address text box. Which of the addresses you use for each of your computers doesn't matter as long as you don't use the same address more than once.

If you don't have a network adapter and instead intend to connect to the Internet through a modem, select PPP from the Connect via drop-down list box (see Figure 2-9). Select Manually from the Configure drop-down list box so that your TCP/IP window looks something like the one shown in Figure 2-9. Enter your computer's permanent IP address, the addresses of name servers to use, and the domain name of which your computer is a member.

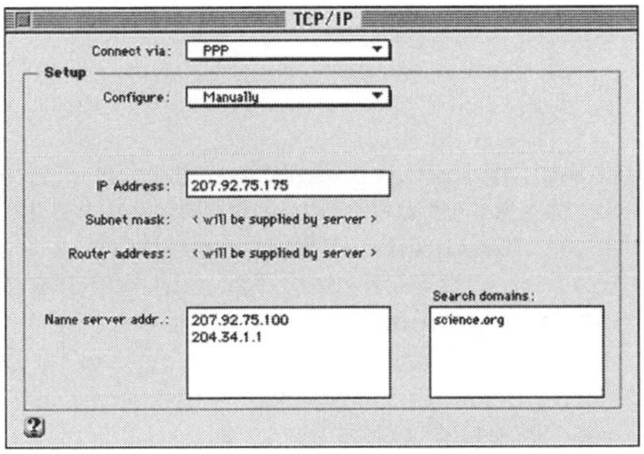

Figure 2-9:
Configure
TCP/IP
settings for
your
dedicated
PPP
connection.

After you're done, close the TCP/IP Control Panel by clicking the window Close box in the upper left-hand corner. A window appears, asking you to confirm that you want to save changes to your current TCP/IP configuration. Click the Save button to save the new TCP/IP settings for your Macintosh. After the save is complete, TCP/IP is ready for your Macintosh to use, either over a modem or through a network adapter, depending on the hardware that you installed.

If you have any trouble installing or configuring Open Transport or a new version of MacOS, somebody at Apple is available to help you at no charge during the week. Call the following number and explain your problem, and the Apple support engineer can assist you: 1-800-SOS-APPL.

Windows 95 Windows Sockets 1.1

Prior to the release of Windows 95, getting TCP/IP to work with your Windows-based PC required a lot of effort. Now, thanks to Plug and Play and Windows Sockets 1.1 for Windows 95, you can configure TCP/IP for your PC in only a few minutes and with few complications. Start by installing your network adapter or modem as described earlier in this chapter and then open the Windows 95 Control Panel. Double-click the Network icon. After the Network Configuration window appears on-screen, click the Add button. The Select Network Component Type window appears, as shown in Figure 2-10. Select Protocol from the list and then click the Add button.

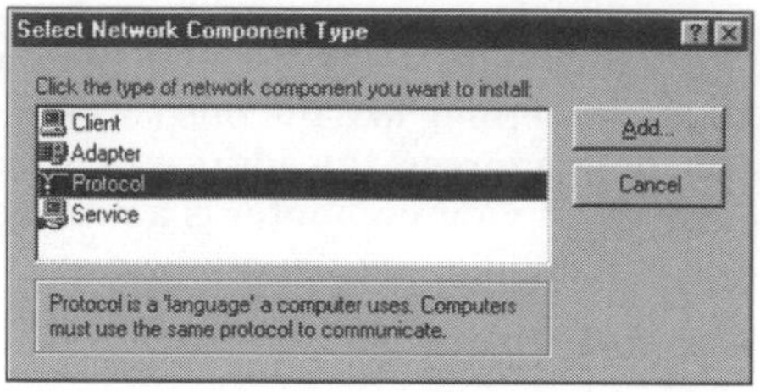

Figure 2-10:
Select
Protocol
to begin
adding the
TCP/IP
network
component.

The Select Network Protocol window appears, as shown in Figure 2-11, and enables you to choose from a list of manufacturers and network protocols. Choose Microsoft as the manufacturer and TCP/IP as the network protocol; then click OK. This action instructs Windows 95 to add Windows Sockets 1.1 with TCP/IP support to your computer.

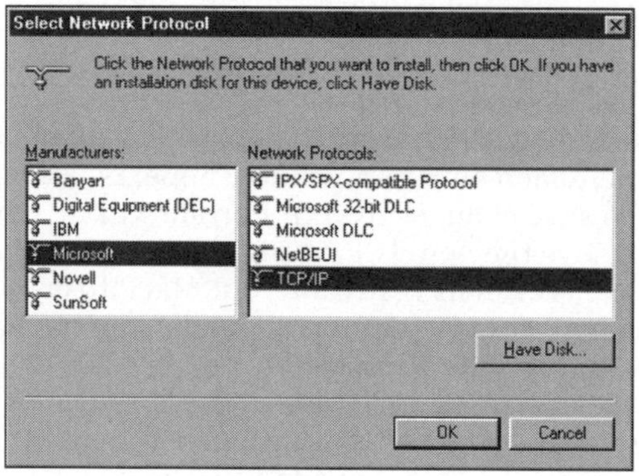

Figure 2-11:
Choose
Microsoft
TCP/IP to
install
Windows
Sockets.

Windows 95 automatically binds the TCP/IP network protocol to your modem or network adapter, whichever is installed in your computer. You don't need to do anything special to tell Windows 95 about the communications hardware with which you intend to use the TCP/IP network protocol. As long as your hardware is correctly installed, the TCP/IP protocol is available for use with the hardware after you're done with the installation.

The only thing left to do now is to configure TCP/IP settings for your computer. Figure 2-12 shows the first TCP/IP configuration screen, which Windows 95 dispays for you automatically, in which you type the IP address and subnet mask that your computer is to use. Your Internet Access Provider can tell you what your computer's permanent IP address is; make sure that you type this address accurately in the IP Address text box.

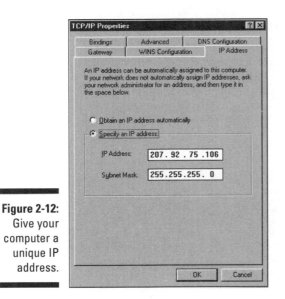

Figure 2-12:
Give your
computer a
unique IP
address.

Next, click the DNS Configuration tab to reveal the screen shown in Figure 2-13. Click the Enable DNS radio button so that your computer can resolve domain names to IP addresses. Type the host name of your computer in the Host text box and type the Internet domain name of which your computer is a member in the Domain text box. Together, your host and domain names are considered your *fully qualified domain name* (FQDN). Other people use your FQDN if they want to refer to your computer by name instead of by IP address. The FQDN of the configuration shown in Figure 2-13 is as follows:

```
helium.science.org
```

To add the addresses of the DNS servers that your computer uses to resolve domain names to IP addresses, enter these addresses one at a time in the DNS Server Search Order text box and click the Add button. The IP address that you enter is added to the list box beneath the entry field. Your Internet Access Provider can tell you which IP addresses to use here. If you decide to set up your own DNS server, as described in Chapter 4, enter the IP address of the computer on which your DNS server is running. Enter the IP address of your own computer if you intend to install and run your DNS server on the computer that you're now configuring.

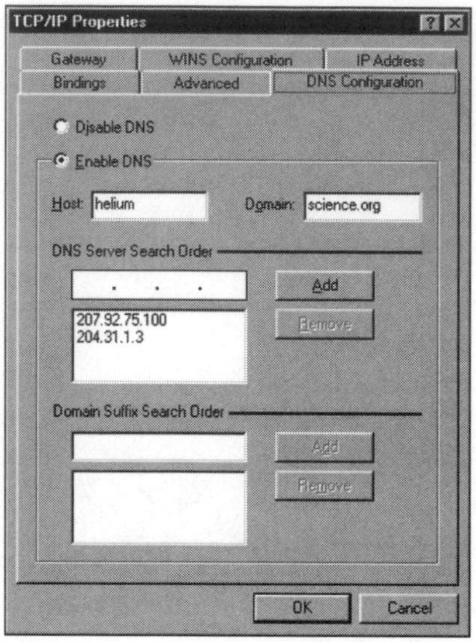

Figure 2-13:
Provide
DNS
Configuration
information
for name
resolution.

Finally, click the Gateway tab to reveal the screen shown in Figure 2-14. In this screen, you must type the IP address of the computer or router that relays TCP/IP packets to and from your computer and the rest of the Internet. If you use a modem to establish your dedicated Internet connection, you should leave the Gateway screen blank. If your modem connects to your Internet Access Provider by using PPP, a new gateway is normally added to your system automatically. If you enter a gateway IP address manually in the Gateway tab and then connect to your IAP by using a modem, this action can cause problems and prevent your computer from communicating with the Internet at all. If you aren't going to use a modem to connect to the Internet, you must enter a gateway IP address in the New gateway text box. Click the Add button to add the IP address of your new gateway to the list of Installed gateways. Click OK to complete your installation of Microsoft TCP/IP.

Your computer is now fully prepared to communicate with the Internet, either through a dial-up PPP connection to your access provider or through your own computer network, depending on the communications hardware you decided to use. Chapter 3 shows you how to connect your computer or computer network to the Internet so that you can internetwork with others on the Internet.

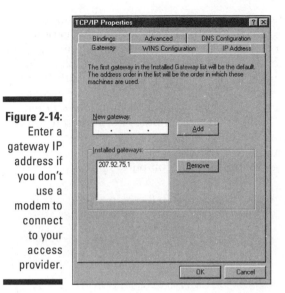

Figure 2-14:
Enter a gateway IP address if you don't use a modem to connect to your access provider.

This LAN Is Your LAN, This LAN Is My LAN

One of the things we strongly suggest is that you build your own computer network as you set up your Internet site. Although you can possibly connect each of your computers to the Internet through a separate modem and phone line and thereby avoid creating your own computer network, such an approach has several serious drawbacks. First, you sink a significant amount of money into modems. For the same price as an average modem, about $150, you can purchase a 10 megabit-per-second Ethernet card. Consider the amount of money that you spend for each kilobit-per-second of communications potential. By using a 28.8 kilobit-per-second modem, you spend upwards of $5 for each kilobit of communications speed. By using a standard 10 megabit-per-second Ethernet adapter, on the other hand, you spend only about 15 cents for each kilobit. Modems are a terrible communications investment compared to network adapters.

Assuming that you already have modems in each of your computers, think about the cost of Internet access for all of them. You pay at least $20 per month to your Internet Access Provider for each computer, and you pay at least $15 per month to the phone company for a telephone line for each computer. As soon as you connect more than three computers to the Internet through modems, you start paying more per month to various service providers than you'd pay if you built a computer network and connected the network to the Internet through a single communications link. Consider also how much more you'd need to spend to upgrade the speed of your Internet connection if you relied on modems and phone lines. You'd need to replace every modem and every phone line with a faster communications technology, such as ISDN, if you set up your Internet site by connecting each computer to the Internet through a standard modem and phone line. If you build a 10MB Ethernet computer network and connect it to the Internet, however, you need to replace only one piece of communications equipment and one Internet access service to upgrade your Internet connection for every one of your computers.

Chapter 3

Internetworking

● ●

In This Chapter

▶ Connecting your computer to the Internet

▶ Creating your own computer network

▶ Connecting your network to the Internet

● ●

Don't skip this chapter! You may be thinking that this chapter is not for you because you have only one PC sitting on your desk, not a network. Not true. A *network* is simply one computer connected to another, and the Internet is a big network of computers. Therefore, setting up an Internet site means setting up your computer, no matter what kind it is, as part of the network. Even if you have only one computer initially, if you turn that one computer into the foundation of an Internet site, you need to learn about networking.

Internetworking Is for Everyone

The Internet is just a large computer network that, aside from its size, is no different from a network you'd have in your office or possibly at home. As you can with all networks, you can do more than just send and receive information on the Internet. Any computer on the Internet can share resources with other computers via the network. Here are some of the resources that users commonly share across a network:

✔ Printers

✔ Disk drives and files

✔ Modems

✔ Backup tape or cartridge devices (such as Iomega Jaz or Zip drives)

✔ Company databases

One of the main reasons people started connecting personal computers with networks was to share printers. In a network, all the computers in an office can use the same printer. The time and money that network-printer sharing save more than pays for the cost of the network.

Only recently, however, did people become aware that their networks were capable of doing much more than just sharing printers. Networks can also be used to share disk drives, company databases, modems, backup tapes, and (most recently) a single dedicated connection to the Internet.

A computer that provides resources (such as a database or printer) to other computers over a network is said to be providing a network *service* and is often referred to as a *server*. The computers that use the services of a server are called *clients*. The idea that clients and servers should work together to accomplish things that neither could do alone is an important technical feature of computer use on the Internet. This approach to computer networking has proved to be so valuable that it has been given a special technical term: *client/server computing*.

All the shared devices or software services that server computers provide on a network must have unique names so that client computers can refer to them without ambiguity. A variety of methods is used to give unique names to network services, but the one that has gained the most popularity is the now-common *Uniform Resource Locator* (URL) for identifying services on the Internet.

If you build a computer network of your own and connect it to the Internet, every machine and every device on your network can provide services. At the same time, each computer can also be a client, using the services that are available on the network. Your computer systems may not be powerful supercomputers, but that doesn't matter much on the Internet. Even personal computers can provide sophisticated services, ranging from running Web server software and providing Web pages to clients all the way up to serving the commerce infrastructure of a business.

This entire book is based on the premise that a good idea is to build your own Internet site so that you are free to do anything you want with the Internet technology of your choice. Computer communication isn't new; computers have been talking with other computers for decades, using much of the same technology that is used today on the Internet. Computer online services aren't new either. Given a modem and the oldest personal computer, people have been able to browse information and use e-mail from nearly any telephone in the world since the 1970s. The procedure wasn't always easy (actually, it was never easy, not even in the early 1990s), but those people who discovered a compelling reason to learn it could do so.

Before the Internet, even the largest computer online services failed to provide a compelling reason for most people to learn how to communicate by using a computer. You know these computer online services; they all offer Internet access now, in addition to their old services, and thanks to the excitement of the Internet, they now have millions of subscribers. The major difference between the old online services and the Internet is simply freedom to internetwork. Anyone can build a site on the Internet and do with it what he pleases. The freedom to build an Internet site is a fundamental expression of the American right to free speech. As amazing as it seems now, the old online services didn't offer customers this capability.

Freedom can't be bought, however; it must be built. As a site builder, you should be able to purchase any Internet software or hardware from any vendor and incorporate it into your Internet site. Your business could purchase an Internet server that enables clients and suppliers to arrange shipping and receiving schedules at their convenience, for example. The Internet scheduling server could automatically adjust your project time lines to reflect delays or other unusual events, such as a supplier's finishing ahead of schedule.

To run such a scheduling server, you need a way to connect it to the Internet 24 hours per day, 7 days per week. You also need the server to be accessible so that you can fix it if it breaks. The best way to meet these needs is to establish a dedicated connection to the Internet for every computer in your organization. One connection can be shared by every computer that you own, including the computers that you use to publish information on the Web or that offer some other information utility, such as automated scheduling.

Many Internet Service Providers offer a co-location service, in which you buy a computer that you want to connect to the Internet and then locate it physically at the office of the ISP. This type of service gives you the best of both worlds; the computer has a dedicated and fast Internet connection at a low monthly rate, and you own and control it. The only drawback is that accessing the computer physically to perform maintenance or fix a hardware failure requires someone to drive to the remote site. Co-location may be an absolute must, however, if cable modems become popular.

Why own when you can rent?

In many places throughout this book, we discuss an alternative method for setting up an Internet site: renting services from an Internet Service Provider. You don't need a dedicated Internet connection if you just want to publish information on the Web. Creating a Web site by using a Web-publishing service provider is almost always less expensive than setting up an Internet site and running your own Web server software. If you don't build your Web site yourself, however, you may sacrifice the freedom to choose the technology that you could use to build the site.

For site builders who are on a limited budget, we recommend a slow and inexpensive dedicated connection combined with a Web site hosted by a Web-publishing service provider. This way, the essential contents of your Web site are available to Internet users at high speed, and you have the freedom to enhance the functionality of your site with other technology and a dedicated connection.

Ultimately, you must decide whether your plans for your Internet site justify the expense for a dedicated connection. If the price of a dedicated connection falls (as we think that it must over the next couple years), this decision is easier to make. Several industries are working to give everyone, everywhere a dedicated Internet connection known as an *Internet dial tone*. These industries recognize how important it is for anyone to be able to use data-communications technology with the same freedom and flexibility that people now use the telephone.

This chapter addresses the critical issues of data communications and networking equipment for your Internet site. The chapter also explores a little further the basic premise of this book and challenges assumptions about cost, utility, and the value of building an Internet site of your own.

A dedicated Internet connection is important

Setting up your own Internet site instead of renting server space from an Internet Service Provider has distinct advantages. For one thing, the only way to have complete control of the technology that your Internet site uses is to set everything up yourself. If anything goes wrong with your Internet site's hardware or software, you know that you can be around to fix the problem quickly. If you want to use a new hardware or software technology, you can incorporate it into your Internet site immediately.

The only drawback of setting up your own Internet site is also a benefit: You typically need a high-speed Internet connection. This type of connection costs more than the low-speed dial-up Internet access that is common among Internet users. As a site builder, your use of the Internet is different from that of a user. Your site provides resources for other people to use (many people, we hope), and it requires dedicated, high-speed Internet access to accommodate all your users around the clock. Of course, if your Internet site has dedicated high-speed Internet access, you and each member of your organization has dedicated high-speed Internet access for your own use as well. Dedicated high-speed Internet access for your Internet site, therefore, is both a drawback, because it costs more, and a benefit, because you and all the other members of your company can surf the Net at high-speed.

Running your own dedicated connection to the Internet enables you to provide many types of services that an Internet Service Provider may not offer; it also enables you to experiment with new and interesting technologies. Most ISPs limit the types of programs that you can run on their machines — for good reason. If you create a program that has bugs and ultimately crashes, it could disable an ISP's entire machine, interrupting Internet service for many people.

Linking Computers

The Internet is just a large network of computer networks. Anyone can build a computer network easily and quickly without spending a great deal of money. The most popular type of computer network today is the *Ethernet* network. Chapter 2 shows you how to install an Ethernet adapter in each computer that's part of your Internet site. Now you need to connect all your computers with network cable so that they can communicate by using the Ethernet protocol.

Building a computer network — even a small one in your home — opens new doors. Many products on the market just plug in to your Ethernet network and go to work for you. Printers, data-storage devices, CD-ROM jukeboxes, modems, fax systems, Internet servers, and many other products don't require you to open your computer to install new hardware; instead, you just plug the equipment into the network and start using it. After your network is connected to the Internet, you can even use the equipment from a remote location.

Before long, consumer-electronics devices such as VCRs are going to work on an Ethernet network, enabling you to use a Web browser to program your VCR from anywhere in the world. To take advantage of this exciting new area of technology (and to set up your own Internet site), prepare each of your computers to work on a network as described in Chapter 2 and then use the following guidelines to link the computers in a typical Ethernet network:

✔ You need a piece of hardware called a *network hub,* which you can buy at most computer stores. You need to purchase a network hub that matches the network adapters that you installed. If you installed network adapters that have transfer rates (throughput) of 10 megabits per second (10MB/sec.), you need a 10MB/sec. hub. Some network adapters and hubs also operate at speeds of 100MB/sec.

✔ You need to purchase network cabling. The most commonly used type of cabling for Ethernet networks is *twisted-pair cable,* called 10baseT and 100baseT for 10MB/sec. and 100MB/sec. networks, respectively. Some adapters and hubs use an alternative type of cabling known as *thin coaxial.* Some network adapters enable you to use either type of cabling, but 10baseT and now 100baseT are by far the most common.

✔ Connect the cables from the network adapters in each of your computers to the network hub.

A feature of most hubs is a status light above each connector. If the connection is made to a computer (turned on) with a network adapter, the status light glows. This feature helps you troubleshoot network problems. If the light is not glowing, you can look for a problem with the physical connection between the network hub and the network adapter. If this connection is okay, the network adapter's connection with the computer may be a problem (the card may not be seated correctly in the card slot), or the network adapter may be defective.

If you create networks that have considerable distance between the computers and the hub, you should refer to your hub's manual for the maximum distance possible between computer and hub. If you need to exceed that distance, you can purchase an additional piece of hardware known as a *network repeater.* A network repeater simply amplifies the signal that it receives from a computer and passes that signal farther down the network.

Connecting Computers to the Internet

After your computer is connected to the Internet, it becomes part of the Internet. The Internet is the sum of all the computers connected at any time. Many computers connect first to a local network and then access the Internet through the local network. Millions of other stand-alone computers access the Internet through a modem.

Connecting a stand-alone computer to the Internet

Chapter 2 shows you how to install a modem in your computer. The next step is to connect your modem to either the phone system or (in the case of cable modems) the cable TV system.

Telephone modems that are installed in your computer (*internal modems*) normally have two female modular phone receptacles, known as *RJ11 receptacles*. You can recognize these receptacles as being the typical phone jacks that you find in most homes. One of these receptacles is used to connect your modem to the phone system; the other is for connecting an optional telephone.

Most modems come equipped with the RJ11-type phone cable that you use to connect the modem to a phone jack. Simply plug one end of the cable into the modem in the receptacle normally labeled *line*. The other receptacle, for the optional phone, normally is labeled *phone*. Plug the other end of the cable into the jack that connects to your phone system. If you connect the optional phone to the modem's phone jack, you should be able to pick up the receiver and hear a dial tone.

 The best setup is to connect your modem to a phone line that does not go through an office phone system. Most phone systems tend to introduce electronic noise, which degrades the performance of most modems. And make certain that your phone line is not equipped with a call-waiting feature. The tones that the call-waiting feature generates to tell the listener that he's receiving an incoming call disrupt modem connections.

Similar instructions apply for connecting a stand-alone (external) modem. These modems generally are connected to your computer by a serial cable. The RJ11 phone connectors generally appear on the back of the modem and usually are well labeled. ISDN modems, whether they are internal or external, are connected in much the same way, except that ISDN uses a larger connector type than the typical RJ11 phone connector does. Cable modems use coaxial cables similar to the one that may connect your TV set to the cable system. The Internet signal can travel over the same cable as your television set without interfering with either the TV or the Internet signal.

After it's connected to the phone system, a telephone modem should dial the telephone number of your Internet Service Provider. The connection software (often PPP, as discussed in Chapter 2) takes over after the modem on the Internet Service Provider's end answers.

Modem connections are sensitive to telephone-line noise. This type of noise can be generated by many sources, such as the following:

- Heavy machinery operating near the phone system.

- Rain, wind, and snow, which often cause terrible line noise.

- Faulty or worn telephone wiring.

- Other phone-company problems. If you don't suspect any of the other sources, you should call the phone company, which should send a service technician to look for additional problems.

Setting up dial-up networking in Windows

After your modem is connected and correctly wired, you need to launch the Windows 95 Dial-Up Networking software to establish the connection with your Internet Service Provider. To set up the software, follow these steps:

1. **Choose Start➪Programs➪Accessories➪Dial-Up Networking.**

   The Dial-Up Networking window appears.

2. **Double-click the Make New Connection icon.**

   The Make New Connection dialog box appears.

3. **In the text box labeled Type a Name for the Computer You Are Dialing, enter a name that you can easily remember (the name of your Internet Service Provider, for example), as shown in Figure 3-1.**

   If you need to configure your modem, which is unlikely, you can click the Configure button. This action displays a new dialog box that enables you to set modem speed, speaker volume, and a few more esoteric modem settings, such as parity.

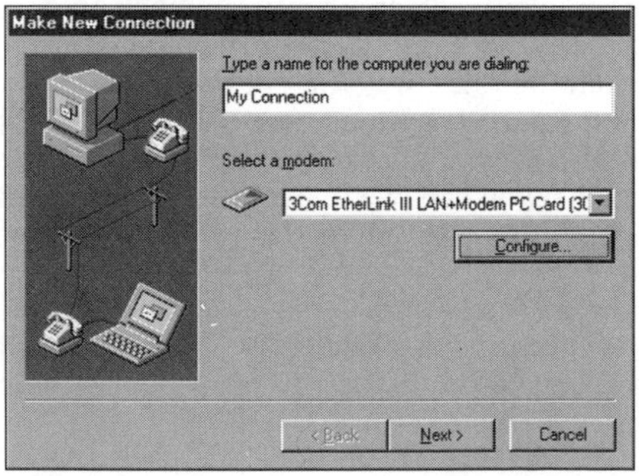

Figure 3-1:
Configure
your
Dial-Up
Networking
connection.

4. Click the Next button.

The Make New Connection dialog box changes, enabling you to enter the telephone number of your Internet Service Provider's modem (see Figure 3-2).

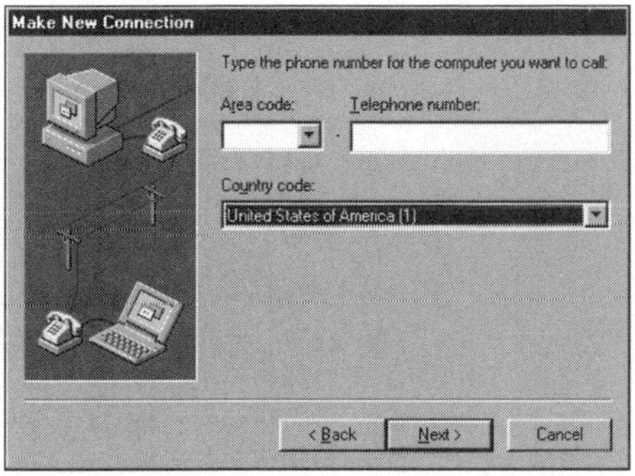

Figure 3-2:
Enter the
telephone
number of
your access
provider's
modem.

5. Enter the area code in the Area Code text box and the modem phone number in the Telephone Number text box.

6. If you're dialing out of country, you may also need to select a country code from the Country Code drop-down list.

The default setting is (1), for the United States.

7. Click the Next button.

The Make New Connection dialog box changes again, verifying that you have successfully set up your new connection.

8. Click the Finish button to end your setup.

After your new dial-up connection is configured, a new icon appears in the Dial-Up Networking window. To start the new connection, double-click the icon; the Connect To dialog box appears (see Figure 3-3). In this dialog box, you specify your user name and password for connecting to your access provider. After you enter these items, click the Connect button to start the connection. You should hear your modem start to dial.

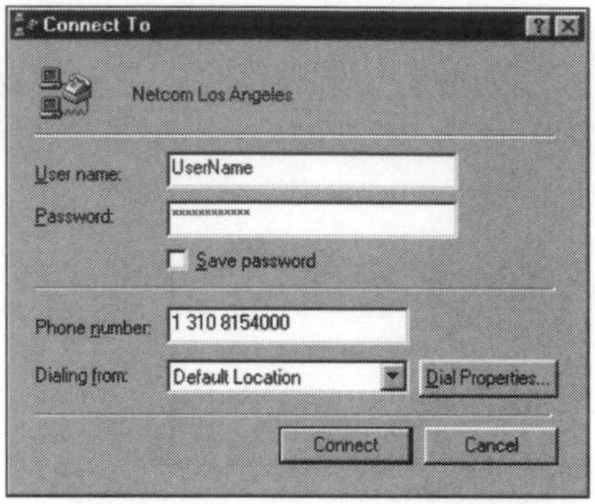

Figure 3-3:
Enter your
user name
and
password
for your
Internet
connection.

After the dial-up connection is established, Dial-Up Networking issues a sound, and a small window appears, telling you that you're connected. A small clock keeps track of how long you stay connected.

Setting up dial-up networking on your Macintosh

Connecting to your Internet Service Provider with a modem and your Macintosh is simple. Chapter 2 shows you how to install and configure a modem and TCP/IP on your Macintosh so that you can establish a dial-up Internet connection to your access provider. After everything is configured correctly, you just launch Mac PPP, the dial-up PPP networking software for Macintosh, and tell Mac PPP where to call. Follow these steps:

1. Choose Apple⇨Mac PPP.

The PPP dialog box appears (see Figure 3-4).

2. Enter your user name in the Name text box.

3. Enter your password in the Password text box.

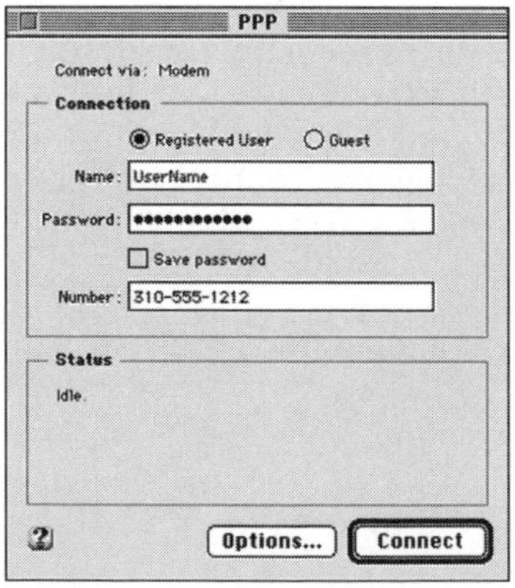

Figure 3-4:
Configure
your PPP
software for
dial-up
networking
on a
Macintosh.

4. **Enter the phone number of your Internet Service Provider's modem in the Number text box.**

5. **Click the Connect button.**

   The connection status appears in the status bar of the PPP dialog box.

Plugging your network into the Net

Connecting your company's computer network to the Internet isn't difficult, and it doesn't need to be expensive. Having your own network connected to the Internet is becoming increasingly important for business communications. As new network-based information appliances become available, a computer network with dedicated Internet access becomes an essential technology for modern commercial activity.

The following sections show you how to connect your computer network to the Internet. Refer to Chapter 2 to find out how to prepare each computer for network communications.

Making the network connection

Your entire network can be connected to the Internet. You can think of this physical connection to the Internet as being a big pipe through which each of the computers on your network can communicate with the Internet. Because your network's connection to the Internet is acting as a pipeline for the other computers, one of the most important considerations is the amount of communications throughput that your connection provides. The amount of communications throughput is commonly referred to as *bandwidth*. Technically, bandwidth is the amount of frequency bandwidth, but in many computer circles, the term has grown to mean throughput (the number of bits per second that can travel through the pipe).

To determine your optimal bandwidth, think about how you plan to use your Internet site and how much Internet traffic it may generate. Remember that this pipe must handle traffic in both directions. You could have only three people on your network, but your Web site may get millions of hits a day from visitors.

Mary, Mary, quite contrary, how do your packets flow?

Because a single pipe to the Internet exists, it must connect to a single point on your network. This single point is a *router* — hardware that routes packets to and from your local network out onto the Internet. Directing the flow of packets is called *routing*. (Packets are described in Chapter 1.)

Many routers are stand-alone pieces of hardware. Figure 3-5 shows a router (the unit on the bottom rack). In other cases, computers have software programs that enable them to act as routers. These programs are known as *software routers*.

Figure 3-5:
Hardware
routers
direct
packets to
computers
on a
network.

Hardware routers are connected to the network hub the same way that any other computer is connected. Normally, a 10baseT or 100baseT connection on the router is used to connect the router to the network. Because hardware routers are most often used on networks that have a dedicated, leased telephone line, such as a high-speed T-1 line that you can lease from the telephone company, an additional connector connects the router to a DSU/CSU (interface equipment on either end of a T-1 phone line), as shown in Figure 3-6.

Both hardware and software routers are designed only to route packets. Packets on your local-area network that are destined for the Internet are directed through the router and out to the Internet. For this reason, your router becomes your gateway to the Internet. In network software that asks you for the IP address of your gateway, you enter the IP address of your router (if it's acting as a gateway).

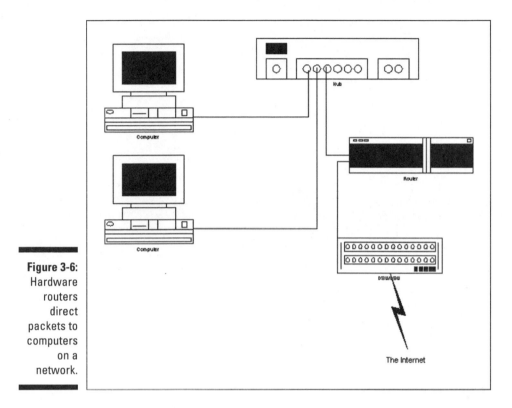

Figure 3-6:
Hardware
routers
direct
packets to
computers
on a
network.

Local- and wide-area networks can use routers without connecting to the Internet. In these cases, routers don't act as gateways; instead, they simply route traffic within the local network.

Packets inbound from the Internet first encounter your router, which delivers the packets to your network hub so that the packets can reach the intended computer on your network. Together, a router and a hub enable every computer on your network to communicate with the Internet simultaneously. The router moves packets to and from the Internet and the hub moves packets to and from the network adapters in each of your computers. After you have a dedicated connection to the Internet for your site, you can begin installing Internet server software and focus on the software side of your Internet site. Chapter 4 shows you how to obtain your own Internet domain name and set up domain name server software for your Internet site.

Chapter 4

What's in a Name?

In This Chapter

▶ Introducing the Internet domain name system

▶ Applying for a domain name of your own

▶ Setting up domain server software

*O*ne of the first things people learn as children is their name. Everything important gets a name. Favorite toys had names. Pets have names. And now, computers have names, too. In this chapter you find out why giving your Internet site a name (called a *domain name*) is important and how you apply for one.

As we mention in Chapter 1, every computer connected to the Internet has a unique IP address. This addressing scheme enables computers to easily identify and communicate with each other. But we're not computers, and humans prefer names to numbers. You can give a name to any computer connected to a network. Your computer's name is known as its *host name*. A host name, such as Buzz or InfoDroid or Walnut, is easier for other people to remember. Network software, such as a Web browser, enables the user to identify a computer by using the computer's name instead of its IP address. Each computer still has an IP address that another computer must use to communicate with it via the network, but people don't need to worry about translating computer names into IP addresses.

The Domain Name System in a Nutshell

Just as a king and queen manage a royal domain, a network server that keeps track of all the host names and IP addresses for a network also is said to manage a domain. A network domain may consist of a single network or several networks within an organization. And, just as in those days of old when each ruler's domain had a name, each network domain has its own name, which is known, naturally enough, as a *domain name*.

You can still refer to individual computers by their host names. This name is that of the computer itself; think of a host name as the computer's first name. Refer to entire networks by their domain names. You then refer to each host within a domain by its host name, followed by its domain name. This situation is much like that of people having a first and a last name. A host's full name is its fully qualified domain name. Suppose, for example, that you name a computer that you call Bruin and that your domain name is `football.com`. The fully qualified domain name of the host computer, therefore, would appear as follows:

```
bruin.football.com
```

In the early days of the Internet (at the time called *ArpaNet*), special text files called *host files* tracked all the computer host names. Any computer connected to the Internet needed a host file that listed every other computer on the network by name. In the 1970s, only a few hundred computers were connected to the Internet, so maintaining a host file wasn't a huge chore. As the number of computers connected to the Internet began to grow rapidly, however, the problems inherent in using the host file system for keeping track of host names quickly became evident. A new system was devised, known as the *domain name system,* or *DNS*.

The DNS is a method of managing domain names on the Internet. DNS groups host into a *hierarchy of authority* (which is actually a hierarchy of responsibility, as you find in most corporations), enabling the distribution of addresses and host information to special name databases around the globe. The software that computers use to manage these databases, which map IP addresses to domain names, is known as a *name server*. Computers all across the Internet employ name servers, although not every computer has such a program installed. Computers contact name servers while looking up domain names. The name servers, which distribute domain name information among themselves, direct the request for information to the name server designated as responsible for keeping track of a particular domain name-IP address.

The domain name hierarchy begins with a *root domain*. In Figure 4-1, the root domain appears at the top of the hierarchy tree; similar to the root directory of a file system (much like the one on your hard drive), the root domain appears in the hierarchy represented as a backslash. Domains that appear directly beneath the root domain are known as *top-level domains*. The top-level domains include the COM, EDU, NET, MIL, GOV, ORG, and two-letter country domains, such as US. An organization known as the *InterNIC* (Internet Network Information Center) is responsible for managing the root domain and several of the top-level domains. *Domain registries* manage the other top-level domains. Table 4-1 lists the major top-level domains and a few of the country domains. More than 250 different country domains currently exist.

Table 4-1	Some Top-Level Domains and Their Descriptions
Top-Level Domain	**Description**
COM	Commercial organizations
EDU	Educational institutions
ORG	Nonprofit organizations
MIL	Military agencies for the United States
GOV	Government agencies for the United States
NET	Networks that provide Internet access or other services
AU	Australia
CA	Canada
IL	Israel
IN	India
US	United States
CA.US	California, United States (Labels exist for all 50 states.)

Don't confuse the two-letter country code domain for Canada with the second-level domain for the State of California. Telling them apart is easy. The U.S. country code (US) domain name always follows the letters *CA* if the latter stand for California.

Domain registries are responsible for knowing where the primary name servers are for all domains within a top-level domain. (Registrars are the people who manage these registries.) Primary name servers are sometimes called *authoritative name servers* because these servers have the authority and responsibility for mapping host names to IP addresses for every computer within a particular domain. If a computer on the network needs to know what the IP address is for a host in a domain, that computer may contact the primary name server for the domain to ask for the address. If the primary name server were the only computer in the world that could answer such a query, however, significant bottlenecks and lots of unnecessary network traffic would result whenever one computer wanted to communicate with another.

Instead, every name server around the world automatically keeps a copy of the host name and IP address information it obtains from another name server. So if the primary name server for a domain stops functioning for a while, many Internet users don't even notice the interruption. Additionally, each domain has an official *secondary name server* that maintains complete copies of the database from the primary server. If you add a new domain to a top-level domain, the domain registry for that top-level domain adds an entry to its database for the primary name server and for all the secondary name servers for the new domain.

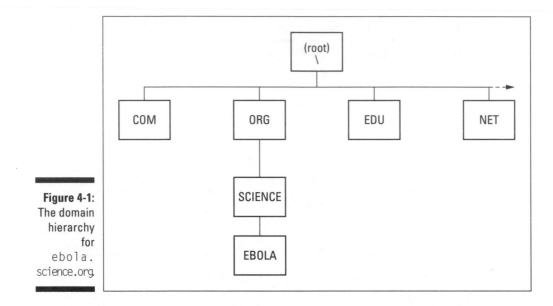

Remember that computers don't know how to deliver information to domain names — only to IP addresses. Aardvark.com contacts the local name server and asks it to provide the IP address associated with Zebra.com. If the local name server knows that information, the server immediately responds by providing the IP address. If the local name server can't resolve the name Zebra.com to an IP address, it must find the name server that can resolve the domain name. This process is a little like playing the card game Fish. One player asks another for a certain card. If the player has the requested card, he hands the card over to the requesting player; if not, the player says, "Go fish!" The player then starts searching for the card he needs.

The local name server then contacts a different name server, one that knows about a greater number of domains. The local name server continues to contact other name servers until, finally, it contacts the primary name server. The primary name server is the ultimate authority for a domain and can normally map the domain name to the IP address for any host within the domain. If the local name server contacts the primary name server and the latter can't provide an IP address for a host name, the local server considers that answer *authoritative* and the host name invalid. After receiving an authoritative answer that a host does not exist, the local name server no longer attempts to contact other name servers.

In other words, the authoritative primary name server has the last word. Either it returns an IP address after another name server asks about a host in its domain, or it indicates that the host does not exist. Because the primary server has the last word, network software knows that asking any other name servers about the host is pointless. If the primary name server can return a valid address, the IP address passes back through the name servers until it finally returns to Aardvark.com, which uses the IP address to communicate with Zebra.com.

The top-level domain COM contains many domains, such as Zebra.com, which in turn can contain many other domains, called *subdomains*. Zebra.com may be the network server of an office in Africa, for example, which may include a subdomain such as Corporate.Zebra.com, whereas the Zebra.com marketing department in New York may use something such as Marketing.Zebra.com. Each of these example subdomains can contain many hosts, including President.Corporate.Zebra.com to identify the president's computer in Africa.

Registering Your Own Domain Name

Every domain name in the entire world is unique. Some domain names may be similar to one another, but no two domain names are identical. The first step on the road to having your own domain name is to decide on your domain name. The first step is to find the registrar who manages the registry that is to contain your domain name. (You find more information on this point in the following section.) The InterNIC (at http://rs.internic.net) is the primary registrar. You can find contact information for all other registrars on this site. The next step is the fun one: coming up with a domain name. In choosing a domain name, you should search the registrar's database to determine whether the domain name you want is already in use. Most registrars provide a mechanism for searching their databases, and some even have a Web query form.

Choosing a domain registry

The InterNIC manages the COM, EDU, ORG, GOV, and NET top-level domains. The InterNIC thus keeps track of any information about these domains (all that end with .com, .edu, .org, .gov, and .net), including contact information and primary and secondary (backup) name servers. Oddly, however, InterNIC and other domain registries aren't responsible for knowing a domain's IP addresses. Instead, the domain registry keeps track of the name servers and the people responsible for knowing the IP addresses that a domain uses. Knowing this fact, you can better understand that one of the steps in applying for a domain name is setting up primary and secondary name servers for the new domain. You then need to provide the IP address of each name server for your new domain at the time you apply to a domain registry. This procedure may seem a little confusing. Say that your adminis-trative assistant is the only one who knows the phone number that someone can reach you on at any one time. The admin assistant becomes like your name server. Anyone who wants to contact you by phone first must contact your admin assistant to retrieve the phone number where you are. As you change numbers, your admin assistant (who keeps track of these things) gives out a new phone number. So anyone who wants to contact you needs to keep track only of your admin assistant's phone number. The admin assistant is then responsible for keeping track of the individual whereabouts of the people for whom the assistant is responsible.

Before you can begin the process of choosing and obtaining a domain name, you need to know where to register as well as what rules the registrar may have for creating and registering domain names. Each country has its own domain registrar. Table 4-2, later in this chapter, lists some countries, their country codes, and contact information.

To determine which organization you need to contact to register a domain name, consider the following points:

- ✔ If you're in the United States and you want a domain name that ends in COM, EDU, ORG, GOV, or NET, contact InterNIC directly.

- ✔ If you're in the United States and want a domain name that ends with US, you need to contact the .US Domain Registry.

- ✔ If you're outside the United States, you need to contact the registry for your country. In this chapter, we provide registration information for Canada and many other countries.

- ✔ If you're a U.S. military organization, contact the Department of Defense.

In this chapter, we mainly offer details on registering a domain name with the InterNIC. The InterNIC has the responsibility of managing the root domain and the NET, COM, EDU, ORG, and GOV top-level domains. You generally find, however, that most registrars in the world require similar information and require its submission via use of a template that's very similar to the InterNIC's template. Fees and regulations vary with each registrar. Contact the registrars directly for more information. (We include contact information in Table 4-2.)

Note: You can register only secondary-level domain names, such as `mysite.com` with the InterNIC. The registrar doesn't create new top-level domains, such as COM or EDU, for you. That's the job of the *Internet Engineering Task Force (IETF)*. Many new top-level domains are currently under consideration. One of the interesting top-level domains in the works is NUM, for using phone numbers as domain names (for example, `6195551212.NUM`). For more information on proposals to the IETF for new top-level domains, you can contact the IETF Web site at the following URL:

```
http://www.ietf.org/
```

You can search the InterNIC database by using the *Whois utility*. To access a Whois utility, you can telnet to rs.internic.net and use the Whois utility on that site.

Start Telnet in Windows 95 or Windows NT by choosing Start⇨Run and entering **telnet** in the Run text box. Then click OK. The Telnet program window then appears. Choose Connect⇨Remote System from the Telnet menu bar to open the Connect dialog box. In the Host Name text box of the Connect dialog box, type **rs.internic.net** and click the Connect button. You get a UNIX prompt that looks like as follows:

```
InterNIC >.
```

Whether you connect to the InterNIC by using Telnet, or you have access to a UNIX machine connected to the Internet, use the built-in Whois utility by typing the following command:

```
whois mydomain.com
```

Follow the command, **whois**, with the name of the domain name that interests you. This name could be the domain name you're interested in registering or any domain name about which you'd like more information. We use this tool to contact people who manage other domains. Most recently, we used it to track down someone sending malicious e-mail. If you're using Telnet, you can now close the Telnet window by choosing Connect⇨Exit from the Telnet menu bar.

In the event that you don't have access to a UNIX machine and the Whois utility that comes with UNIX, you can always use the World Wide Web Whois utility provided by InterNIC at the following address:

```
http://rs.internic.net/cgi-bin/whois
```

The Whois Web page has a single field in which you enter the domain name you want to register. If Whois finds a match for a domain name, the display tells you that information. If no one has that name currently registered, the Whois program returns a NO MATCH message. A search on peanutbrittle.com, for example, returns the following message:

```
No match for peanutbrittle.com
```

Note: Not finding a match in the InterNIC domain database is not a guarantee that your desired domain name is available. A certain name may not appear for several reasons. Perhaps the name is already applied for but not yet activated. The name also may be in dispute and was removed from the database until the dispute is settled.

Becoming a domain contact

One step in obtaining a domain name is becoming the official contact person for your domain. Only official contacts may apply for, change, or remove a domain name. The InterNIC is very cautious about enabling just anyone to request domain name changes. For this reason, the registry has devised a foolproof security system, known as *Guardian*. You're not required to use Guardian to apply for and maintain your domain name, but for security reasons, we highly recommend that you do. The coming section "Registering as a contact" describes how to use Guardian for registering yourself as a contact.

Each domain has the following three kinds of contacts:

- **Administrative contact.** The *administrative contact* is the official representative of an organization. These contacts don't need to have technical knowledge; they just must to be able to answer questions about the organization's use of the domain name.

- **Billing contact.** Quite simply, the *billing contact* gets the bill. Registering domain names with the InterNIC involves paying an anual registration fee. The billing contact is responsible for seeing that the fees are paid.

- **Technical contact.** The *technical contact* is usually the person who manages the primary name server for your domain. Often, this contact is actually your Internet Service Provider. If your organization runs its own name server, however, whoever manages this software is probably the technical contact.

If you're the person in charge, you pay the bills, and you manage your company name server, you can be any or all three of these contacts.

You and your NIC handle

The InterNIC gives contacts a special identification number, known as an *NIC handle*. This situation is a little like that of CB radio, where everyone has a handle. ("This is the Boll Weevil. What's your 20, good buddy?") Unfortunately, NIC handles aren't quite as fanciful and fun as CB handles.

The InterNIC assigns you a NIC handle that consists of your first and last initials and a sequential number. The sequential number follows the last person to register as a contact that had your initials. If you do a Whois search on the name Coombs, for example, you see that Ted Coombs has a NIC handle of TC150. That means that Ted was the 150th person with the initials TC to get an NIC handle. Jason Coombs, on the other hand, has an NIC handle of JC, because Jason was the first JC in the InterNIC database and so doesn't have a sequential number.

Registering as a contact

You can register as a contact in two ways. The simplest way, but also the least secure, is to simply add contact information into your application for a domain name. Registering in this fashion doesn't enable you to register your domain name in a secure fashion or to secure your entry from changes by unauthorized and devious people. A much safer choice is to register yourself as a contact before registering your domain name.

To apply as a contact, you simply fill out a request, which you format by using a contact registration template that InterNIC provides. You can download a copy of the template from the following site:

```
ftp://rs.internic.net/templates/contact-template.txt
```

You must make the request in ASCII text format. In other words, you can't submit a request in Microsoft Word format or in WordPerfect format. Most word-processing programs, including the two we just mentioned, can save files in text (TXT) format.

If you want to refer to an already-completed sample template, you can download it from the following URL:

```
ftp://rs.internic.net/templates/contact-template-
examples.txt
```

If you want your contact information to remain private, you can make this request to keep your contact information provate in your contact registration. The last question on the contact registration template asks you whether you want your information publicly accessible.

The InterNIC offers an additional security feature to protect your domain record from accidental or nefarious changes as part of the contact registration. One question you should answer Yes to is the one that asks whether you want to receive notification of all change requests made to your domain record. This feature may keep you from scratching your head one day, wondering why the Whois lookup for your domain shows someone else's name on it.

After you complete the request, answering all the questions in the template, you must secure it in one of the ways described in the section "The InterNIC Guardian," later in this chapter. Then you can e-mail your request to the InterNIC registrar. The registrar's e-mail address is as follows:

```
hostmaster@internic.net
```

Applying to InterNIC

The instructions we offer for registering a domain name are specific to InterNIC. If you register with any other domain registry, you need to contact that registrar for more information about its registration procedures. With the exception of the Guardian security system, you find that most domain registries use the same application template and similar application procedures.

Registering a domain name is quite simple. Prepare your application; secure it by using one of the procedures discussed in the section "The InterNIC Guardian," later in this chapter; e-mail your application — and wait. You receive notification by e-mail after your domain name is registered. This process usually takes a couple days.

Registering a domain name does not give you any legal right to that name. To guarantee your right to a domain name, you must trademark the name. At the same time you perform your search to find out whether a domain name is available, you also should try to determine whether the name is trade-marked. If you apply for a particular domain name, you must certify that, to the best of your knowledge, the name you want to register isn't trademarked by another person or company. If you violate someone's trademark, you could be in for a very expensive legal battle. Check out `http://www.micropat.com/` for a Web-searchable trademark database.

Preparing your application

Preparing your application for a domain name is similar to registering as a contact. You must follow the registration template exactly. Of course, you can use the online form at the InterNIC Web site, and your completed registration request is e-mailed back to you, formatted correctly.

Follow these steps to prepare your application:

1. **Make sure that you've arranged for both a primary and secondary name server.**

   The InterNIC requires that you (or your service provider) have both name servers configured at the time you submit your application.

2. **Register the administrative, billing, and technical contacts.**

   See the section "Becoming a domain contact," earlier in this chapter, for details.

3. **Choose a domain name.**

   See the section "Registering Your Own Domain Name," earlier in this chapter. Make sure that you first check the registry database to ensure that the domain name you want is available.

4. **Create a text file and import the empty template or access the Web registration form.**

   You can open the template in a text editor such as Notepad or WordPad. Make changes and save the template as an ASCII text file. The alternative to this procedure is to use the Web form on the InterNIC site. You get the correctly formatted text file through e-mail. To use the Web form, go to the following URL:

   ```
   http://rs.internic.net/cgi-bin/domain
   ```

Simply filling in the Web registration form doesn't complete your application for a domain name. InterNIC e-mails a completed and correctly formatted application to you. You *must* e-mail this application back to InterNIC to complete your registration process. Otherwise, you could wait forever, believing that the wheels of progress turn slowly, when actually you need to take the next step.

The InterNIC Guardian

To keep your domain name record safe from unscrupulous people or even accidental changes, InterNIC uses a system by which it accepts applications and updates only from an authenticated contact. Guardian contact authentication ensures that only authorized representatives can make changes to a company's domain record.

The Guardian system consists of the following three contact authentication methods, also called *authorization schemes*:

- ✔ **Mail-from:** InterNIC checks the From field of any e-mail message sent to the registry against the From field of the e-mail message that contains the contact registration form. Be warned, however, that altering the contents of a From field *is* possible in many e-mail client programs, enabling others to pretend that they are you by doing so. This authorization scheme is the least secure and is also the default scheme used if you request no other scheme.

- ✔ **Crypt-password:** This authorization scheme employs a password that you encrypt by using the UNIX crypt program. (The InterNIC Web site provides a Web interface for the crypt program.) You supply your password whenever you send correspondence to InterNIC requesting changes to a domain record. This password is the one you submitted as part of the contact registration process.

- ✔ **PGP:** Pretty Good Privacy is a program that enables you to digitally sign any correspondence sent to InterNIC by using public-key cryptography. (Chapter 11 gives you complete instructions on using PGP.) This scheme affords the highest degree of security and is the one that we recommend.

Choose which authorization scheme you want to use by entering a choice in the AUTH-SCHEME field of any templates you submit to InterNIC.

Make sure that you remember what authorization scheme you request as part of your contact registration. This scheme is the one the InterNIC expects you to use in any future correspondence. Not using the scheme that you originally selected results in the InterNIC ignoring your correspondence — and may even cause the InterNIC to send a warning message to the domain contacts, telling them that someone has tried to send correspondence using an incorrect authorization scheme. (If InterNIC doesn't send such a warning, it should.)

Paying for Your Domain Name

No such thing as a free lunch? Well, the same goes for free domain names. You must pay $50 per year to maintain a domain name with InterNIC. At the time you first register a domain name, the registry bills you for two years — $100. You don't need to pay right at the time you register, however; InterNIC generously bills you or your billing contact within a few months. After two years, the invoice comes annually.

InterNIC accepts several payment methods. You can use your MasterCard or Visa; you can pay by check; and now, you can even use First Virtual's Virtual PIN to pay your InterNIC fees. Some people feel more comfortable using a First Virtual PIN instead of entering their credit card number. For a small fee of $2 a year, you can maintain a First Virtual account. You can apply for your First Virtual PIN at the following URL:

```
http://rs.internic.net/cgi-bin/fv/apply
```

If you're a school (with an EDU label) or a government agency (with a GOV label), InterNIC picks up the tab. (The plan is that, at some time in the future, government agencies are to pay their own way.) Military agencies (MIL) register by using a different service, and the U.S. Department of Defense pays all fees.

If you're curious about the anniversary date for your domain name, you can find this information by performing a Whois search on the domain name. Remember that you receive your bill every year around the domain's anniversary. What an anniversary present!

Where does the money go?

You may be happy to know that a full 30 percent of the money you send to InterNIC goes toward building the intellectual infrastructure of the Internet. InterNIC uses the other 70 percent to support its network services. This money goes to cover the cost of staffing, hardware, software, and all normal overhead. The U.S. National Science Foundation (NSF) controls the amount of money that InterNIC can charge. Back when the NSF operated the InterNIC, domain-name registration was free. The NSF isn't in the business of operating public data networks, however, so the foundation contracted out the duties of running InterNIC to a private company, Network Services.

What happens if you don't pay

If problems arise — as they often do — make sure that you contact InterNIC as soon as possible. You're better off starting a dialog instead of ignoring the problem and letting your domain name expire. The registry's rules are stringent. You must have your payment in no later than midnight of the due date. (You find the due date on your invoice.) If you don't make that date, all contacts receive a 15-day deactivation notice, sent by e-mail and also by regular mail to the domain name user. Many times, however, the user of the domain name is not the contact person. This situation occurs mainly if Internet Service Providers register the domain names for their customers. If you receive one of these notices, you have 15 days to get your payment to the InterNIC. If you miss this date, the registry removes your domain name from its database.

Even if InterNIC deactivates your domain name, you haven't lost the name yet. You have an additional 60 days to get your money to InterNIC to reactivate your domain name. After 60 days, the registry returns your (former) domain name to the pool of available domain names for someone else to snatch up.

Accessing your account information

What good would having a computer connected to the Internet be if you couldn't check the status of your InterNIC account online? Doing so is simple enough. Contact the InterNIC's Web-tracking system by using the tracking number found in your latest correspondence from the registry.

You can find the Web-based tracking system at the following URL:

```
http://rs.internic.net/cgi-bin/finger
```

If you have trouble using the Web form, don't know your tracking number, or need additional information not found online, you may send an e-mail requesting additional information to `mailto:billing@internic.net`.

Sending in your payment

In paying your InterNIC invoice, send your payments to the following address:

Network Solutions, Inc.
P.O. Box 17305
Baltimore, MD 21297-0525
USA

If you're making a payment that's not from an invoice, you need to use a different P.O. Box number and zip code, as follows:

Network Solutions, Inc.
P.O. Box 17304
Baltimore, MD 21297-0524
USA

Making Changes to Your Domain Later

Things change. That's both the nature of life and, possibly, of your Internet domain name or company information. You need to update your domain name record with the InterNIC whenever you change name servers, corporate information, or contact information. (You may wonder why you'd ever want to change name servers. But because Internet Service Providers run most name servers, you're likely to need to change name servers if you ever change Internet Service Providers.)

To minimize your amount of downtime in making such server changes, coordinate the change in your name server carefully between your existing name service provider and the new name service provider.

You're unlikely to need to change information very often, but if you do, you must make all changes to your domain name record by using a template similar to the one you use to register your domain name.

Registering a US domain

The .US Domain Registry administers the .US Domain Registration Services at the Information Sciences Institute of the University of Southern California (USC), under the Internet Assigned Numbers Authority (IANA). You can find its Web site at the following URL:

```
http://www.isi.edu/in-notes/usdnr/
```

The US domain is a top-level domain the same as that of any other country domain in the InterNIC registry. Using the US domain is a little different from using a COM or ORG domain. The US domain uses second- and third-level domains. The last row of Table 4-1, earlier in this chapter, shows an example of a second-level domain that the US domain uses. Second-level domains consist primarily of two-letter state labels, such as TX for Texas or CA for California. In addition to states, the second-level domain can be FED, STATE, K12, LIB, CC, TEC, GEN, DST, COG, MUS, ISA, and NSN. Figure 4-2 illustrates part of the US domain hierarchy.

Figure 4-2:
The US domain is a top-level domain with several domain levels beneath it.

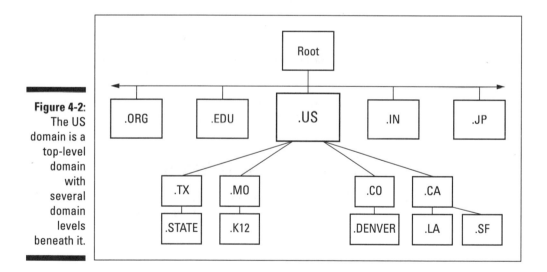

The third-level domain specifies a specific locality. IBM, for example, maintains offices all across the United States. You can easily determine which office uses which domain name by its second- and third-level domains. `IBM.Armonk.NY.US`, for example, could be the domain name for IBM's Armonk, New York, office. The locality can also be the name of a county or a city. If a domain name uses a county name, a fourth-level domain label, `CO`, precedes the county name. The label `CI` precedes city names. `CO.SanDiego.CA.US` is an example of a possible county domain name.

All domain names must be unique, because every domain name eventually points to a single IP address. Every computer connected to the Internet has at least one unique IP address.

Applying for a US domain name

You can request a template for applying for a US domain by sending an e-mail request to the U.S. Domain Registrar at the following address: us-domain@isi.edu. You're likely also to be applying for a domain name within a specific locality, also known as a *delegated branch*. You need to look up the delegated branch contact information by pointing your Web browser to the following URL:

```
http://www.isi.edu/in-notes/us-domain-delegated.txt
```

This Web page contains contact information for every single delegated branch in existence. If you apply for a location that's not currently delegated, you can fill in the Web page form found at the following address:

```
http://www.isi.edu/cgi-bin/usdomreg/template.pl
```

You can also find a text version of the template on the US domain's home page.

Currently, the US domain administrator charges no fee for delegating a locality or other branch of the US domain at that level.

Paying for a US domain name

The delegated branch managers determine the amount of the registration fee. Most of them currently do not charge for this service. If the branch in which you're interested does charge, the fee is usually nominal. Regulations don't prohibit a branch manager from charging a fee — requiring only that the fee is fair and applies equally to all customers.

If you apply for a locality-level domain, you may be relieved to know that the US domain registrar does not currently charge a fee for its services.

Registering a Canadian domain name

CA is the two-letter country code for Canada. The .CA Domain Committee and the University of British Columbia administer the CA domain. The process for applying for a domain name in Canada is a little different from applying through the InterNIC or the US domain registrar.

The structure of the CA domain is similar to the that of US domain. Figure 4-3 shows the CA domain as a top-level domain, with all the other domain levels beneath it.

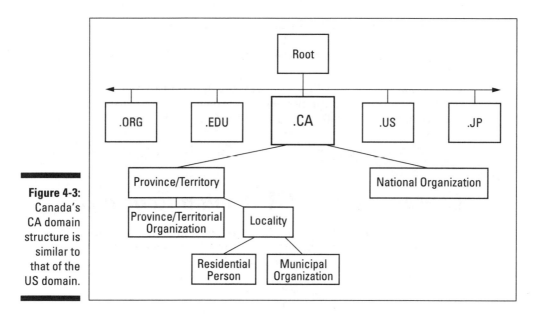

Applying for a CA domain name

One of the first things you want to do in applying for a CA domain name is to make sure that the domain name you want to register is available. The .CA Domain Registrar maintains a list of domain names in Gopherspace. (Remember that Gopher is an Internet information-publishing system similar to the WWW.) Contact the following URL in your Web browser to search the list of domain names already in use:

```
gopher://nstn.ns.ca:7006/7
```

In applying for a Canadian domain name, you work with a member of the domain committee who helps you with your application. The committee member then checks the application by submitting it to the following URL:

```
mailto:ca-domain-checker@relay.cdnnet.ca
```

A syntax checker looks for errors in the application. After the application is error free, it's sent along to the committee for approval.

The committee takes about a week to either approve or deny an application. The committee may contact the applicant for further information. On approval of the application, the registry registers the domain name and the committee notifies the applicant.

The application template is located at the following URL:

```
http://www.canet.ca/canet/templates/ca-domain.application.template
```

The template appears with sample registration information. You simply replace the sample information with your own. Complete instructions for completing this template are online at the following URL:

```
http://www.canet.ca/
```

Contacting the .CA Domain Registrar

For information regarding an application for a Canadian domain name, you can contact the .CA Domain Registrar at the following postal or e-mail address or the listed phone or fax number:

> Department of Computer Science
> University of British Columbia
> Vancouver, BC, Canada V6T 1Z4
> Tel: +1 604-822-6724
> Fax: +1 604-822-5485
> E-mail: ca-registrar@cdnnet.ca

Registering domain names around the world

In most countries of the world, domain registrars are available to accept your domain name registration. Some smaller countries work directly through the InterNIC or one of the larger European domain registrars.

RIPE (Réseaux IP Européens) is a European organization dedicated to the administration and technical coordination necessary for a European IP network. The organization's home page URL is as follows:

```
http://www.ripe.net/
```

The RIPE Network Coordination Centre has utilities for searching the RIPE domain name database. The organization offers a Web-based Whois utility as well as an interface to WAIS (the Wide Area Information Service). The RIPE

Network Coordination Centre does not register domain names. You must apply with the particular country's domain registrar. Table 4-2 lists contact information for many of the countries of the world.

Table 4-2	Domain Registrar Contact Information for Various Countries
Country	*Contact Information*
AT - AUSTRIA	mailto:domain-admin@univie.ac.at
BE - BELGIUM	http://www.dns.be
BG - BULGARIA	http://www.digsys.bg/bg-nic/
CZ - CZECH REPUBLIC	mailto:ors@eunet.cz
DK - DENMARK	http://www.nic.dk/
FO - FAROE ISLANDS	http://www.nic.fo/
FR - FRANCE	http://www.nic.fr/
GA - GABON	mailto:dfk@ripe.net
DE - GERMANY	mailto:dolderer@nic.de
GR – GREECE	mailto:pr@forthnet.gr
GL – GREENLAND	http://www.nic.gl/
HU – HUNGARY	mailto:hostmaster@nic.hu
IS – ICELAND	mailto:hjons@isnet.is
IE – IRELAND	mailto:hostmaster@ucd.ie
IL – ISRAEL	http://www.isoc.org.il/
IT – ITALY	http://www.nis.garr.it/netdoc/TLD-RA/
JO – JORDAN	http://www.nic.gov.jo/
LV – LATVIA	http://www.nic.lv
LI – LIECHTENSTEIN	mailto:huber@switch.ch
LT – LITHUANIA	mailto:daiva@sc-uni.ktu.lt
LU – LUXEMBOURG	http://www.dns.lu/
MD – MOLDOVA	mailto:domain-admin@roearn.ici.ro
MC – MONACO	mailto:noc@rain.fr
NL – NETHERLANDS	mailto:hostmaster@cwi.nl
NO – NORWAY	mailto:hostmaster@uninett.no
PL – POLAND	http://www.nask.pl/

(continued)

Table 4-2 *(continued)*

Country	Contact Information
PT – PORTUGAL	`http://ww.dns.pt/dns/`
RO – ROMANIA	`http://www.rnc.ro/`
RU – RUSSIAN FEDERATION	`http://www.ripn.net/`
SM - SAN MARINO	`mailto:lvianello@intelcom.sm`
SK – SLOVAKIA (Slovak Republic)	`http://www.eunet.sk/sk-nic/`
ES – SPAIN	`http://www.nic.es/whois`
SE – SWEDEN	`mailto:ber@sunet.se`
CH – SWITZERLAND	`mailto:schneider@switch.ch`
TN – TUNISIA	`mailto:hostmaster@Tunisia.EU.net`
TR – TURKEY	`mailto:hostmaster@knidos.cc.metu.edu.tr`
YU – YUGOSLAVIA	`http://ubbg.etf.bg.ac.yu/yu-tld/`

Setting Up a DNS Server

As we mention in the section "The Domain Name System in a Nutshell," earlier in the chapter, most organizations depend on their Internet Service Providers to maintain a DNS server and provide domain name service to the organization. Some advantages to running your own DNS server do exist, however. The two main reasons to do so are for greater flexibility and lower cost.

Running your own DNS server enables you to maintain complete control over your domain names. This situation is known as *managing your domain name space,* or more commonly, as *managing a zone*. When you're ready to register a domain name, you can quickly add the domain name to your DNS server (which you must do before registration). This way, you can avoid the hassle and wait of having your ISP add a domain name to its own DNS server.

Most ISPs charge a monthly fee for managing a domain name (even though the word *managing* is a bit of an overstatement). The ISP performs no additional work on a monthly basis to maintain a domain name in its DNS database. Many ISPs charge per domain name. If your organization maintains several domain names, monthly fees can become costly. Maintaining your own DNS server enables you to avoid any additional charges beyond possible annual fees to a domain name registrar such as the InterNIC.

What is a DNS server?

The first section of this chapter "The Domain Name System in a Nutshell," gives you a detailed overview of what a domain name is and how name servers work to map domain names to IP addresses. The heart of the DNS service is the *DNS server,* or simply the *name server.*

Name servers are specialized databases of zone information. Name server databases contain records, known as *resource records,* that specify many different types of domain information. Table 4-3 lists most currently used resource record types and a brief description of each one.

Table 4-3	Resource Record Types
Record Type	*Description*
AA host	An address.
AFSDB	Special name service specifier for the Andrew File System.
CNAME	Canonical name for an alias.
HINFO	A text string specifying the operating system and CPU type for a particular domain name.
ISDN	Specifies the direct dial-in ISDN number for a given domain name.
MB	A mailbox domain name.
MG	A member of a mail group.
MINFO	Domain names specifying a mailbox responsible for a mailing list and a mailbox responsible for receiving error messages.
MR	A domain name that specifies the new name of a renamed mailbox.
MX	Domain name of a host serving as a mail exchange.
NS	Domain name of the authoritative name server.
NULL	A null resource record. (Nothing is in this record.)
PTR	A *pointer* domain name. PTR points to some domain name within the domain name space.
RP	A domain name that specifies the mailbox of a responsible person. You can also query related TXT records by specifying the domain containing the TXT resource records.
RT	Intermediate domain names to reach a host, with an integer specifying the priority.

(continued)

Table 4-3 *(continued)*

Record Type	Description
SOA	Start of Authority record, which is a complex record specifying the server name of the data source for this zone, the mailbox of the person responsible for the zone, the version number of this copy of the zone information, the refresh rate, retry rate, expiration date, and the minimum Time to Live (TTL).
TXT	A text comment.
WKS	Specifies the address of a Well-Known Service.
X.25	Specifies the PSDN (Public Switched Data Network) address.

Other databases share the information of a zone database. This sharing of information is what makes the DNS system distributed. One DNS server shares its zone information with every other DNS server. The capability of a DNS server to query another's zone database determines the method the databases and servers use in sharing this information. You can see from Table 4-3 that a DNS server's database can contain all types of information, including other name servers, names of persons responsible for the databases, mail exchangers, and, of course, the IP addresses of hosts within the server's domain space (zone).

Configuring a DNS server

If you use the Windows NT Server, you can access a DNS server that's already installed in your operating system. To do so, click the Start button and choose Programs⇨Administrative Tools (Common)⇨DNS Manager from the menus that appear. This sequence starts the Domain Name Service Manager (DNS Manager), as shown in Figure 4-4.

In the DNS Manager, choose DNS⇨New Server from the menu bar to open the Add DNS Server dialog box. Then enter the Name or IP address of the DNS server in the appropriate text box in this dialog box. Click OK.

If you see an icon with a red X through it in the Domain Name Service Manager Window, the DNS Manager was unable to connect to the DNS service on the server you specified. You can delete a server that you may have entered incorrectly by right-clicking the icon and choosing Delete from the pop-up menu that appears.

After the DNS Manager connects to your DNS server, statistics information appears in the list box on the right side of the Manager window (see Figure 4-5). At this point, you can begin setting the properties for your name server. To

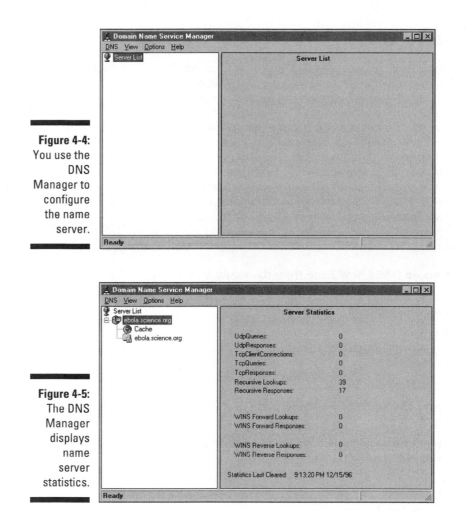

Figure 4-4:
You use the
DNS
Manager to
configure
the name
server.

Figure 4-5:
The DNS
Manager
displays
name
server
statistics.

do so, choose DNS⇨Properties from the Manager's menu bar. You see the IP address of the name server in the Server Properties dialog box. To set the DNS server's properties, follow these steps:

1. **In the Server Properties dialog box, select the Interfaces tab.**

2. **Enter the IP address of the name server you're adding in the text box.**

3. **Click the Add button to return to the DNS Manager window.**

   The new IP address appears in a list in the DSN Manager Window.

Adding a zone

Two types of zones are possible: *primary* and *secondary*. (Remember that a *zone* is the domain space for which a server is responsible.) If a name server has primary responsibility for a zone, that server is a *primary name server* (or *authoritative name server*). Each zone also has at least one secondary name server that acts as a backup to the primary server. The secondary name server periodically queries the primary name server for the most current zone information. In the event that other name servers can't reach the primary name server, these servers query the secondary name server, which they expect to have the most current information. Companies running their own primary DNS servers commonly have their ISP provide secondary name service.

To add a zone for your DNS server to manager, follow these steps:

1. **Choose DNS⇨New Zone from the menu bar.**

2. **Select either Primary or Secondary, depending on the type of zone you're setting up.**

   If you select Secondary, you need to add both the Zone name and Server domain name. (The following instructions are for setting up a Primary zone.)

3. **Click the Next button.**

4. **Enter the name of your new zone in the Zone Name text box (see Figure 4-6).**

   The Zone name is the name of the domain. The name of our domain, for example, is `science.org`.

   Note: Pressing the Tab key takes you to the Zone File text box, which the program automatically fills in for you. We recommend that you accept the default value.

5. **Click the Next button.**

   Another dialog box appears, explaining that you've entered all the zone information.

6. **Click the Finish button.**

The DNS Administrator automatically enters all the basic resource records into the zone database. After finishing the last step in creating a new zone, the basic zone information appears on-screen for you. In Figure 4-7, you can see that three types of resource records are entered: the *start of authority* (SOA), *name server* (NS), and *address* (A) records.

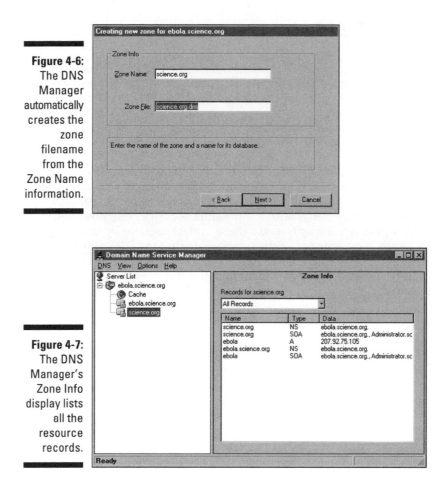

Figure 4-6:
The DNS Manager automatically creates the zone filename from the Zone Name information.

Figure 4-7:
The DNS Manager's Zone Info display lists all the resource records.

You can continue updating your zone information by adding new domains, hosts, and records. Choose the corresponding menu command from the DNS menu. Enter any information for which the program prompts you. The DNS Manager tests each of your entries to see whether it's valid. An invalid entry, however, doesn't prevent the DNS Manager from accepting the record. Instead, you receive an error message if the DNS Manager doesn't think you entered a valid value. As you enter new records, the Manager also prompts you for the resource record type. You want to refer to Table 4-3 for these record types whenever you add new records.

The Future of DNS

Competing technologies to DNS do exist. Competition is good, however, because it drives stagnant systems to change and grow. What some of the competing technologies offer that is currently lacking in DNS is dynamic update capability, the capability for DNS to update itself whenever domains change, and security, where authentication enables DNS servers to be certain from whom they're receiving information.

Currently, Internet drafts are circulating that propose new standards for DNS, including a dynamic update capability. Such capability would enable domain name servers to dynamically insert and delete resource records. Because this capability brings with it a possible security hole, however, another draft proposes a way to make these updates secure by using digital signature technology. Another proposal suggests that the DNS system is an ideal vehicle for managing personal public keys across the Internet. (See Chapter 11 for a complete discussion of digital signatures and public key cryptography.)

Part II
Publishing Information on the Internet

The 5th Wave — By Rich Tennant

"Children- it is not necessary to whisper while we're visiting the Vatican Library Web site."

In this part . . .

An Internet site is much more than just a World Wide Web home page. The Internet's open nature means that your site is limited only by the type of server software that you use, and Internet software companies are producing (at a surprising rate) new server programs that enable everything from video conferencing to virtual worlds.

The key to turning your Internet site into a competitive advantage, a functional virtual workplace, or a useful public relations tool is to add enabling server software. To communicate with others automatically through e-mail, set up an automated e-mail server. To form a cohesive community surrounding a special interest (even if that special interest is you), create a new automated electronic mailing list or run your own Internet BBS. To exchange files easily and securely with others, set up your own FTP server. And if you're serious about making your Internet site something special, examine options available to you other than the World Wide Web.

You're going to invest lots of time and money in your Internet site; it should be at least as easy to set up and maintain as using your favorite word-processing program. The enabling tools discussed in this part make an effort to do just that.

Chapter 5

Publishing on the World Wide Web

*T*he World Wide Web is the most important way for users to navigate the Internet. The Web is a trap, however, for Internet-site developers who don't understand that the Web is just one application of the Internet. In the words of Sir Walter Scott from *Marmion,* "Oh, what a tangled web we weave, when first we practice to deceive!" Don't be deceived by high-profile claims that the World Wide Web is *the* operating system for the Internet. The Web is not an operating system, and it is *not* the Internet.

This chapter shows you how to set up your own World Wide Web site and create Web pages that anyone on the Internet can view in a browser. Some unfortunate and completely unnecessary complexities make Web publishing a little tricky. This chapter points out these complications and clears up confusion before it has a chance to flourish and invade your Web-publishing effort.

You have more than one way to build a Web site:

> ✔ You can build your site the hard way by writing Web pages manually and figuring out the Web-page formatting language, known as *HyperText Markup Language* (HTML).

> ✔ You can build your site the *really* hard way by taking advanced programming classes and then writing your own Web server program and constructing Java applets to display each page.

> ✔ You can build your site the easy way by using a set of software tools that makes building a complex and interactive Web site simple.

So many ways to build a Web site and publish Web pages are now available that the variety is truly amazing. If you understand how the World Wide Web works technically, you can much more easily decide which option is most appropriate for your needs.

Understanding Web Technology

The World Wide Web is a deceptively simple mechanism. The Web is simpler than your computer, and a computer is just a bunch of electrons flowing into a hunk of material that manipulates those electrons to perform calculations. As your computer often does, the World Wide Web seems to be much more complicated than it truly is because of the amazing things that it does.

As does all Internet software, the World Wide Web enables computers to conduct meaningful conversations. The Internet all by itself can provide only the potential for computers to talk with one another; for these computer conversations to have meaning, software must make sense of them. If somebody shows up on your doorstep and rings the doorbell, you answer the door. That's what the Internet provides for computers — one computer can "show up on the doorstep" of another computer and ring the doorbell. What happens next depends on the Internet software that you're using. If the person at the door just stands there and stares at you, nothing happens, and you close the door (or maybe you call the police). Regardless, you can't have a meaningful conversation with somebody who just stands at your door and stares at you. The same is true of computers.

Perhaps the person on your doorstep starts speaking a language that you don't understand. You may attempt to communicate with the person and try to comprehend what he's saying, but without a common language, having a meaningful exchange is difficult. Computers aren't as clever as people; they can't wave their arms or speak louder in an attempt to convey a message to the foreign computer at the doorstep. If computers don't speak a common language, they can't communicate at all about anything. The job of Internet software such as Web browsers, therefore, is to facilitate meaningful intercomputer communication.

How Internet software works

You may already know about the difference between clients and servers on the Internet (especially if you've read other chapters of this book). Any computer that provides information or services to other computers is a *server,* whereas a *client* is any computer that uses the services of a server. A given computer can even act as both a client and a server in different capacities. The behavior of Internet software is what determines whether a computer provides a service to other computers or uses a service provided by other computers.

Network cabling, network cards, modems, telephone lines, and other pieces of equipment in the data-communications grid work to transport bits to and from every computer on the Internet. With all this hardware in place, any computer that has an active connection to the Internet can listen for incoming requests from client computers and respond to those requests. In addition, any computer that has an active Internet connection can contact servers and ask those computers for information or ask them to do something. Special software known as *server software* enables a computer to interpret certain bits as a request from a client. The server software then sends bits back to the client, and special software known as *client software* interprets the bits that it receives as a response from a server.

The agreement between the client software and the server software, which governs how each interprets the bits that it receives across the network, is known as a *protocol*. A protocol is made up of a set of commands that client software sends to server software and a set of responses that the server software sends to the client software. For client software and server software to work together over the network without a common protocol to use for communication is impossible.

How the Web works

The World Wide Web is based on a communications protocol and a page-layout language. The protocol is called *Hypertext Transfer Protocol* (or *HTTP*). HTTP is the set of commands that a World Wide Web client uses to make requests of a World Wide Web server. You're probably familiar with the most common type of client program: the World Wide Web browser. Other types of client programs exist, too, such as World Wide Web spider programs, which automatically traverse and index pages for Internet search utilities. (Refer to Chapter 14 for more information on spiders.)

The page-layout language is called *Hypertext Markup Language* (or *HTML*). HTTP takes care of transferring Web pages across the Internet from server to client, and HTML makes sure that users can view the pages in any browser. Together, HTTP and HTML form the initial foundation of the World Wide Web, but other ways for you to write and deliver Web pages are available. We discuss those other options in Chapter 6.

Web browser programs must use HTTP to communicate with Web servers. Web servers aren't complicated pieces of software. Servers receive requests for files and deliver those files (or deliver error messages, if the files don't exist). Servers also receive data from Web browsers if users fill out HTML forms and submit the forms for processing. You see just how simple Web servers are in the section "Setting Up Your Own Web Server," later in this chapter, as you actually install a server on your personal computer.

At the core of the World Wide Web is an idea within a concept wrapped in a language on top of a standard. The *idea* is that every Internet resource of any kind be accessible from a single easy-to-use, familiar interface. Your World Wide Web browser acts as this interface. Furthermore, the idea proclaims that every Internet resource of any kind should have a simple, consistent address structure, known as a *Uniform Resource Locator* (or *URL*). The URL for an FTP server looks as follows:

```
ftp://science.org/
```

The URL for an HTTP server, commonly known as a Web server, looks like this:

```
http://science.org/
```

Notice in both URL examples that the Internet domain name, `science.org`, is the same. A domain name simply identifies a particular computer on the network. Domain names do not specify which server software to contact on the computer. A given computer can have both an FTP server, which is ready and waiting to have FTP conversations with clients, and an HTTP server, which is ready and waiting to have HTTP conversations with clients. To specify which of the servers to contact as part of a URL address, someone invented the convention of the letter prefix, followed by `://`. This standard turned out to be a really confusing way for computer users around the world to exchange Internet addresses, so a trend is building toward hiding the prefix from users and having them instead think in terms of domain names. Domain names, with all their dots and `multipleletterwordsnotseparatedbyspaces`, also are confusing to many people, of course. We can't speak from personal experience, but some people say that phone numbers were confusing to many people after the telephone came into widespread use.

The concept at the core of the Web is *hypertext* — that is, text with links to text in documents located on computers distributed throughout the Internet. The hypertext concept has been around for ages. Ever since the first person decided to place a reference to another work within his own creation (see, for example, the cave paintings in Vallon-Pont-d'Arc, France), people have been placing references to other writings within their own. A cross-reference enhances the value of writing for those readers who choose to learn more about the subject matter.

What makes hypertext in the World Wide Web different from simple cross-references is that, by using hypertext, you can actually create a link to another document instead of simply referring to it. You aren't limited to text documents, either; you can create links to images, sounds, movies, searchable databases, FTP servers . . . anything at all. Because you use URL syntax to create the link, a World Wide Web hypertext link can point to any Internet resource of any kind. People sometimes use the term *hypermedia* to refer to the diverse resources that link via World Wide Web hypertext, which enables you to access many forms of media beyond just text.

The *language* at the core of the Web is Hypertext Markup Language (HTML). HTML is a special text-formatting language that World Wide Web browsers read to display a document, along with its links to other Internet resources. Creating HTML documents is the key to publishing pages on the World Wide Web.

The *standard* at the core of the Web is Hypertext Transfer Protocol. HTTP enables a World Wide Web browser or other HTTP client program to retrieve HTML documents from an HTTP server. Any images, sounds, or other files associated with an HTML document you can also retrieve through HTTP. Software that combined the URL idea with the hypertext concept, the HTML language, and the HTTP standard finally resulted in the birth of the World Wide Web.

You can integrate all the resources on the Internet through the World Wide Web. Ideally, the Web is a single user interface to all Internet resources that are available to surfers on the Net. Although this goal has some way to go to full implementation, Internet users already rely on Web browsers so heavily that, from their perspective, the World Wide Web *is* the Internet. For users to believe that the Web is the Internet is okay, provided that site builders know and understand the truth behind the magic.

Remember that, from the user's perspective, the World Wide Web *is* the Internet. Any resource that you provide on the Internet *must* be easily accessible through the use of a common Web browser for the average Net surfer to access that resource. If you decide to set up information or busi-ness services that don't integrate well within a Web browser, you must give visitors to your site detailed instructions and even offer live technical support for many of them to step outside the Web to use your resource. With this new understanding, you're ready to join the World Wide Web without getting stuck.

Setting Up Your Own Web Server

Every Internet site should have at least one Web server. We highly recom-mend that you set up your own Internet site rather than rent space on somebody else's servers. The following two sections show you how to set up your own Web server software under Microsoft Windows 95 or Apple's Macintosh operating system. As soon as you install your Web server, you can immediately begin to promote your Internet site and give out the URL to your Web server. See Chapter 15 for detailed instructions on promoting your Internet site so that people can visit it.

Spinning a web in Windows

Installing a Web server in Windows 95 is simple. The best Web server software to use for personal or small-business sites is the Microsoft Personal Web Server, which you can download for free from Microsoft's Web site (at http://www.microsoft.com/). After downloading the software, install it and then restart your computer. The installation is self-explanatory; just follow the on-screen prompts, and everything is set up for you.

The first thing that you notice after restarting your computer is a new icon in the right-hand portion of your taskbar. The Microsoft Personal Web Server icon — the icon that vaguely resembles a computer floating above the Earth — shows you that your Web server is now running.

Microsoft Personal Web Server comes with a default Web home page preinstalled. To see what the default home page looks like in a Web browser, right-click the taskbar icon; then choose Home Page from the shortcut menu that appears. Internet Explorer (or your default Web browser, if not Internet Explorer) opens and receives instructions to contact your Personal Web Server. Figure 5-1 shows what the default home page looks like after your Web browser appears.

Again right-click the Personal Web Server taskbar icon, and this time, choose Properties from the shortcut menu. The Personal Web Server Properties dialog box appears, as shown in Figure 5-2. This dialog box enables you to configure various properties for the operation of your Personal Web Server. Notice that the location of the default home page on your computer's hard drive appears in this dialog box.

You can always click the taskbar icon (not shown in Figure 5-2) if you want the taskbar to appear.

To see start-up options for Personal Web Server, click the Startup tab. Figure 5-3 shows the Startup tab of the dialog box, which indicates whether the Web server is currently running and enables you to select your settings for the two start-up options. If you don't want Personal Web Server to begin running automatically after your computer boots up, make sure that you deselect the Run the Web Server Automatically at Startup check box. If you ever need to start or stop Personal Web Server, remember that this dialog box is the place to do so.

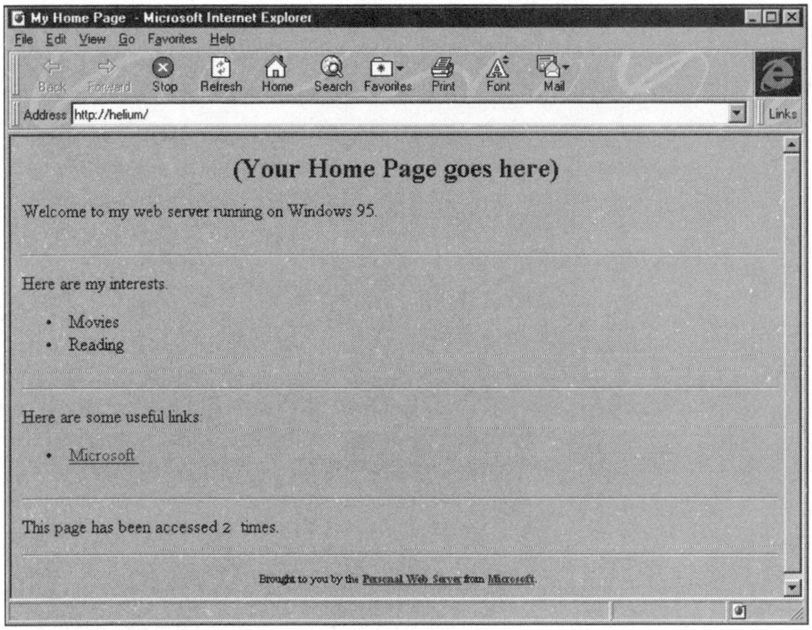

Figure 5-1:
Examine
the default
Web home
page that
Personal
Web Server
provides.

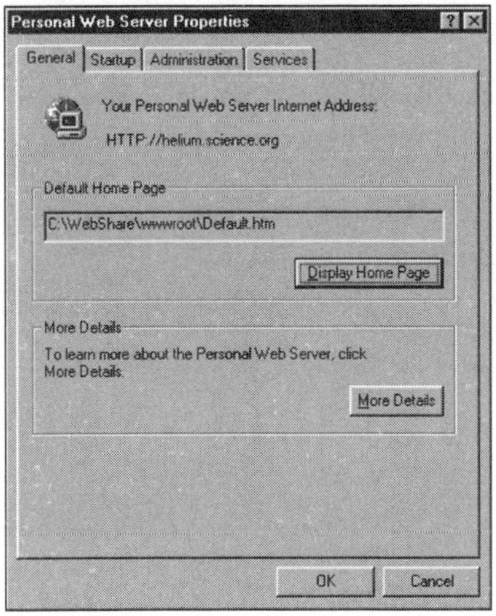

Figure 5-2:
Set
operating
parameters
for your
Personal
Web Server
in this
dialog box.

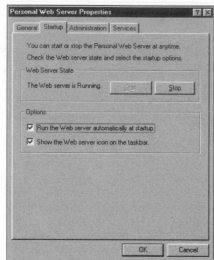

Figure 5-3:
Configure
start-up
options for
your
Personal
Web Server
in this tab
of the
Personal
Web Server
Properties
dialog box.

The Administration tab contains only one button: <u>A</u>dministration, as shown in Figure 5-4. Click the button to start a Web-based application that enables you to more completely administer the Personal Web Server. A *Web-based application* simply means that you use a Web browser to interact with the program, to see its information screens and enter data in its forms, or click its configuration buttons. After you click the Administration button, your Web browser again communicates with the Personal Web Server, but this time, the browser receives instructions to contact the Web server's special Administration system.

Figure 5-4:
Click the
Administra-
tion button
to continue
Web-server
configuration.

When your Web browser appears on-screen this time, it displays the Microsoft Personal Web Server Internet Services Administrator (for Web-based Server Administration), as shown in Figure 5-5. Use this administration tool to configure the remainder of the features that you find in Microsoft Personal Web Server. The server has the capability, for example, to support local user accounts and to add an FTP service that enables your computer to receive files or Web pages from elsewhere on the network.

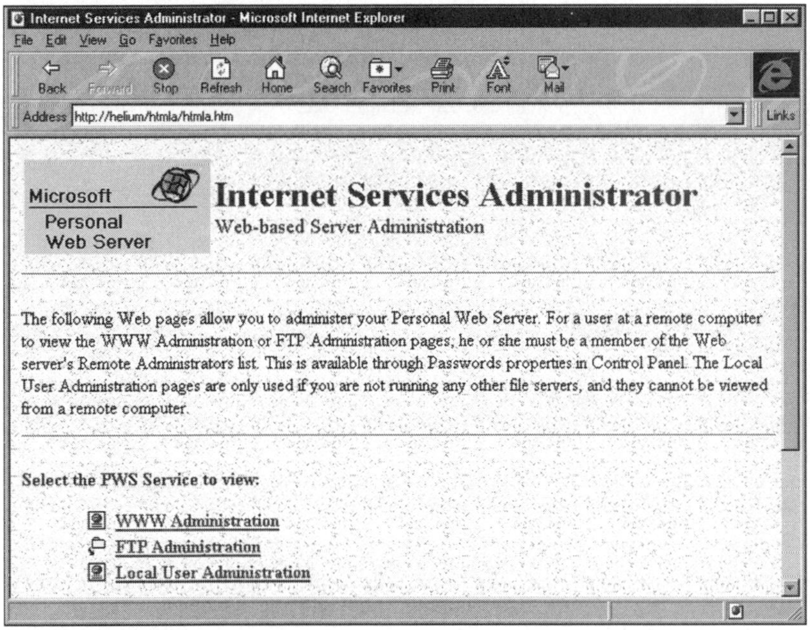

Figure 5-5:
Use the Web-based Internet Services Administrator to manage your server.

Clicking the WWW Administration link takes you to the WWW Administration screen, as shown in Figure 5-6. By using this screen, you can set properties for the Web server, including the password-authentication method for users, the directories that the server uses, and logging configuration.

On the Service tab of this page, you see a Connection Timeout setting, which is a measure of how patient the server is while waiting for Web browsers and FTP clients. Increasing the value of this setting enables Web users who have slow or unreliable Internet connections to retrieve the content of your Web site more easily — provided, of course, that the user is also very, very patient. In most cases, the default setting (600) works just fine.

Another setting in the Service tab is Maximum Connections. This setting determines how many simultaneous connections the server can handle on the network. Each file (including every graphic and every HTML page) that someone retrieves from your Web server by using a Web browser is a separate connection between the browser and the server. A setting of 300, as shown in Figure 5-6, means that users can simultaneously retrieve 300 files. This setting doesn't limit the number of connections that are possible over time, and changing the value normally isn't necessary, because 300 simultaneous connections is a substantial number for your personal computer to serve.

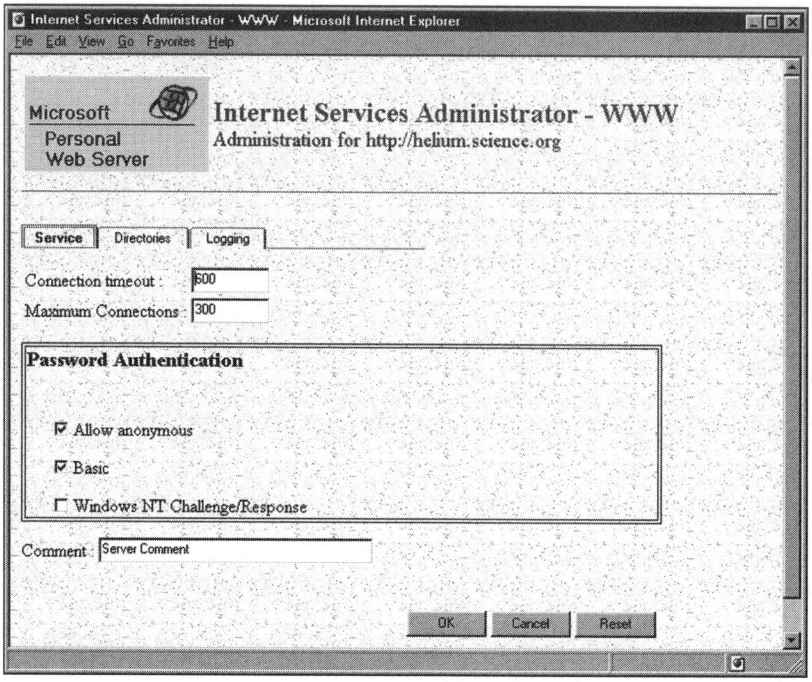

Figure 5-6: Configure the rest of the Web server's settings by using the WWW Administration screen.

The Password Authentication check boxes enable you to pick the type of user identity that you want the server to use in verifying the user IDs and passwords of registered users. You don't need to change these settings unless you decide to implement user accounts and restrict access to your Web site to registered users only. If you deselect the Allow Anonymous check box, every visitor must enter a valid user ID and password to obtain pages from your Personal Web Server.

The Directories tab, as shown in Figure 5-7, usually doesn't require any changes either, but your understanding of what each of these settings means is critical.

The table in this tab has two important columns: Directory and Alias. For each row in the table, the Directory column lists a directory on your hard drive. In this case, each of the directories listed in the column is on the C

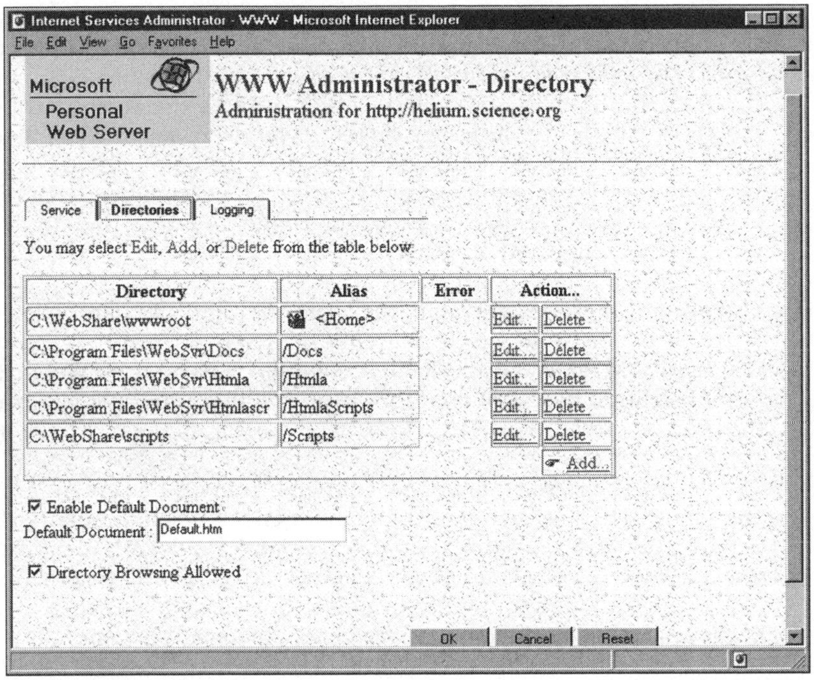

Figure 5-7:
Add, edit, or delete directories and aliases by using the Directory Administrator.

drive. For each of the directories, the Alias column indicates the name of the directory from the user's perspective. As you may have noticed, a URL never contains the drive name, any spaces, or the like. So if a Web user wants to access a file from the C:\WEBSHARE\WWWROOT directory on your computer's hard drive (the DEFAULT.HTM file that contains your Web server's home page, for example), the user can't type something such as the following example, even though doing so makes some sense to a human:

```
http://your.computer C:\WebShare\wwwroot\Default.htm
```

Instead, the Web user must enter something like the following line:

```
http://your.computer/Default.htm
```

If you look at things this way, you see that the entire process is clearly easier for the user if he doesn't need to think about what drive letter and directory your Web site's home page is in. As is true of any Web server, if the user just types a URL such as the following, the Microsoft Personal Web Server home page appears by default:

```
http://your.computer/
```

So the Directory table shown in Figure 5-7 is what the Microsoft Personal Web Server uses to determine which directory to look in for files of certain types. The server considers the preceding example — the C:\WEBSHARE\WWWROOT DIRECTORY — to be the default, or Home, directory. The Home directory is where you eventually place all your Web pages and create additional directories that can help organize your Web site. Whenever a Web user requests a file from the Personal Web Server, the first thing that the server does is check the Home directory to determine whether the requested file exists.

The other directories shown in the table contain files that the Personal Web Server uses for handling special requests. Each of the directories located in C:\PROGRAM FILES\WEBSVR\, for example, is part of the Web-based Administration tool. The directories for executable scripts, such as those that you use to process HTML form data, appear as the last rows of the table.

The two check boxes that appear at the bottom of the screen also are important. The Enable Default Document check box and Default Document text box tell the Web server whether to look for a default file if the user doesn't specify a filename. If, for example, a Web user types the following URL in a Web browser, the Personal Web Server needs to know what to do, because the user didn't specify which file she wanted to see:

```
http://your.computer/
```

By default, the Web server looks for a file named DEFAULT.HTM that's located in the specified directory. In the case of the preceding example, the server searches the Home directory for a file named DEFAULT.HTM, which you saw in Figure 5-1. You can change the name of the default document file, if you want; what you call it doesn't matter as long as the Web server can find the file in each directory. If you don't provide a default document for a given directory on your Web site, the last check box in the Directories tab determines what the Web server can do. The server can either display a complete list of all the files in the directory, or reply to the Web user with an error message. If you want the server to show Web users a list of every file in any directory for which you don't provide a default document, select the Directory Browsing Allowed check box. Otherwise, deselect the box, and make sure that you provide a default document in each of the directories in your Web server's home directory.

The final tab in the WWW Administrator — the Logging tab — enables you to configure Web-server logging preferences, as shown in Figure 5-8. If you don't care to keep a log of accesses to your Web server, you can turn off this feature by deselecting the Enable Logging check box. Otherwise, decide how often you want the server to create a new log file, and pick a directory in which you want the server to create log files. Make sure that you click the OK button after changing settings in any of the WWW Administrator tabs.

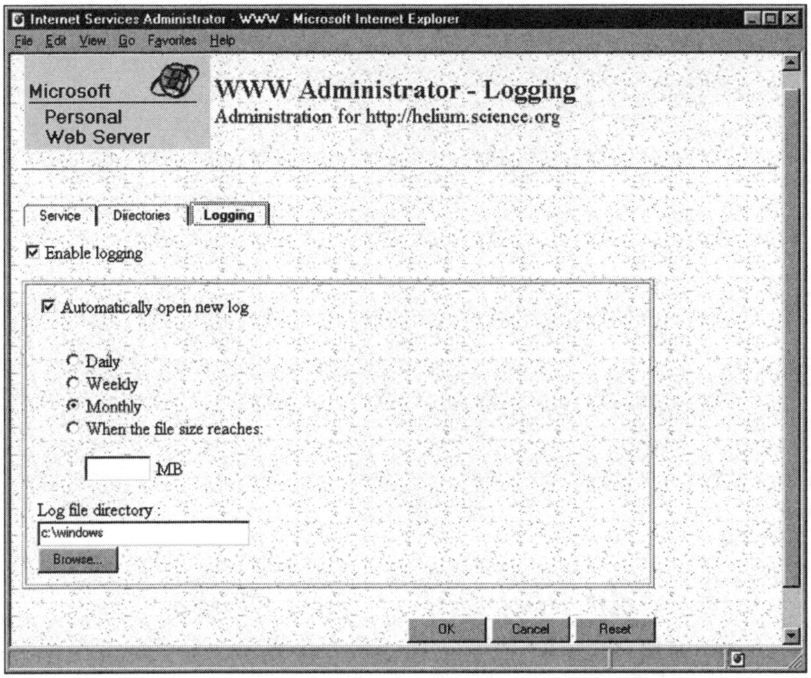

Figure 5-8:
Choose
Logging
preferences
for
recording
Web-server
activity in
this tab.

One last setting is worth looking at; you find it back in the Personal Web Server Properties dialog box. The Services tab enables you to start or stop the two services that Microsoft Personal Web Server provides, as shown in Figure 5-9. By default, after you install the server, the FTP server is disabled. You can determine whether to launch each service automatically as soon as your computer starts or whether to start the service manually every time.

Microsoft Personal Web Server satisfactorily supports a small Web site. The server even offers you the capability to write your own Web programs by using CGI scripts (Common Gateway Interface, an old Web programming standard that doesn't see much use today), ISAPI programs (the Internet Server Application Programming Interface), and IDC (the Internet Database Connector). If you're not interested in Web programming, the Personal Web Server enables you to use Microsoft FrontPage extensions instead to create powerful Web applications.

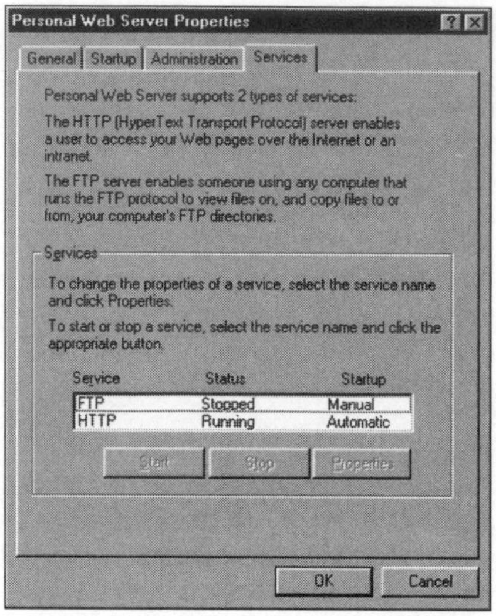

Figure 5-9:
Start or
stop the
Web and
FTP
services in
this tab
of the
Personal
Web Server
dialog box.

What do you get if you cross an Apple with a spider?

With all the cloning and other genetic experiments that are going on these days, it shouldn't be long before somebody crosses an apple with a spider. The result, we predict, should resemble StarNine Quarterdeck's Personal WebSTAR server. You can download the WebSTAR server from StarNine's Web site (at `http://www.starnine.com/`). Installing WebSTAR is self-explanatory; just follow the on-screen prompts.

After you install Personal WebSTAR, launch the program by double-clicking its icon. The window shown in Figure 5-10 appears, enabling you to turn on or off the serving of files through the server. A slide bar enables you to adjust the performance of the server to optimize it for faster serving or faster status updates. Notice also that the Internet address of your computer appears. If your computer doesn't have a permanent, registered Internet domain name, you (and users of your Web site) must use your computer's IP address.

Three buttons also appear in the Personal WebSTAR window. The Open Users & Groups button enables you to update the user and group accounts that your WebSTAR server recognizes. Click the Open Users & Groups button to open the window. You add, remove, or modify Users and Groups for WebSTAR by adding, removing, or modifying Users and Groups for Macintosh file and printer sharing. Personal WebSTAR uses the same users and groups facility as your Macintosh does.

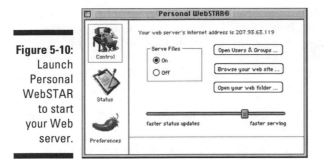

Figure 5-10:
Launch
Personal
WebSTAR
to start
your Web
server.

After you install Personal WebSTAR, the program automatically creates a default Web page and places it on the server. Click the Browse Your Web Site button in the Personal WebSTAR window, or launch a Web browser manually and then enter your computer's IP address to see your server's default Web page. Figure 5-11 shows what the default Web page looks like inside a browser. This page helps you confirm that the server is functioning correctly and gives you the chance to see how your server responds to and communicates with your Web browser.

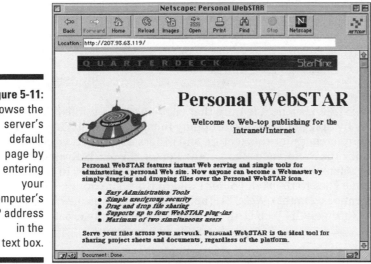

Figure 5-11:
Browse the
server's
default
page by
entering
your
computer's
IP address
in the
text box.

The third and final button in the Personal WebSTAR window gives you an easy way to go right to the folder on your hard drive in which you save Web pages. Click the Open Your Web Folder button to look at the contents of your WebSTAR folder.

In this folder, you must place folders and files that you want to make available to other people via the WebSTAR server. Any folder that you create within your Web folder creates a subdirectory on your Web site. If you create a new folder called ANNUALREPORTS, for example, users of your site access the contents of this directory by using a URL similar to the following example:

```
http://your.computer.name/annualreports/
```

Click the Status icon in the Personal WebSTAR window if you want to see current statistics for your Web server. Figure 5-12 shows a typical Status screen within Personal WebSTAR. Both the current number of connections and the total number of connections received from Web clients appear in this window. A graph shows you the percentage of current usage on a scale of 0 to 100.

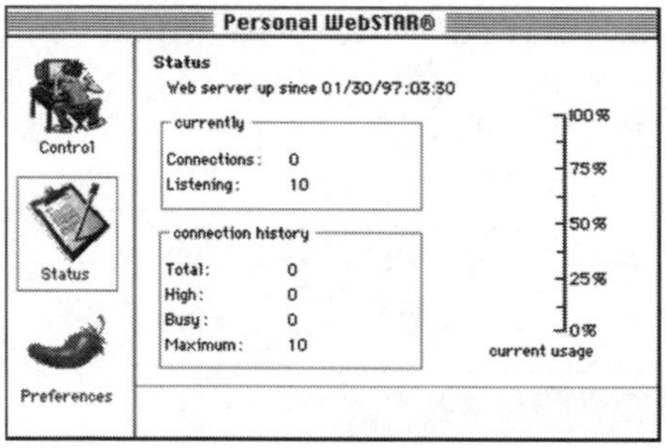

Figure 5-12:
Monitor your Web server's performance by using the Status screen.

Personal WebSTAR has a neat feature that enables you to publish new Web pages simply by dragging files and dropping them on the WebSTAR program icon. To set preferences for this feature and others associated with WebSTAR, click the Preferences icon in the Personal WebSTAR window to display the Preferences screen. Click either the Create Aliases in the Web Folder or Move Files to the Web Folder radio button. The option that you choose determines whether WebSTAR automatically moves new Web-page files that you drop on the WebSTAR program icon or simply creates an alias to the files.

A program called Internet Config also comes along with Personal WebSTAR. Internet Config enables you to set certain Internet preferences in one place and have any Internet program use the Internet Config settings. This program makes configuring new Internet software to work correctly on your Macintosh much easier. Some applications may not need any configuration at all, other than those settings that are already configured in Internet Config.

Click the Open Internet Config button to access the Internet Preferences window, as shown in Figure 5-13. The only Internet Config preference that you need to set for use with WebSTAR is the one in the section for the World Wide Web. Click the World Wide Web icon in the Internet Preferences window, and confirm that the settings that appear meet your needs. You can set other Internet Preferences for e-mail, news, or file transfer if you want.

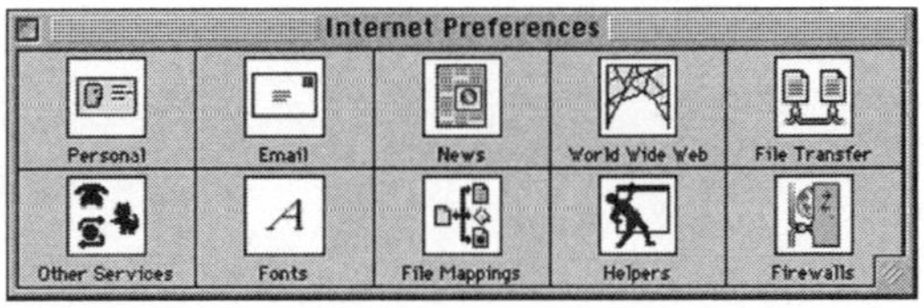

Figure 5-13:
Use Internet Config to set both client and server preferences for your Macintosh.

Setting up your own Web server program on your Macintosh is simple, because Web server programs are simple. Now that the server software is running on your computer, the only thing left for you to do is to create Web pages and publish them. If you don't have dedicated Internet access for your computer, you must rent space on somebody else's Web server. The next chapter shows you how to create and publish pages on your Web site, whether you run your own server or rent Web space.

Chapter 6

Creating Web Pages

● ●

In This Chapter

▶ Using a Wizard to create a Web page

▶ Constructing a Web page by using FrontPage

▶ Going for the Gold — using Netscape Navigator Gold

● ●

*A*nybody can discover how to create Web pages in only a few minutes. You don't need an entire book about creating Web pages; all you need is to see how easy the process is. The key to creating Web pages is to use a software program that can generate and save HTML files. Such a program takes away all the complication of figuring out HTML itself and enables you to concentrate on style and content for each page. You need the following things to create and publish information on your Web site:

✔ At least one HTML document to publish.

✔ A World Wide Web (HTTP) server through which you can publish your HTML documents and other files.

You can either set up your own HTTP server on your personal computer or subscribe to a World Wide Web publishing service on the Internet. Unlike the case with setting up an FTP server, you enjoy no obvious advantage in setting up your own HTTP server on your personal computer, aside from the fact that you avoid paying fees to a World Wide Web service provider. Even this advantage may be offset, however, by the cost of the dedicated Internet connection that you need if you want your HTTP server to be accessible to other users at all times.

Keep in mind also that the World Wide Web is evolving rapidly; standards are changing, and developers are creating new technologies all the time (to enable you, for example, to conduct true electronic financial transactions by using the World Wide Web). If you set up your own HTTP server, you may need to keep up with these changes and continue to update your HTTP server software or buy add-ons to take advantage of these new technologies. On the other hand, if you're using a Web-publishing service provider, the provider should do all these things for you; if it doesn't, you should change service providers.

Whether you set up your own HTTP server or subscribe to a publishing service, you need to create at least one HTML document to publish on the World Wide Web before you consider other options for expanding your presence on the Web. The following sections explain how to create content for your Web site and then send that content to a Web server via the network.

In the past, creating content for the Web was difficult and time-consuming. Today, however, creating Web content is as easy as using a word processor. In fact, by using Microsoft Office 97 and Microsoft FrontPage, you can create sophisticated interactive Web content without doing any programming; FrontPage provides software robots that program the Web for you. Whether you want to receive feedback from your Web visitors or create an online order page that receives and stores product or service orders from customers, FrontPage makes Web interactivity simple to build.

This chapter introduces Microsoft Office 97 and FrontPage and shows you how to build Web content by using these programs. The chapter also briefly covers Navigator Gold, the Netscape Web-page authoring tool, which isn't as fancy as FrontPage and Office 97 but offers an easy way to create Web pages.

Using Microsoft Office 97

The easiest of all the easy ways to create Web pages is to use Microsoft Word 97 and its built-in Web Page Wizard. If you use Word 97, creating Web pages is as easy as typing a regular letter, preparing a flyer, or drafting a memo. Start by launching Microsoft Word 97 and choosing File⇨New. The New Document dialog box appears. This dialog box gives you a way to specify what type of new document you want to create.

Click the Web Pages tab and double-click the Web Page Wizard.wiz icon; then click the OK button. The Word 97 Web Page Wizard guides you through the process of creating a new Web page, including choosing a graphical layout and presentation style.

Creating a page by using the Web Page Wizard

After the Web Page Wizard first appears, it automatically generates a simple Web page and fills that page with sample content. Then the wizard asks you to decide what type of Web page you're going to create. Select a page type from the list and then click the Next button to go on to the next step.

Now that the Web Page Wizard knows what type of page you want to create, it offers the capability to select a visual presentation style. Choose the visual style that you prefer from the list box. As you select styles from the list, the Web Page Wizard shows you in the background what each visual layout looks like. After you make a visual style selection, click the Finish button.

Now you can edit the text of the new Web page and insert any additional graphics or hyperlinks that you want to use in the page. Figure 6-1 shows what a Web page may look like in its final form, after you add your text to the page. To add a hyperlink to the new page, choose Insert⇨Hyperlink. To add a new graphic image to the page, choose Insert⇨Picture and then choose an option from the Picture submenu. You can insert a picture from clip art, from a file, directly from a scanner, from a chart, or by selecting a picture from the Web Art page.

Saving the Web-page file

Before you insert hyperlinks or pictures, Word 97 recommends that you save the new Web-page file. One nice feature of Office 97 applications, including Microsoft Word 97, is the capability to save files directly to an FTP

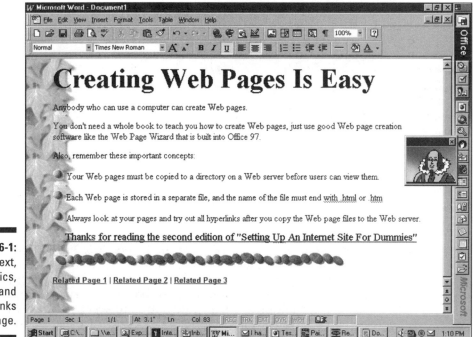

Figure 6-1:
Add text,
graphics,
and
hyperlinks
to the page.

server on the network. (FTP is an abbreviation that stands for File Transfer Protocol, and it's the standard way to transfer files from one computer to another on the Internet.) If you use a Web-publishing service provider instead of running your own Web server program, you're likely to use FTP to deliver Web-page files to your service provider's computer.

Choose File⇨Save As in Word 97 to access the standard Save As dialog box. Now click the Save In drop-down list box and select Internet Locations (FTP) from the list. This action reveals an Add/Modify FTP Locations entry.

Double-click the Add/Modify FTP Locations entry in the Save As dialog box or choose the item from the Save In drop-down list to open the Add/Modify FTP Locations dialog box, shown in Figure 6-2. The Add/Modify FTP Locations dialog box enables you to configure FTP sites for use in saving files from the Save As dialog box. After you configure an FTP Location entry, you can choose the entry from the Save In drop-down list, just as you can any local hard drive or file folder while you save files in Office 97.

Remember that, if you run your own Web server on the same computer that you use to create Web pages, you needn't worry about sending files to your Web server by using FTP. Instead, just save the files on your hard drive in the directory where your Web server expects to find Web pages and directories.

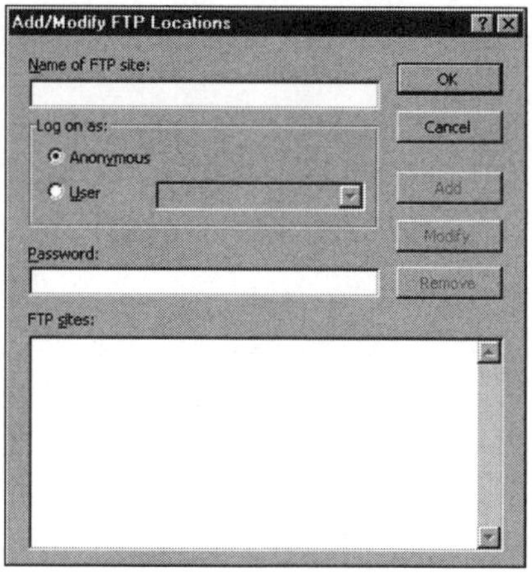

Figure 6-2:
Add or modify FTP locations in this dialog box for easy remote file storage.

Type the domain name of an FTP server in the text box. If you need to supply a particular user name and password after you contact the FTP server that you specify, click the User radio button and then type the user name and password in the appropriate text boxes. Otherwise, click the Anonymous radio button. Click the Add button to accept the new FTP Location entry. After you finish adding FTP site entries, click OK to return to the Save As dialog box.

After you add an FTP Location entry, you see an `ftp://` URL appear in addition to the Add/Modify FTP Locations entry in the Internet Locations (FTP) list. Select the FTP site from the list to access the folders on the FTP server. Word 97 automatically connects to the FTP server and logs in by using the user name and password that you supplied.

Now you can specify the remote FTP server directory in which to save your Web-page file. After you select an FTP location, the dialog box looks normal except for the `ftp://` URL in the Save In drop-down list.

Navigate to the folder in which you want to save your Web page, just as you'd navigate through folders on your local hard drive. After you locate the correct folder, give your file a name in the File Name text box and click the Save button.

Microsoft Word 97 doesn't automatically copy graphics files and the like to the Web server. Instead, the program saves the files to a temporary directory for you to transfer to the Web server.

The final step, because Word saves each of the graphic files associated with the Web page to a local directory, is to use an FTP client program to send these graphic files to the FTP server. Make sure that you send the IMAGE.GIF files to the same directory on the FTP server in which you save the Web page HTML file.

Whether you save the new Web page and its associated graphics files to your hard drive or transfer them over the network to a Web server, an important step is to use a Web browser to verify that your page is accessible.

You can see this file on the Web by visiting the following URL:

```
http://www.science.org/creating_web_pages.html
```

You just saw how easy Microsoft Word 97 is to use for creating and publishing a simple Web page. Microsoft provides another tool, called FrontPage, that makes creating entire Web sites with multiple pages — and even interactive features — just as easy. FrontPage, as is Microsoft Word 97, is a commercial product that you must purchase to use. Contact the Microsoft Web site (at `http://www.microsoft.com/`) for more information.

Using Microsoft FrontPage

You may be surprised to find out that the best Web-site construction kit we've seen is Microsoft Office 97, with its Microsoft FrontPage Web publishing add-on product. (Other products are unacceptably difficult and time-consuming for the typical Web-site construction project.) By using Office 97, you can build a complete Web site in minutes by using built-in interactive forms that enable you to receive information from visitors. Best of all, thanks to the Microsoft FrontPage *bots* (software robots that eliminate the need for Web programming), the information that you receive from users of your Web site — such as contact information or detailed product orders — you can automatically open in Microsoft Excel 97, Microsoft Word 97, or a variety of other programs. And if you know how to write Excel 97 or Word 97 macros, you can easily automate the processing of this Web information. Interactive Web publishing is never going to get any easier than it is today, thanks to Office 97. For more information on these products, see *FrontPage For Dummies,* by Asha Dornfest, and *Microsoft Office 97 For Windows For Dummies,* by Wallace Wang (IDG Books Worldwide, Inc.).

Microsoft FrontPage takes Web publishing to a new level of simplicity. Instead of providing just a Web-page authoring tool, FrontPage gives you extensions to your Web server, which enable FrontPage software robots to interact with your Web visitors. The FrontPage robots eliminate most of the complex Web programming that other programs require to add interactive features to your Web site.

To edit individual Web pages in your Web site, you use the FrontPage Editor. FrontPage Editor works much like a regular word-processing program, and as you may expect, the Editor looks a great deal like Microsoft Word 97. You can use the FrontPage Editor all by itself to create and modify Web pages, or you can use the Editor in conjunction with the FrontPage Explorer to work on a collection of pages, known together as a *Web.* A single Web site can have many Webs, and FrontPage makes managing all of them easy — including any hyperlinks that you may have between Webs.

To manage your Web site and to enable FrontPage to assist you in constructing each page of a new Web, you use the FrontPage Explorer. If you're using FrontPage for the first time, you should start with the Explorer. The Explorer contains several Web wizards that create a complete Web site or a specialized Web section within your site, all automatically. You need only answer a few questions about your preferences for the new Web pages; the Wizard does the rest. The Wizard is fairly simple, but if you have more questions or want to find out more about FrontPage, refer to *FrontPage For Dummies.*

Many, but not all, Web servers work with the FrontPage server extensions. If you use an Internet Service Provider to host your Web site, you must ask the provider whether its Web server supports the Microsoft FrontPage server extensions before you begin. If you run your own Web server, check with Microsoft to find out whether the FrontPage server extensions work with your server or with a Microsoft server such as the Personal Web Server, discussed in Chapter 5.

After your files are sent to the Web server, you can use FrontPage to easily manage them. The FrontPage Explorer displays an interesting graphical view of the pages in your Web. Instead of showing a single page at a time or a list of pages, the Explorer draws a diagram of your site. Each page and each hyperlink appears as part of the diagram. A couple of additional views are possible in the FrontPage Explorer, which makes this feature a useful tool for managing the content of your site.

By choosing Tools⇨Editor to switch to the FrontPage Editor, you can edit the contents of any of the pages in your Web. The FrontPage Editor shows both regular text, which the Editor enables you to edit just as a word processor does, and the FrontPage robots that the Corporate Presence Web Wizard installed. The area of the page shown in Figure 6-3 that reads Company Logo is actually a software robot, as is the navigation bar that appears below the Home title graphic. You can alter the properties of any of the software robots in your page by clicking one and then clicking the robot icon in the toolbar. (The robot icon appears just below and slightly to the right of the Help menu in the FrontPage Editor window.)

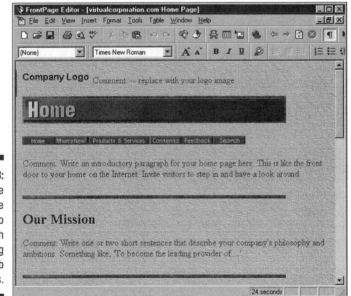

Figure 6-3:
Use the FrontPage Editor to finish customizing your Web pages.

Using the FrontPage Editor takes some practice, but if you're comfortable using a word processor, you don't need long to figure out FrontPage. If you want additional help, we recommend *FrontPage For Dummies,* by Asha Dornfest (IDG Books Worldwide, Inc.).

If you choose to save your new Web to a file instead of directly to a FrontPage-enabled Web server, you must send your Web to the server to publish it for others to access. Choose File⇨Publish FrontPage Web. The dialog box shown in Figure 6-4 appears, enabling you to specify the destination Web server and the name of your FrontPage Web in the dialog that appears. After you finish, click OK to send your Web to the server so that other people can access it across the network.

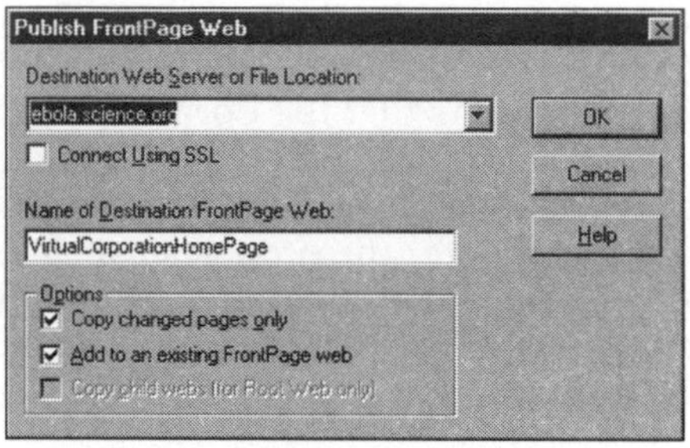

Figure 6-4: Publish your FrontPage Web by filling out this dialog box.

Whether you save your Web directly to the server or choose to publish your Web from your hard drive, an important next step is to try to view your pages in a browser. The only way to know for certain that your Web site is accessible to Internet users is to try to contact it yourself by using a browser. If your Web site appears as you expect, other Web users probably can see everything, too. Don't assume, however, that everything works just because it works for you. Ask somebody else to try your site and report back to you.

Figure 6-5 shows the Virtual Corporation home page that the Corporate Presence Web Wizard creates. Notice that the URL of the Virtual Corporation home page refers to `ebola.science.org`, which is the specified FrontPage-enabled Web server and includes the name that we assigned to the new FrontPage Web.

You can use your own Internet domain name in your URL instead of the domain name of the computer on which your Web server is running. The easiest way to accomplish this task is to ask your Internet Service Provider to configure his server to enable you to use your own domain name. If you run your own Web server, however, you need to know how to configure the server to act as a *virtual server,* which means, essentially, that the server provides Web pages for multiple domain names instead of just one. This feature is sometimes known as *virtual hosting,* but your server software may call the feature something else entirely. See the following Web site for updated information about configuring Web-server software from a variety of software vendors to support multiple domain names:

`http://computers.science.org/internet/site/setup/`

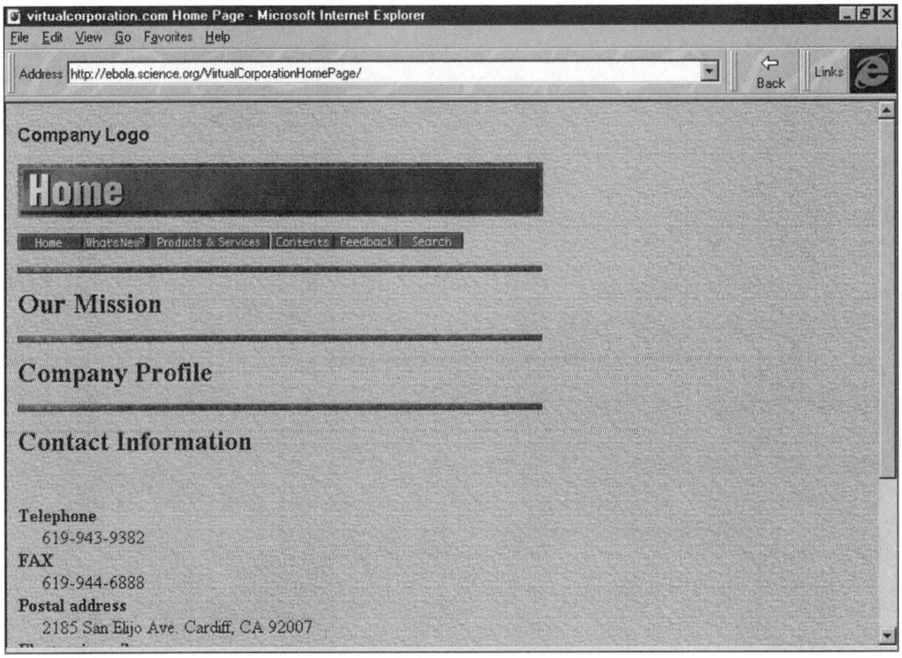

Figure showing the virtualcorporation.com Home Page in Microsoft Internet Explorer:

> **Company Logo**
>
> **Home**
>
> Home | What's New? | Products & Services | Contents | Feedback | Search
>
> **Our Mission**
>
> **Company Profile**
>
> **Contact Information**
>
> Telephone
>   619-943-9382
> FAX
>   619-944-6888
> Postal address
>   2185 San Elijo Ave. Cardiff, CA 92007

Address: http://ebola.science.org/VirtualCorporationHomePage/

Figure 6-5:
Verify that your Web is accessible from the server.

Using Netscape Navigator Gold

Netscape Communications Corporation offers an HTML-authoring tool that isn't as flashy as Microsoft FrontPage or as easy to use as Microsoft Word 97, but the program does work well. The Netscape HTML authoring tool, called Navigator Gold, is a fully functional Netscape Navigator Web browser combined with an HTML editor called Netscape Editor. As you first run the Navigator Gold program, the Web browser appears and looks just like Netscape Navigator, except for an Edit button added to the toolbar.

Click the Edit button or choose File⇨New Document⇨Blank to start the Netscape Editor. A new blank document appears, and you're now ready to begin typing and formatting text in the new Web page. To insert images, hyperlinks, or tables, choose one of those options from the Insert menu.

To demonstrate how easily you can create a simple HTML document by using the Netscape Editor, we used the Editor to construct the INDEX.HTML file on the *Setting Up An Internet Site For Dummies* CD-ROM. You can open the INDEX.HTML file in Navigator Gold simply by choosing File⇨Open File in Netscape Editor or in Navigator. Figure 6-6 shows Netscape Editor constructing the *Setting Up An Internet Site For Dummies* CD-ROM's table of contents document.

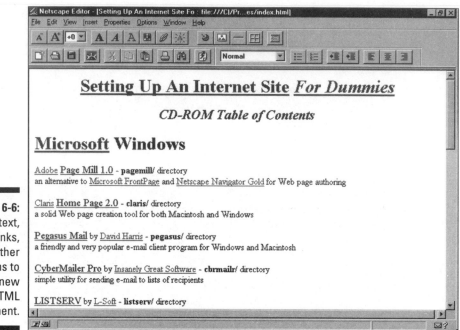

Figure 6-6:
Add text,
hyperlinks,
and other
items to
your new
HTML
document.

To insert a hyperlink into a Web page, select the text that you want to use as the link and then choose Insert⇨Link. A Link Properties dialog box appears, similar to the one shown in Figure 6-7. You see the linked text and a text box, in which you can type a URL to which to link the text. Click OK after you enter a URL, and you see the linked text change color and get an underline to reflect its new hyperlinked status. You can also use a graphic as a hyperlink instead of text. Simply click the graphic that you want to turn into a link and then choose Insert⇨Link. The same Link Properties dialog box appears, enabling you to enter a URL to which to link the graphic.

Make sure that you give a title to each of the Web pages that you create by using Navigator Gold. Choose Document in the Properties dialog box; then click the General tab to access the dialog box shown in Figure 6-8. Type a title for the Web page and then click OK. Visitors to your page see this title at the top of their browser screens.

Overall, Navigator Gold gives you a simple and reliable way to create Web pages. This program is yet another example of the sophisticated Web-authoring tools that are now commonly available. You no longer need to memorize HTML and keep up with the newest changes to HTML to create quality Web pages. Instead, you can have an authoring tool worry about the complex details for you.

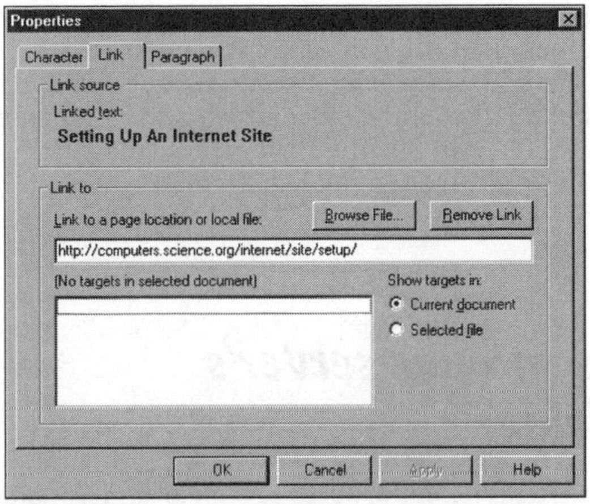

Figure 6-7:
Set the Link
Properties
of the text
or a graphic
to use as a
hyperlink.

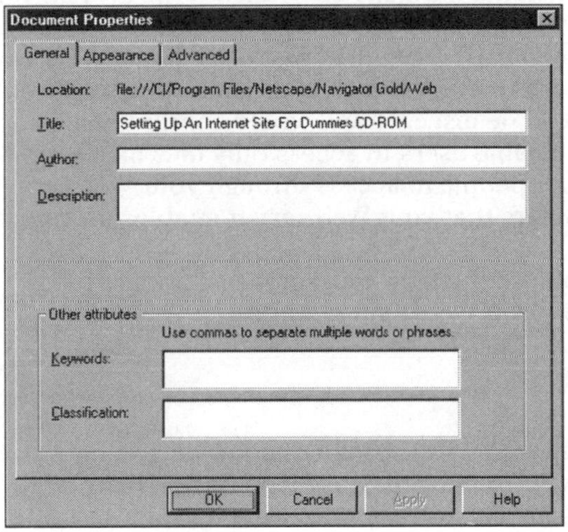

Figure 6-8:
Give each
of your
Web pages
a title.

Publishing Files on Your Web Site

After you finish creating the pages for your Web site, you must send the
pages to the Web server so that other people can access your pages through
a Web browser. You can send content to a Web server in several ways.
Depending on the services that your Web-publishing service provider offers
or the features that your Web server software provides, you may have a
different set of options for getting your Web pages onto your Web server.

The simplest way to send content to your Web server is to copy the files to a folder on your computer's hard drive in which you configure the Web server to look for files. This method works only if you run your own Web server software on your computer. If you use a Macintosh and run the Personal WebSTAR server, as described in Chapter 5, you could also drag and drop files on the WebSTAR program icon to publish them. If you don't run a Web server program on your computer, you must send Web pages to a Web server over the network.

Putting files in your server's Web-page folder

We can't emphasize enough the importance of a clear understanding of this last step in publishing content through your Web site. For privacy reasons, other people on the Internet normally can't access the files on your computer's hard drive, but a Web server does give other people access to files on your computer's hard drive. The Web server doesn't give other people unlimited access to every file on your computer, however, because that arrangement would be insecure and would compromise your privacy. Instead, Web servers enable users to access only files in certain folders. Any file that you want other people to access through your Web server, you must place in one of the folders that your Web server enables users to access.

You could, for example, configure a Web server to use the following directory as the default (or *root*) Web-content folder:

```
C:\INETPUB\WWWROOT\
```

Any file or folder in the WWWROOT folder is now accessible to other people through the Web server. To publish a new Web-page HTML file through your Web server, you save the file and any associated graphics or other items in the WWWROOT folder or one of its subfolders. You could, for example, save a new Web-page HTML file in a folder named SAMPLES that's a subfolder in WWWROOT.

Your new Web page then is available from your Web server to anyone who uses a URL similar to that of the following example:

```
http://your.computer/samples/newpage.html
```

Note: Because the WWWROOT folder is your Web publishing home directory, it is considered the "root" or (\) of your Web publishing directory hierarchy and therefore is not included in the URL of your Web page.

If you decide not to run your own Web server software, you must rent space on a Web server maintained by an Internet Service Provider. To publish your Web-site content through your rented Web server, you still must put files in a special folder. Your service provider's Web server operates exactly the same way as the Web server software that the chapter describes. Your service provider's Web server looks in a particular folder for all your Web-page content, as does the Web server software that you can run on your own computer. The following section explains the issues involved in using a Web-publishing service provider.

Using a Web-publishing service provider

Rather than run your own server, you can subscribe to a Web publishing service, meaning that your Web pages reside on someone else's computer. That computer attaches to the Internet full time and runs a Web server program similar to the ones shown in Chapter 5. This arrangement ensures that your documents are available through the Web all the time — normally, via a fast Internet connection.

Most World Wide Web service providers charge by the number of bytes that you publish and/or by the amount of network traffic that your publishing generates. More people reading your World Wide Web material means more work for your service provider, so the provider passes on the cost to you. You may reach a point at which setting up your own HTTP server is more cost-effective than paying a World Wide Web publisher. You must balance your needs against your resources to decide on the best approach.

After you subscribe to a World Wide Web publishing service, your service provider gives you at least the following things:

- ✔ A user ID and password.
- ✔ A directory in which to place your files so that they're available at your Web site.

Your service provider also gives you instructions on logging in by using your user ID and password and on sending files to your World Wide Web directory. To publish your HTML documents and other Web files, simply follow your service provider's instructions to send the files to your Web directory.

The most common way to send files to your Web directory on your service provider's server is to use an FTP (File Transfer Protocol) client program. WS_FTP, an FTP client program, is one of the most popular FTP programs for Windows; Fetch is a similar FTP client for the Macintosh. (Macintosh programs always have friendlier names than Windows programs do.)

The first thing that you do in using your FTP client program to send files to your Web directory is to tell your FTP client program which FTP server to contact. Your Internet Service Provider tells you the domain name of the FTP server to which you need to send Web files. Figure 6-9 shows how WS_FTP asks you which FTP server to contact (in this case, `ftp.science.org`). The Macintosh FTP client, Fetch, or a different Windows FTP client has a different way of asking you to enter the name of the FTP server to contact.

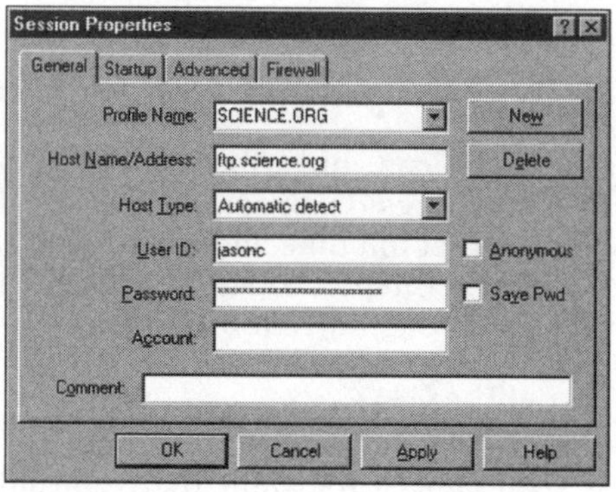

Figure 6-9: Contact your ISP's FTP server by using an FTP client.

After your FTP client program successfully connects to the FTP server, you must locate your remote Web directory and tell the FTP client program to send your Web files to that directory. Every FTP client program works differently, but Figure 6-10 shows how WS_FTP works. The WS_FTP ChgDir button on the Remote System side (the right side) of the WS_FTP window enables you to specify the full name of your Web directory.

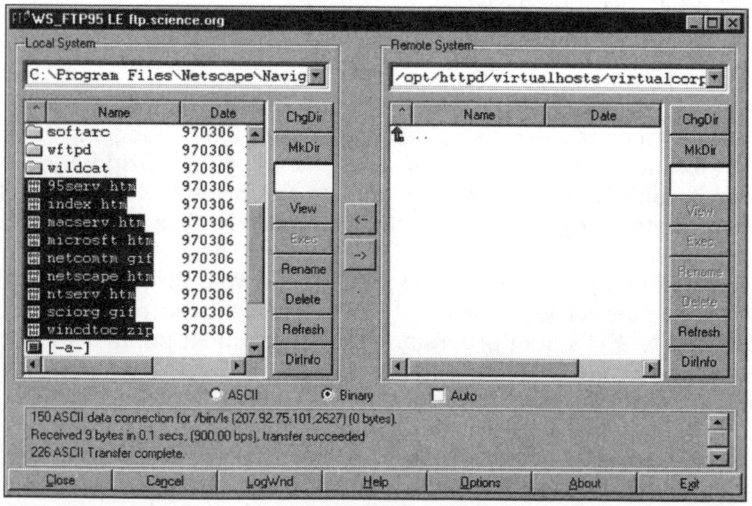

Figure 6-10: Locate your remote Web directory by using your FTP client program.

In the sample screen shown in Figure 6-10, the full name of the sample remote Web directory is as follows:

```
/opt/httpd/virtualhosts/virtualcorp
```

This directory is the one in which we must put Web files if the files are to become accessible to visitors to our Web site. Save any files you want publicly accessible to Web site visitors in this directory. Be aware that the full name of your remote Web directory is going to be something different.

You also want to locate, on your local system, the directory in which you save all the files for your Web site. You must send these files to your remote Web directory so that the files are published on your Web site. At this point, all the files have successfully transferred from the local system directory to the remote Web directory. Now these files should be accessible to our Web-site visitors.

You definitely want to check to make sure that the files that you just sent to your remote Web directory are available through your Web site. Start a Web browser and point the browser at the URL of your site to make sure that the files are accessible. If everything is in order, you can exit your FTP client program. In WS_FTP, you exit the program by clicking the Exit button.

If you're using Microsoft FrontPage to create your Web pages, you don't need to worry about all this complicated FTP nonsense. We highly recommend that you use FrontPage and subscribe only to a Web publishing service that supports FrontPage.

Chapter 7

Setting Up an Automated Electronic Mailing List

● ●

In This Chapter

▶ Creating a mailing list for your Internet site

▶ Using an Internet Service Provider to run a mailing list

▶ Turning your mailing list into an interactive information resource

● ●

*S*ince the days of jungle drums and smoke signals, man has looked for ways to broadcast information to groups of people. Automated mailing-list software is this century's answer to that age-old challenge. Send e-mail to an automated mailing list, and it distributes the mail automatically to everyone who subscribes to that list.

An *electronic mailing list* is exactly what it sounds like: a list of e-mail addresses. Similar to traditional mailing lists filled with postal addresses, an electronic mailing list is a compilation of electronic addresses. You can use electronic mailing lists to send the same message to many people at the same time, just as you use a traditional mailing list to send a printed letter to many people. The only difference between an electronic mailing list and a traditional postal mailing list is the way in which these lists deliver messages to the recipients.

Anyone can create an electronic mailing list simply by gathering a list of e-mail addresses. Many e-mail programs enable you to easily create and send messages to electronic mailing lists. Your e-mail program may, for example, enable you to define special groups such as family members, corporate departments, or project work groups to which you send e-mail on a regular basis. You simply type the e-mail addresses of each person who is part of the group and then tell your e-mail program to send e-mail to the entire group rather than to just one person.

This type of electronic mailing list is so straightforward that we're not going to go into detail in this chapter on how to set one up. Make certain that you refer to the manual that comes with whichever program you choose. If you want to create this type of electronic mailing list, start collecting e-mail addresses of people to whom you want to send e-mail. After you have a list of e-mail addresses to which you want to send a message, just determine how to use your particular e-mail program to send a message to the entire list. Every e-mail program works differently, but most e-mail programs today enable you to create such lists.

You can't prevent people from adding your e-mail address to their mailing lists. The fact that e-mail is inexpensive to send (free, in most cases) makes electronic junk mail (unwanted e-mail) a fact of life that isn't going to change any time soon. Be considerate of other people, and don't send e-mail that people may resent. Remember what your mother said when you were young: Don't talk to strangers — unless, of course, you have a good reason to do so and both you and the stranger enjoy the conversation.

This chapter covers a type of electronic mailing list that's more useful than the old manual type of list: *automated electronic mailing lists*, which are managed by a special server program called a *list server*. A list server still manages a list of e-mail addresses, but with a few twists, as the following list describes:

- ✔ Anyone can add his e-mail address to an automated mailing list by sending a special *subscribe* request via e-mail.

- ✔ Anyone can remove an address from an automated mailing list by sending an *unsubscribe* request through e-mail.

- ✔ The list server enables anyone to send a message to everyone on the mailing list without compromising the privacy of the mailing-list subscribers.

People choose to be part of an automated mailing list. If they no longer want to receive e-mail through the mailing list, they remove their e-mail addresses from the list. This sense of freedom makes people much more comfortable with the idea of subscribing to the list in the first place. In some cases, people experience difficulty in removing their names from a list, but after they begin sending complaints to everyone on the list, the problem usually resolves itself quickly.

If you want to create your own electronic mailing list, seriously consider using a list server to start an automated electronic mailing list. A list server is a valuable information resource for the members of its mailing list. And because people choose to be on the list, they don't consider the e-mail that they receive to be junk. Some mailing lists that list servers manage include tens of thousands of subscribers. Such mailing lists are an excellent way to deliver timely Internet content.

Creating Automated Mailing Lists for the Listless

You can set up an automated electronic mailing list in two ways: You can establish a mailing-list service by using a service provider on the Internet, or you can set up your own automated electronic-mailing-list server on your personal computer. Either way, the setup process is straightforward if you know the anatomy of an automated mailing list.

One of the mailing list's vital organs is its e-mail address, which is known as the *mailing-list address*. This address is where people send e-mail if they want that mail to go to the entire mailing list. A mailing-list address can look something like the following example:

```
computers.enthusiast@science.org
```

The mailing-list address connects to the *list-request address* — the address to which people send subscribe and unsubscribe requests for the mailing list. Remember that all the messages sent to a mailing list end up in all subscribers' electronic mailboxes. No one wants a mailbox full of "Please add me to the mailing list" requests, so you need to send commands of this sort to the list-request address instead. The list-request address usually is the name of the mailing list, followed by `-request`, although many mailing lists also have a list-request address that includes something such as `majordomo` or `listproc`, as shown in the following example:

```
listproc@science.org
```

The list-request address connects to a *mailing-list server* — the program that makes the mailing list possible. The server maintains the list of e-mail addresses for the mailing list and responds to commands sent to the list-request address. If you subscribe to mailing lists on the Internet, you may have encountered two common mailing-list-server programs: *majordomo* and *listproc*.

The mailing-list server connects to the mailing-list manager's (or administrator's) e-mail address. The *mailing-list manager* is the person who oversees the operation of the mailing-list server. Members of a mailing list need to know who the mailing-list manager is so that they can send messages to a human being if problems occur. The mailing-list server software also needs to know the address of the mailing-list manager so that the program can send error reports and other useful information to the administrator.

If the mailing list is a *moderated* one, the mailing-list moderator's e-mail address also connects to the mailing-list server. A *mailing-list moderator* is a person who reads each message that anyone sends to the mailing list and then approves or rejects the message. If the moderator approves the message, that message goes to everyone on the mailing list; otherwise, members of the mailing list never see the message.

Mailing-list moderators can be valuable — if they do their jobs. By reviewing all the mail that comes to a list before the messages go out to everyone, a moderator can screen messages that not everyone on the entire list needs to read. The moderator may choose to eliminate duplicate messages on a subject, messages that have nothing to do with the subject of the mailing list, and solicitation posts (product sales, announcements, and so on) that the moderator deems to be wasteful of the reader's time. The work of a good list moderator can save the members of the list a great deal of time, because members don't need to weed through unnecessary or irrelevant e-mail.

Using an Internet automated-mailing-list service

Alternatives to running your own list server are available. Several companies on the Internet can host your mailing lists for you. Using a list-hosting service is much like posting your Web pages on someone else's server; you get the benefit of a fast connection, support staff, and expertise.

Many Internet Service Providers offer automated-mailing-list services. Best Internet Communications (at `www.best.com`) hosts one of the most popular mailing-list services, called *bestserv*. To set up a new mailing list through `best.com`, you simply fill out a form on a Web page (see Figure 7-1). Users still interact with your mailing list by using e-mail; `best.com` just simplifies the process by enabling you to establish a new list through a Web page.

Other service providers' mailing-list services may not be as easy to use as `best.com`'s, but you shouldn't have too much trouble as long as the provider that you choose gives you reasonable instructions. Unfortunately, all the services provide different mailing-list server programs and give you different instructions for creating a new list; otherwise, we'd tell you exactly how to set up a mailing list by using a service provider. Just remember the following key elements of setting up a list:

- ✔ Your mailing list needs a name and a mailing-list address.
- ✔ Your mailing list needs a list-request address.
- ✔ You must provide the mailing-list manager's e-mail address at some point.
- ✔ You need to decide whether to set up a moderated or an unmoderated mailing list.

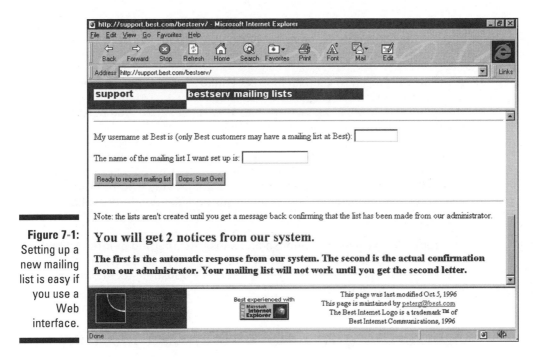

You probably want your mailing-list address to use your registered domain name. This setup makes the process much simpler for people trying to associate your list with your organization. Using your registered domain name is something that you need to work out with your service provider. (See Chapter 4 for information about domain names.) Typically, you need to send the provider a monthly fee in exchange for using the provider as your domain-name server. Your domain-name service also applies to other services that your provider may offer, such as Web-publishing service.

L-Soft offers a list hosting service called EASESM. Using EASESM (or another list-hosting service) is a convenient way to run electronic mailing lists on the Internet without running your own server. One reason why using a list-hosting service can be a good idea is that list servers can become resource hogs while running mailing lists with many subscribers. These servers become resource hogs because every time someone sends a message to a list, an e-mail message must go out to each subscriber on the list. Continually sending e-mail messages to an active list can burden an underpowered server. The other advantage of using a service is the fact that an expert sets up and manages the mailing list for you.

Unlike other Internet server programs, list servers don't need a dedicated connection to the Internet. The list server retrieves e-mail bound for any of the lists it manages each time a connection to the Internet is established. You can send outgoing messages while you're connected to the Internet or queue the messages for delivery at another time. For busy lists, however, placing the list-server software on a machine with a dedicated connection provides superior results.

Note: You still need to keep an Internet e-mail account, even if you use someone else's list-hosting service. Your continued participation in the lists that you run is vital. Remember that to keep a list active, you need to seed the list with information on a regular basis.

Of all the Internet information utilities that you may run, a list server is one of the easiest and most effective. List servers already follow the publish-and-subscribe paradigm that Web technologies are moving toward. Running electronic mailing lists enables you or your organization to broadcast information efficiently and effectively.

List servers have used the publish-and-subscribe method of Internet broadcasting for several years. This method has proved to be so successful that the technology is creeping into other Internet-publishing technologies, such as the World Wide Web.

Subscribing to your automated mailing list

Mailing lists can be *public* (advertised to the public) or *private* (reserved for family members or internal company communications, for example). Chapter 14 provides tips on how to advertise your mailing list to the public.

Whether your mailing list is public or private, Internet users normally need to join your mailing list before they can send or receive mailing-list messages. To join your mailing list, a user must send to your list-request address an e-mail message that contains a command such as that shown in the following example:

```
subscribe ListName
```

`ListName` is the name of the mailing list to which the user wants to subscribe. Giving instructions to people on how to subscribe to your mailing list is simple. The following text provides instructions on subscribing to a mailing list at `science.org` **called** `computers.enthusiast`:

```
To join the SCIENCE.ORG mailing list for computer enthusi-
        asts, send e-mail to listproc@science.org and
        include, in the body of your message, the fol-
        lowing:
subscribe computers.enthusiast FirstName LastName
```

Another option is to tell people how to obtain help on using your mailing list. Your mailing-list software responds to a request for help automatically by sending instructions to the user. Here is an example of instructions that you can give to people so that they can get help from your mailing-list server:

```
For instructions on using SCIENCE.ORG s automated elec
        tronic mailing list server, send e-mail to
            listproc@science.org, and include, in the body
            of your message, the following word:
HELP
```

After a person subscribes to your mailing list, he can send a message to the other subscribers on the list by sending e-mail to the mailing-list address. After a person subscribes to the `science.org` mailing list `computers.enthusiast`, for example, that person can send e-mail to `computers.enthusiast@science.org` to communicate with the other mailing-list subscribers.

Running Your Own Mailing List

To get started creating your own electronic mailing lists on your personal computer, you need the server software that can manage your lists. This list-server software enables people to perform such tasks as these:

✔ Subscribe and unsubscribe from lists.

✔ Get a Help file via e-mail.

✔ Obtain a list of mailing lists that the list server manages.

✔ Obtain a list of other list subscribers. (You can turn off this option for security reasons.)

✔ Tell the list to send e-mail messages in a batch rather than one message at a time. (This method of sending e-mail is called *archiving*.)

An *automated-mailing-list-server program* is a cross between an automatic-reply e-mail system and a simple electronic mailing list. Instead of responding to file requests, however, the automatic-reply component of a mailing-list server accepts subscription and cancellation requests from Internet users.

Setting up an automated-mailing-list software package involves the following two general steps:

1. **Configure an automatic-reply account.**

2. **Create a mailing list.**

The following sections show you how to perform these steps in detail by using Windows and Macintosh mailing-list software.

Setting Up a Mailing List for Windows

The same software that enables you to run a full Internet e-mail server on your Windows-based PC — SLmail — also enables you to set up automated mailing lists. (For instructions on setting up SLmail, see Chapter 9.) The following sections describe how to use SLmail to set up a mailing list.

Using SLmail to set up the list

In this section, you use SLmail to set up a list called `setupshop` — a mailing list for discussions about setting up shop on the Internet. Follow these steps:

1. **Run SLmail and then choose Configuration⇨Users.**

   The System Users dialog box appears.

2. **In the User ID text box, type the user ID for the new mailing list.**

   In this case, type **setupshop**.

3. **In the User Type area of the dialog box, select the Mailing List radio button.**

4. **In the Mailing List Name text box, type a descriptive name for the mailing list.**

   Make sure that you verify that the Mailing List text box contains a valid path and filename.

5. **Click the Add button to add your new mailing list.**

   The System Users dialog box appears, as shown in Figure 7-2.

Configuring the mailing list

Now follow these steps to configure your new mailing list:

1. **Click the Show Configuration button in the System Users dialog box.**

   The Configure Mailing List dialog box appears (see Figure 7-3).

2. **Select or deselect configuration item check boxes to set up your mailing list.**

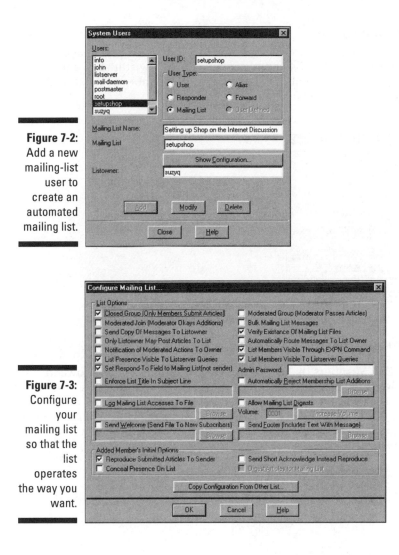

Figure 7-2:
Add a new
mailing-list
user to
create an
automated
mailing list.

Figure 7-3:
Configure
your
mailing list
so that the
list
operates
the way you
want.

The settings shown in Figure 7-3 are good ones for a typical mailing list. Make sure that you select the Send Welcome and Send Footer check boxes; then select a file to send for each. Your software automatically adds a welcome message and footer information to each message that it sends.

3. Click OK.

You return to the System Users dialog box.

Your mailing list is ready.

Editing the mailing list

To manage the mailing list, choose System⇨Mailing List Maintenance. The dialog box shown in Figure 7-4 appears, displaying a few statistics and enabling you to edit the member list manually. (Remember that list members usually add their own names to your list.)

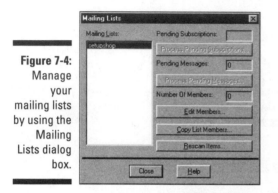

Figure 7-4:
Manage
your
mailing lists
by using the
Mailing
Lists dialog
box.

To manually edit the member list for one of your mailing lists, select that mailing list in the Mailing Lists list box and then click the Edit Members button. The Edit Members dialog box appears. (Notice that, as shown in Figure 7-5, the dialog box's title includes the name of your list.) This dialog box displays the member list and enables you to add, modify, and delete members. Notice that no members of the list appear in Figure 7-5. As soon as you enter a name and address, that action enables the Add button.

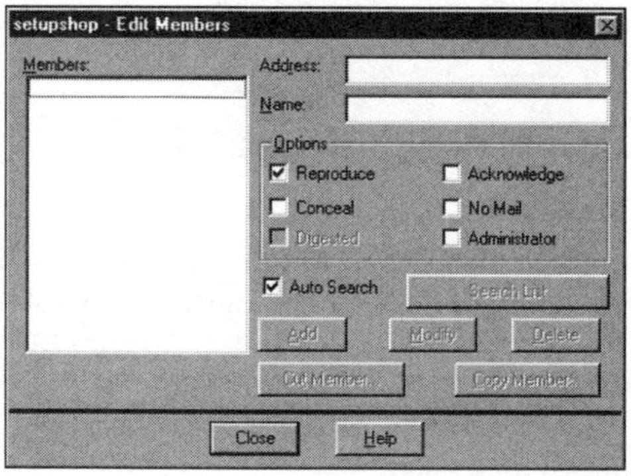

Figure 7-5:
Add,
modify, or
delete
members
manually by
using the
Edit
Members
dialog box.

To add a new mailing-list member manually, follow these steps:

1. Type the new member's e-mail address in the Address text box.

If the Address text box is already filled in, type over its contents.

2. **Type the member's full name in the Name text box.**

3. **Set any options you want for this new user by making selections in the Options area.**

4. **Click the Add button to add the new member.**

Deleting a member is easy; just click the member's e-mail address in the Members list box and then click the Delete button. To modify a member's entry, select the member in the Members list box, make your changes, and then click the Modify button.

Using LISTSERV to set up a list server

Another automated-electronic-mailing-list software package for the Windows environment is LISTSERV, an L-SOFT product. Created in 1986 for IBM mainframes, LISTSERV is now available for several operating systems, including Windows NT, Windows 95, and UNIX. You can download LISTSERV from the following URL:

```
http://www.lsoft.com/
```

You configure LISTSERV during installation. The first dialog box that appears during installation explains the three modes in which LISTSERV can run.

The following list describes these modes:

✔ **Networked.** This mode enables LISTSERV to interoperate with other list servers running on the Internet.

✔ **Tableless.** This mode sets up LISTSERV to run as a slave to a master list server. Slave LISTSERV programs can support master LISTSERV programs.

✔ **Standalone.** This mode is the recommended one for most business and personal operations. This mode is also the only one in which you can run if you don't have an Internet connection.

After you have LISTSERV set up to run in one of the modes described in the previous list, you must finish configuring LISTSERV. The next window that appears is the LISTSERV configuration dialog box. Each subsequent configuration dialog box appears automatically as you click the Continue button. Follow these steps to finish configuring LISTSERV:

1. **Enter the e-mail address of the LISTSERV maintainer (that is, the person who's going to manage the list).**

You perform this action so that LISTSERV can notify the maintainer of any problems that the program experiences. Knowing how to contact the mail server is the most important part of configuring LISTSERV. Click the Continue button whenever you're ready to continue.

2. **Enter the name of the machine running the mail server in the Hostname text box and then click the Continue button.**

   A final dialog box appears at the end of the installation process, telling you what to do if you're notified, on installation, that your license has expired. This dialog box kindly gives you the URL from which you can download a new, unexpired copy of LISTSERV. Click OK to continue.

Configuring LISTSERV

Start the LISTSERV Configuration program from the Windows Start menu. After the LISTSERV Configuration Utility window appears, you can change the basic configuration parameters by clicking the Basic Configuration button, as shown in Figure 7-6. The Configure LISTSERV window appears (see Figure 7-7).

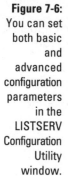

Figure 7-6: You can set both basic and advanced configuration parameters in the LISTSERV Configuration Utility window.

The Configure LISTSERV window enables you to set the name of the machine (NODE), the domain name of the machine (MYDOMAIN), the domain name of the mail server (SMTP_FORWARD), the person to contact in case of problems (POSTMASTER), and the password for creating lists (CREATEPW).

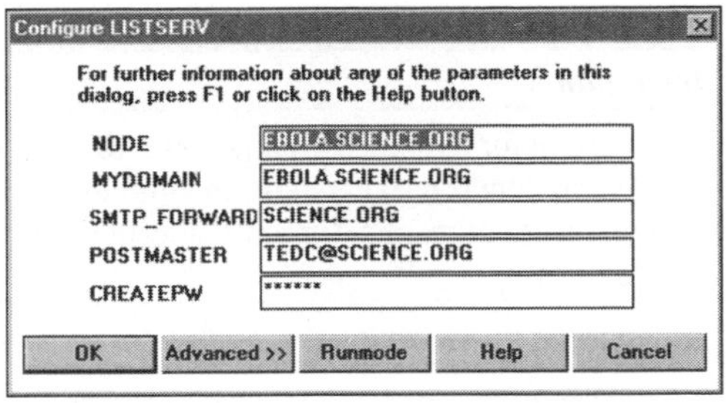

Figure 7-7:
You can set
all the basic
configuration
parameters
in the
Configure
LISTSERV
window.

By clicking the Advanced button in the Configure LISTSERV window, you can view and set all the LISTSERV parameters (as described in Table 7-1).

Table 7-1	Advanced LISTSERV Parameters
Parameter	**Description**
BITNET_ROUTE	This parameter is important only if you have a gateway to BITNET. Most Internet sites can ignore this parameter.
CREATEPW	This parameter is the password set by the administrator for creating new lists. (**Warning:** Giving this parameter to the public may not be a good idea. Your list server could quickly become swamped.)
DEFAULT_SPLIT	If your site is behind a firewall or if your mail server has a maximum mail-file size, set this parameter to something less than that maximum size so that you can split mail files into smaller files.
FILTER_ALSO	This parameter defines a list of users whom you want to block from using your list server.
FIOC_TARGET	You normally set this parameter, which defines the size of the cache in kilobytes, by clicking the Optimize For button in the LISTSERV Configuration Utility window.
FIOC_TRIM	You also set this parameter by clicking the Optimize For button in the LISTSERV Configuration Utility window. This parameter sets the point at which the program aggressively trims the cache to free virtual memory.
FIOC_WARNING	Defines the cache size in kilobytes.
LIST_ADDRESS	Ignore this parameter, which is for BITNET machines migrating to Windows.

(continued)

Table 7-1 *(continued)*

Parameter	Description
LIST_EXITS	This parameter (which is an advanced topic) specifies special custom programs that run whenever a list exits. See the product manual for more information on using this feature.
LOCAL	This parameter identifies the domain for local hosts.
MAILMAXL	This parameter specifies the maximum size of incoming e-mail messages.
MAXBSMTP	This parameter sets the maximum number of recipients for a single e-mail message. You normally set this parameter by clicking the Optimize For button in the LISTSERV Configuration Utility window.
MAXDISTN	Ignore this parameter, and leave the default value (1000) alone.
MYDOMAIN	This parameter is a list of all possible Internet domain names for the machine running LISTSERV. If you have only a single domain name, this parameter is the same as the NODE parameter.
MYORG	This parameter is the name of your organization. The parameter appears in the header of e-mail messages sent from the list server.
NODE	This parameter is the Internet host name of the machine running LISTSERV.
POSTMASTER	This parameter is a colon-delimited list of e-mail addresses of the maintainers of the list server. If bad things happen, these people automatically receive notification by e-mail.
PRIMETIME	This parameter specifies when the machine running LISTSERV is busiest. LISTSERV can delay sending e-mail until a time other than prime time.
RUNMODE	You set this parameter only in the Windows NT version. This parameter defines the three modes discussed in the preceding section.
SMTP_FORWARD	This parameter lists the host name of the machine running the mail server.
SMTP_FORWARDn	For a busy site, you can use this parameter to spread e-mail delivery among several mail servers.

Parameter	Description
SMTP_RESET_EVERY	If your mail server is running on a UNIX system and using Sendmail, this parameter enables Sendmail to run more efficiently by resetting the connection on a regular basis. (Sendmail is the program that many UNIX machines use to correctly direct e-mail messages.)
SORT_RECIPIENTS	This parameter enables mail servers running on UNIX machines to receive the recipient list in presorted form. You normally set this parameter by clicking the Optimize For button in the LISTSERV Configuration Utility window.
TRAPIN	This parameter is a list of blacklisted addresses from which LISTSERV is not to accept e-mail.
TRAPOUT	This parameter is a list of blacklisted addresses to which LISTSERV is never to send e-mail.

Most of the parameters in Table 7-1 are set automatically by LISTSERV, have default values that are sufficient to run LISTSERV, or are set by clicking the Optimize For button in the LISTSERV Configuration Utility window. A handy thing to know is that you can view or change these settings in the configuration utility. You may want to make a note of the default values of these parameters in case you accidentally set a value that causes the LISTSERV program to misbehave.

Creating an electronic mailing list by using LISTSERV

The first step in creating an electronic mailing list is deciding what topic your mailing list covers. No one is going to subscribe to a mailing list unless the list covers a topic of interest. Topics can range from personal family mailing lists to end-user and product support lists. Many special-interest groups also find that electronic mailing lists are an excellent way to disseminate information to people who are interested in their cause.

Your excitement about running your own list, now that you have LISTSERV installed, may lead you to start electronic mailing lists that already exist on the Internet. Don't reinvent the wheel. No law or technical reason prevents you from starting electronic mailing lists on a topic that's identical to someone else's, but you may want to simply subscribe to that group and start your own list on a different topic. (Trying to steal subscribers from someone else's mailing list is never a good idea.) The spirit of cooperation has helped Internet information systems, such as mailing lists, become as successful as they are.

An easy way to determine whether someone else is running a group similar to the one that you want to start is to send an e-mail message to a list server running at L-SOFT. Put the following line in the body of the e-mail message:

```
LIST GLOBAL <search_string>
```

Address the e-mail to the following address:

```
LISTSERV@LISTSERV.NET
```

You then receive a long list of existing electronic mailing lists by e-mail.

The following list describes some additional ways to find out what lists already exist:

- Visit the Mailing Lists section of Yahoo! on the World Wide Web at the following URL:

  ```
  http://www.yahoo.com/
  ```

- Obtain a copy of the Interest Groups List of Lists, which is maintained by a company called SRI. Point your FTP-enabled Web browser to the following address:

  ```
  ftp://sri.com/netinfo/interest-groups
  ```

- You can also use an FTP client program and access the FTP site at `sri.com`. Change `directory` to **netinfo** and download the file INTER-EST-GROUPS. (See Chapter 10 for more information on using an FTP client.)

Using commands to control LISTSERV

You create mailing lists and perform all other administrative functions by sending e-mail messages to the LISTSERV software. The e-mail messages that you send to the list server contain command words and parameters that tell LISTSERV what to do. You can send the following seven types of command keywords to LISTSERV:

- **Access control.** These command keywords specify who can post to the list, who can obtain the list of subscribers to a list, and whether the list is open to general subscription.

- **Distribution.** These command keywords determine how LISTSERV distributes postings to subscribers. Some of the settings determine whether posters receive acknowledgments. Other settings specify the maximum number of postings that can go through the list daily and indicate whether the list is available in digest form (messages that the server sends out in a group instead of delivering one at a time).

- **Error handling.** This group of commands sets automatic deletion, loop checking (when e-mail sent from the server ends up returning only to be sent again and again and again), and the e-mail address of the list administrator.

✔ **List maintenance and moderation.** These commands set the list owner, list editor, and list archive notebook (which tells you about archived copies of the list). The commands also set other subscription parameters, such as the person to contact if users subscribe or unsubscribe.

✔ **Security.** These keywords control who can view the list and whether a list is password protected.

✔ **Subscription.** These keywords determine whether a list is open to general subscription and what user options are set as the default if someone subscribes.

✔ **Other.** These keywords include miscellaneous and rarely used commands.

Note: The LISTSERV software comes with complete documentation on the command keywords that you use to control LISTSERV. Refer to the LISTOWNR.MEMO file in the MAIN directory for detailed information on creating lists.

Giving birth to the new list

The PUT command is the one that you specifically use to create a new electronic mailing list. Only the person you designate as the postmaster or anyone you authorize to create new lists can use this command. Creating a new mailing list makes you the list's *list owner.* You use this list as shown in the following example:

```
PUT <listname>
```

A good idea for protecting your list is to password-protect the list-header information by using the PW command, as follows:

```
PW=xxxxxxx
```

Making changes to your list

If you want to change your list's configuration parameters, first fetch a copy of the list's header information by using the GET command, as in the following example:

```
GET <listname> PW=yourpassword
```

The GET command returns a header file that looks something like the following example:

```
PUT SUPPORT.SAWBLADES PW=XXXXXXXX
* This is a list for the support of saw blades
*
* Owner= TEDC@SCIENCE.ORG (Ted Coombs)
* Notebook= Yes,A,Monthly,Public
* Errors-To= Owner
* Subscription= Open,Confirm
* Ack= Yes    Confidential= No    Notify= No
* Files= No  Mail-Via= Distribute  Validate= No
* Reply-to= List,Respect Review= Public Send= Public
* Stats= Normal,Private X-Tags= Yes
* Default-Options= NoFiles,NoRepro
*
* This list installed on 97/01/01, running under L-Soft s *
            LISTSERV-TCP/IP version 1.8b for Windows NT.
*
* Comments:
```

Edit this header file and send it back to the list server. This file is what instructs the list server to set a list's configuration.

You modify a list's configuration by using the GET and PUT commands in concert. First, you GET the list's header file. Next, you make any modifications. Finally, you include the PUT command in the first line of the header file to replace the current header with the new, modified version.

Using a list server

Sending the INFO command to a LISTSERV list server in the body of an e-mail message returns a list of commands that are available to subscribers and potential subscribers. This information can vary from server to server, depending on how the postmaster configures the list server. You can activate and deactivate the digest feature, for example. (The *digest* feature is the capability to receive postings as a group in a single e-mail message on a regular basis.) How you configure this feature affects whether a subscriber can have messages sent in digest form instead of receiving many e-mail messages at random intervals.

Almost all list servers support the SUBSCRIBE command. The SUBSCRIBE command always includes the name of the mailing list as its first parameter. Some list servers require that you enter your name and sometimes your e-mail address as second and third parameters. Other list servers grab this information from the e-mail header.

Obtaining subscriber information from the e-mail header has its pros and cons. On the pro side, no one can enter your subscription to various mailing lists without your knowledge or approval; all e-mail automatically goes to the e-mail address in the From field of the e-mail header. The downside of this setup is the confusion that sometimes results from a company's e-mail server configuration. If you subscribe from one machine, and the e-mail address includes the name of the machine, this machine is the only one that you can use to post messages to the mailing list. Postings from a different machine, even in the same domain, aren't acceptable.

After you subscribe to a list, you automatically receive messages from the list. You can respond to messages in one of the following ways:

✔ **Respond only to the person who posts the message.** You accomplish this action by sending e-mail to the sender's personal e-mail address, which usually is part of the original message.

✔ **Respond or send new e-mail to the list address** (which usually is `listname@domain.com`). These messages go out to everyone on the list.

To unsubscribe from an electronic mailing list, you must send the `UNSUBSCRIBE` command (usually including the name of the list as a parameter) to the same e-mail address that you used to subscribe — *not to the e-mail address of the list.* The address of the list server depends on the type of list-server software the list owner uses, as shown in the following examples:

`majordomo@domain.com`

`listserv@domain.com`

`macjordomo@domain.com`

You send all commands to the list server, including the `UNSUBSCRIBE` command. The list server e-mail address is probably going to look like one of the examples we just listed. Sending a wrong command or a badly formatted command usually results in an error message sent back to you. The error message usually includes instructions for receiving help from the list server. Sometimes, you can start receiving help by sending either the word `HELP` or the word `INFO` within the body of the message. (By the way, sending both words, just to make sure that you get help, is a safe bet.)

Most list servers ignore or just complain about words in the body of the e-mail message that the server can't understand. If your e-mail client includes a signature file along with each of your e-mail messages, for example, the list server may complain that it doesn't understand each of the words in your signature file. If you can send e-mail without sending a signature, the list-server software is much happier (if a list server can even *be* happy).

Setting Up a Mailing List for Macintosh

Two good Macintosh mailing-list software packages are available on the Internet. AutoShare (which you can read about in Chapter 9) and Major-domo (which we introduce in this chapter) are complete automated mailing-list servers.

Macjordomo uses a different approach to receiving incoming e-mail. AutoShare relies on Apple Internet Mail Server (AIMS) to put new e-mail in the Filed Mail folder. Macjordomo, on the other hand, uses POP (Post Office Protocol) to retrieve new e-mail from any e-mail server. You can use Macjordomo with any e-mail server that supports POP, not just AIMS. AutoShare is ideal if you also use Apple Internet Mail Server and want to run a mailing list. If you don't use AIMS, Macjordomo is a good alternative.

The following sections show you how to use these software packages to create and run an automated mailing list on your Macintosh.

Creating a mailing list in AutoShare

AutoShare mailing lists (which are similar to AutoShare automatic-reply accounts) rely on Apple Internet Mail Server accounts that store incoming e-mail in the Filed Mail folder. To use AutoShare as an automated mailing-list server, you first must create an Apple Internet Mail Server account named AutoShare. This account serves as the subscription- and cancellation-request address for all the mailing lists that you create in AutoShare.

Creating the AutoShare account

To create the AutoShare account in Apple Internet Mail Server, follow these steps:

1. **Switch to Apple Internet Mail Server (already running on your computer) and choose Server⇨Account Information.**

    The Server Account dialog box appears.

2. **Click the Add button to add a new account.**

3. **Type** AutoShare **in the User Name text box.**

4. **Enter a password in the Password text box.**

5. **Type** AutoShare Listserver **in the Full Name text box.**

6. **Select the Account Enabled check box.**

7. **Deselect the Login Enabled check box.**

8. **Select Save as Files from the Forwarding drop-down list.**

9. **In the text box below the Forwarding list box, type the Filed Mail folder name.**

   This name should match that of the Filed Mail Folder selection that you made when you configured AutoShare. (Figure 7-8 shows the completed dialog box.) Make sure that you leave off the trailing colon.

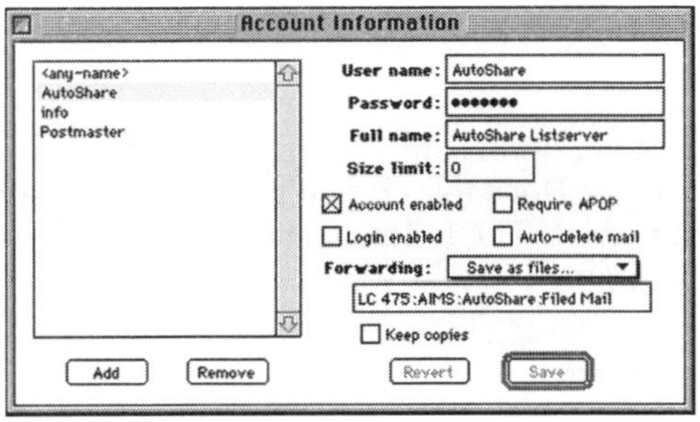

Figure 7-8:
Create an
Apple
Internet
Mail Server
user
account
named
AutoShare.

10. **Click the Save button to save the AutoShare account.**

Just as an automatic-reply account in AutoShare does, the special account that you create in Apple Internet Mail Server needs a corresponding folder in the DOCS directory. The difference is that this account is a special AutoShare account that needs more than a few simple files in its folder; the account needs many special script files that have specific names. Fortunately, the AutoShare user-account folder and its required script files are already installed in your DOCS folder (see Figure 7-14). This AutoShare folder is provided for you as you copy the Auto folder from AutoShare Samples.

Customizing the AutoShare account

The Default file in the AutoShare user-account folder contains helpful instructions, including a full list of commands that the AutoShare mailing-list server recognizes. Messages that don't contain a valid command receive this file in reply. Edit the contents of the Default file to customize the file for your setup. Double-click the Default icon on the desktop to open the file and then follow these steps:

1. **Replace the domain name in the e-mail address (**autoshare@*yourdomain***) with your computer's full domain name.**

2. **Replace** listmaster@*yourdomain* **with your full e-mail address.**

3. **Notice the address** <list>@*yourdomain***; you need to replace this address with the address of your mailing list.**

If you don't know the address of your mailing list yet, remember to come back to this step later.

4. Add a few pleasantries to make the message friendlier.

5. Save the file.

Another file, named Help, exists in the AutoShare user-account folder. Unfortunately, the Help file isn't as helpful as the Default file. Delete the Help file so that the Default file goes out in reply to messages that contain the HELP command.

With the AutoShare account set up in Apple Internet Mail Server and the AutoShare folder present in the Docs folder, you're ready to create a mailing list. Creating a mailing list is easy. The following sections show you how to create a sample mailing list named fun-l.

Creating accounts for the list

First, you must create three Apple Internet Mail Server accounts for the mailing list. Follow these steps:

1. Switch to Apple Internet Mail Server and choose Server⇨Account Information.

2. Type fun-l **in the User Name text box.**

3. Type a password for the account in the Password text box.

4. Type something in the Full Name text box.

What you type here doesn't matter.

5. Deselect the Login Enabled check box.

6. Make sure that the Account Enabled check box is selected.

7. Select Save as Files from the Forwarding drop-down list.

8. In the text box below the Forwarding list box, type the full name of the Filed Mail folder (see Figure 7-9).

9. Click the Save button.

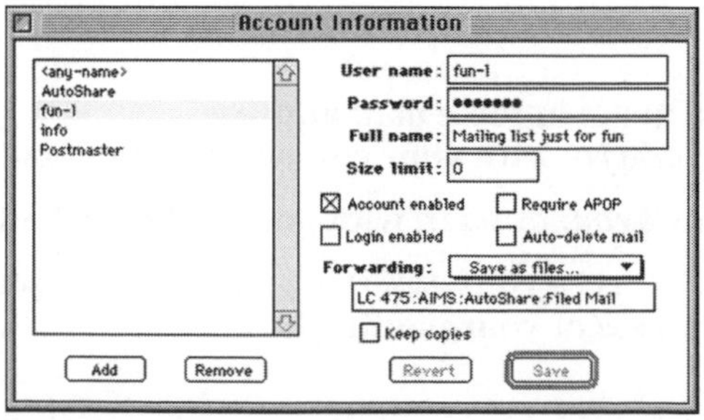

Figure 7-9:
Create a
user
account for
your mailing
list.

The fun-l user account is the e-mail account for the fun-l mailing list. This account needs two support accounts, named fun-l.m and fun-l.d. Every AutoShare mailing list needs three Apple Internet Mail Server accounts, as in this example. The names of the mailing-list support accounts must contain .m and .d extensions, also as in this example.

Creating support accounts for the list

To create the two support accounts for the fun-l mailing list, follow these steps:

1. **From the Apple Internet Mail Server menu bar, choose Server⇨Account Information.**

   An account information dialog box appears.

2. **Type** fun-l.m **in the User Name text box.**

3. **Type a password in the Password text box.**

4. **Type a name in the Full Name text box.**

5. **Select Mailing List from the Forwarding drop-down list.**

6. **In the text box below the Forwarding list box, type the following line:**

   RootFolderName:AutoShare:LS:fun-l.m

   RootFolderName is the name of the root folder on your hard drive (see Figure 7-10).

7. **Click the Save button.**

8. **Repeat Steps 1 through 7 to create a fun-l.d account.**

9. **Open the LS folder in AutoShare, and create a file named fun-l.**

   This file stores the list of subscribers to the mailing list. The LS folder may already contain a fun-l file. If so, double-click the file to edit its contents. Remove the sample e-mail addresses and save the empty file.

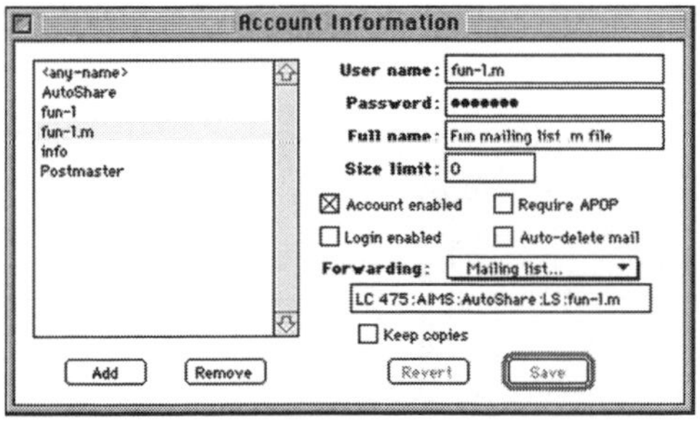

Figure 7-10: Create an .m support account.

Using the mailing list

Now the fun-l mailing list is ready to use. To subscribe to the mailing list, Internet users need to send a message to AutoShare@*your.domain.name* (the AutoShare e-mail address, of course, uses your computer's domain name instead of *your.domain.name*), including the following command:

```
SUBSCRIBE fun-l FirstName LastName
```

FirstName and *LastName* are the user's first and last names. To get help on using your AutoShare mailing-list server, a user can send a message that contains the HELP command — or no command at all — to the AutoShare e-mail address.

Serving a delicious mailing list by using Macjordomo

Using Macjordomo with Apple Internet Mail Server to run a mailing list is easy. The first step is creating a Macjordomo user account in Apple Internet Mail Server. The Macjordomo user account serves the same purpose as the AutoShare user account that we describe in the preceding section; the account acts as the automatic-reply account for the mailing-list server, enabling Internet users to subscribe to and unsubscribe from your Macjordomo mailing lists.

To create a Macjordomo account, follow these steps:

1. **Switch to Apple Internet Mail Server and choose Server⇨Account Information from its menu bar.**

2. **Create a new user account named macjordomo by following the steps in the section "Creating the AutoShare account," earlier in this chapter.**

3. **Select both the Account Enabled and Login Enabled check boxes.**

4. **Leave the Forwarding drop-down list set to No Forwarding (see Figure 7-11).**

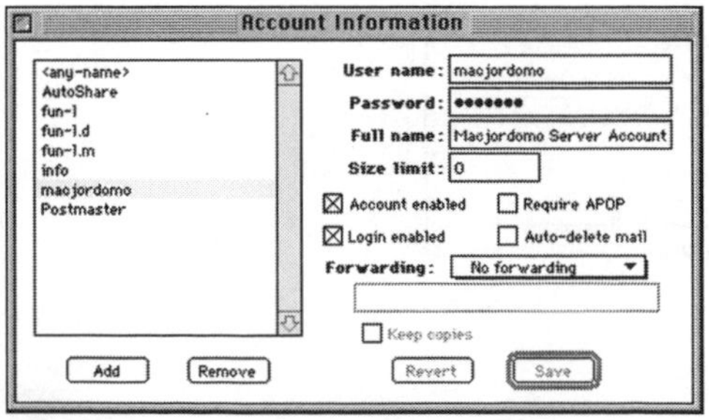

Figure 7-11: Create a Macjordomo AIMS user account.

5. Click the Save button to save the Macjordomo account.

Note: Remember the password that you give this user account; you need this password to configure Macjordomo.

Configuring Macjordomo

To configure Macjordomo for your subscription list, follow these steps:

1. Start Macjordomo and choose Lists⇨Subscription List from the Macjordomo menu bar.

A Macjordomo configuration dialog box appears (see Figure 7-12). This dialog box is the most important configuration dialog box in Macjordomo. In this dialog box, you specify the macjordomo account name and password, the name of your SMTP (e-mail) server for outgoing mail, and an e-mail address to which users can send messages if a problem occurs.

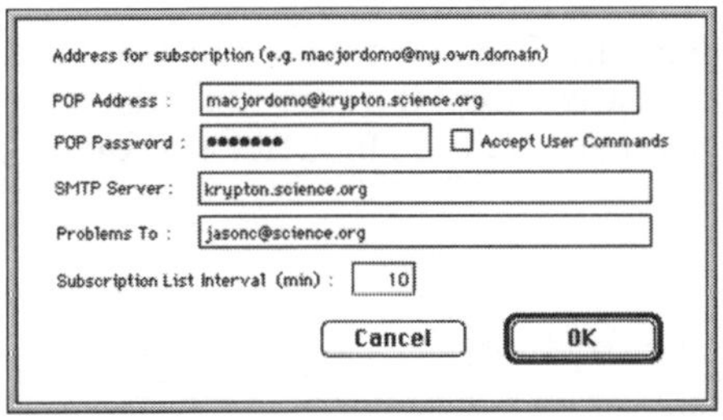

Figure 7-12:
Configure Macjordomo by entering values in this dialog box.

Address for subscription (e.g. macjordomo@my.own.domain)

POP Address : macjordomo@krypton.science.org

POP Password : •••••••   ☐ Accept User Commands

SMTP Server : krypton.science.org

Problems To : jasonc@science.org

Subscription List Interval (min) :   10

Cancel   OK

2. In the POP Address text box, type the full e-mail address of the Macjordomo AIMS account that you created in the steps described in the preceding section.

In the example shown in the figure, the e-mail address is the name of the Apple Internet Mail Server account (`macjordomo`), followed by the @ sign and the full domain name of our computer, as follows:

```
macjordomo@krypton.science.org
```

3. In the POP Password text box, type the password that you assigned to the macjordomo AIMS account.

Note: Each character in the password appears as a dot as you type, so be careful to enter the password exactly as you entered it as you set up the Macjordomo account.

4. Select the Accept User Commands check box to enable command processing in Macjordomo.

5. In the SMTP Server text box, enter the full domain name of your computer.

For this example, we entered **krypton.science.org** — the name of the computer on which we run Apple Internet Mail Server. Remember that Apple Internet Mail Server is your SMTP server as well as your POP server, so nothing is wrong with using the same domain name in the POP Address and SMTP Server text boxes.

6. **In the Problems To text box, enter a valid e-mail address to which users can send problem reports.**

7. **Click the OK button.**

Creating a user account

To create a new user account in Apple Internet Mail Server, follow these steps:

1. **Switch back to Apple Internet Mail Server and create a new user account for your mailing list.**

   (See the section "Creating accounts for the list," earlier in this chapter, for more information.)

   In the example shown in Figure 7-13, we named our mailing list `coffee-talk`. (All we need now is a digital picture of Mike Myers wearing a wig, and we'll have a head start on the Internet edition of "Saturday Night Live.")

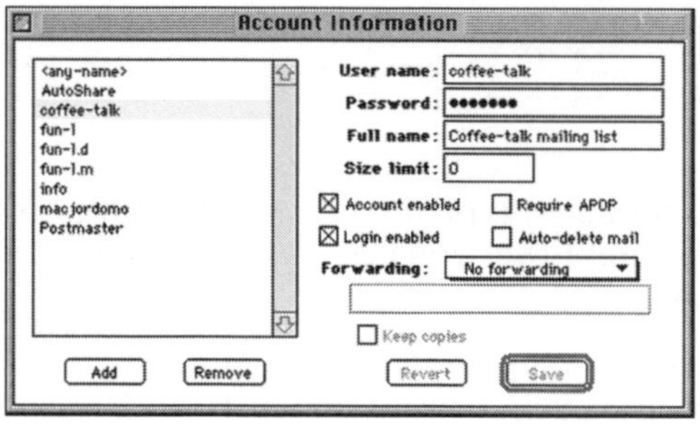

Figure 7-13:
The account is named coffee-talk.

Note: After you select a password for the mailing-list account, make sure that you remember it; you need this password later.

2. **Make sure that the Login Enabled check box is selected.**

3. **Click the Save button to save the new Apple Internet Mail Server account.**

Creating the mailing list

To create a Macjordomo mailing list, follow these steps:

1. **Switch back to Macjordomo from AIMS, and choose Lists⇨New List.**

   The new list window appears (see Figure 7-14). Use this window to configure your new mailing list.

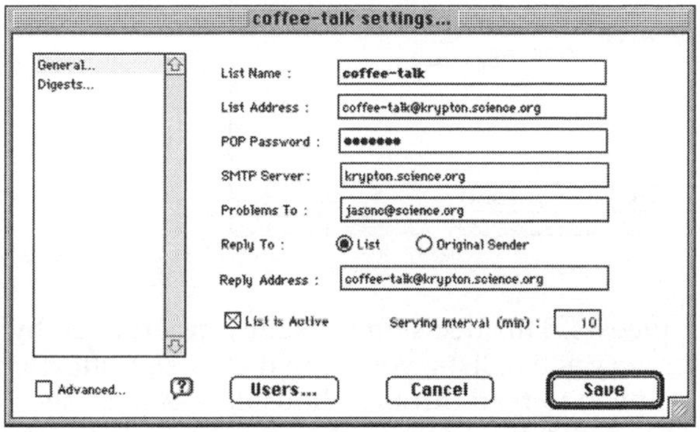

Figure 7-14:
Configure
your
Macjordomo
mailing list.

2. **Type the name of your mailing list in the List Name text box.**

   In our example, the list name is coffee-talk.

3. **Type the e-mail address of the mailing list in the List Address text box.**

4. **In the POP Password text box, type the password that you assigned to the mailing-list user account.**

5. **In the SMTP Server and Problems To text boxes, enter the same values that you entered when you configured Macjordomo.**

   In Figure 7-14, the SMTP Server name is krypton.science.org, and the Problems To e-mail address is jasonc@science.org.

6. **Select the List is Active check box.**

7. **Click the List radio button and enter the e-mail address of your mailing list again in the Reply Address text box.**

   This address is the address to which subscribers reply if they respond to a mailing-list message.

8. **Select Digests in the list box on the side of the window; then select the Create Digests check box that appears and type a digest name in the Digest Name text box that also appears (see Figure 7-15).**

   A digest is like a summary file that collects mailing-list messages during the specified Digest Interval and sends the summary file to any mailing-list subscriber who instructs Macjordomo to send digests. You can set the default digest interval by changing the value in the Digest Interval text box. You may choose to select daily or even weekly intervals to

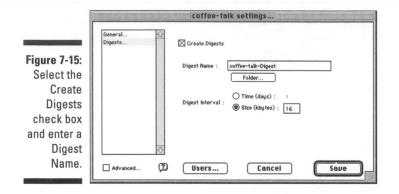

Figure 7-15:
Select the
Create
Digests
check box
and enter a
Digest
Name.

receive your digests. This decision is usually determined by how active the list is. For very active lists, you should choose a shorter interval so that you don't need to read through thousands of messages at once. Many users prefer digests, because they receive a single, large e-mail message periodically instead of many e-mail messages continually.

9. Click the Save button to save these mailing-list settings.

Customizing response messages

You probably want to customize the messages people receive from your list server. You can tell them about your organization, what to do if they're having trouble, and some notes about using your list server. To customize the Macjordomo response messages, follow these steps:

1. Choose Special⇨Edit Generic Messages.

The Edit Generic Response dialog box appears.

2. From the Edit Generic Response drop-down list, select the response message that you want to edit.

3. Click the Edit button.

Figure 7-16 shows the generic Help message that appears in the Edit window. Each mailing list can have its own version of each response message.

4. To edit the mailing-list-specific versions of these response messages, choose Special⇨Edit List Messages from the Macjordomo menu and add a custom message for each type of response by using the editor that appears on-screen (refer to Figure 7-16).

This feature enables you to use some of your creative-writing talent to inspire and instruct the users of your mailing list. Customizing these mailing-list response messages is important so that the overall impression given to users of your mailing list is consistent with the purpose of your organization and/or the list.

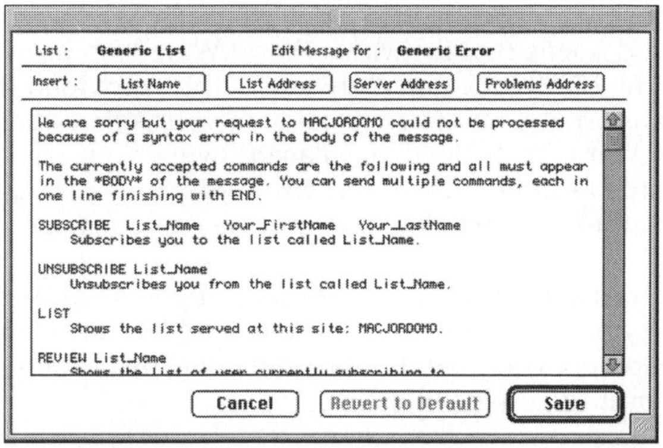

Figure 7-16:
Edit the
Help
response
message to
provide
your own
helpful
insights.

| List : | **Generic List** | Edit Message for : | **Generic Error** |

Insert : [**List Name**] [**List Address**] [**Server Address**] [**Problems Address**]

We are sorry but your request to MACJORDOMO could not be processed because of a syntax error in the body of the message.

The currently accepted commands are the following and all must appear in the *BODY* of the message. You can send multiple commands, each in one line finishing with END.

SUBSCRIBE List_Name   Your_FirstName   Your_LastName
    Subscribes you to the list called List_Name.

UNSUBSCRIBE List_Name
    Unsubscribes you from the list called List_Name.

LIST
    Shows the list served at this site: MACJORDOMO.

REVIEW List_Name
    Shows the list of user currently subscribing to

[Cancel] [Revert to Default] [Save]

Using Your Automated Mailing List

Automated mailing lists are excellent interactive tools, and running a list of your own presents several interesting possibilities. Two possibilities that we're excited about (and that we describe in the following sections) are using your mailing list to serve World Wide Web pages and to distribute files.

Sending World Wide Web documents to the mailing list

One of the best aspects of a mailing list is the fact that you can send World Wide Web documents to all the subscribers. You can send any World Wide Web HTML document to any mailing list without requiring additional configuration or any special type of mailing-list service. The HTML documents simply end up in the electronic mailboxes of the list's subscribers.

Why would you want to send Web documents via a mailing list? The answer is access. Remember that the World Wide Web is not available to all people on the Internet. The graphics that Web pages use place a heavy load on connections to the Internet. Dial-up connections to the Internet over older, slower modems make surfing the Web a painfully slow and annoying process. In many cases, surfing the Web is not even a viable option because of the time that downloading a graphically rich page takes.

If your objective is to distribute information, you find that an automated mailing list is an efficient and widely accessible means of delivery. The connection demands of e-mail file distribution can be insignificant compared with those of delivering the same information via the Web. The Web may be more glamorous, but e-mail can be more effective in delivering information to a larger user base of Net surfers.

To view a World Wide Web document, a subscriber simply saves the e-mail message to a file and opens that file with a World Wide Web browser. Any hyperlinks within the HTML document are accessible, provided that the subscriber has an Internet connection. If some of your subscribers don't have access to the World Wide Web, they can still view your basic World Wide Web documents as long as they have browsers; they just can't access any of the links to other Internet sites that may be on your page.

A mailing list becomes even more like a magazine if you send World Wide Web documents to your subscribers. Using a mailing list this way gives you a great deal of flexibility in content, format, and advertising, and also opens new possibilities for interactive publishing.

Distributing files by using a mailing list

Another great use for a mailing list is the distribution of binary files (such as word-processing documents). To send a binary file through e-mail, you first must convert the file to text-only format; e-mail can handle only text. The most common way to perform this conversion from binary to text is to use a program called *UUEncode*. After you uuencode a binary file (turn it into text), you can send the file to your mailing list, and the file ends up in the electronic mailboxes of the list's subscribers. Users must uudecode the file to return it to its original binary form.

More information on UUEncode and on sending files via e-mail is available on the Setting Up an Internet Site page on the World Wide Web, at the following address:

```
http://computers.science.org/internet/site/setup/
```

Making Money by Using Your Automated Mailing List

An automated mailing list is similar to a traditional magazine: A mailing list has subscribers, each message sent to the mailing list is like a magazine article, and a successful mailing list can attract advertisers. If your mailing list is especially useful, you may be able to charge for subscriptions to the list.

You can charge for subscriptions in several ways. One popular means of charging for information is the voluntary approach. Put the information out there and indicate that, if the information is useful, the user may elect to pay a specified fee. You can collect the money via traditional snail mail (you know — the mail that the guy in the uniform delivers while walking down the street with the dogs at his heels) or through some type of online commerce system.

The voluntary approach is a low-pressure means of generating revenue from your mailing list. A more aggressive method involves requiring a subscription fee before you distribute information. In this method, you structure your mail-delivery system to provide information on how to subscribe to your list as part of the autoresponse system (the message that they receive after they contact you). After a person subscribes, you add that person's name to the list; then the person can begin receiving your information. How you decide to collect fees for your information depends on the information that you have to deliver and on the methods that you use to attract interested users to your site.

Other money-making opportunities exist with an automated mailing list, depending on how you configure your list. If you use a moderated list, you can charge to distribute messages to the mailing list. If you distribute World Wide Web documents through the mailing list, you can charge users a fee for including hyperlinks to their Internet resources in your documents. If you're going to charge, of course, you need a loyal subscriber base, and your mailing list must offer enough value to support fees or advertising.

Mailing lists have a great deal to offer, both to potential subscribers and to your Internet site. An automated electronic mailing list is, in some ways, better than the World Wide Web. You can reach anyone who has an e-mail account, for example, and you know exactly who subscribes to your list — capabilities that the World Wide Web doesn't offer yet.

A mailing list is more interactive than most World Wide Web sites are. And, a list has a greater chance of becoming a regular tool for its users, because mailing lists rely on the one resource that all users have in common: e-mail. Remember that, to extend the capabilities of your mailing list and make the list even more useful to you and your business, you can distribute World Wide Web documents to the subscribers, thus combining the benefits of a mailing list with the power of the World Wide Web. Take advantage of the fact that e-mail is easy for people to read and respond to and that list servers are simple to set up and easy to maintain. A mailing list is an important addition to any Internet site.

Chapter 8

Setting Up an Internet News Server

● ●

In This Chapter

▶ Getting a handle on Internet News

▶ Starting a global Usenet newsgroup

▶ Creating local newsgroups

▶ Setting up your own News server

● ●

*I*nternet news, commonly referred to as *Usenet news,* is a simple resource that enables people around the world to carry on conversations and exchange information. The term *news* implies a professional, journalistic source of information, as is true of most television news; but Usenet news rarely resembles anything professional. The reason for this lack of professionalism is that the vast majority of the global Usenet is uncontrolled, which means that anyone who wants to can post a message about anything. As a result, having a real conversation about a particular topic is difficult; even more difficult at times is keeping the conversation focused on the original topic.

Nonetheless, Usenet news remains a valuable resource for global topical conversation and information and is one of the aspects of using the Internet that some people find to be most rewarding. The uncontrolled nature of Usenet is part of the reason for its popularity. People can (and do) discuss anything — anything at all — in Usenet newsgroups.

Using Internet News

Internet News is a software system that enables people to read and post messages in topic-specific message areas called *newsgroups*. Some newsgroups, such as `alt.alien.visitors` or `alt.destroy.the.internet`, are strange or useless. Many other newsgroups are serious interactive tools that provide indispensable resources for technical and scientific professionals. To understand the difference between a local newsgroup and a global one that is part of Usenet, you need to know a little about how people read newsgroups, how you distribute news messages through the Internet, and how the news system operates.

Internet News is a client/server system, with the News server managing the newsgroups. Participants use client software, called a *newsreader,* to read and post messages to the groups. Until recently, people used news almost exclusively as a distributed, global Internet system known as *Usenet.* Each News server within the Usenet system forwarded new message postings to other News servers until the messages propagated to every News server in the world that participated in Usenet.

More recently, people with Internet sites have provided public access to local newsgroups published from their own News servers rather than start new newsgroups within the global Usenet system. Providing public access to your own News server is simpler and more flexible than participating in Usenet. The process of starting a new group within the Usenet system is cumbersome and political, and you shouldn't attempt to do so unless you're already a big Usenet fan. (For instructions on creating a new global Usenet newsgroup, see the section "Creating a global newsgroup with the seal of approval," later in this chapter.)

This chapter describes the technical function of Internet News in an easy and simple-to-understand manner. The chapter also explores ways in which you or your company can establish a presence on Internet News and integrate this valuable interactive resource into your Internet site. Although creating a new global Usenet newsgroup is possible, and although we describe the process that you must go through to do so, we recommend that you instead set up your own Internet News server at your Internet site. This chapter also shows you how to add an Internet News server to your site.

Looking at Both Sides of the News

As does every other type of Internet server, News servers use protocols, and protocols usually have weird acronyms. The Internet News protocol, for example, is *NNTP,* or *Network News Transport Protocol.* In this chapter, we show you how to configure your own NNTP News server, set up newsgroups, and configure your local News server to either contribute to the global Usenet News system or keep newsgroup postings to itself so that users must come to your site to read and post to your newsgroups. Setting up an Internet News server, however, is only half the story. As a News server provider, you need to know about the software that people are likely to use to read and post messages in your newsgroups.

For too long, reading and contributing to Usenet News was a clumsy and tedious process that frustrated all but the most devoted users. The problem was simple: To access Usenet, a user needs a special program known as a newsreader. Most Internet users don't have newsreaders or find the programs to be difficult and complicated to install and use. This situation has changed now that both Netscape and Microsoft provide easy-to-use newsreaders. Netscape provides a newsreader as a component of the Navigator browser, and Microsoft provides a stand-alone newsreader called Internet News that runs under both Windows 95 and Windows NT.

Configuring and using newsreaders — the Netscape or Microsoft products, or some other brand — is a fairly standard process. Users must undertake the following two primary configuration tasks before they can read news:

- Configure the newsreader to contact a News server that enables you to connect to it.
- Download the list of newsgroups offered by the News server and choose which ones to view.

The first configuration step — telling a newsreader which News server to connect to — is one of the things about newsreaders that has changed recently. Formerly, a user needed to configure a newsreader just once for use with his Internet Service Provider's Usenet News server — and that was that. The user then had access to all the Usenet newsgroups provided by the ISP. Now, however, many companies or people who provide newsgroups that you don't find in Usenet run their own News servers. Many of these News servers provide newsgroups on product-specific topics or topics that complement the offerings of an Internet site. Other servers provide newsgroups with particular topic categories. The `science.org` News server, for example, provides publicly accessible science- and technology-related newsgroups. To access these newsgroups, a user simply uses a Web browser to access the following URL:

```
news://news.science.org/
```

The user's Web browser launches a newsreader program whenever the browser encounters a URL that begins with the `news://` prefix, such as the one in the preceding example. You're probably familiar with URL syntax by now, but this prefix may be news to you (sorry about the pun). (We discuss the `news:` URL syntax in more detail later, when we show you how to include a link to your Internet News resource on your World Wide Web site.)

More and more people are abandoning the Usenet groups, which tend to fill with ads that less-considerate people leave in unrelated newsgroups. You also find much of the pornographic content on the Internet in these newsgroups. Parents who are concerned about explicit content are especially concerned about their children having access to Usenet newsgroups.

The `news:` URL prefix has a special meaning to many Web browsers. Some older browsers don't understand the `news:` URL at all and give the user an error message, but the majority of Web browsers in use today do understand the `news:` URL. A user can type a `news:` URL just as he can type an `http:` URL or can click a hyperlink in a Web page. If the user enters `news:` in a Web browser all by itself, a newsreader program usually appears on-screen. To access a particular newsgroup automatically after the newsreader appears, a user can type the name of the newsgroup that he wants to access immediately after the `news:` prefix. The following URL for example, accesses the global newsgroup `news.answers` (see Figure 8-1):

```
news:news.answers
```

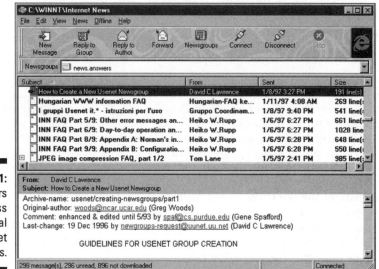

Figure 8-1:
Newsreaders
can access
global
Usenet
newsgroups.

Now comes the tricky part. The URL shown in the preceding example is a valid URL for the `news.answers` newsgroup, but unlike the URL for your Web site, the `news:news.answers` URL doesn't specify a unique resource on the Internet. Remember that the URL of your Web site is a unique address; whenever anyone on the Internet accesses your Web site, that person sees the exact same Web page that everyone else sees. With the `news:news.answers` URL, however, each person sees something different and accesses a different News server. (Remember that a *News server* is a program that maintains newsgroups and news messages and that communicates with newsreaders.) The newsgroup `news.answers` is an example of a global Usenet newsgroup that each user accesses on his local News server. (Think globally, act locally.)

After a user posts a message to a global newsgroup, that message enters the global news stream, beginning with the News server that the user's Internet Service Provider (ISP) maintains. Then the message is distributed automatically to other News servers on the Internet. Not every message that you post to a global newsgroup makes its way to every News server, so people who read a global newsgroup can't necessarily access every message that people post to the newsgroup.

For most newsgroups, this situation isn't a big deal. The kinds of conversations that occur in global newsgroups don't require 100 percent reliability. But the unreliable nature of global newsgroups does preclude your company from offering customer support or other important business electronic conferencing through a global newsgroup. The answer to this problem is to create a local newsgroup instead.

A *local newsgroup* is one that exists only on a single News server. Because a local newsgroup doesn't distribute globally, as do other groups, anyone on the Internet who accesses a local newsgroup sees precisely the same messages that every other person sees. This situation enables you to use local newsgroups to conduct important discussions in which every participant must access every message, as is the case in a customer-support group.

To access a local newsgroup, you use the familiar URL format of a prefix followed by a colon and two forward slashes (as in `news://`), followed by the domain name or IP address of the server. The URL `news://news.science.org`, for example, points to the Internet News server at `science.org`. You can also specify a specific newsgroup on `news.science.org`, as in the following URL, which points to a newsgroup for genetics students:

```
news://news.science.org/science.org.genetics.student
```

Figure 8-2 shows the Microsoft newsreader program after the program contacts the `news.science.org` News server and accesses the `science.org.genetics.student` newsgroup. This newsgroup is a local newsgroup that you can access globally.

Thousands upon thousands of Usenet newsgroups are available on the Internet, and you may wonder how they all got there, especially if you want to create one yourself. The following section answers this question; later sections show you how to create a Usenet newsgroup, how to set up your own News server program, and how to create your own local newsgroups.

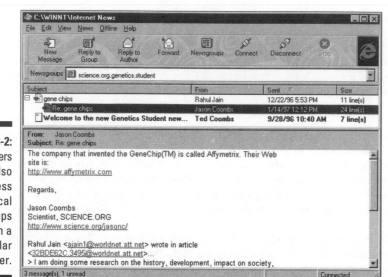

Figure 8-2:
Newsreaders
can also
access
local
newsgroups
from a
particular
server.

Where do little newsgroups come from?

You may have seen some of the Usenet newsgroups, such as those mentioned earlier in this chapter, and wondered how people came up with those odd names. And what's with all those dots in the names? Newsgroup creators organize their newsgroups, whether those newsgroups are part of the Usenet system or available only on your local News server, in a *newsgroup hierarchy*. The people who wrote the first News-server software decided to organize newsgroups in categories. The categories were given short symbolic names, such as `news`, `comp`, and `sci`. This naming convention forms the newsgroup hierarchy. A newsgroup with a name that begins with one of those category names is part of that newsgroup hierarchy. Following are a few samples of different newsgroup hierarchies:

- `news.answers`
- `comp.forsale`
- `sci.energy`

Each newsgroup category serves a particular purpose. Table 8-1 shows the seven major categories that comprise the core of the global Usenet newsgroup hierarchy.

Table 8-1   The Seven Major Global Usenet Newsgroup Categories

Hierarchy	Purpose
news	Groups that pertain to the Internet News system itself.
sci	Scientific newsgroups for serious discussions.
rec	Newsgroups for discussion of recreational activities.
comp	Computer-related newsgroups.
misc	Miscellaneous discussion groups (no focus).
soc	Groups for socializing or talking about social issues.
talk	Debates about controversial topics.

Organizations that run News servers create local newsgroups. Most universities, for example, have News servers and provide local newsgroups for discussion of campus-specific issues. Internet Access Providers have local newsgroups to provide technical support or to give their customers a place to talk among themselves.

The names of local newsgroups don't need to adhere to the global Usenet News naming convention. The Internet access provider Netcom, Inc. (at `http://www.netcom.com/`), for example, provides several local newsgroups with names that begin with `netcom.`, such as `netcom.support`. Because these newsgroups are local and not distributed globally throughout the Internet, they need not comply with the global Usenet News naming scheme.

Organizations create and name global newsgroups in two ways, depending on the type of group that is involved in the process. "Official" Usenet newsgroup categories are very strict about new-group names. The "official" global Usenet newsgroup categories listed in Table 8-1 earlier in this section rely on a voting process. During this voting process, participants select — or possibly even vote on — the exact name for the group. The "unofficial" Usenet newsgroup categories, such as `alt.`, rely on anarchy for group creation. These "unofficial" Usenet News categories don't impose any naming restrictions, so these groups can use just about any name imaginable.

Move over, Larry King and Art Bell: Moderated groups

Most newsgroups allow anyone to post anything. The quality of the people who participate by posting messages determines the quality of the messages in a newsgroup. If a person posts an offensive message, he usually receives endless e-mail messages spouting disapproval, and a great deal of discussion about the offending message often occurs in the newsgroup. The person who posts the message never forgets the flood of angry messages (called *drive-by hatred*) that he receives and usually posts more appropriate messages in the future. Flooding the offender with angry e-mail is an after-the-fact method for ensuring that people post only quality content to newsgroups.

Waiting for someone to post an offending message and then blasting that person is, at best, a clumsy way to prevent inappropriate postings. At worst, this method is ineffective, and inappropriate postings become the norm for that newsgroup. A special type of newsgroup solves this problem by enabling someone to approve or reject articles before a user can post an article in the newsgroup. This type of newsgroup is known as a *moderated newsgroup*.

One person — usually the creator of the newsgroup — becomes the moderator for that group. Articles that people post to the newsgroup go directly to the moderator instead of to the group. The moderator reads each message and then approves or rejects the article. If the moderator rejects a message, he usually sends an e-mail message to the author, offering a reason why he considers the message to be unsuitable for posting.

Moderating a newsgroup is an excellent way to maintain a question-and-answer format or to establish a level of editorial quality. This arrangement is also effective for newsgroups that function as one-way news and information sources. In these newsgroups, the moderator is the sole supplier of information to the newsgroup; all other postings, he rejects.

The following section shows you how to create both moderated and unmoderated global and local newsgroups. The information in this section (and earlier sections of this chapter) should enable you to decide which type of newsgroup is most appropriate for your needs.

Note: Global newsgroups are essentially public property. You can't control a global newsgroup, even if you moderate it; therefore, you don't own that group, even if the group was your idea in the first place.

Giving Birth to a Newsgroup

The idea for a newsgroup can come from anywhere. Often, a newsgroup idea springs from the release of a new product or from a special-interest group that's just discovering Internet News. Any topic that interests people is a valid newsgroup idea.

After you give birth to the idea, the group needs a name. Make sure that the name of your newsgroup is interesting and descriptive, because the name of your newsgroup is the single most important factor in determining its content. In a newsgroup that you name `alt.cold.fusion`, people expect to read about and discuss advancements in this area of research. Carrying on serious conversations about cold fusion in a newsgroup that you call `alt.cold.fusion.silly.idea`, however, may prove to be difficult.

Newsgroups are either local or global. A local newsgroup exists only on a single News server, whereas global newsgroups are available on nearly every News server that participates in Usenet. Messages that you post to a local newsgroup exist on only one News server, whereas messages that you post to a global newsgroup propagate around the Internet and are available on many (although not necessarily all) News servers.

Make sure that you scan the list of current newsgroups to make sure that your newsgroup name is available and is not already in use for exactly the type of conversation that you have in mind. Also read the newsgroups `news.groups`, `news.announce.newgroups`, and `alt.config` to verify that someone else hasn't recently recommended a newsgroup similar to the one you're proposing. If you want to start a moderated newsgroup, consider adding the extension `.moderated` to the end of your group's name.

Creating a global newsgroup with the seal of approval

You create global Usenet newsgroups through a voting process. The first step is submitting a *Request for Discussion* (or *RFD*) for your newsgroup idea to the committee that ultimately either creates your newsgroup or turns you down. Read the newsgroup `news.announce.newgroups` to find a good RFD example and copy the format as you create your newsgroup. Then post your RFD to the following newsgroups (which is how you submit your proposal):

- `news.groups`
- `news.announce.newgroups`

You also should post the RFD to any other newsgroups or mailing lists that relate to your newsgroup idea. The goal is to elicit discussions among those people who are most likely to use the new newsgroup. Don't overdo your postings, however. Keep the number of newsgroups to a minimum out of consideration for others, and never post your RFD to newsgroups that are unrelated to your newsgroup proposal.

If you have trouble posting to `news.announce.newgroups`, you can e-mail your RFD to `newgroups@uunet.uu.net`, which posts the RFD for you. You also should look for a message with the title "How to Create a New Usenet Newsgroup," which appears regularly in `news.groups` and `news.answers`.

After you submit your RFD, someone reviews your proposal and, if everything is in order, posts the RFD to each of the newsgroups that you specify. In response to the RFD, discussion ensues in the newsgroup `news.groups`. After enough time passes to give people a chance to think about and comment on your newsgroup idea, you (or the volunteer vote takers, a group of people that helps keep group Usenet going) must post a *Call for Votes* (CFV) to the same newsgroups. This posting triggers a voting process, the result of which determines whether the Internet community approves or denies your group proposal.

When the time comes for a Call for Votes, send e-mail to the Usenet Volunteer Votetakers (UVV) for advice on how to proceed. The e-mail address for the UVV is as follows:

```
uvv-contact@amdahl.com
```

This tedious, involved, official process of creating a global newsgroup is a holdover from the days before the World Wide Web. Internet News was one of the only global Internet information resources, and people expended a great deal of energy to keep the newsgroup resource valuable and usable for serious discussion. Computer network managers who were in charge of administering News servers for universities, research institutions, and government offices were overwhelmed by the task of managing huge volumes of newsgroup traffic. These managers needed a simple way to prevent an endless stream of useless newsgroups from consuming their time and network resources.

Instead of improving Internet News technology and creating innovative tools to solve these problems and make Usenet easier to manage, however, these network managers devised a political solution. If you find this political system to be unfriendly, ignore it and create a local newsgroup or use the `alt.` newsgroup hierarchy. The following section describes how to create an `alt.` newsgroup.

Starting a global newsgroup the alternative way

A way around this tedious voting process exists. One global-newsgroup hierarchy — the `alt.` hierarchy — doesn't require public approval for its newsgroups. Many people believe that *alt* stands for *alternative*. The name has taken on that meaning over time, but it originally stood for *anarchists, lunatics, and terrorists*. This hierarchy quickly became one of the most popular and diverse of the many hierarchies.

The `alt.` newsgroups range from `alt.sexy.bald.captains` to `alt.comp.shareware.for-kids`. Forget the phone book; if you can't find something here, it *really* doesn't exist.

Creating an `alt.` newsgroup is simple: Just post a message to the `alt.config` newsgroup, suggesting the new group. Also post a copy of the newsgroup suggestion to groups that are similar to the one you want to start, so that discussion of the new group idea is widespread. If the administrators of Internet News servers around the world like the idea, they create the new `alt.` group.

Make sure that you read a few other proposals before posting your own to get a general idea of what to include in a proposal. You should also read a message titled "So You Want to Create an Alt Newsgroup," which posts periodically to `alt.config` and `alt.answers`. This message provides up-to-date instructions on creating an `alt.` newsgroup.

Forming a local newsgroup

The organizations that control News servers create local newsgroups. Because an organization has total control of the groups that exist on its News server, that organization can create any group instantly. Contact your Internet Service Provider to find out whether it can create a local newsgroup for you and, if so, whether users elsewhere on the Internet can access the local newsgroup.

If you're searching for a host for your local newsgroup, keep the following two points in mind:

- ✔ The entire local-newsgroup concept is somewhat new on the Internet. Don't be surprised if your local ISP has never received such a request.

- ✔ The name of your local newsgroup shouldn't conflict with the name of a global newsgroup. Identical names may cause serious technical problems. The news administrator is likely to resolve this conflict by dropping your group in favor of the global one. This resolution keeps the News server software from getting confused.

Until recently, most people used local newsgroups only for local discussions. These included universities, Internet Access Providers, and ISPs that provide News servers with local groups for use by their members. Outsiders were prevented from accessing the local newsgroups or simply never tried to access them, because gaining access wasn't easy. Now that most Web browsers support the news://hostname/groupname URL syntax, however, you can host a local newsgroup that people can access globally.

Still, creating a local newsgroup isn't common yet. Be patient and be persistent if you encounter a confused response to your request to create a local newsgroup. (If all else fails, buy the news administrator a copy of this book.)

Any idea for a newsgroup is valid. Some Usenet newsgroups have become famous. The rec.food newsgroups, for example, are renowned as a rich source of recipes. Other groups have loyal followings. Companies such as Microsoft and Netscape provide local News servers to which thousands post daily, discussing their products. What makes these newsgroups popular is the involvement and feeling of community that surrounds the group. Creating a newsgroup on a topic that interests not only you, but also many other people, can be an excellent way to make new friends or meet colleagues.

Running Your Own News Server

Running a News server on your Internet site can be one of the most rewarding aspects of maintaining an Internet site. If you work with Web servers and list servers, you find that people come and go from your site, sometimes leaving little more than log entries. A great number of people who use your News server may post information there, however, thus participating in your Internet resource. Throughout the earlier chapters of this book, we tell you how important taking part in providing information on the Internet is. Newsgroups often provide more important information than Web pages do. These resources, in fact, are the ones that people use if, for example, they need to share important technical information with one another.

Instead of burdening yourself by creating static content, as you do in a Web page, you generally find that the moment you fire up your News server and start a newsgroup, you have an important, vital Internet resource at your fingertips.

If you want other people to participate in your newsgroups, you and other people in your organization must actively participate in the newsgroup. Seed the newsgroup initially with topics of interest, demonstrating the type of information that you hope to see in the newsgroup. High-quality postings beget more high-quality postings. Set your standards early. Changing later — or, more important, regaining disillusioned visitors to your News server — is almost impossible.

News servers have the following two primary capabilities:

✔ **To give users access to all Usenet newsgroups (or to a subset of newsgroups).** This capability is one that you may want to provide, whether or not you choose to start your own newsgroups. To give your users access to Usenet newsgroups, you need someone who's running a News server that provides Usenet newsgroups to agree to forward the newsgroup messages to your server on a regular basis. Getting your newsgroup messages in this manner is known as *having a feed*. The other provider feeds messages to your News server regularly.

✔ **To provide local newsgroups.** You create these newsgroups locally, and they aren't considered to be part of the Usenet news hierarchy. After you create local newsgroups, you must decide whether to enable visitors from the Internet to view your local newsgroups or restrict access to these groups, enabling only users on your local intranet to view your newsgroups. (Remember that an intranet is a Local Area Network that runs network applications, such as News and the World Wide Web.)

The Windows 95/NT News server that we discuss in the following section has an additional capability: sucking the newsgroup messages from a News server (much as a newsreader program does). Newsreaders download message headers from a News server and normally leave the full text of the message on the server until the newsreader requests the text. The News server that we discuss requests from another News server the full text of every message in each newsgroup. All you need to provide your users with newsgroups in this manner is normal read access to a News server.

Getting started

To serve up your own newsgroup, you first need to install a News server. We chose DNews for Windows 95/NT and Macintosh as the News server to demonstrate in this book. This News server is simple to install and maintain; has a full list of features; and has the sucking capability described in the preceding section, which enables you to provide Usenet newsgroups without a feed. (DNews is shareware, so remember to send in your license fee if you intend to keep using it.)

You can download your Windows 95/NT version of DNews from the following URL:

```
http://netwinsite.com/dnews.htm
```

You can download your Macintosh version from the following URL:

```
http://world.std.com/@tdnetwin
```

You perform most of the work involved in setting up your DNews News server during installation. We walk you through each step of the installation in detail in this section. Just follow these steps:

1. **Start the setup program on your PC or Macintosh.**

   After specifying where to install the files, the first dialog box that appears requests your fully qualified IP name or number. (Refer to Chapter 4 for a complete description of fully qualified domain names and IP numbers.) Figure 8-3 shows the dialog box with a `science.org` machine name, which you must replace with your computer's fully qualified domain name. This dialog box usually appears with this text box already filled in for you.

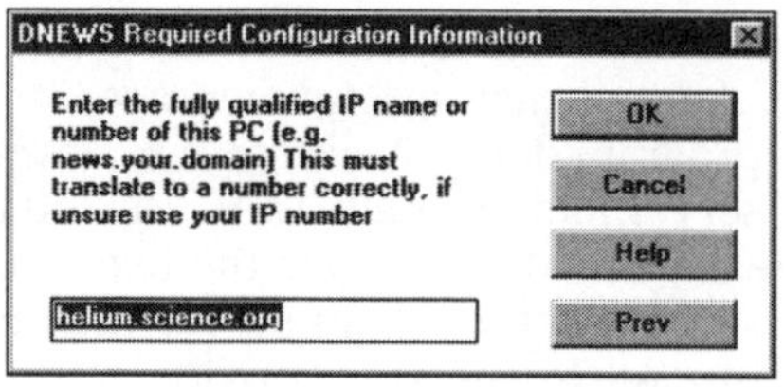

Figure 8-3:
Enter your
fully
qualified
domain
name.

2. **Correct the entry in the dialog box, if necessary; then click OK.**

   The next dialog box asks whether you have a feed or whether your News server is going to suck its News messages from a News server. By default, the Yes I'm going to SUCK news check box is selected (see Figure 8-4).

3. **If you have a feed, click this check box to deselect it and then click OK; if not, just click OK and skip to Step 5.**

Figure 8-4:
Decide
whether
your News
server is
going to
suck news
or not.

4. **If you chose to receive news by using the suck method, enter the fully qualified domain name of the News server that DNews needs to contact to request news; then click OK.**

   Replace the default sample shown in Figure 8-5 with the correct domain name.

5. **Supply the domain name of your e-mail gateway and click OK (see Figure 8-6).**

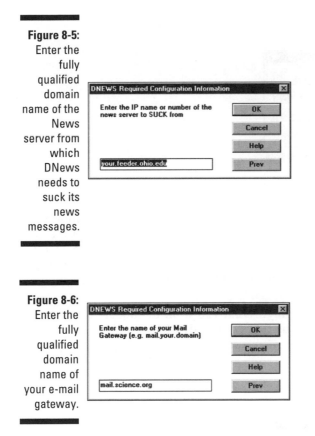

Figure 8-5:
Enter the fully qualified domain name of the News server from which DNews needs to suck its news messages.

Figure 8-6:
Enter the fully qualified domain name of your e-mail gateway.

News works closely with your e-mail system. You can find the information that you need to complete this dialog box in the properties of your e-mail client program; alternatively, ask your network administrator. You must supply this information so that the News server can send reports to the news administrator and also send postings to moderators of moderated newsgroups for approval. Your e-mail client program has a menu choice for setting and viewing properties. Start your e-mail client at this time and view the properties to retrieve this information.

In the following step, you get to designate who is to receive reports and complaints from the DNews server program.

6. **Enter the e-mail address of the News administrator in this dialog box and click OK (see Figure 8-7).**

   Note: Please don't enter `tedc@science.org`, as shown in Figure 8-7. Ted doesn't want to receive messages from your News server. He likes e-mail, but not *that* much.

Figure 8-7:
Designate a News administrator and enter the administrator's e-mail address here.

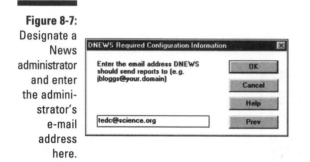

Note: Take extra care at this point, because the next step is important. This step is where you tell the News server how much disk space it can use on your hard drive to store newsgroup information. Specifying too much can leave you without room for other programs; specifying too little can leave you with inadequate space to store newsgroup information.

7. **Enter the number of megabytes that you want to allocate to the News server for storage in the text box; then click OK.**

   The default value is 100 (see Figure 8-8). You may need to adjust this number later.

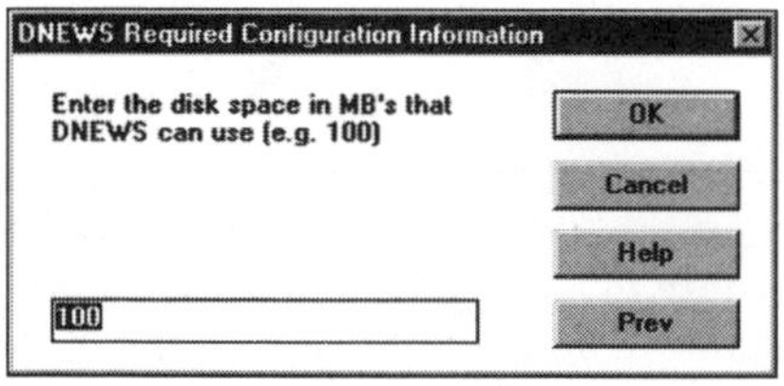

Figure 8-8:
Allocate hard-disk space to store newsgroup information.

Some Usenet newsgroups, especially the alt.binary hierarchy, can use a considerable amount of hard disk space. Make sure that you have the processing power, bandwidth, and hard-disk space to support the storage and transfer (to and from the server) of large binary files. Not heeding this warning could overload your computer to the point where it can't function until you reboot. Be warned, too, that many Usenet alt.binary files contain graphically explicit material that may not be suitable for children.

Note: The next dialog box is a little tricky to fill out, so take care in doing so.

8. **In the next dialog box, enter the domain to which DNews needs to send e-mail confirmations; then click OK (see Figure 8-9).**

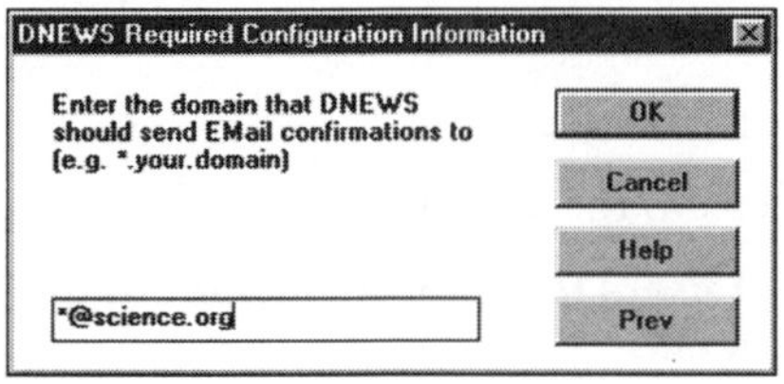

Figure 8-9:
Specify
who the
local users
are so that
they can
receive
e-mail
confirmations
of their
postings
from
DNews.

> **DNEWS Required Configuration Information**
>
> Enter the domain that DNEWS
> should send EMail confirmations to
> (e.g. *.your.domain)
>
> *@science.org
>
> OK
> Cancel
> Help
> Prev

The information that you enter in this dialog box gives DNews an idea of who the local users are so that the program can send e-mail confirmations to them. These confirmations tell the users that their postings were successfully sent to a nonlocal newsgroup. The example in the figure uses the wildcard character * to designate all users in the science.org domain. Entering ***@yourdomain** works here, but entering ***.yourdomain** doesn't. (Don't follow the directions shown in the dialog box. We found a way to make it work correctly.)

The next dialog box is where you get to restrict access to your News server. The * shown in Figure 8-10 specifies access for the world. Providing world access may be your choice if you're providing only local newsgroups and want everyone able to access these groups. But whoa — think hard. Do you *really* want to provide news to the world?

Believe me, if you provide it, seekers *will* come! Access to a majority of the Usenet hierarchy appeals to many people who enjoy having free access to newsgroups. (Several free Usenet servers already exist on the Internet. Providing Usenet for free may be nice but isn't necessary.)

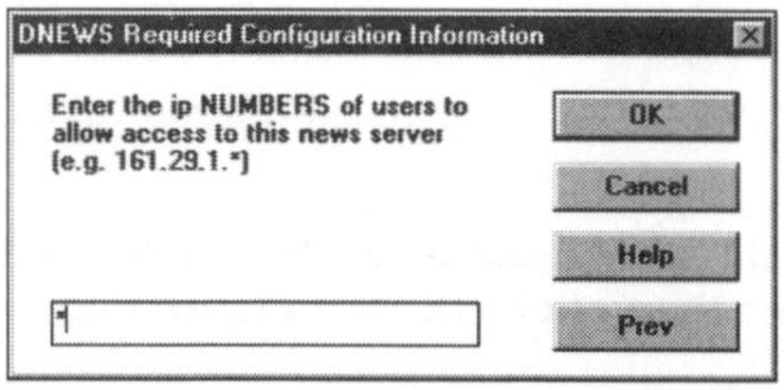

Figure 8-10:
Enter the IP address of users who can access your News server.

DNEWS Required Configuration Information

Enter the ip NUMBERS of users to allow access to this news server [e.g. 161.29.1.*]

OK
Cancel
Help
Prev

9. **If you want to restrict your newsgroups to users in your intranet, enter the IP address of your domain with an asterisk (*) in the last (host) portion of the IP address in this dialog box; then click OK.**

   You could enter, for example, **207.92.75.***.

   If you want to provide access to the world, enter a * in this field.

10. **Enter the domain names of users to whom you want to give access to your News server and click OK.**

    This step is similar to Step 9. Figure 8-11 shows an example in which you allow only computers within the `science.org` domain to access the DNews server. Using a domain name may be more inclusive where the domain incorporates several blocks of IP addresses.

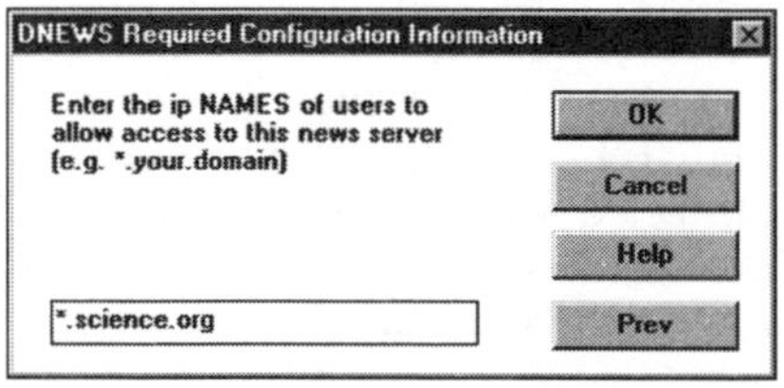

Figure 8-11:
Enter the domain name of users who can access your News server.

DNEWS Required Configuration Information

Enter the ip NAMES of users to allow access to this news server [e.g. *.your.domain]

OK
Cancel
Help
Prev

*.science.org

This step completes your setup. The main DNews administrator window appears, as shown in Figure 8-12. Should you ever want to set up these parameters again, you can click the Setup Wizard button in the administrator window. The Setup Wizard takes you through the same steps that you went through during installation. You can always choose to administer your News server by running the News Administrator.

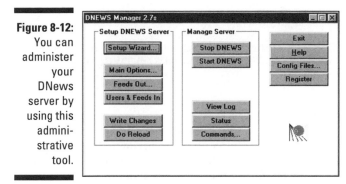

Figure 8-12:
You can administer your DNews server by using this administrative tool.

Setting up an incoming feed

A feed is the traditional way that a News server receives Usenet news. This setup is known as operating an *IHAVE* feed. News servers that have an IHAVE feed passively listen for the *upstream* or *provider* News server to send News messages to them, which is the way that Usenet is primarily set up. (The upstream News server is the program that provides news to your server.) Each News server that participates in Usenet has a feed from some other News server; no central server or structured hierarchy for the delivery of Usenet news exists. If you were to diagram the delivery of news this way, the diagram might appear to be similar to a cotton ball under a microscope — a great cloud of fiber, strung every which way.

Getting active

Each News server that operates with an IHAVE feed must have a list of the active newsgroups on the upstream News server. You store this list of newsgroups in a file with a name such as ACTIVE or ACTIVE_FILE. Before you can begin receiving your feed, you need to load this file onto your local machine.

You can FTP (that is, use the File Transfer Protocol program to transfer) the ACTIVE file from the upstream machine and save the file on your local hard drive. You can get instructions from the news administrator of the upstream server for downloading a copy of the ACTIVE file. Save the file to the following path and filename:

```
\DNEWS\SPOOL\ACTIVE.DAT
```

If you can't get an active file from the upstream machine, you can load one from the following FTP site. (***Note:*** The file may have a slightly different name, with the word *active* in the filename.)

```
ftp.std.com
```

You can also find a FAQ (Frequently Asked Questions) document for DNews at the preceding FTP site. Look in the /FTP/VENDORS/NETWIN/DNEWS directory.

Sending an outgoing feed

DNews has a feature called Live Links that automatically sends messages that you receive on your site on to a recipient machine downstream. (A downstream machine is any computer to which you send news. This designation, of course, makes your computer the upstream machine.) This setup operates differently from — and more efficiently than — the setups of other News servers. Instead of reading the messages from the hard disk and then sending them downstream, DNews forwards the messages immediately, even before storing them on your hard drive. This setup enables you to support multiple machines downstream, with little effect on your Internet site.

Set up your NEWSFEEDS.CONF file with the following entry for each downstream machine that you want to support:

```
site qualified.domain.name
type live
groups *
```

Edit the NEWSFEEDS.CONF file by using any text editor, such as Notepad. You can find the NEWSFEEDS.CONF file in the \DNEWS directory. The qualified.domain.name is the fully qualified domain name of the downstream machine. As you become more familiar with DNews, you can add parameters to further customize your outgoing feed.

Sending local posts upstream

Because DNews can provide a News server without having an IHAVE feed, you can post messages back to upstream machines by using a workaround. We call this a *posting feed*. To enable you to send messages this way, DNews pretends to be a newsreader. Messages that you post to the upstream machine go out looking as though they were sent by a newsreader.

The important step in preparing DNews to post messages in this manner is setting the exclude parameter in the NEWSFEEDS.CONF file to exclude your provider. Use a text editor to add the following lines to the NEWSFEEDS.CONF file:

```
site me
Groups *
site $nntp_feeder
```

```
type built in
posting
groups *
exclude news.provider.net
```

Posting with an IHAVE feed

The IHAVE feed is the normal way to send articles upstream. To convert a posting feed to an IHAVE feed, simply remove the word `posting` from your NEWSFEEDS.CONF file. Removing this word sets up DNews to post messages in a more conventional manner.

Controlling the News Server

You control the DNews News server by sending it commands. Clicking the Commands button in the DNews administrator window displays a complete list of commands and short descriptions of the commands. (*Note:* Before its designers created this Windows interface, DNews had a command-line interface called Tellnews, which is why the commands in DNews are still known in its documentation as Tellnews commands.) Select the command that you want to execute by double-clicking the command name in this list. If the command requires parameters, a dialog box appears, asking you to fill in the required parameters. To ease any possible confusion, the dialog box includes a description of each parameter.

One of the commands in the list that appears after you click the Commands button is EXPIRE. If you issue the EXPIRE command, DNews begins deleting all expired newsgroup messages. Other important commands include the following:

- ✔ EXIT. This command shuts down the DNews server.
- ✔ GETGROUPS. This command retrieves newsgroups in a sucking DNews configuration.
- ✔ KEY. You use this command to enter your license key given to you at the time that you register the program. (Remember that DNews is shareware, and you should license the program as soon as possible.)
- ✔ KILLGROUP. This command removes a group from the active file.

If you want a longer description of each command and its use, the DNews documentation includes a full list of commands in the COMMANDS.HTM file, located in the \DNEWS\MANUAL\ directory.

Now that your News server is set up and running, the next step is to create some local newsgroups.

Creating Local Newsgroups

Earlier in this chapter, we discuss setting up DNews to provide Usenet news. A much more exciting use for a News server is setting up local newsgroups. A good idea is to plan your local newsgroup hierarchy *before* you begin creating newsgroups. You don't need to follow the Usenet hierarchy if you never intend for other News servers to host your local newsgroups.

Creating your own hierarchy of newsgroups is easy: Think about a broad topic heading, and make this heading the first hierarchical level. *Support,* for example, may serve as a topic heading for newsgroups that support your company's products. The next level of the hierarchy may use the name of your products. If your company makes saw blades, a newsgroup that you may decide to create is `support.saw_blades`.

To set up local newsgroups on your News server, follow these steps:

1. **Start the DNews administrator by launching it from the Windows 95 Start menu and then click the Commands button in the DNews administrator.**

   A list of commands appears.

2. **Double-click the Newgroup command.**

3. **Fill in the name of the newsgroup in the Group text box.**

4. **If your newsgroup is moderated, enter m in the next parameter text box; otherwise, for unmoderated groups (normal groups), enter y.**

5. **Enter your name as the creator of the newsgroup in the field provided for that purpose.**

6. **Enter a short description of the newsgroup in the Description text box and then click OK.**

   This description appears in the ACTIVE.NAMES file.

This process is all you need to do to get going. Completely administrating a News server is beyond the scope of this chapter.

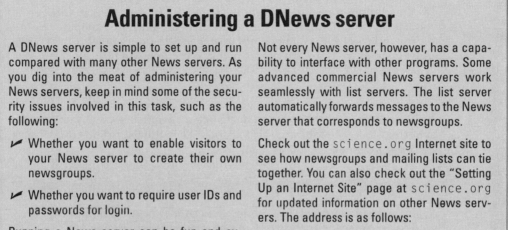

Administering a DNews server

A DNews server is simple to set up and run compared with many other News servers. As you dig into the meat of administering your News servers, keep in mind some of the security issues involved in this task, such as the following:

✔ Whether you want to enable visitors to your News server to create their own newsgroups.

✔ Whether you want to require user IDs and passwords for login.

Running a News server can be fun and extremely rewarding. As you become familiar with the intricacies of setting up and running a News server, you find new, creative ways to interface your News server with other network programs, such as your list server.

Not every News server, however, has a capability to interface with other programs. Some advanced commercial News servers work seamlessly with list servers. The list server automatically forwards messages to the News server that corresponds to newsgroups.

Check out the `science.org` Internet site to see how newsgroups and mailing lists can tie together. You can also check out the "Setting Up an Internet Site" page at `science.org` for updated information on other News servers. The address is as follows:

```
http://computers.science.org/
      internet/site/setup/
```

Internet News and the World Wide Web

The newsgroups that exist around the world today — whether they are global and part of Usenet or local and provided by a single organization — offer an incredible amount of information and serve as a forum for dialogue on just about any topic. Until recently, however, using Internet News at all was difficult for most people, and accessing the local newsgroups provided by an organization's News server was impossible. The newest Web browser and newsreader programs, however, are easier than earlier programs for people to use to participate in News as part of their Internet experience. Current Web browsers even support embedded `news://` URL hyperlinks in Web pages, so that users need only click a link to read a newsgroup on your News server.

In constructing a Web page, you can place a newsgroup reference as a hypertext link in an HTML document by using the following code:

```
<a href= news:alt.surfing >alt.surfing</a>
```

This HTML syntax provides a hyperlink that a user can click to launch a newsreader program and go right to the `alt.surfing` Usenet newsgroup. If you use a visual HTML editor program such as Netscape Navigator Gold or Microsoft FrontPage, you need not even concern yourself with the HTML code. Instead, you can just create a link to the following URL:

```
news:alt.surfing
```

Another method enables you to designate a specific News server with a hypertext link. The following HTML code takes the user right to the News server at `science.org`:

```
<a href= news://news.science.org >news://news.science.org</a>
```

Again, instead of using HTML code, you can just create a link to the following URL in Netscape Navigator Gold or Microsoft FrontPage:

```
news://news.science.org
```

Taking this technique one step further, you can create a link to a specific News server and newsgroup by using the following HTML code:

```
<a href= news://news.science.org/
science.org.general >general</a>
```

Linking directly to your News server and newsgroup is particularly advantageous if you have a local newsgroup for customer support or product feedback. Putting such a link right in your Web page makes your news resource a significant part of your Web presence. Consider printing the `news://` URL for your news resource, along with your `http://` URL for your Web site, in company brochures or on business cards.

Usenet news is one of the most valuable interactive information resources on the Internet. People enjoy and benefit from the discussions that occur in newsgroups. Starting a new global Usenet newsgroup or running your own local News server is a superb extension to your existing Web site. The potential of newsgroups to serve as simple, powerful, global business tools is finally being realized, now that Web browsers support the integration of Internet News into the World Wide Web. Setting up your own Internet News server is also one of the best ways to move beyond the World Wide Web in the construction of a multifaceted Internet site.

Part III
Setting Up Basic Internet Services

The 5th Wave   By Rich Tennant

THE MODERN JAMES BOND

The name is bond.com,
JAMES bond.com.

In this part . . .

The best thing about the Internet is that it's an unlimited communications resource. Software designed to work on the Internet can be made to do just about anything that you can imagine a computer doing. This part introduces several more Internet software packages that add functionality and appeal to your Internet site.

As with any Internet resource, the average user must be able to access these services easily. Until something better comes along, this concept means simple integration into the existing World Wide Web. Real-time communications software is rapidly emerging. Two other resources featured in this part, Gopher and Usenet news, already offer seamless integration into the Web.

Chapter 9
Electronic Mail Service

· ·

In This Chapter

▶ Creating your own electronic mailboxes

▶ Responding to e-mail automatically

▶ Providing information through an e-mail information service

▶ Setting up an e-mail information server on your PC or Mac

· ·

*E*lectronic mail remains the number-one Internet application, even taking into consideration the huge success of the World Wide Web. Although the World Wide Web dominates the media coverage of the Internet, the basic tools available to Net surfers and site developers are what bring the Internet to life. This chapter closely examines another Internet tool that you should consider whenever you develop an Internet site.

More people use electronic mail, also known as *e-mail,* than any other Internet utility. Current estimates place the number of e-mail users in the tens of millions. All commercial online services — such as CompuServe, America Online, and Prodigy — provide Internet e-mail service to their customers. Furthermore, organizations of all sizes are creating links between their internal e-mail systems and the Internet.

Reasons for Using E-Mail

E-mail isn't as fancy as the World Wide Web, but in many ways, e-mail is a more practical and useful way to distribute information, especially if your site appeals to Net surfers who can't support the additional bandwidth demands of the Web.

Consider international visitors to your site. In some countries, the Web is barely usable, because the communications network can't handle the flow of graphics through the system. On recent trips to India and Indonesia, we found that using the World Wide Web in those countries was tedious, with many interruptions because of connection loss and slow Internet connections. The Internet backbone in many countries is slower than the average ISDN connection. Yet you must make allowances for delivery of information to such locations even if the Web is not appropriate for the task.

Knowing that the Web is not available to everyone on the Internet makes e-mail an even more interesting tool for the Internet site developer. Keep in mind that although e-mail is not as glamorous as the World Wide Web, e-mail is the single most widely used tool on the Internet. On the Net, new users and old-timers alike know and understand e-mail, and they use it every day.

The enormous number of people who use e-mail as part of their businesses makes the number of World Wide Web users seem to be insignificant. If you want to reach as many people as possible and provide information in a way that works for the average user, e-mail is the answer.

Many forward-thinking companies realize the important role that e-mail plays in communicating with other Internet users. A telecommunications engineering company called Qualcomm, for example, uses e-mail to distribute information about job opportunities. Anyone who wants information about Qualcomm jobs can send e-mail to `jobs@qualcomm.com`. This special e-mail address illustrates several advantages of e-mail compared with other Internet information resources. Internet e-mail addresses are

- ✔ Easy to remember
- ✔ Simple to advertise
- ✔ Accessible to every person who has e-mail access
- ✔ Less complicated to use than Gopher, FTP, and the Web

Another common use for e-mail is providing contact information and a basic introduction to Internet users who want to know more about an organization. Companies often use a special e-mail address for this purpose, such as `info@science.org`. The info-and-jobs e-mail addresses are excellent examples of the power and importance of e-mail for every Internet site.

By providing information through special e-mail addresses, you can target a specific audience for a specific purpose. Other information resources, such as the World Wide Web, are like your storefront and large-scale advertising efforts, whereas communicating with people through e-mail is like having a conversation on the telephone or giving somebody your business card.

If you have plenty of time on your hands, the only thing that you need to provide information through e-mail is an e-mail account of your own. You can respond to each piece of incoming e-mail manually and return whatever

Providing information through your existing e-mail account

E-mail accounts are like opinions: Everyone has one, and they're all different. Because e-mail accounts vary so greatly, your existing account with MCI, CompuServe, or America Online — or even your corporate e-mail account — probably doesn't enable you to respond to incoming e-mail automatically. This limitation doesn't mean that you should ignore the possibility, however; it just means that giving detailed instructions for non-Internet e-mail systems is beyond the scope of this book.

Regardless, you don't need to give up your existing e-mail account. If you're like most people, you've already added your e-mail address to business cards and stationery. You can obtain a new e-mail service to provide information on the Internet but keep your existing account for your personal e-mail.

information the sender requires, but this approach is unwieldy, especially if you receive a large number of e-mail messages. One of the primary reasons to provide information through e-mail is to automate the process of communicating directly with people via the Internet. Without automation, providing information through e-mail is little better than using the telephone to speak with each caller personally.

The idea that manually replying to each e-mail request provides a bit of class and a human touch is a tempting one. Initially, to anyone who is new to business on the Internet, taking such a course does seem to be classy. What this strategy really says, however, is that you're not using your resources effectively. You have better things to do than to send your electronic brochure to every person who asks for it. So automate your responses to repetitive e-mail requests.

Getting the Most Out of E-Mail

The first step in using e-mail as part of your Internet site is establishing electronic mailboxes, either by setting up your own e-mail server program or by using an Internet Service Provider. After you create electronic mailboxes, you can provide information through e-mail in either of the following ways:

 ✔ Reply automatically, with a predefined message, to incoming e-mail

 ✔ Use an Internet e-mail information service to fulfill specific information requests

Of these two options, replying to e-mail automatically may be the more useful. This method is simple, yet powerful, and you can set up the system very quickly. The following section shows you how to reply to e-mail automatically, and a later section of this chapter, "Using Your Personal Computer as a Mail Server," shows you how to set up an electronic mail server for your Internet site. If you're not going to run your own e-mail server program, you don't need to concern yourself about how to construct electronic mailboxes. As you read the following sections, however, assume that you've decided to use an Internet Service Provider for your electronic mailboxes.

Replying Automatically to Incoming E-Mail

If you ever sent e-mail that never reached its destination or that wasn't replied to for weeks, you know how useful an automatic reply is. An *automatic reply* tells people who send e-mail that their mail was received. The reply can also contain references to other information sources or tell people how to contact you in other ways.

 An automatic reply is especially useful as a way to communicate with customers. If you run a store with walk-in business, for example, you can use an e-mail address that sends an automatic reply as a way to tell people what your hours of operation are and to give directions to your store. You always want to add your automatic-reply e-mail address to your advertising, especially to your ad in the phone book.

You can create an automatic-reply e-mail address in any of the following ways:

- ✔ Subscribe to an automatic-reply e-mail service on the Internet
- ✔ Use a mail client program that has new-mail filtering capability
- ✔ Set up a UNIX shell account with an Internet Service Provider

Responding automatically through a service provider

If you subscribe to an automatic-reply e-mail service, follow these steps to create an automatic reply:

1. **Create a text file containing the message that you want to send as the automatic reply.**

You can use any text editor or word-processing program to create this document, as long as you save the message as a text-only file.

2. **Send the text file to your service provider.**

   Your provider gives you instructions for this process. All providers are different. Some accept the message through e-mail; others enable you to fax the message to them and then retype the text for you.

3. **Give out the e-mail address that the provider assigns to you.**

   This e-mail address is different from the one you normally use to receive e-mail. If people contact this e-mail address, they automatically receive your automatic reply.

If you have access to e-mail, test the automatic reply by sending a message to the e-mail address yourself.

Your service provider should ask whether to save the e-mail that's sent to your automatic-reply account. If you choose not to save the e-mail, make sure that you mention in your reply message that no human being reads the sender's e-mail. Otherwise, people may assume, even after receiving an automatic reply, that a human eventually reads their messages and replies personally.

If you decide to save the e-mail that's sent to your reply account, find out from your service provider exactly where the service saves incoming e-mail. If you have another e-mail account, most service providers can forward e-mail messages to that account. If you prefer, you can ask your provider to keep the messages in a separate mailbox. Your provider can tell you how to access those messages. Many e-mail client programs, such as Microsoft Outlook, enable you to specify multiple mailboxes from which to retrieve mail. Such a feature simplifies retrieval of e-mail from several places.

Whether you save or discard the e-mail sent to your automatic-reply account ultimately depends on how you use the service. If you create a simple text file that contains your store's hours of operation and gives directions to your customers, you can safely discard every message sent to the automatic-reply account. If, on the other hand, you use your automatic-reply account as a first contact for potential clients, you want to save the e-mail that's sent to the automatic-reply account so that you can follow up later with a more involved e-mail message. Your detailed reply can answer any questions posed in the original message and take your marketing efforts even farther.

Creating a do-it-yourself automatic-reply e-mail account

The following sections describe two options for creating your own automatic-reply e-mail account. One option is to use a mail client program that has new-mail filtering capability; the other option is to use a UNIX shell account.

Using a mail client

New-mail filtering is the capability to have your e-mail client program figure out what to do with your incoming mail, based on your instructions. Not all e-mail client programs have this capability. A popular e-mail client program for Windows that has new-mail-filtering capability is called Pegasus (see the following sections). A version of Pegasus is available for the Macintosh as well.

In addition, the popular e-mail program Eudora supports new-mail filtering in its commercial version. You may want to read the following sections on Pegasus anyway, however, because they give you a good idea of what to look for in an e-mail client program.

The Setting Up An Internet Site World Wide Web page always has the most up-to-date information on e-mail client programs and anything else that affects your Internet site. The address is as follows:

```
http://computers.science.org/internet/site/setup/
```

Replying automatically by using a large, winged horse

Pegasus, a mail client written by David Harris, is a popular full-featured Windows e-mail client program. After you define mail-filtering rules, Pegasus can filter and respond to new mail as the messages arrive in your mailbox. A *rule,* in this context, is a directive that you give to your computer, just as you give an instruction to an assistant. You may tell someone, "If Bob calls, tell him I went golfing." A mail-filtering rule is similar: "If you get mail from George, file it under New Business." You don't get to type the rule in plain English, but constructing rules for handling your e-mail is simple in Pegasus.

Setting e-mail rules in Pegasus

You create rules to control what Pegasus responds to and what is done as a response. To set e-mail-handling rules in Pegasus, follow these steps:

1. **In the Pegasus program, choose <u>T</u>ools⇨Mail fi<u>l</u>tering rules⇨Edit <u>n</u>ew mail filtering rules; then you must choose between the Rules applied when folder is <u>o</u>pened and the Rules applied when folder is <u>c</u>losed options.**

Selecting the Rules applied when folder is <u>o</u>pened option preprocesses your e-mail. Selecting the Rules applied when folder is <u>c</u>losed option processes rules after you finish reading your e-mail.

The Rules for new mail window appears, as shown in Figure 9-1.

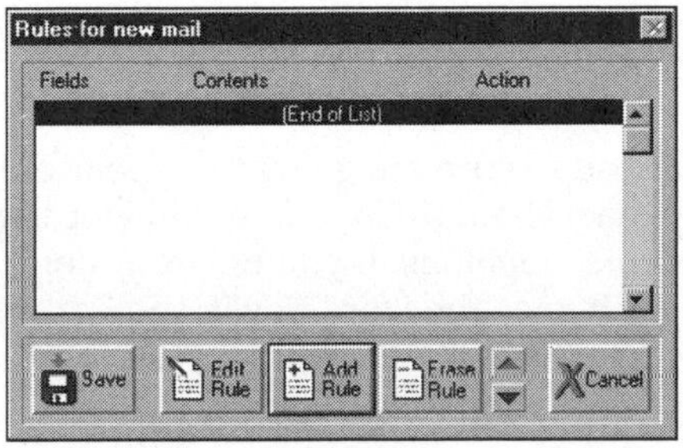

Figure 9-1:
The Rules
for new
mail
window.

2. To create a new rule, click the Add Rule button.

The Edit Rule dialog box appears, enabling you to define or change rules. Your rule can tell Pegasus to look for text in either the header or body of the mail message.

3. Click either the In these <u>h</u>eaders check box or the As an E<u>x</u>pression radio button (see Figure 9-2).

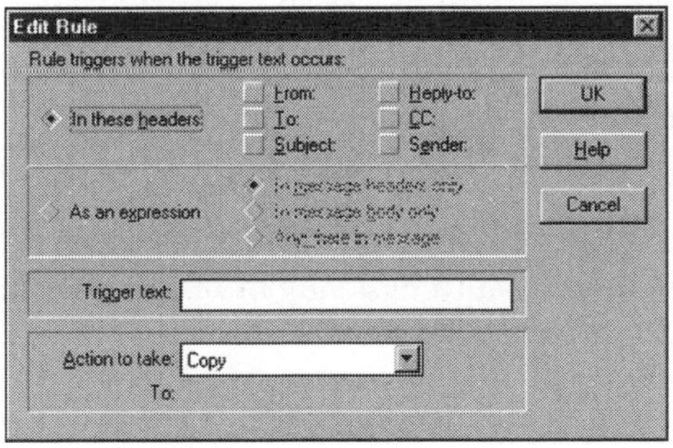

Figure 9-2:
Create
rules by
using this
easy-to-use
dialog box.

By selecting the In these <u>h</u>eaders radio button, you tell Pegasus to look for keywords in the selected parts of the e-mail message. After receiving mail, Pegasus automatically looks for the words that you specify in the <u>F</u>rom, <u>T</u>o, <u>S</u>ubject, <u>R</u>eply-to, <u>C</u>C, or S<u>e</u>nder header by selecting the appropriate check boxes. You can select more than one check box to have Pegasus look for the text that you identify in any of the areas that you indicate.

If you select the As an expression radio button, you give Pegasus permission to look for information in a more global manner. Depending on what option you then select, Pegasus looks for information In message headers only, In message body only, or Anywhere in the message.

4. In the Trigger Text box, enter the text that triggers the rule.

This text can be someone's name, a product name, or some keyword or command that's unique enough for your computer to answer appropriately.

Try to choose words that you're sure are going to appear only in the messages in which you expect them to appear. Avoid words that are too generic or that have multiple meanings. If you tell your computer to send love letters whenever it sees the word *Sue* in the body of the message, for example, you may get an interesting reaction from an unfriendly lawyer.

5. Now tell the computer what action to take by selecting an action from the Action to Take drop-down list.

Pegasus can do many things with the incoming e-mail, including move messages to a particular folder, delete messages automatically, and reply to messages automatically. To create an automatic-reply filter, select either Send Text File or Send Binary File.

After you select a send option from the Action to Take list, the Select a File dialog box appears, enabling you to select the file that you want to send automatically in response to the incoming e-mail message.

6. Choose a file in the Select a File dialog box by clicking the filename and then click the OK button.

You return to the Edit Rule dialog box, where the full path of the file now appears below the Action to Take drop-down list.

7. Click the OK button to accept your new automatic-reply rule.

Now the selected file goes out automatically in response to messages that contain the specified trigger text.

Obviously, before you can select a file to send via this automatic-response method, you need to create this file. To do so, you need to use your word-processing program and type the information that you want to deliver automatically. After you finish typing the information, save the file as text. Most word processors offer the capability to save a document as text if you choose the File⇨Save or File⇨Save As menu commands. You normally see a list of file types from which to choose, and selecting Text saves the file, sometimes adding a TXT extension to the filename.

Pegasus is not a full e-mail information server, but the program has valuable features that enable you to use your personal e-mail account more effectively. Pegasus is simple to use and is also a great e-mail client program.

Replying from a UNIX shell account

If you're a do-it-yourself type, you can create your own automatic-reply e-mail account by obtaining a UNIX shell account from a service provider. A UNIX shell account comes with its own e-mail address, and you can use a special UNIX utility, called the `vacation` *program,* to reply to incoming e-mail automatically.

To use the `vacation` program to reply to incoming e-mail automatically, you need a UNIX shell account from an Internet Service Provider. Your ISP must give you access to the `vacation` program, so make sure that you ask ahead of time whether a `vacation` program is available.

To use the `vacation` program to reply to incoming e-mail automatically, follow these steps:

1. **Before doing anything else, verify that your UNIX shell account has access to the** `vacation` **program by logging in to your UNIX shell account.**

   You normally use the telnet client included with most operating systems. If you're using Windows 95 or Windows NT, start telnet by choosing the Start menu's <u>R</u>un command. Enter the word **telnet** in the Run dialog box, click OK, and the telnet program starts running. Select Connect to Remote Host from the telnet menu and enter the IP address of your ISP. After clicking OK, a login prompt should appear. Enter your login id and password after you're prompted for that information. If you successfully logged into your UNIX shell account, you most likely see a UNIX command prompt (%).

2. **Type the following command at a command prompt:**

   ```
   which vacation
   ```

   This command tells your UNIX shell account to search for the `vacation` program. If the account locates the program, you see something like the following line:

   ```
   /usr/ucb/vacation
   ```

   If your UNIX shell account can't find the `vacation` program, you see something like the following line instead:

   ```
   no vacation in /usr/local/bin /usr/ucb /usr/bin
   ```

If your UNIX shell account responds with a suggestion such as `Caribbean Cruise` or `Hawaii`, or with `which:Commandnotfound`, the program probably misunderstood your request. Ask your ISP for help.

3. **After you're sure that your UNIX shell account can locate the** `vacation` **program, type the following command at the command prompt:**

```
touch .vacation.msg
```

This command creates a new file called .VACATION.MSG, which contains the automatic-reply message for the `vacation` program to use. Because editing a file in a UNIX shell account is easier said than done, we show you a way to create your reply message without editing a file. (This method isn't the only one — just the easiest.)

4. **Type the following command at the command prompt:**

```
cat >> .vacation.msg
```

After you type this command, your UNIX shell account doesn't display anything; it just sits there, waiting for you to type some text.

5. **Type the message that you want to send as your reply to incoming e-mail.**

Make sure that you press Enter at the end of each line. To leave a space between paragraphs, simply press Enter twice. To include a subject in the e-mail reply, type the subject in the first line. Following is an example that a company called Virtual Corporation might use as its reply message:

```
Subject: Automatic reply from Virtual Corporation
Thank you for sending e-mail to Virtual Corporation.
Because of the volume of e-mail we receive, it
may take a few days for a human being to read
your message. If you need to contact us immedi
ately, you can call (800) 555-1212 to reach any of the
following departments:

Sales: ext. 216; Marketing: ext. 840
Public Relations: ext. 408; Human Resources: ext. 600


Be sure to check out our other Internet information
       resources at:

WWW: http://www.virtualcorporation.com/
Gopher: gopher://gopher.virtualcorporation.com/
```

```
FTP: ftp://ftp.virtualcorporation.com/

Thank you for your interest in Virtual Corporation.
```

6. **After you finish typing your reply message, press Ctrl+D.**

   This action saves your reply message to the .VACATION.MSG file and returns you to the command prompt.

If you make a mistake while typing your message, press Ctrl+D to save the incorrect message. Erase the .VACATION.MSG file by using the following command:

```
rm .vacation.msg
```

Then repeat the preceding instructions, beginning with the command `touch.vacation.msg`.

Creating your reply locally

If you prefer, you can create your reply message on your personal computer and then send the message to your UNIX shell account. (Contact your service provider for help on sending a file to your UNIX shell account.) Follow these steps:

1. **Perform the steps in the preceding section.**

2. **After you send the text file, rename the file by using the following command (because you can't create filenames on PCs and Macs by using a period as the first character):**

   ```
   mv TextFile .vacation.msg
   ```

3. **Replace *TextFile* in this command with the name of your file.**

4. **Type the following command to activate the** `vacation` **program:**

   ```
   vacation
   ```

   After typing this command, you should see something like the following:

   ```
   This program can be used to answer your mail automati-
       cally when you go away on vacation.
   You have a message file in .vacation.msg. Would you
       like to see it?
   ```

If you don't see a similar response after typing the `vacation` command, contact your UNIX-shell-account service provider for assistance.

The last line asks whether you want to see your reply message.

5. Type y **and press Enter to view your message.**

After displaying your message, vacation asks whether you want to edit the message.

6. Unless you know how to edit a file in your UNIX shell account, type n **and press Enter.**

Next, vacation asks whether you want to enable the vacation feature by creating a .FORWARD file.

7. Type y **and press Enter.**

The vacation program creates the special .FORWARD file to activate the vacation feature and then displays the following message:

```
Vacation feature ENABLED. Please remember to turn it
  off when you get back from vacation. Bon voyage.
```

Now your vacation program is ready. Anyone who sends e-mail to your UNIX shell account receives an automatic reply from the program.

To turn off the vacation program, type the following command to remove the .FORWARD file:

```
rm .forward
```

The vacation program is one way to create your own automatic-reply e-mail account. If you already have a UNIX shell account on the Internet, using the vacation program doesn't cost you a penny or require a new account with an Internet Service Provider.

Modifying the vacation program

One last thing you need to know is that, by default, the vacation program sends the reply message only once per week to a given e-mail address. If the same person sends e-mail to your UNIX shell account twice in one week, that person gets a reply only the first time. To change this situation, you must modify the .FORWARD file. If you know how to modify files in your UNIX shell account, make the change that we describe in the following section; otherwise, keep reading for a simpler way to modify the .FORWARD file. (See the following section.)

Changing the .FORWARD file in UNIX

To modify the .FORWARD file in your UNIX shell account, look at the original file. The original version of the .FORWARD file should have a line that looks something like the following example:

```
\youruserid,   |/usr/ucb/vacation youruserid
```

The change that you need to make is small. Immediately following `vacation`, insert the following segment:

```
-t2s
```

Your new .FORWARD file looks something like the following example:

```
\youruserid,   |/usr/ucb/vacation -t2s youruserid
```

This change tells the `vacation` program to wait two seconds, instead of one week, before sending the reply message to the same e-mail address. This way, the program responds to every message that it receives, even if a particular user has already received a reply within the past week.

Creating a new .FORWARD file

If modifying this file in your UNIX shell account proves to be too difficult, you can erase the file and create a new one by following these steps:

1. **View the current .FORWARD file by typing the following at the command prompt:**

   ```
   cat .forward
   ```

2. **At the command prompt, remove the current .FORWARD file by typing the following:**

   ```
   rm .forward
   ```

3. **Now type the following command to create a new .FORWARD file:**

   ```
   cat > .forward
   ```

   After you type this command, your UNIX shell account waits for you to type the text for the new version of the file.

4. **Type the following (making sure that you replace *youruserid* with your UNIX shell account login ID and */path/vacation* with whatever was there before in the old .FORWARD file):**

   ```
   \youruserid,   |/path/vacation -t2s youruserid
   ```

5. **Press Ctrl+D to save the new .FORWARD file.**

Starting Your Own E-Mail Information Service

Automatic-reply e-mail accounts are great if you have only one message to send to people on the Internet. If you want to distribute many messages and files through e-mail, however, you need an *e-mail information server* — a program that reads incoming e-mail and responds to special commands within the message.

One command that most e-mail information servers respond to is the following request for help:

```
help
```

If an Internet user sends a message that contains the command help to an e-mail information server, the server replies with a message that contains instructions. Following is another command to which most e-mail information servers respond:

```
get filename
```

Sometimes, users type the send command instead of the get command, as follows:

```
send filename
```

After an e-mail information server receives a message that contains a command of this sort, the server checks to see whether a file named *filename* exists in its file archive. If *filename* does exist, the server replies to the e-mail message by sending a copy of the file. If *filename* doesn't exist in the archive, the server replies with an error message.

Many e-mail information servers are smart enough to send help if the incoming message doesn't contain a valid command.

You can provide information through an e-mail information server in two ways:

- Subscribe to an e-mail information service on the Internet
- Set up your own e-mail server on your personal computer

The next few sections describe these two options.

Using an Internet e-mail information service provider

E-mail information service providers vary greatly in terms of the services that they offer and in the ways in which their services operate. The two commands mentioned in the preceding section — help and get (or send) — have become informal standards for e-mail information servers on the Internet. If the service offered by your provider doesn't support these commands, or at least the help command, your e-mail information service may be difficult for people to use. Before you subscribe to an e-mail information service on the Internet, ask for a demonstration, and make sure that the service supports the help command.

The basic idea behind subscribing to an e-mail information service offered by a service provider is that you rent space for your files on the provider's computer. The provider gives you a new e-mail address, and anyone who wants to receive one of your files by e-mail sends a command to that e-mail address. The procedure is a bit like that of FTP, but instead of an FTP client program, the service uses e-mail messages to transfer files. (See Chapter 10 for more information on the File Transfer Protocol.)

Providing files through e-mail has one major advantage over traditional FTP: Internet users can receive copies of your files through e-mail rather than directly from your FTP server. Because you don't need direct Internet access to receive e-mail, people still can access your files. If you use only FTP to transfer files to interested visitors to your site, you may eliminate a large number of potential visitors who can't access FTP.

To subscribe to an e-mail information service on the Internet, ask a service provider for a demonstration of its e-mail service. This demonstration typically involves sending an e-mail message to a demonstration server, so you need access to an e-mail account of your own. If you like the way that the provider's server responds to your message, sign up!

Your service provider gives you the following items after you subscribe:

- The e-mail address of your new e-mail information server
- Instructions on adding files to your e-mail information server

One file that you want to add to your server is a text file called INDEX, which normally contains a list of all files available from your e-mail information server. This file enables users of your e-mail information server to retrieve a list of available files by sending the following command to your e-mail information server:

get index

Depending on the service provider, you also may need to create or modify the file that goes to users after they ask for help. After you do that, your e-mail information server is ready to respond to messages and send files through e-mail to anyone on the Internet.

Telling others how to use your e-mail information server

To tell other people how to access your e-mail information server, give them the e-mail address of your server. You also may want to provide simple instructions, similar to the following example:

```
Virtual Corporation has an e-mail information server. To
access it, send e-mail to infobot@virtualcorporation.com,
with the word  help  in the body of the message.
```

You can use a special type of hyperlink in the World Wide Web to create a link to an e-mail address. This special type of hyperlink is called a mailto: link. Here's an example:

```
mailto:infobot@virtualcorporation.com
```

To turn a mailto: link into a World Wide Web hyperlink, create an anchor by using the mailto: syntax. The following HTML line creates such an anchor:

```
<A HREF= mailto:infobot@virtualcorporation.com >Send us
          e-mail</A>
```

The mailto: syntax doesn't serve any purpose outside the World Wide Web. Adding a mailto: link to your stationery or to your business card, for example, wouldn't make sense. Simply give people your e-mail address so that they can request more information about your site by using the help command.

Making money by using your e-mail information server

E-mail information servers are similar to FTP, World Wide Web, and Gopher servers in that anyone on the Internet can obtain information from them. You normally can't charge for access to your files, but you can charge for the use of your files.

Some e-mail information service providers offer a special type of e-mail information service that does enable you to charge for access to your files. By using this service, you create user accounts and passwords for each person who accesses your e-mail information server. To retrieve a file from your e-mail information server, a user must include a password in the e-mail message, along with the file request. If the password is valid, the server sends the file and bills the user's account accordingly.

Using Your Personal Computer As a Mail Server

If your computer has a direct connection to the Internet, you can set up your own e-mail server. An *e-mail server* is a program that receives e-mail from other computers and then routes the mail to its destination. By using an e-mail server of your own, you can create both automatic-reply e-mail accounts and e-mail information servers without paying extra to your Internet Service Provider. You don't need to worry, therefore, about breaking open the piggy bank if you need to provide many types of information through several automatic-reply e-mail accounts.

Best of all, because your computer acts as an Internet e-mail server, you can create as many normal e-mail accounts as you need at no extra charge. If you run a small or medium-size business, this method is the best way to give your employees Internet e-mail accounts of their own.

All e-mail servers on the Internet speak the same language: *Simple Mail Transfer Protocol,* or *SMTP* (pronounced *ess-em-tee-pee*). Don't confuse an *e-mail server,* which actually speaks SMTP, with an e-mail *information server,* which simply reads incoming e-mail and responds to commands within the message. Because an e-mail server speaks SMTP, that type of server can receive e-mail directly from other e-mail servers. E-mail information servers, which can't speak SMTP, must rely on an e-mail server to function. An e-mail server is like the postman who delivers the mail. You, the receiver of the mail, are more like an e-mail information server, responding to the mail the postman delivers.

To run your own SMTP-based e-mail server on your personal computer, your computer must have a direct connection to the Internet. You need a domain name of your own (as explained in Chapter 4), and your Internet Access Provider must provide domain-name service for your domain to enable people on the Internet to send mail to your e-mail server.

How to set up an e-mail server without a direct Internet connection

SMTP e-mail servers on the Internet deliver mail directly to their intended recipients. These servers have a motto similar to that of their physical counterparts: "Neither line noise, nor network congestion, nor power outages shall keep an e-mail server from its appointed tasks." If your e-mail server isn't available when another e-mail server wants to deliver a message, however, your e-mail could end up in Larry's closet in Argentina or who knows where else on the planet.

SMTP is meant for use in delivering mail between e-mail servers that reside on the Internet. If your e-mail server is available on the Internet for only a few minutes each day because you don't have a dedicated Internet connection, other SMTP servers may have trouble delivering your e-mail. A few Internet Access Providers have special e-mail services that eliminate this problem, but this new type of SMTP e-mail service isn't common yet. You need to talk with your access provider about the implications of running your own SMTP e-mail server without dedicated Internet access before you ever attempt to do so.

If you don't have a direct Internet connection, SMTP isn't the best way to receive e-mail from your service provider. *UNIX to UNIX Copy (UUCP)* — a communications protocol that exchanges files between two computers automatically — is a much better option for receiving Internet e-mail if you're going to connect to the Internet only occasionally. UUCP is designed to do what SMTP has trouble with: deliver e-mail to computers that don't have a direct connection to the Internet.

At least one UUCP software package is available for MS-DOS and Macintosh, but it's complicated, and we don't like using it. Other UUCP packages for Windows and Macintosh should be available soon; these packages should enable you to do everything described in this chapter without a direct Internet connection. More important, Internet Access Providers everywhere should soon be offering SMTP e-mail service that's reliable even if your connection to the Internet isn't.

Besides communicating with other Internet e-mail servers by using SMTP, an e-mail server provides normal e-mail accounts to individual users. While delivering e-mail to individual users, an e-mail server acts a little like an electronic post office. E-mail messages arrive at the post office and then go out to each person's electronic mailbox. To pick up their e-mail, users must request their e-mail from the e-mail server by using the *Post Office Protocol (POP)*.

E-mail servers that speak Post Office Protocol are known as *POP servers*. *POP* is an important term to remember, because the people who have e-mail accounts on your server must use a program known as a *POP client* to retrieve e-mail from their electronic mailboxes. The most common POP client is a program called Eudora, although many POP clients exist for every type of computer. For the most part, no difference exists between a POP client and a normal e-mail client, because most e-mail clients use the Post Office Protocol.

Are you blown away by all these abbreviations — SMTP, POP, UUCP? If so, the following list should help clear things up for you:

- ✔ An e-mail server is a program that receives e-mail from other computers and then routes the mail to its destination.

- ✔ Post Office Protocol (POP) is the protocol that sorts and delivers mail on an SMTP server to the appropriate user's mailbox.

- ✔ Simple Mail Transfer Protocol (SMTP) is the language that all e-mail servers on the Internet speak.

- ✔ An e-mail information server is a program that reads incoming e-mail and responds to special commands within the message.

- ✔ The `vacation` program is a UNIX utility that you use to reply automatically to incoming e-mail.

- ✔ An automatic-reply e-mail account is a service that you set up to send mail to interested parties who request information. You can use your Internet Service Provider or your own system to set up this account.

- ✔ Larry's closet is the place where your e-mail goes if the electronic post office misplaces it.

Setting up a Windows e-mail server

One of the software packages that inspired this book is SLMail, written by Jack De Winter and now owned by Seattle Lab. SLMail is a complete Windows SMTP server that supports both automatic-reply and e-mail information server e-mail accounts. The server also is a functional POP server, which you can use to set up as many e-mail accounts as you want.

To run SLMail, you need Windows 95 or Windows NT and TCP/IP access to the Internet. Make sure that you communicate extensively with your Internet Access Provider as you set up your e-mail service so that the provider fully understands what you're doing. This communication helps your provider configure its computers to work correctly with your SLMail server and keeps your e-mail from getting lost.

To begin, obtain the SLMail software and install the program on your computer. You can find SLMail on the World Wide Web at the following address:

```
http://www.seattlelab.com/
```

The SLMail main window appears after you install and run the SLMail program on your computer.

After you start SLMail for the first time, the program uses the settings in your existing Internet software to configure itself; the main window shows you some of the settings that the program chooses. Even if SLMail gets everything right, checking the detailed configuration, just to make sure that everything is okay, is a good idea.

Configuring SLMail

To configure SLMail, follow these steps to verify and correct the SLMail system configuration:

1. **Choose Configuration➪System.**

   The System Options dialog box appears, as shown in Figure 9-3. For SLMail to work, you must set up the four areas of the System Options dialog box correctly.

2. **In the Local Node text box, verify or enter the fully qualified domain name of the computer on which you're running SLMail.**

   In the example shown in Figure 9-3, the computer's name is `krypton.science.org`. Make sure that the Local Node text box contains the full domain name of your computer.

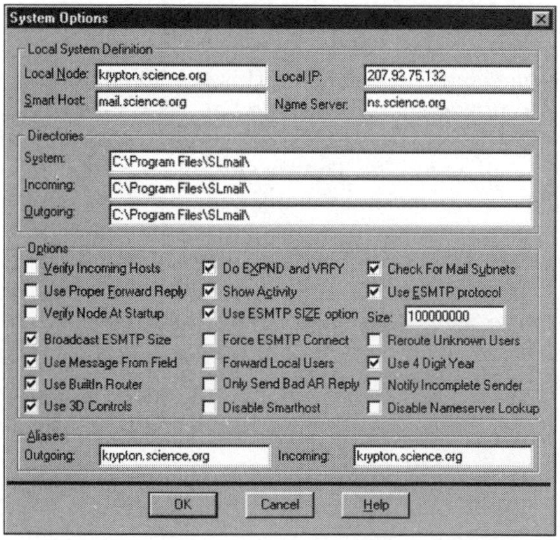

Figure 9-3:
Configure SLMail in the System Options dialog box.

3. **Enter your computer's IP address in the Local IP text box.**

4. **In the Smart Host text box, enter the full name or the IP address of your Internet Access Provider's e-mail server.**

   This host is the computer to which the program directs outgoing e-mail, if SLMail decides to have another e-mail server help deliver certain messages.

5. **Make certain that each of the directories listed in the Directories area of the dialog box is valid.**

   System is the directory in which you install SLMail. The Incoming and Outgoing directories determine where SLMail stores e-mail as the program processes it. The same directory can appear in all three boxes.

   You probably don't need to change anything in the Options area unless your Internet Access Provider tells you to do so. If you don't want to see a play-by-play narration of everything that SLMail does, you can deselect the Show Activity check box, but leave the other settings alone unless you have a good reason to change them.

6. **If you entered something other than your registered domain name in the Local Node text box, enter your registered domain name in both the Incoming and the Outgoing text boxes in the Aliases area of the dialog box.**

   Entering your registered domain name in both text boxes tells SLMail that sending and receiving mail by using your real domain name, instead of the name that you enter in the Local Node field, is okay.

7. **If you made any changes in the settings in the System Options dialog box, exit and restart SLMail so that your changes can take effect.**

A few other configuration dialog boxes may be important if you have a complex network or an unusual mail-transfer mechanism. You can access these dialog boxes through the SLMail Configuration menu. If you're setting up a standard system, however, you can move on to the best part: creating user e-mail accounts.

Creating user accounts

You can choose Configuration⇨Users to display the System Users dialog box, shown in Figure 9-4. Every time you see this dialog box, think about all the people in the world who pay unreasonable rates for a single e-mail account through an online service. This dialog box releases you from the prison of online-service e-mail by enabling you to create your own Internet e-mail accounts on your SLMail e-mail server.

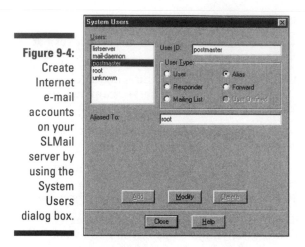

Figure 9-4:
Create
Internet
e-mail
accounts
on your
SLMail
server by
using the
System
Users
dialog box.

The System Users dialog box enables you to create five types of e-mail accounts. By creating different types of accounts, you can do more with your SLMail server than simply receive e-mail. The five account types are

- ✔ Alias
- ✔ User
- ✔ Responder
- ✔ Forward
- ✔ Mailing List

We cover each of these account types in the following sections. You may want to set up some of or all these account types for your Internet site.

Alias accounts

Alias accounts, which are the simplest type, provide other names by which particular users can receive e-mail. Figure 9-4, in the preceding section, shows that the postmaster account is an alias for the user named Root, which means that any e-mail sent to postmaster actually goes to Root.

You can create as many Alias accounts as you need by following these steps in the System Users dialog box:

1. Type a user ID for the new Alias account in the User ID text box.

The User ID is the name that other people use to send e-mail to this user. The user's full e-mail address is his user ID, followed by @ (the *at sign*) and then by your registered domain name, as shown in the following example:

```
UserID@krypton.science.org
```

Note: The user ID should not contain spaces.

2. **Click the Alias radio button in the User Type area.**

3. **In the Aliased To text box, type the user ID of the existing user for whom you want to create an alias.**

4. **Click the Add button to create the new alias.**

   In Figure 9-4, you notice that you can add only one postmaster. In other cases, the Add button isn't deactivated.

User accounts

User accounts are the normal e-mail accounts through which people send and receive mail. Each person who has a User account on your SLMail server can use a POP client, such as Eudora, to access his mailbox.

To create a User account, follow these steps in the System Users dialog box (see Figure 9-5):

1. **Type a user ID for the new account in the User ID text box.**

   Note: The user ID should not contain spaces.

2. **Click the User radio button in the User Type area of the dialog box.**

3. **Type the user's full name (or any other descriptive text) in the User Name text box.**

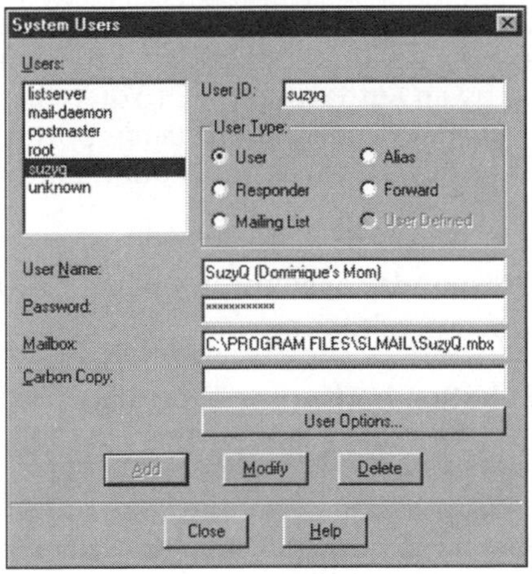

Figure 9-5:
Add User accounts to create individual mailboxes for your e-mail users.

4. **Enter a password for the account in the _P_assword text box.**

The user must supply this password to access the account on your SLMail server. As you type the password, each character appears as an asterisk (*), so enter the password carefully.

5. **Verify that the _M_ailbox text box contains an acceptable filename.**

The mailbox file usually has a name similar to the user ID. This file is the file in which the program stores e-mail for this user.

6. **Enter an e-mail address in the _C_arbon Copy text box if you want to send a copy of the messages that this user receives to another e-mail address.**

If you're the boss in your company, please don't enter your own e-mail address in the _C_arbon Copy field so that you can read all your employees' e-mail. We consider e-mail to be private communication if it's addressed to an individual. If you feel that keeping tabs on all business communication is important, assign a separate e-mail address that is clearly of a business nature (such as `webmaster`, `jobs`, or `accounting`), and enable one or more of your employees to receive business-related e-mail at that address instead of a private one. Recognize and respect the privacy rights of your workers.

7. **Click the _A_dd button to accept the new user.**

The _A_dd button activates after you fill everything in correctly.

Responder accounts

Responder accounts enable you to set up an automatic-reply e-mail account or a full e-mail information server by using SLMail. This account always responds to e-mail automatically. Don't use this account as a regular e-mail account unless you always want the computer to respond for you. The Responder account is managed by an auto responder. (You're likely to see this term written as both *auto reponder* and *autoresponder*. Both versions mean the same thing.) To create a new Responder account, follow these steps in the System Users dialog box:

1. **Type the user ID for the Responder account in the User _I_D text box.**

The ID in this example is `info`.

2. **Click the Responder radio button in the User _T_ype area (see Figure 9-6).**

3. **Enter a descriptive name for the Responder account in the _R_esponder Name text box.**

The Responder _N_ame is just for decoration, so use any name that you want.

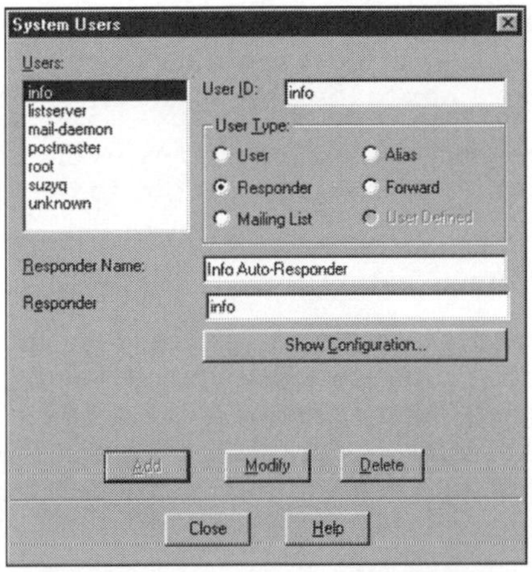

Figure 9-6:
Create a
Responder
account to
set up an
automatic-
reply
account or
an e-mail
information
server.

4. **Verify that the filename in the Responder field is OK; then click the Show Configuration button to open the Configure Autoresponder dialog box (see Figure 9-7).**

   The Responder file is the file in which you want to store the configuration information for this Responder account.

5. **To use this Responder account as an e-mail information server, select the Send Files Only On User's Request check box.**

   This default option tells the Responder account not to respond with a file unless the incoming e-mail contains a valid file request. Otherwise, deselect this check box so that the responder account replies to any incoming e-mail by sending the file or files that you specify.

6. **Change the other settings to meet your needs.**

   If you want the autoresponder to send files as attachments instead of as normal e-mail messages, for example, select the Send Files As Attachments check box.

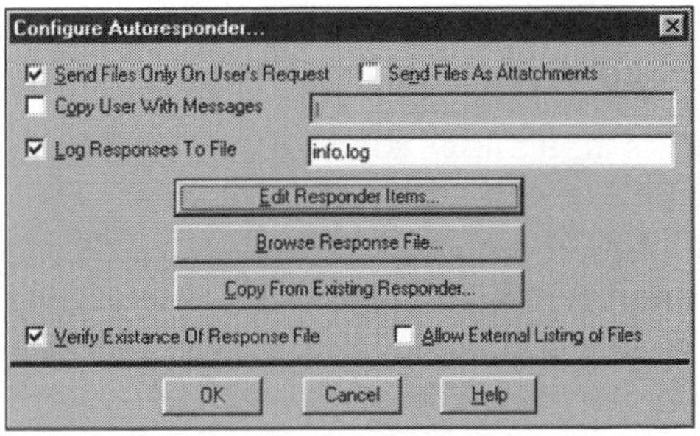

Figure 9-7:
Configure
your auto-
responder
so that it
can reply to
incoming
e-mail
correctly.

To send a copy of the incoming e-mail messages to another e-mail address, select the Copy User With Messages check box and then enter the e-mail address in the text box to the right of the check box.

To log responses to a file, select the Log Responses To File check box and then enter a name for the log file in the text box to the right of the check box.

7. Click the Edit Responder Items button.

The Configure Auto Responder dialog box appears (see Figure 9-8). You use this dialog box to tell the autoresponder which files to send. If you selected the Send Files Only On User's Request check box in the preceding dialog box, the autoresponder sends a file only if it receives an e-mail message containing a command such as the following, in which *filename* appears in the dialog box's File List:

```
send filename
```

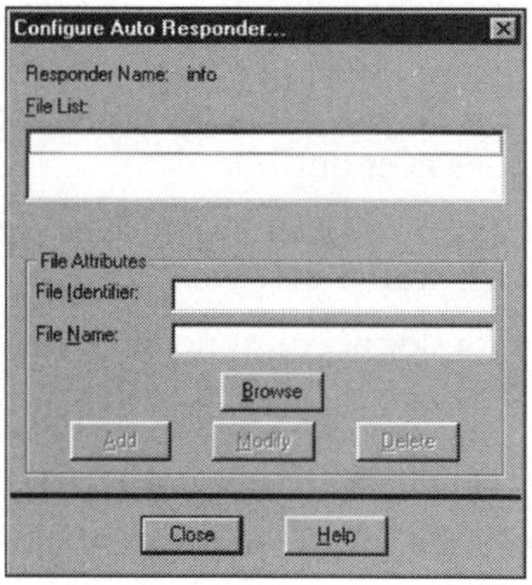

Figure 9-8:
Configure
your auto-
responder
by adding
filenames to
the File List.

Configure Auto Responder...

Responder Name: info

File List:

File Attributes
File Identifier:
File Name:

Browse

Add   Modify   Delete

Close   Help

8. To add an item to the File List, enter a file identifier and a filename; then click the Add button.

If you don't know the name of the file, click the Browse button to select one from the Open dialog box that appears.

9. After you finish adding files to the File List, click the Close button.

The Add button appears active after you correctly enter all the information.

10. Click the OK button in the Configure Autoresponder dialog box to accept your changes and return to the System Users dialog box.

Forward accounts

Sometimes, you need to forward mail for a particular user to a new e-mail address. If an employee named John leaves your company and goes to work for another company, for example, you may want to forward his mail to his new e-mail address (depending, of course, on how much you like John and on his reason for leaving your company).

To forward mail to another e-mail address, you create a *Forward account*. To create a Forward account with the same name as an old User account (as in the case of your ex-employee, John), you first must delete the old User account. Select the User account from the list in the System Users dialog box, click the Delete button, and then follow these steps to add a new Forward account:

1. **Type a User ID for the new Forward account.**

   If you're replacing an old User account, make the user ID the same as the one for the old User account.

2. **Click the Forward radio button in the User Type area.**

3. **In the Forwarded To text box, enter the address to which you want to forward e-mail.**

4. **Click the Add button to accept the new account.**

Wrapping up

After you finish adding any of the accounts, click the Close button. This action returns you to the main application window. Administering an e-mail server isn't difficult. You can add any of these account types whenever you need them.

Enabling POP in SLMail

Finally, to enable the capability for e-mail client programs to use the Post Office Protocol (POP) to contact the SLMail server and retrieve the contents of electronic mailboxes, choose Configuration⇨Remote Access to open the System Access Options dialog box, as shown in Figure 9-9. Verify that Pop3 Mailbox Access is enabled. As long as check marks appear in both check boxes in the System Access Options dialog box, POP is enabled.

You've probably used Internet e-mail yourself in the past without understanding completely what your Internet Service Provider needs to do for you to use your electronic mailbox. Well, after you set up your own Internet e-mail server and configure mailboxes, you'll know exactly what an ISP does for every one of its customers who has an Internet e-mail address.

Note: Chapter 7 describes the Mailing List account type in detail, so we don't go into that type of account here.

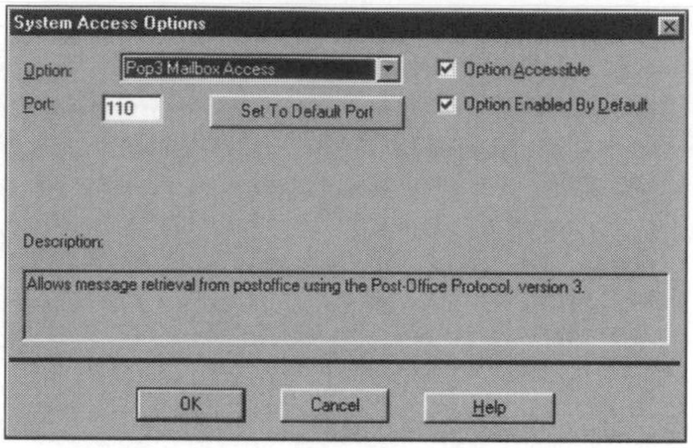

Figure 9-9:
Enable POP
access to
the SLMail
server.

System Access Options

Option: Pop3 Mailbox Access ▾   ☑ Option Accessible
Port: 110   Set To Default Port   ☑ Option Enabled By Default

Description:

Allows message retrieval from postoffice using the Post-Office Protocol, version 3.

OK   Cancel   Help

Setting up an e-mail server on a Macintosh

A great e-mail server package called *Apple Internet Mail Server (AIMS)* is available free for the Macintosh. AIMS, written by Glenn Anderson, is a full Simple Mail Transfer Protocol and Post Office Protocol server program that makes your Macintosh a complete Internet e-mail server. (See Chapter 7 for more information.) To set up automatic-reply, e-mail information server, and Mailing List accounts, you need an add-on product called AutoShare. To find more documentation on AutoShare and a link to download AIMS on the Web, go to the following URL:

```
http://computers.science.org/internet/site/setup/
```

To run AIMS and AutoShare, you need a Macintosh running System 7 or later. You also must have MacTCP 1.1.1 or later, and you need TCP/IP access to the Internet. Make sure that you communicate extensively with your Internet Access Provider after you start using Apple Internet Mail Server so that the provider knows what you're doing and can better meet your needs.

Installing Apple Internet Mail Server

To configure AIMS, follow these steps:

1. **Obtain the AIMS software and install the program on your computer.**

2. **Double-click the AIMS icon to start the program.**

   The program starts and displays a Debug window that tells you more about your MacTCP configuration.

3. **If any of this information seems to be incorrect, check the configuration of MacTCP by using the MacTCP Control Panel; close the Debug window after you're satisfied that everything's correct.**

The Debug window also gives you important messages while AIMS is running, particularly if something goes wrong. Check this window often to make sure that your e-mail server is functioning correctly.

4. **Choose Server⇨Account Information to set up user accounts on your e-mail server.**

   The Account Information dialog box appears (see Figure 9-10).

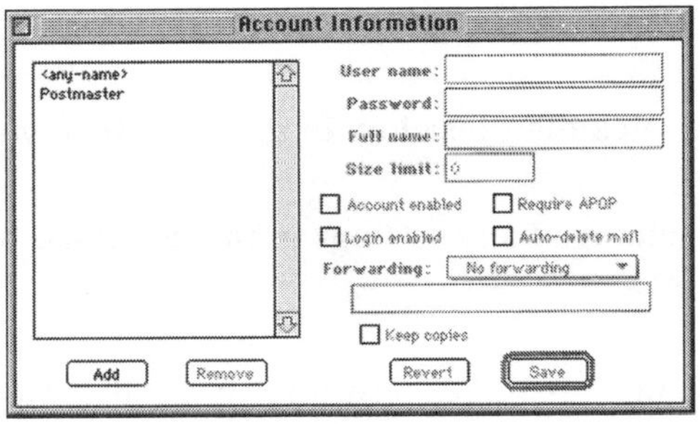

Figure 9-10:
Add, edit,
or remove
user
accounts in
the Account
Information
dialog box.

```
┌─────────────────── Account Information ──────────────────┐
│ ┌──────────────────┐  User name : [                    ] │
│ │ <any-name>     ⇧ │  Password : [                    ]  │
│ │ Postmaster       │  Full name : [                    ] │
│ │                  │  Size limit : [0    ]              │
│ │                  │  ☐ Account enabled  ☐ Require APOP │
│ │                  │  ☐ Login enabled    ☐ Auto-delete mail │
│ │                ⇩ │  Forwarding : [ No forwarding   ▼]  │
│ │                  │  [                              ]   │
│ └──────────────────┘  ☐ Keep copies                     │
│  [  Add  ] [ Remove ]    [ Revert ]  [  Save  ]          │
└──────────────────────────────────────────────────────────┘
```

5. **Click the Add button to add a new user.**

6. **Enter a name in the User Name text box.**

   Note: This name should not contain spaces, because it is part of the address to which other Internet users send e-mail.

7. **In the Password text box, type a password for this user account.**

   The user must specify this password to access his e-mail by using a POP client.

8. **Enter the user's full name in the Full Name text box.**

9. **Select the Account Enabled check box.**

10. **Select the Login Enabled check box.**

11. **Click the Save button to save the new user.**

    This step closes the dialog box and returns you to the main window.

12. **Choose Server⇨Preferences.**

    This command opens the AIMS Preferences window, shown in Figure 9-11.

13. **Verify that the settings shown in the dialog box — especially the default server name — are acceptable.**

    The default server name shown in the Server names list box should match the name of your computer.

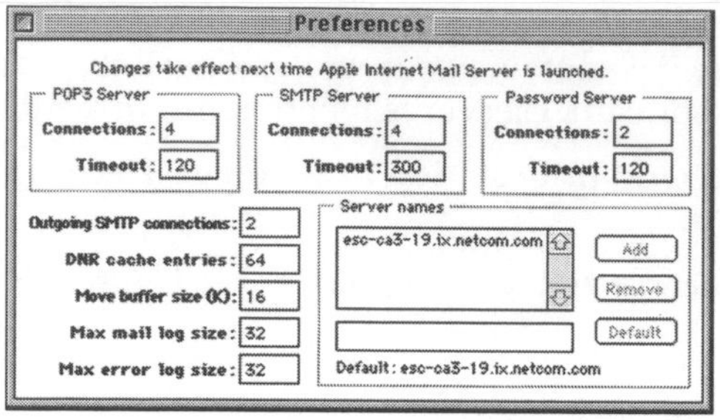

Figure 9-11:
Verify your
AIMS
preferences.

14. **If everything is OK, click the Close box in the top-left corner of the window.**

15. **Restart AIMS if you changed any settings in this window.**

Using AutoShare

Next, you need to obtain the AutoShare software and install it on your computer. The AutoShare folder contains three other folders:

✔ The AutoShare folder contains the main AutoShare software.

✔ The Samples folder contains important files that you use to configure AutoShare.

✔ The Documentation folder contains further instructions for installing and using AutoShare.

Installing AutoShare

The first step in installing AutoShare is checking the Map Control Panel. To check the panel and then install AutoShare, follow these steps:

1. **Open the Apple Control Panel and choose Map by double-clicking the Map selection.**

   AutoShare uses the Control Panel's Map window to determine the time and date in your area of the world (see Figure 9-12).

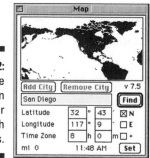

Figure 9-12:
Choose the
city in
which your
Macintosh
lives.

2. **Click the map or click the Find button to choose a city near you.**

   Your selection appears filled in. After you finish making your selection, click the Set button to close the Map window.

3. **Now go back to the Macintosh finder and locate and open the Samples folder; then open the Auto folder.**

4. **Select all the folders inside the Auto folder and drag those folders to the main AutoShare folder.**

5. **Now open the AutoShare folder that's located within the main AutoShare folder; then open the 68K folder.**

6. **Double-click the AutoShare icon to start the AutoShare program.**

After AutoShare starts, a blank window titled Status appears. A warning message is likely to appear at the bottom of this window, instructing you to reconfigure AutoShare. Because you haven't yet configured AutoShare, this warning is not surprising.

Configuring AutoShare

After you start AutoShare, the first thing that you need to do is to tell AutoShare where to find the AutoShare folders. The AutoShare folders are the ones that you moved from the Auto folder to the main AutoShare folder in the preceding section. To give AutoShare that information, follow these steps:

1. **Choose Preferences⇨Folders.**

   The AutoShare folders configuration window appears (see Figure 9-13).

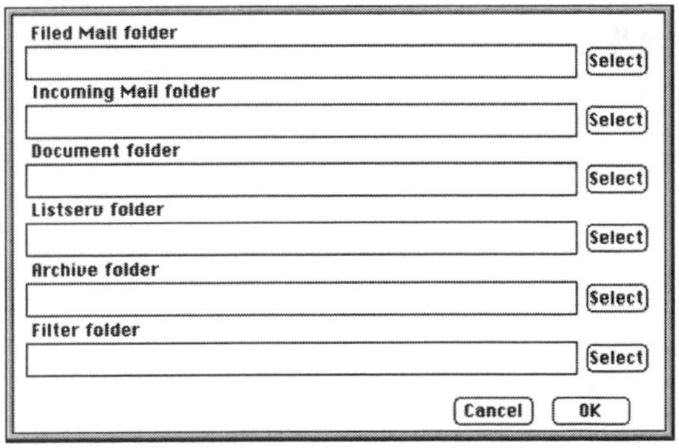

Figure 9-13:
The AutoShare folders configuration window appears empty at first.

Filed Mail folder | Select

Incoming Mail folder | Select

Document folder | Select

Listserv folder | Select

Archive folder | Select

Filter folder | Select

Cancel | OK

2. **Click the Select button (next to the Filed Mail folder field) and choose the Filed Mail folder inside the main AutoShare folder (see Figure 9-14).**

   This action tells AutoShare which folder to use for incoming e-mail.

3. **Then click the Select "Filed Mail" button to select the folder.**

   This action tells AutoShare which folder to use for incoming e-mail.

4. **Select the Incoming Mail folder inside the AIMS folder named Mail Folder, which is located in your System folder.**

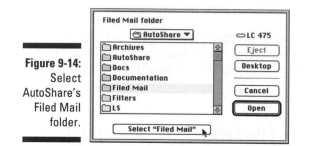

Figure 9-14:
Select
AutoShare's
Filed Mail
folder.

5. **Click the Select button next to the Incoming Mail folder field and choose the Incoming Mail folder inside the Mail Folder.**

   Look in your System folder for these folders.

6. **Click the Select "Incoming Mail" button to select the Incoming Mail folder (see Figure 9-15).**

7. **Choose Docs, LS, Archives, and Filters to set up the remaining four folders that you need.**

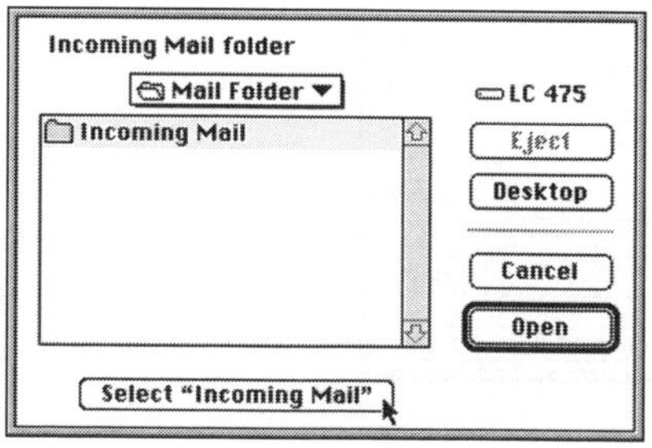

Figure 9-15:
Select the
AIMS
Incoming
Mail folder,
located
inside the
System
folder.

You find these files inside the main AutoShare folder.

Now your screen should look something like that shown in Figure 9-16, with all the folder fields filled in.

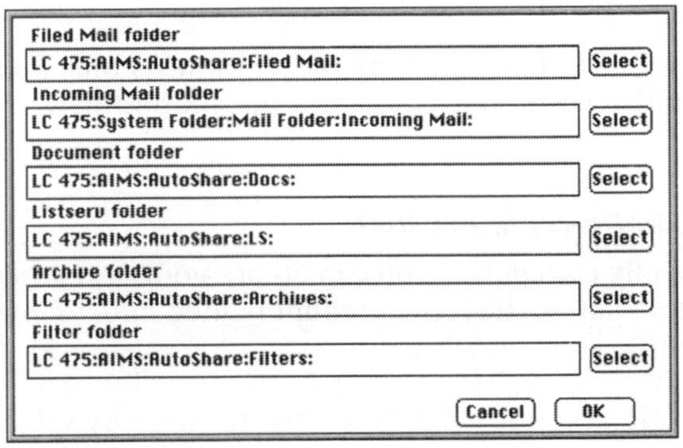

Figure 9-16:
You now
have a
folder listed
for each of
the folder
fields.

Filed Mail folder	
LC 475:AIMS:AutoShare:Filed Mail:	Select
Incoming Mail folder	
LC 475:System Folder:Mail Folder:Incoming Mail:	Select
Document folder	
LC 475:AIMS:AutoShare:Docs:	Select
Listserv folder	
LC 475:AIMS:AutoShare:LS:	Select
Archive folder	
LC 475:AIMS:AutoShare:Archives:	Select
Filter folder	
LC 475:AIMS:AutoShare:Filters:	Select

Cancel   OK

8. **Click the OK button to accept these folders.**

   The Status window reappears, no longer displaying the reconfigure warning.

9. **Choose Preferences⇨Miscellaneous.**

   The AutoShare Preferences window appears (see Figure 9-17).

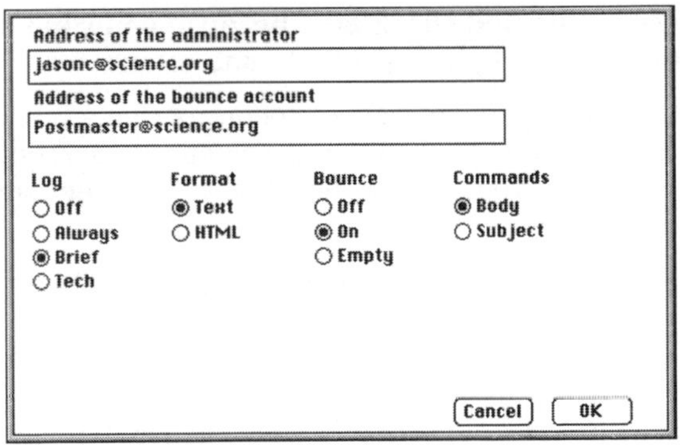

Figure 9-17:
Configure
miscellaneous
AutoShare
preferences
in this
window.

Address of the administrator
jasonc@science.org
Address of the bounce account
Postmaster@science.org

Log	Format	Bounce	Commands
○ Off	◉ Text	○ Off	◉ Body
○ Always	○ HTML	◉ On	○ Subject
◉ Brief		○ Empty	
○ Tech			

Cancel   OK

10. **Change the Address of the Bounce Account text box to some e-mail address that you're certain to check often.**

This account notifies you each time a message bounces (that is, does not reach its destination).

Note: Make sure that the Address of the Administrator text box contains your correct e-mail address; otherwise, important AutoShare messages can't reach you.

The remaining preferences most likely are acceptable as they appear by default. After you finish editing, you can click the OK button to close this window.

Creating an automatic-reply account

After AutoShare is fully configured, you can create your first automatic-reply account. To create an automatic-reply account named info, follow these steps:

1. **To create an info account in AIMS, switch to AIMS by selecting it in the Finder and choose Server⇨Account Information.**

   The Account Information dialog box appears.

2. **Type** info **in the User Name text box.**

3. **Type a password in the Password text box.**

4. **Type a name in the Full Name text box.**

   You may want to use a name such as **Auto-reply info account**.

5. **Make sure that the Account Enabled check box is selected.**

6. **Deselect the Login Enabled check box, because you can't access this automatic-reply account by using a POP mail client.**

   You need Login Enabled only for e-mail accounts that a human being uses to receive e-mail. If Login Enabled is selected, a person can retrieve his e-mail from your server by using a POP client such as Eudora.

7. **From the Forwarding drop-down list, select Save as Files.**

   This selection tells AIMS to save all incoming e-mail for the info account as individual files in the location that you specify.

8. **In the text box below the Forwarding list, type the name of your Filed Mail folder, just as the name appears in your folder preferences in AutoShare (refer to Figure 9-16 earlier in this chapter).**

   Note: Make sure that you leave off the trailing colon from the Filed Mail folder name as it appears in the configuration window; AIMS doesn't accept folder names that end with a colon.

Figure 9-18 shows how your Account Information window appears at this point. (Remember to use your own Filed Mail folder line instead of the one that appears in this figure.)

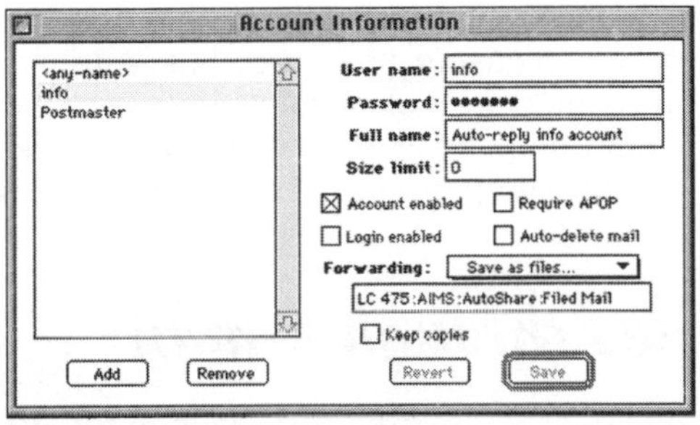

Figure 9-18:
Create
account
information
in AIMS.

9. **Switch to the Finder, and open the main AutoShare folder on your hard drive.**

10. **Open the Docs folder within the main AutoShare folder by double-clicking it and create a new folder by choosing File⇨New Folder.**

11. **Change the name of the new folder to Info.**

12. **In the Info folder, create a new file named Default.**

   AutoShare sends the contents of the Default file automatically in reply to any e-mail message someone sends to the info account.

This procedure is all that you need to do to set up an automatic-reply e-mail account by using AutoShare and AIMS. To set up an e-mail information server account — one that provides many files and sends only the ones that users request — simply create an automatic-reply e-mail account and add files to the account's AutoShare folder.

To request a file, an Internet user need only send to your automatic-reply account an e-mail message that contains the name of the file. AutoShare looks in the automatic-reply account's folder within the Docs folder, and if the program locates the requested file, it sends a copy to the requester. AutoShare sends the special file named Default automatically in reply to any e-mail message that doesn't contain a valid file request, which is why the sample info account works as an automatic-reply account.

Using Your E-Mail Information Server

Immediately upon setting up an e-mail information server, you can begin doing several creative things. Whether or not you do what this section describes, you should at least incorporate your e-mail information resource into your World Wide Web page by using a `mailto:` link. Adding an e-mail information server to your home page makes your Internet presence more interactive and also sets your company apart from those that believe that the World Wide Web is the only thing on the Internet that matters.

Send binary files through e-mail

To send binary files through e-mail, you first must encode the file by using a utility such as BinHex or UUEncode. If you encode a binary file (most programs are binary files), you convert that file to a text-only format. You can then send this text-only file through e-mail, and all that the recipient needs to do is decode the message to end up with a binary file again. Many e-mail readers decode the message automatically, enabling people to receive and use your binary files easily.

Several programs that are available on the Internet enable you to encode and decode files. You can obtain more information about UUEncode and UUDecode online. The Setting Up An Internet Site home page can also help you. You can reach this page at the following URL:

```
http://computers.science.org/internet/site/setup/
```

The entire process of sending a binary file via e-mail sometimes confuses the receiver. With so many people just coming on to the Internet, one more step in receiving and sending files may be too much for many people to handle.

For documents that do not rely on specific formatting and for those documents that don't include graphics, consider sending them in text format. This procedure eliminates the need for you to UUEncode or BinHex-encode the file — and, more important, relieves the recipient of the responsibility of knowing how to deal with the strange-looking file that you sent.

Provide World Wide Web documents

One of the most clever things that you can do with your e-mail information server is provide World Wide Web documents. After Internet users retrieve one of your Web documents through e-mail, they can save that document on their personal computers and then view the file by using their Web browsers. If the users have TCP/IP connections to the Internet, they can click any hyperlink in your document; their Web browsers respond exactly as they would had they contacted your HTTP server to retrieve the document. This method is a creative way to provide World Wide Web documents without running an HTTP server or paying a Web publishing service to host your Web pages.

Thus, an e-mail information server is just as important to your Internet site as a World Wide Web home page. You can find no better way to distribute information than via e-mail, because e-mail enables you to reach more people cheaper and faster than other methods do. In addition, e-mail enables you to find out exactly who contacts you. E-mail is true two-way communication — something that any psychologist or business professional knows is an essential part of any relationship (even an electronic one).

Chapter 10

Exchanging Files on the Internet

· ·

In This Chapter

▶ Understanding how FTP works

▶ Providing files to others on the Internet

▶ Receiving files from others by using FTP

▶ Setting up a permanent FTP site

· ·

*T*he Internet is the ultimate in diverse computing environments. After you connect to the Internet, you join a computer network that integrates everything from Cray supercomputers to computerized Coke machines. This diversity works because all the computers speak the same set of languages to transfer and store executable and data files.

Transferring files is an important function of the Internet. If your computer can't transfer files, you can't get the latest software programs or send files to your associates. An important aspect of almost any program that runs on the Internet is the way in which this transfer occurs.

Programs transfer files in several ways. Some programs use simple network communications (known as *socket programs*) to transfer files; others use a *protocol* (that is, a set of commands) known as *File Transfer Protocol* (or *FTP*).

Understanding How FTP Works

By setting up your own FTP server, you can send files to and receive files from other people on the Internet or on a local-area network. Anyone who uses a World Wide Web browser, such as Netscape Navigator, can send and receive files through your FTP server.

FTP is a protocol that enables computers to transfer files across the Internet. An *FTP client program* (or *FTP client*) sends a request to an *FTP server program* (or *FTP server*), asking to exchange information and transfer files. The server then verifies that the user is authorized to send or receive files and responds to the request accordingly. World Wide Web browsers that support FTP can support both file uploading and downloading or, in some older browsers, file downloading (retrieval) only.

One desirable feature of FTP is the fact that the protocol maintains the original formatting of the file it transfers. Unlike other file-transfer techniques, such as those that you use to attach a file to an e-mail message, FTP doesn't require the user to decode received files before she can use those files. You must convert files that you transfer through e-mail to text-only formats. Several programs can perform this conversion; the most common is *Uuencode*. To decode a file that someone uuencodes, you must configure the e-mail client receiving the e-mail that contains the encoded file to use the Uudecode program.

Using the FTP client

Many graphical FTP client software programs are available as freeware or shareware. One of our favorite FTP clients available on the Internet is WS_FTP (available for Windows 3.1, Windows 95, and Windows NT). You can find this program on the Web at the following address:

```
http://www.tucows.com/
```

The top of the window shown in Figure 10-1 has a text box for the *profile name*, which simply is a name that you give this connection setup so that you can use the same setup again without reconfiguration. You can use anything for the profile name; the name is solely for your benefit and doesn't affect the way that WS_FTP operates. For the sake of simplicity, you can enter as the profile name the name of the host to which you're connecting.

The host name can be either a registered Internet domain name or the IP (Internet Protocol) address of an FTP server. In Figure 10-1, the host name of the FTP server is `ftp.cdrom.com`.

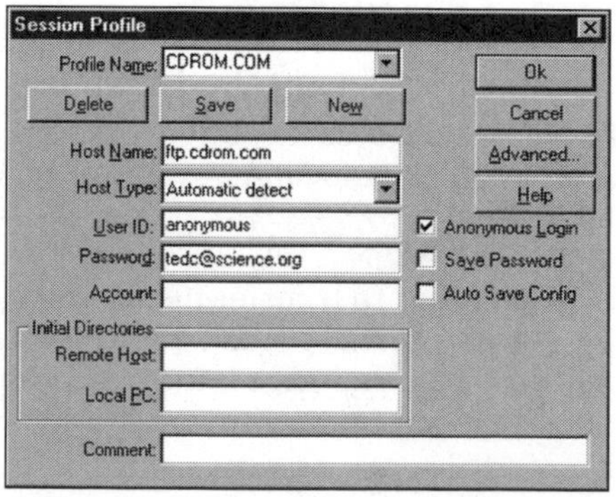

Figure 10-1: Connecting to an FTP server by using the WS_FTP client program.

Enter the appropriate user ID and password (or select the Anonymous Login check box to have the program fill in these spaces automatically); then click OK to establish the connection to the server.

Using anonymous FTP

Can you imagine handing out a password to every single person who wants access to your FTP site? You probably don't know most of the people who send or receive files through your FTP server, and you certainly don't have time to give them all personal accounts with passwords.

Many FTP server programs use a special login account called *anonymous FTP* to enable anyone on the Internet to log in and transfer files. Users can enter the word **anonymous** as the user ID and then enter their e-mail address or the word **guest** as the password. But does this setup mean that the Internal Revenue Service can access financial records on your computer to see how accurate your tax return is? No. You can set up FTP server software so that the public can access only those files that don't compromise your computer or your private information. (Whew!)

After a successful connection to the desired FTP server, the file transfer dialog box shown in Figure 10-2 should appear. This dialog box shows the local file system (the one running the FTP client) and the remote file system (the one running the FTP server). In Figure 10-2, you see the local file system in the list on the left side of the dialog box and the remote file system displaying directories in the list on the right side of the dialog box.

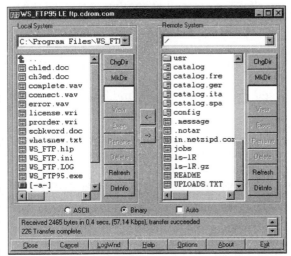

Figure 10-2: Select files to send or receive and click the arrow buttons to begin the transfer.

The next step before you use WS_FTP to transfer files is selecting the files that you want to transfer. To download files from the FTP server to your local machine, highlight the files that you want to transfer by clicking their names in the Remote System column (right column) of the file transfer dialog box. To navigate the directories, you can either double-click a directory name that appears as a file folder (refer to Figure 10-2) or click the ChgDir button and then type the full path of the directory that you want to access in the text box in the Change Directory dialog box that appears. Clicking the OK button causes the directory to change and the Change Directory dialog box to close.

Often, directories have hundreds of files, and searching for the files that you want to transfer can become tedious. The small text box below the MkDir button is for entering a *template*. This template consists of a wildcard (*) and a file extension. If you want to view only files with a .WAV extension, for example, enter ***.WAV** in the text box. The display of files adjusts to show only files that have the .WAV extension.

Two arrows appear between the local file system column and the remote file system column. You use these arrows to send selected files between the two file systems. Highlighting a file on the local file system and clicking the arrow that points toward the remote file system initiates a file transfer between the file systems.

To download files to your local system, highlight the files you want downloaded in the remote file system column and then click the arrow between the two lists that points from the remote system list to the local file system list (the arrow on top). To upload files to the server, you follow the same procedure, except that you need to highlight the files to upload in the local file system and then click the arrow that's pointing toward the remote system, or server, list (the bottom arrow).

An important selection in WS_FTP — and even more important in using a text-based FTP client — is the type of file transfer to use. WS_FTP offers two radio buttons and a check box for file-type selection: ASCII, Binary, and Auto. Choose between ASCII (for text files) and Binary (for most word-processing files, graphics, executable programs, and sound files). Because text files that you transfer in binary format remain text after being transferred, we recommend that you always use binary file transfer. Text files that you transfer as ASCII remain text, although binary files that you transfer as ASCII are no longer usable. In using a text-based FTP client, either from the DOS or UNIX prompt, you can select binary mode by entering the letter **I** at the FTP prompt. Text-based FTP clients start in ASCII mode by default.

A dialog box then appears if you're using WS_FTP as you transfer files. If you have a sound card in your computer, a sound tells that you that the file is being transferred. WS_FTP makes an "uh-oh!" sound in the event that an error occurs. After the file finishes transferring, you hear a strange sound and the dialog box goes away. If an error occurs, you may need to restart the file transfer.

Deciding whether FTP is right for you

Something strange — something that we don't fully understand — is happening on the Internet. In the rush to create new Internet products, many companies seem to be overlooking the basics, as though all the electronic trees are obscuring the view of the forest. One of the best examples of this is Internet file-transfer technology. Although FTP works well for some people, the majority of us need a better file-transfer tool. Tools that measure up to these expectations are slow in coming.

Some of the options for transferring files on the Internet are as follows:

- ✔ FTP
- ✔ World Wide Web
- ✔ E-mail file attachments
- ✔ Socket communications

FTP is a great way to exchange files with someone on a regular basis. You can run your own FTP server or purchase FTP services from your Internet Service Provider. You can provide password-protected user accounts for accessing your files instead of providing public access to them.

One of the simplest, yet most insecure, ways to transfer files is to provide them from your World Wide Web site. Placing a file in the publicly accessible Web publishing directory (see Chapter 5 for more information on Web publishing) and then sending someone a URL for accessing the file provides a simple way to retrieve files by using a Web browser. Unfortunately, anyone can access publicly accessible files. If your files are of a private nature, Web file transfer is not the solution for you.

People now use e-mail file attachments a great deal to transfer files. This method is the easiest way to transfer files but is also plagued with the greatest amount of restrictions and problems. Many e-mail servers place restrictions on the maximum size of a file that you can transfer through e-mail. Depending on e-mail to transfer files lets you down as soon as you have a large file to send. Plus file attachments are encoded in text, and the mechanism for changing the text back into the original file format is not always compatible between e-mail clients.

Programmers can actually build robust file-transfer technologies by using socket communications. The priority to build this type of technology is low, however, because a mechanism for transferring files over the Internet already exists, even if it is overkill. Today, we see more simple-to-use and robust file-transfer mechanisms appearing in various Internet-ready applications.

Providing Files by Using FTP

The potential uses of FTP are limitless. Some companies use an FTP server to provide customer support; other companies use FTP for communicating with employees at remote sites. A construction company, for example, can use FTP to transfer construction drawings back and forth from remote construction sites. If the foreman in Montana requests a drawing change, he can use FTP to transfer the file to the home-office FTP site. The home office then makes the change and places the corrected drawing on its FTP site for the remote employee to download.

You can easily fulfill numerous needs by providing files to the general public or to specific people via FTP. The applications of FTP file transfer are endless.

Using an Internet FTP service provider

The simplest, quickest, and least painful way to provide files through FTP involves using an existing FTP service provider. FTP service providers come in all shapes and sizes. Nonetheless, all providers have a few things in common, as described in the following list:

✔ Their Internet connections are probably faster than yours.

✔ They enable you to provide files on the Internet through their FTP servers, so that you don't need to set up and maintain your own server.

✔ They like being paid.

Using an FTP service provider should enable you to bypass many initial hassles and set up a good FTP site immediately. This method is the suggested strategy if you currently have limited resources, such as a low-bandwidth Internet connection, or if you aren't connected to the Internet with a dedicated connection running up to 24 hours a day, 7 days a week.

Companies that are concerned about security can opt to have their FTP sites provided by an FTP service provider. This course reduces the need for a protective firewall by increasing the security of corporate machines and also reduces the manpower necessary to administer an FTP server, as well as the hardware and bandwidth necessary to provide this service. Companies should conduct a serious cost-benefit analysis to see whether using an FTP service provider is more cost-effective than running their own sites.

The company that you use to connect to the Internet may also offer FTP service. If not, you can always subscribe to an FTP service provided by another organization. Some service providers even give you a graphical interface to make setting up and maintaining your FTP service easy (although having a graphical interface certainly isn't essential).

Your FTP service provider tells you the following two important things when you set up FTP service:

- ✔ Which directory to store files in so that users can access those files though anonymous FTP. (You call this directory, appropriately enough, your *anonymous FTP directory*.)
- ✔ How to put files in your anonymous FTP directory.

The pathway to your anonymous FTP directory should look something like the one in the following example:

```
/PUB/YOURUSERID
```

The PUB directory (short for public directory) is a standard directory set up by FTP administrators as part of anonymous FTP sites. The next directory establishes where you can find files associated with your account; service providers typically name this directory with your user ID. This directory is where you place publicly accessible files and subdirectories. Files in this directory are publicly accessible through the Internet, meaning that anyone who can access this directory can download files.

Getting a UNIX shell account

If you request FTP service from an Internet Service Provider, you can also request a UNIX shell account that any computer with a telnet client can access. *Telnet* is a network application that enables you to log in remotely to a UNIX machine. After you log in, you can work as though you were sitting in front of the UNIX machine. The UNIX shell account makes maintaining the files in your FTP directory simpler, assuming that you're familiar with UNIX. A UNIX shell account is also useful for many of the other services that this book discusses. If you aren't familiar with UNIX, you can pick up a copy of *UNIX For Dummies,* 2nd Edition (IDG Books Worldwide, Inc.) — an excellent resource.

Putting files in your FTP directory

You generally have two ways to put a file in your anonymous FTP directory:

- ✔ Beg and plead your FTP service provider to do the job for you. (Remember, however, to have the provider show you how.) Then send in a disk with the files on it.
- ✔ Send the file by using FTP. To do so, log in to the FTP server from your local computer by using your user ID and password; then send the file to your anonymous FTP directory.

If your FTP service provider set everything up correctly, you can transfer files into and out of your FTP directory. You can have special security set up, enabling you alone to upload files to your FTP directory and enabling other users only to download files. The next few sections explain how to accomplish these tasks. We also describe how to create directories and set the security permissions for special upload-only or download-only directories.

Removing files from your anonymous FTP site

To remove a file from your anonymous FTP site, simply delete the file by using one of the following options:

✔ Using WS_FTP, highlight the file that you want to remove by clicking the filename in the server-side list; then click the Delete button. (Refer to the section "Using the FTP client," earlier in this chapter.)

✔ Using a UNIX text-based FTP client, type the following command at the FTP prompt:

delete filename

✔ From a UNIX shell account, remove files from the anonymous FTP directory by typing the following `rm` command at the UNIX prompt:

rm filename

Receiving files from others

Your FTP service provider probably also gives you a special subdirectory called INCOMING. The full path name of the directory usually looks something like the following example:

```
/PUB/YOURUSERID/INCOMING
```

FTP users can send files to the INCOMING directory but can't download files from this directory. This arrangement gives you a secure way to receive files from other users through FTP. One of our service providers (CTSNet, at http://www.cts.com/) calls this directory an *FTP drop-box*; some providers also refer to this subdirectory as your *incoming directory* or your *FTP inbox*. (For Windows 95 users, directories are folders.)

Checking the security of your incoming directory

Some FTP server programs enable people to get files out of an incoming directory if they know the exact names of the files. This setup is not very secure, however, because anyone who guesses the name of a file in your incoming directory can download a copy of that file. To find out whether your incoming directory behaves this way, follow these steps:

1. **Use your FTP client program to connect to your FTP server.**

   (If you're using WS_FTP refer to the section "Using the FTP client," earlier in this chapter.)

2. **Log in as** anonymous.

3. **Send a file to your incoming directory.**

4. **Try to get the file out of the incoming directory by using its filename.**

If you can get the file, anyone else on the Internet can also get the file as long as that person knows (or can guess) the filename. Your incoming directory has a minor security hole, although it may be one that you can live with.

If the INCOMING directory in your FTP service comes with the security hole that we describe in this section, you can use that hole to your advantage. If you need to give files to a particular person, you can place the files in your incoming directory and then tell the other person the specific names of the files, so that the person can retrieve those files from your incoming directory. To anyone who doesn't know the filename, the incoming directory appears to be empty.

If possible, you can create an incoming directory and name that directory OUTGOING. This approach keeps the names of the files in your outgoing directory from appearing. Again, anyone who knows the name of a file in the outgoing directory can retrieve that file. This approach is one of the simplest ways to control access to files in directories that an FTP service provider provides. The alternative is to give a user ID and password to each person who wants secure access to your service.

Telling others how to access your anonymous FTP directory

You can tell other people how to access your FTP directory in one of the following ways:

✔ Write out a Uniform Resource Locator (URL) so that others can access your site by using a Web browser.

 ✔ Give other users long, drawn-out instructions on how to use a conventional FTP client to access your site.

A URL can look like something that a cat typed by walking across your keyboard, as the following example shows:

```
ftp://ftp.science.org/pub/internetsite/info.txt
```

Yet using a URL is probably the most direct and simple way to tell someone how to connect to your site. The long, drawn-out alternative explanation goes something like this: "Connect to the FTP server at `ftp.science.org`, and log in as **anonymous**. Use your e-mail address as the password. Change the directory to /PUB/INTERNETSITE/. Then download the INFO.TXT file."

Setting Up Your Own FTP Server

Although using an FTP service provider is convenient, we think that nothing can beat setting up your own FTP server. With your own FTP server, you can set up user accounts so that business associates and friends can log in to your FTP site securely. You can receive files from other users directly rather than through a third party, and you can provide files to others simply by copying those files to your FTP directory.

Setting up your own FTP server has one drawback: Your FTP server is available only while you're connected to the Internet. If you don't have a dedicated 24-hour connection, you probably should use an Internet FTP service provider. Using a provider is a great way to establish a permanent FTP site on the Internet, is also much less expensive than establishing your own dedicated connection and requires less maintenance.

If your computer can communicate with the Internet by using TCP/IP, you can set up and run your own FTP server. You need only access to the Internet and FTP server software that works in the operating system that you're using. Most FTP server software is straightforward — just install it and away you go.

The following sections provide detailed instructions on setting up FTP server software for either a Macintosh or a Windows-based personal computer.

Using a Macintosh NetPresenz FTP server

The best shareware FTP server software available for your Macintosh computer is NetPresenz, by Peter N. Lewis. The price is $10, and the program is worth every penny. You usually find the software distributed as a StuffIt archive, so your first step is to obtain the software and unStuffIt onto your hard drive.

Uniform Resource Locator (URL) review

Uniform Resource Locators (*URL*) are standardized addresses that people use to refer to Internet resources.

The first group of letters, ending in a colon, identifies the type of server that is providing the resource. You identify a file on an FTP server, for example, by the first three letters in the URL: `ftp:`.

The second portion of the URL, which normally begins with a double forward slash (`//`), identifies the domain name of the computer on the Internet that offers the Internet resource. In this example, the computer is running an FTP server.

Following the domain name is the path name of the directory that contains the resource. (By the way, a *resource* is usually a file of some type.) In the case of a file on an FTP server, that portion of the URL may appear as follows:

`/pub/internetsite/`

The URL for an FTP resource can also include a specific filename. The following URL points to a file called INFO.TXT in an anonymous FTP directory on the FTP server named `ftp.science.org` at `ftp://ftp.science.org`:

`ftp://ftp.science.org/pub/`
`    internetsite/info.txt`

Some computers on the Internet don't have domain names, but every computer on the Internet has a unique address called an IP *address*. You can use the IP address in place of a domain name. The following example, using the IP address, also is a valid URL:

`ftp://207.92.75.100/pub/`
`    internetsite/info.txt`

NetPresenz enables your Macintosh computer to send and receive files through FTP and can also serve Web pages through its built-in Web server. Unlike many other programs that perform only one task, NetPresenz is a multifaceted server system. In addition to FTP and Web service, NetPresenz can also provide files through the Gopher protocol, an old precursor to the World Wide Web. You can find out how to download the most current version of NetPresenz at the following address:

```
http://computers.science.org/internet/site/setup.html
```

To use NetPresenz, your Macintosh must have System 7 (or later) and MacTCP Version 1.1 (or later), and you must have enabled file sharing. To enable Internet users to access your FTP server, you need some kind of Internet IP access, such as PPP or (if you're special) a direct network connection.

Checking security

Before you install NetPresenz, you need to check the security of your computer system. Follow these steps to prepare for the installation of the FTPd server on your computer and to check the computer's security:

1. **Make sure that you have file sharing enabled.**

   Use the Sharing Setup control panel to determine the status of file sharing. Remember that you access your Macintosh control panels through the Apple menu. After you finish, close the Sharing Setup control panel.

2. **After you ascertain that file sharing is enabled (Step 1), configure sharing for your drives and folders by using the Finder to locate and click a drive or folder icon; then choose File➪Sharing.**

   A sharing configuration dialog box appears.

3. **If you don't want anonymous FTP users to access a particular drive or folder, make sure that you deselect (remove the check mark from) each of the three check boxes to the right of Everyone.**

You can change all your folders at the same time by selecting the Make all currently enclosed folders like this one check box.

Installing NetPresenz

After you check the security on your computer, you can install the NetPresenz server. After you install NetPresenz on your Mac, you see the following program icons in the FTPd folder:

- ✔ NetPresenz
- ✔ NetPresenz (Background)
- ✔ Register

Don't click any of these icons yet; just admire their beauty. The NetPresenz Setup program enables you to configure NetPresenz. NetPresenz is the actual FTP server program. The Register program gives you a simple and flexible way to register and pay for the NetPresenz program.

You need to do a few things before you configure NetPresenz. The following four steps show you how to prepare your Macintosh to run NetPresenz:

1. **Run the Internet Config program.**

   You find the Internet Config program in the NetPresenz folder. After you run the Internet Config program, the program enables you to determine the general settings for use in many Internet applications, including NetPresenz. You don't need to click each of the buttons in the Internet Preferences window — just the interesting ones. The important thing is that you run the application at least once so that you install the

Internet Config extension (part of the program). NetPresenz uses the Internet Config extension later. Close the Internet Preferences window after you complete your setup.

2. **At some point, run the Register program (by choosing it from the NetPresenz menu) to register and pay for NetPresenz.**

   Make sure that you look at the neat payment methods that are available!

3. **If you want to enable anonymous FTP logins, use the Users & Groups control panel to set up the** ⟨Guest⟩ **user and enable File Sharing for** ⟨Guest⟩.

   The *Guest user* is anyone who visits your FTP site anonymously.

4. **Double-click the NetPresenz Setup icon to get started with NetPresenz.**

   The About window appears, telling you a little about the program. Close this window by clicking the Close box in the top-left corner. You're now ready to start configuring NetPresenz.

Configuring NetPresenz

After you install the NetPresenz server, you must configure the NetPresenz server correctly by using the NetPresenz Setup window. The Setup program starts after you double-click the NetPresenz Setup icon (as the preceding section describes). If you haven't done so, double-click this icon in the NetPresenz folder now.

To configure general NetPresenz settings, follow these steps:

1. **Click the FTP Setup box in the NetPresenz Setup window.**

   The FTP Setup window appears.

   The most important settings in this window are the File Access privileges, which offer the following levels of access:

   - **None:** No access.

   - **Read Only:** Receive files only.

   - **Upload:** Send and receive only.

   - **Full:** Send and receive files and delete, rename, or modify files and folders.

   You can set the access privileges independently for each of the following types of users:

   - **Owner:** The user whose name appears in the Sharing Setup control panel as the owner of the Macintosh.

   - **User:** Any other user you define in the Users & Groups control panel.

- **Guest:** Anyone who uses anonymous FTP to access the
  NetPresenz server.

2. **Choose an access-level privilege for each of the user types by making
   selections from the drop-down lists.**

   Another important setting in the FTP Setup window is Remote Mounting, which enables an FTP user to access shared file systems on other
   Macintosh computers on your network. To access file systems on other
   computers, the FTP user sends a command similar to the following
   example from an FTP client program:

   ```
   quote smnt MacFileServer
   ```

3. **To enable Remote Mounting, select the Enabled check box in the
   appropriate user-type column.**

   Enable remote mounting, however, *only* if you have a good reason to do
   so. Typically, you disable remote mounting.

   Enabling Remote Mounting for guests is dangerous if you have an
   AppleTalk network. If you enable Remote Mounting for guests, anyone
   on the Internet can access files from any Macintosh on your network. If
   you don't have a good reason to enable Remote Mounting, disable this
   feature by deselecting the Enabled check box.

   Other than disabling Remote Mounting, leaving the default settings for
   the other options in the FTP Setup window should work fine for your
   setup.

4. **Click the Save button after you're done making changes.**

5. **Now check the default login directory for FTP users by clicking FTP
   Users in the NetPresenz Setup window.**

   The FTP Users window appears, enabling you to set up the login
   directory and login commands for each FTP user. You also can set up
   defaults that apply for every FTP user.

   Login Directory is the drive or folder that you want FTP users to see
   initially after they connect to your FTP server. If you want the
   Macintosh Desktop to appear first after a user connects to your FTP
   server, set the Login Directory option to a single forward slash (/).

   The Login Commands box enables you to define commands to execute
   after a user logs in. This option enables users to perform such tasks as
   mount remote shared folders and drives automatically or display usage
   statistics. You can include any SMNT or SITE command in the Login
   Commands box; see the NetPresenz documentation for details.

Creating an anonymous FTP directory

Your FTP server is easier for others to use if you create a /PUB directory. To
create a /PUB directory, follow these steps:

1. **Use the Finder to create a new folder that you name PUB.**

2. **Create the PUB folder on the Desktop or place an alias of the PUB folder on the Desktop.**

3. **Click the PUB folder and choose File⇨Sharing.**

   The File Sharing dialog box appears, titled with the name of the folder.

4. **Select the check box labeled Share this item and its contents.**

5. **In the File Sharing dialog box, you can change the owner of the folder by selecting a different owner from the drop-down list box.**

   Changing the owner is handy if a user other than the owner of the Macintosh is responsible for maintaining the FTP server.

6. **Deselect the Make Changes check box for Everyone and for each User/Group as you want.**

7. **Close the window by clicking the Close box in the top-left corner.**

8. **Start NetPresenz Setup and click FTP Users.**

9. **Change the Login Directory for Default User to /PUB.**

10. **Click the Save button.**

Now put some files in the PUB folder. Remember that some computer operating systems don't permit spaces in filenames. A good idea is to avoid using spaces in the names of the files that you make available in your FTP server. That way, everyone on the Internet can access these files without trouble.

Creating special files

NetPresenz enables you to create special files to help FTP users find the files that interest them. (You must give these special files specific names so that NetPresenz knows that these files are special.) You can, for example, create in any folder a file named !Folder Info; the contents of this file appear automatically after an FTP user enters the folder. Then you can create in the PUB folder a !Folder Info file containing the following message (or something similar):

```
This is the PUB folder. In this folder, you find files and
folders that you may want to download. If you need help,
send mail to help@domain.com. (Don t blame us if your
computer blows up after you use files from this folder.)
Enjoy!
```

You also can create a startup file — another type of special file that appears after an FTP user logs in to the FTP server. You must store startup files in a Startup Messages folder, which you must put in one of the following two places:

✔ The NetPresenz folder

✔ The NetPresenz Preferences folder, which you place in the System Preferences folder

You can create a default startup file as well as startup files for each type of user. NetPresenz can display a file named Anonymous Startup, for example, after an anonymous FTP user logs in to the FTP server. If NetPresenz doesn't find a startup file for a particular user type, the program displays the default startup file (if one exists).

Make all your special files, including the !Folder Info and startup files, text-only. And press Enter at the end of each line in the file instead of using word wrap. Some FTP client programs don't perform word wrap correctly, so you must insert line endings into your files yourself for the benefit of those programs. Try to keep these special files small to improve performance. If you have a good idea of which files are most likely to catch your FTP users' interests, provide simple, direct instructions on retrieving those files. These instructions make your FTP server much easier to use.

Configuring security settings

The Security window of NetPresenz Setup controls several security settings (see Figure 10-3). Click the Security button in the NetPresenz Setup window.

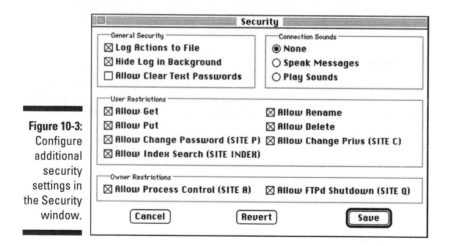

Figure 10-3: Configure additional security settings in the Security window.

You may want to disable (clear) any of the following three Security settings, because the average user doesn't need these settings:

✔ **Allow Change Password (SITE P):** Enables users to change their passwords

 ✔ **Allow Change Privs (SITE C):** Enables users to change their file privileges (file-level security restrictions)

 ✔ **Allow Process Control (SITE A):** Enables the owner to control processes

The rest of the settings are optional. Enabling a Connection Sounds option can prove to be helpful if you plan to be nearby as people connect to your FTP server. Connection sounds may be annoying in a busy office, however.

NetPresenz is also a fully functional World Wide Web server program. If you decide to use the Web server as well, you want to click the WWW Setup icon in the NetPresenz Setup window. The WWW Setup window appears on-screen. Select the WWW Enabled check box to turn on your NetPresenz Web server.

Checking the setup

The last step in the setup process is clicking the Summary button in the NetPresenz Setup window to open the Summary window. If you need to do anything else, the Summary window tells you what else you still need to do.

Using NetPresenz

Start the NetPresenz program by double-clicking the NetPresenz icon. This icon starts the FTP server and displays the Log Window. After you use your FTP server for a while, your Log Window should look something like the one shown for the Windows Vermillion FTP program in Figure 10-4, later in this chapter.

To quit NetPresenz, start NetPresenz Setup by double-clicking its icon. Then hold down the Option key as you quit NetPresenz Setup. This action closes both NetPresenz Setup and the active NetPresenz program.

Using a Windows FTP server

Many good FTP server programs are available for Microsoft Windows. In fact, if you've installed Windows NT Server 4.0 or later, you have access to Internet Information Server (IIS), which includes an FTP server.

The process of setting up most FTP servers is similar. We chose to demonstrate the setup of two FTP servers one called Vermillion FTP (VNETPRESENZ), written by Matte Kalinowski and another called WFTPD, by Alun Jones. These programs include added security features that you don't find in other FTP servers. VFTPD, for example, has an IP-checking feature that can verify an account by IP address as well as by username. This feature is a powerful one, but remember that many people access the Internet by using *dynamic IP addresses* (which means that they get a different IP address each time they connect to the Internet).

To use Vermillion FTP or WFTPD, you must be running a Windows operating system such as Windows 95 or Windows NT, with TCP/IP communications correctly configured in your Windows 95 or Windows NT network applet. You must also have Internet access so that other people can access and use your FTP server. For additional help in setting up TCP/IP in Windows 95 or NT, open the Control Panel, start the Network applet, and choose Help. You need this setup, along with dial-up networking or some other TCP/IP access to your service provider, such as PPP or a direct network connection.

Getting started with Vermillion FTP

The first step in installing Vermillion FTP is obtaining the software, which you usually find distributed in ZIP format. You can download the Vermillion FTP server program from the TUCOWS site at http://www.tucows.com/. After you contact the TUCOWS main page, select a mirror site closest to you. (A *mirror site* is an Internet site with identical information. Mirror sites are located geographically to limit the amount of international network traffic.) TUCOWS offers a Search button, which you can click, or you can follow the links to the Server Daemon page, which lists Vermillion and several other good shareware FTP servers.

Using WinZip, extract the Vermillion FTP software into a directory in which you want the program to reside permanently. Unlike other Windows software, Vermillion FTP requires no installation process. After you extract Vermillion FTP from its ZIP file, it's ready to run.

Note: You can get a copy of WinZip by downloading it from http://www.winzip.com/.

In Windows 95 or Windows NT, choose Start⇨Run to launch Vermillion FTP. After you start Vermillion FTP, you see a status screen, shown in Figure 10-4.

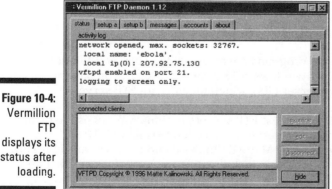

Figure 10-4:
Vermillion FTP displays its status after loading.

If you want Vermillion FTP to launch each time you boot your computer, add a shortcut to the program in your Start folder. Remember that all program shortcuts in your Windows Start folder launch each time you start Windows 95 or NT.

Setting up Vermillion FTP

Vermillion FTP is extremely easy to set up. Click the tab labeled Setup A in the main Vermillion screen. The Setup a tab opens (see Figure 10-5).

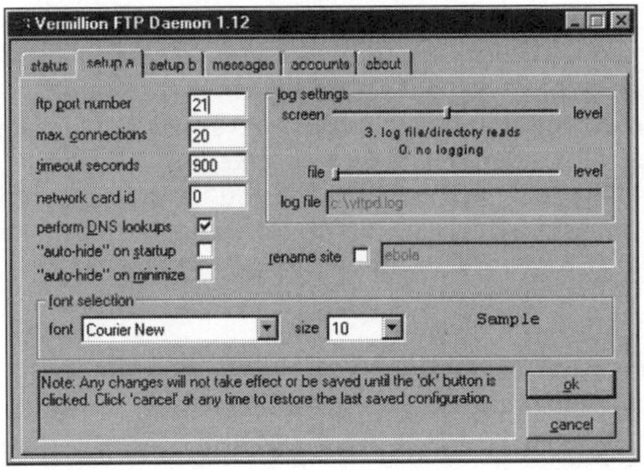

Figure 10-5:
Vermillion
FTP is easy
to set up.

The Setup A tab contains the following options:

✔ **Ftp Port Number.** This option is set to 21 by default. Changing this value is not a good idea. If you change this number, no conventional FTP client programs can contact this server. All FTP clients try to contact an FTP server on port 21.

✔ **Max Connections.** This setting determines the maximum number of simultaneous connections to your server by client programs. The default is 20, which is a nice round number. Unless your machine is fast and has quite a bit of memory, stick with 20 as the maximum number of simultaneous connections.

✔ **Timeout Seconds.** Just how long do you want your FTP server to hang around waiting for a valid response from a connected client? The default setting — 900 — is 15 minutes, which seems to be a little long. You may consider changing this value to something shorter, such as 600.

✔ **Network Card ID.** The default setting is 0. This is a default value that should be left alone.

✔ **Perform DNS Lookups.** Select this option if you want Vermillion FTP to look up domain names from IP addresses.

✔ **"Auto-Hide" on Startup.** Select this option if you want Vermillion FTP to run in the background, hiding itself as soon as it starts. This way, you can get on with your work without being bothered by the FTP server.

✔ **"Auto-Hide" on Minimize.** Select this option if you want to hide Vermillion FTP manually by minimizing the Vermillion FTP window. This option is handy if you regularly administer the FTP server.

✔ **Font Selection options.** These options determine the font type and size that Vermillion FTP uses to display status and log messages. This font is not the one that the client sees.

✔ **Log Settings options.** Logs are an important way of knowing who's accessed your FTP server, what they did when they logged in, and any problems they may have encountered. By moving the slider, you can select one of seven log detail settings. The 0 setting turns logging completely off. (This setting is not recommended.) The 7 setting logs every bit of detail. (Choose this setting if you're having problems you need to troubleshoot.) Choose the amount of log detail that makes you feel comfortable. You want to watch the size of your log file so that the file doesn't fill your hard drive.

Continuing the setup, click the Messages tab of the main screen. (Notice that we're skipping the Setup B tab. These features have not been implemented yet.) You can use two messages to customize your FTP server: a welcome message and a goodbye message. Before you get all pensive trying to think of just the right thing to say, we probably should mention that only text-based FTP clients can ever view these messages. In modern, graphical clients such as WS_FTP, these messages scroll across your screen, almost unseen, in a small status window.

If you decide to construct a message, you can also use a number of *insertable variables* (or *tokens*). These variables are placeholders for information the computer automatically fills in for you. You can insert the time, the number of bytes that are free in the current working directory, the path of the current working directory, the remote host, the local host, the username, the maximum number of simultaneous connections, and the current number of client connections.

This next set of instructions, setting up User accounts, is the most important part of setting up your FTP server. Click the Accounts tab. The dialog box shown in Figure 10-6 appears. Enter a username in the Users text box, and click the Add button. A new dialog box opens to enable you to enter the details for the User account (see Figure 10-7).

Before you get into creating user accounts, you may consider creating a *template*. A *template* is a saved profile that you can use over and over in creating new accounts. You can create templates that act as defaults for new User accounts. This approach enables you to have several classes of users

Figure 10-6:
Adding
User
account
information
in the
Accounts
tab is the
most
important
part of
setting up
an FTP
server.

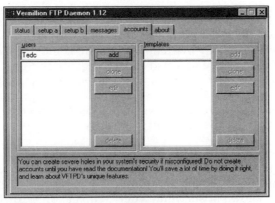

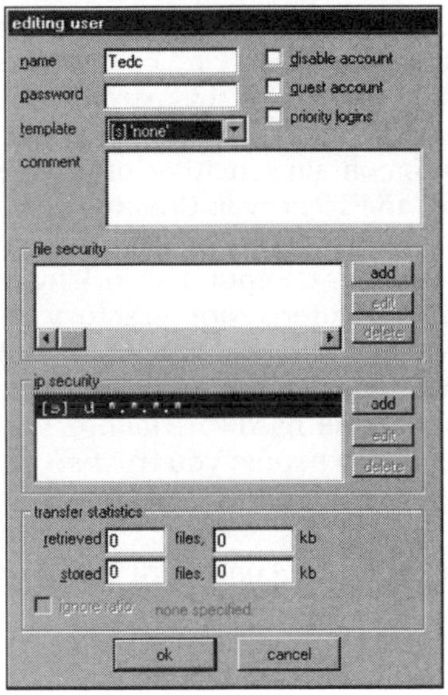

Figure 10-7:
Enter the
detailed
information
for each
user
account in
this dialog
box.

while keeping administration of user accounts fairly simple. To add a new template, add a name for the template in the Template text box and click the Add button. This action launches the Template dialog box. You create settings in this dialog box that act as defaults whenever you create new accounts of the type you specified as you entered a name for the template. You may, for example, enter a name of **Administration**. You use this template each time you want to create an account for someone in administration. All the security settings are set by default.

If you're wondering what the upload-to-download ratio in the template dialog box is all about, this feature is a throwback to the electronic bulletin-board (BBS) days. To promote file uploads to the bulletin board, someone who wanted to download files also needed to participate in uploads. In other words, for every so many bytes uploaded, you could download some number of bytes. This practice was also known as getting credits. Credits were highly sought after and became similar to a monetary exchange.

Creating a new user account requires two additional parameters (other than the account name): file permissions and IP security permissions.

The IP Security permissions setting can remain at its default, enabling connections from any IP address. You may want to change this parameter only if your company has fixed IP addresses, and you want to restrict access to the FTP server to known hosts within your company or to trusted clients.

File security is a little more involved. Clicking the Add button next to the File security text box launches a File Permissions dialog box. Specify only those directories and files that you want this new user to visit. Granting permissions that aren't restrictive enough opens security holes in your system. PCs are fairly impervious to hacker attack, except for this parameter.

Carefully select directories that don't contain sensitive information in setting up access to your PC though an FTP server. Creating new directories and making copies of files to which you want to give users access makes more sense than permitting access to your computer's working directories. Giving someone else access to your computer's root directory (normally, C:\) is never a good idea. Grant write and delete access to only the most trusted users. Writing programs that can launch themselves, destroying important information or causing computer hardware failure, is all too possible. You're best off limiting access to people you trust so as not to inflict these types of programs on your computer.

Carefully follow the detailed instructions that come with your Vermillion software for creating new users and templates. You have no Help button. You need to launch WordPad or Microsoft Word to read the manual that you find in the directory in which you store VFTPD.

The Windows FTP server WFTPD

FTP server software runs very well on a Windows-based computer. Although this type of setup doesn't provide the kind of performance that you obtain from a high-end UNIX workstation, the simplicity of set-up and maintenance you enjoy offsets the reduced performance you experience in using Windows as your Internet-server operating system. That's why we're excited about showing you how to set up your own FTP server in Microsoft Windows NT/95.

WFTPD stands for *Windows FTP daemon*. To use WFTPD, you must be running a Windows operating system, such as Windows 95 or Windows NT, with a TCP/IP communications program that's compatible with WinSock Version 1.1 or later. If you want Internet users to access your FTP server, you need some kind of Internet access, such as PPP or a direct network connection.

Installing WFTPD

The first step in installing WFTPD is obtaining the software, which usually is distributed in PKZIP format.

You must download the program, unzip it onto your hard drive, and then execute the program. After you execute the WFTPD program, the main WFTPD window appears.

Setting up WFTPD security

The first and most important thing to do after you get WFTPD is to beef up your security. As soon as you start WFTPD, you add a new level of complexity to your Internet presence. Now you need to secure your computer against unwanted intruders. WFTPD doesn't fail you in this regard, because the program provides excellent security features.

To begin establishing general security settings, follow these steps:

1. **Choose Security⇨General from the menu bar.**

   The General Security dialog box appears, enabling you to establish basic security preferences.

2. **Establish the level of security preferences that you want by selecting the appropriate check boxes in the General Security dialog box.**

   The most important of these preferences is the Enable Security check box. If you select this check box, every FTP user must enter a user name and a password to use your FTP server. Selecting the Enable Security check box also means that the system enforces access restrictions according to additional security settings that you make.

   If you don't select the Enable Security check box, anyone on the Internet can copy or delete any file on your system. This possibility may seem interesting if you're studying psychology or criminal behavior and want to know what some Internet users may do if they encounter a defenseless FTP server. If you conduct such a study, intentionally or otherwise, please send us the conclusions.

   The other three check boxes in the General Security dialog box are less extreme in their effect, although they're still important to your security considerations. These options function as described in the following list:

- *Allow Anonymous.* Select this check box if you want to enable anonymous FTP access to your FTP server.

- *Allow Uploads.* Select this check box if you want to enable FTP users to upload (send files).

- *Allow Anonymous Upload.* Select this check box if you want to enable anonymous FTP users to upload.

An FTP server accepts two types of users: *anonymous users* and *users who have specific login IDs.* Users with login IDs have password-protected access to files in their home directories or the directories to which you give them access. The server is like a museum. You enable the public to view, touch, and feel the displays in the public viewing area. Employees, on the other hand, have a key to the back room, where you keep displays that aren't for public viewing.

3. **To limit the number of FTP users who can connect to your FTP server simultaneously, enter a number in the Maximum Number of Users field.**

A zero in this field means that no limit applies. (If you enter a zero here and you don't want anyone to connect to your FTP server, don't run it!)

4. **Enter a number in the Timeout for inactive connections (seconds) field.**

Establishing a time-out period for inactive connections is a good idea. An *inactive connection* is an FTP user who hasn't issued any FTP commands to your FTP server in a while. Rather than having these inactive connections just sit there, consuming memory and processing time on your computer, you can tell WFTPD to boot them off after a certain number of seconds of inactivity. If you enter zero in this field, no FTP users are ever disconnected, no matter how long they're inactive.

5. **Click OK to close the dialog box after you finish setting General Security options.**

Next, you need to adjust your settings in the User Security Settings dialog box. This dialog box enables you to set up FTP user accounts and to control the directories that each user can access. To establish settings in this dialog box, follow these steps:

1. **Choose Security⇨User/Password from the menu bar.**

WFTPD provides one default user name: anonymous.

2. **To change the directories that anonymous FTP users can access, select anonymous from the User Name drop-down list; enter a directory name in the Home directory field; and select the Restrict to home check box.**

A user's home directory is the one that user sees after initially logging on to your FTP server. If you restrict users to their home directories (by selecting the Restrict to home check box), you prevent those users from accessing files in any directory that's not a subdirectory of the home directory. FTP users you restrict in this way can still access directories within their home directories. Think of the procedure as similar to grounding a child; you restrict the child to home, but he can still access the refrigerator there.

We usually restrict anonymous FTP users to the C:\WFTPD directory. This type of setup protects important files on your computer but, at the same time, enables anonymous FTP users to access files and directories within the C:\WFTPD directory.

If you enable anonymous FTP users to connect to your FTP server without restricting these users to a certain directory, anyone on the Internet can access every directory and every file on your computer.

3. **After you finish making changes for anonymous users, click the Add/Update button.**

You also can add specific users. If you have a company, you may want to give your employees their own user accounts. These accounts give the employees password-protected FTP access to their own files. To add a new user, follow these steps:

1. **Enter a user name in the User name field.**

2. **Enter a password in the Password field.**

   The password remains hidden as you type.

3. **Re-enter the password in the Verify field.**

   This entry confirms the password that you enter in Step 2.

4. **Type a directory name in the Home directory field.**

   This directory is the one that users see first after they log in.

5. **If you want users to have full access to your computer's files and directories, leave the Restrict to home check box deselected; otherwise, select that check box.**

6. **Click Add/Update to save your new FTP user.**

Now that you can add users, you may also want to delete them at some point. To delete an existing user, open the User Security Settings dialog box and select the user in the User Name list; then click the Delete button. After you finish adding, deleting, and updating users in this dialog box, click the Close button.

As a final level of security, you can deny access to certain hosts or certain networks on the Internet. Suppose, for example, that a nasty hacker breaks into your system from IP address 127.0.0.1 and steals some important files. This act upsets you, so you send e-mail to the Computer Emergency Response Team (CERT), informing the team about the break-in. You then deny access to anyone on any host or network that begins with the number 127 by following these steps:

1. **Choose Security⇨Host/Net from the menu bar.**

   The Host Security Settings dialog box appears.

2. **Type the following line in the Host address field:**

   127.*.*.*

3. **Click the Deny radio button to the right of the Host address field.**

4. **Click the Add/Update button.**

You also can reverse your security approach. Rather than wait until a hacker breaks into your system, you can deny access to *every* host and network by clicking the Deny radio button in the Default action section of the dialog box. Then you can selectively grant entrance to certain hosts and networks that you trust by entering their IP addresses, one at a time, in the Host address field and then clicking the Allow radio button next to the field. Make sure that you click the Add/Update button after you type each address. Click the Close button after you finish making changes.

Configuring other WFTPD settings

Several WFTPD settings are both interesting and useful. First, take a look at the Messages menu. The Greeting and Farewell messages have defaults that you can't change until you pay for the software. This situation is your incentive to honesty. (Not that *you* need an incentive, of course, but many people may not pay for the software without some encouragement.) After you obtain the official version of WFTPD, you can change the Greeting and Farewell messages by choosing those commands from the Messages menu.

The MESSAGE.FTP option in the Messages menu enables you to turn on or off the display of special messages for each directory. If you choose the MESSAGE.FTP option in the Messages menu, for example, the special text file MESSAGE.FTP appears whenever an FTP user changes to a directory that contains this special file. You may want to create, in your C:\WFTPD directory, a MESSAGE.FTP file that contains the following text:

```
This is the FTP directory. Here you find several files that
        may interest you, as well as a few directories
        to explore. If you have questions or need help
```

```
                        using this FTP server, send e-mail to
                        ftphelp@domain.com.
```

The C:\WFTPD directory then displays the following message to any FTP user who accesses it.

Make sure that you press Enter at the end of each line as you create your text file for this message. Many FTP client programs don't word-wrap correctly, so you must mark the line endings in your message for these programs yourself.

If you want WFTPD to keep a log of activity on your FTP server, such as logins and file transfers, choose Logging⇨Log Options from the menu bar. The Logging Options dialog box appears. To turn logging on, select the Enable Logging check box; then select the check box for each of the items that you want the program to log. Click the OK button after you finish.

To log activity to a file rather than just to the screen, choose File⇨Open Log from the menu bar to access the Open dialog box. Choose an existing log file or type the name of a new one and then click the OK button.

To close an open log file, choose File⇨Close Log from the menu bar. To shut down your FTP server, choose File⇨Exit from the menu bar.

Figuring Out What to Do with Your FTP Server

You can do many things with your FTP server. Whether you set up your own server or subscribe to an FTP service the possibilities are almost endless. The following sections present some ideas that may not have occurred to you yet.

Providing World Wide Web documents

Yes, you can provide hypertext World Wide Web documents through your FTP server. Although this method isn't a common (or ideal) approach to providing World Wide Web documents on a World Wide Web server, it works in most cases. Create your HTML document and put the file in your anonymous FTP directory. Anyone who has a Web browser can retrieve and view your HTML document as though she had contacted a Web server.

Providing intracompany file transfer

In addition to providing files to customers, an FTP server can provide the useful function of intracompany file transfer. One of the most useful features of FTP is its capability to limit site access to users who have passwords. This capability enables a company to set up an FTP site that only authorized employees can access.

An FTP site can be a valuable resource, enabling your employees to transfer files among themselves. The FTP site also can serve as a forum where you can post valuable files — such as employee manuals and general employment policies — that all employees can access and use.

Setting up a public file-exchange area

By giving anonymous FTP users permission to send and receive files through your FTP server, you can create a useful public exchange forum. Swapping files among family members, friends, and strangers around the world has its roots in early bulletin board systems (BBSs) — online forums that require user IDs — that existed before the Internet. FTP users can exchange messages and files through your FTP server just as they do by calling a BBS.

If you decide to set up a public file-exchange area for whatever reason, consider talking to a lawyer about your potential liability. A lawyer can help you create a good disclaimer that makes clear to all users of your exchange area that they use the area at their own risk and that you do not control the content or tolerate illegal activity.

Currently, no better tool than FTP exists for transferring files on the Internet, either for personal or business purposes. Depending on your requirements and skill level, you can provide FTP service by using a service provider or by running your own server on a Mac or Windows machine. The FTP system is a valuable tool and usually is essential in setting up an Internet site.

Chapter 11

Encryption and Privacy

● ●

In This Chapter

▶ Getting to know encryption basics

▶ Using PGP to encrypt and decrypt files

▶ Uncovering privacy

● ●

Can you keep a secret? Maybe so . . . maybe not. Things that you think are secret and held in confidence between you and others may be information that you're broadcasting freely to the world. From the early days of communication, people have transferred information by using codes.

In this chapter, we talk about some of the basics of encoding information — both pitfalls and solutions. Understanding how you encrypt electronic information, and also understanding the products that encrypt and decrypt that information, helps you build a more secure Internet site. A secure Internet site is one of the foundations of a secure electronic commerce site (as we discuss in Chapter 13).

Encryption Basics

Encrypting printed or electronic information involves replacing the characters that you use to read the information with a version that's unrecognizable as the original message. The following example offers a simple version of the difference between original and encrypted messages:

▶ **Original message:** The big brown fox ate the ugly black bear.

▶ **Encrypted message:** Uifacjhacspxoagpyabufauifavhmzacmbdjacfbs>

This example is an extremely simple version of a form of encryption that uses an *encryption algorithm*. This algorithm simply replaces each character with the following character in the alphabet and replaces spaces with the letter *a*. This algorithm may take a cryptographic expert about two minutes to decode.

An Introduction to Encryption

Encryption means the scrambling of information into a form that's entirely unreadable by human beings. (Many books on encryption achieve this goal without actually being encrypted.) The purpose of encryption is to prevent unfriendly or untrustworthy people from reading the encrypted material. Encryption forms the heart of all Internet commerce, and you need a working knowledge of encryption to understand the technology that you use to generate secure online sales.

Following are a few encryption facts that you need to know:

✔ The study of encryption is known as *cryptography*.

✔ Unencrypted information is called *plaintext*.

✔ You encrypt plaintext by using an *encryption key* (a passcode).

✔ The encrypted result is called *ciphertext*.

✔ You can decrypt ciphertext only by using a *decryption key*.

Codebreakers — software that can gain unauthorized access to information by figuring out the code used to encrypt text — repeatedly guess at the decryption key until they stumble on the right one. The number of possible decryption keys that you can use in a particular encryption determines how difficult the encryption is to break. Encryption is sort of like a combination lock; the more digits you have in the passcode, the better is the lock. The number of possible decryption keys that you can use to encrypt a piece of text is its *encryption strength*.

Two primary types of encryption exist: secret key and public key. *Secret-key encryption* relies on a single key for both encryption and decryption. The secrecy of the key is of critical importance in this type of encryption. *Public-key encryption* uses a different key for decryption than for encryption. The two keys form a *key pair*, in which you keep secret the private key and make the public key available to the public. Any message that you encrypt by using the public key, someone can decrypt only by using the corresponding private key. This technique ensures reliable encryption without the need to distribute a secret key.

If you use secret-key encryption (which involves the use of a password), the encryption key is also the decryption key. Secret-key encryption is inherently vulnerable, because in addition to sending the encrypted message to the recipient, you must send the recipient the secret key (the password). If you fail to communicate the secret key securely, the entire point of encrypting the message is lost: Unauthorized users can get their hands on the key and thus decipher the encrypted information. If you have a secure way to communicate the secret key, however, why bother with encryption in the first place? Why not just send the message (as plaintext), sans encryption, by way of the secure communications link that you use for the secret key?

Using secure communications is, in fact, much easier and safer than using a secret key. During World War II, codebreakers (men and women who stayed up far too late and drank way too much coffee) found out how to decode almost all encrypted information simply by figuring out the code used to encode the documents. Today, with modern, powerful computers on the desktop, breaking encryption codes is a relatively simple task for anyone who is interested in that sort of thing. The alternative is to use public-key encryption (which we discuss in the following section).

Using public-key encryption

Public-key encryption uses a pair of keys: a public key and an associated private key. The owner of a key pair distributes the public key to the general public. Anyone who wants to send an encrypted message encrypts it by using the recipient's public key. The recipient uses the corresponding private key to decrypt the messages. This technique ensures that only the owner of a private key can decrypt the messages that anyone encrypts by using the public key.

Ideally, everyone should eventually have a public-key/private-key pair. This combination is the only way to ensure privacy, especially as online shopping becomes a part of everyday life. After just about everyone has a key, millions or even billions of keys may exist. Sending your public key to everyone you think may need it is one way to publish your public key. People need a simpler way to find and use the public key that the person or company to which they want to send a secure message owns, so they must have *public-key directories* — centralized databases of public keys. These directories are a little like phone directories. You find the listing of the person with whom you want to communicate in the directory; then you discover that person's public key so that you can communicate securely (that is, in a private manner, by using encryption).

Not only are people going to have public and private keys, but software products requiring secure communication also are going to have keys. Soon, you can expect all Web sites to use public-key encryption for secure online Web communications. This same capability is being built into e-mail software, FTP software, Usenet news software, and banking applications.

Using Pretty Good Privacy

A popular program called Pretty Good Privacy (PGP), originally created as freeware by Phil Zimmerman, is available on the Internet. PGP enables you to create both public and private keys. You can download a copy from the Massachusetts Institute of Technology site at the following URL:

```
http://web.mit.edu/network/pgp-form.html
```

At this site, you're asked to fill out a form that says you're an American citizen and that you don't intend to use this product for commercial purposes. After submitting this form, you receive an e-mail message containing a password for downloading the PGP program.

Freeware PGP versions are available for many platforms. Windows users must use the DOS version, however, and access the program through an MS-DOS shell.

After you download and unzip the program, it's ready to run. The PGP program, however, isn't one that enables you to make choices from a menu. Instead, PGP is a *command-line program,* which means that each time you run the PGP program, you tell it what you want to do by adding parameters as you launch the program.

The PGP program enables you to perform two basic types of tasks: encrypt/decrypt files and manage keys. You store encryption keys in special files called *keyrings*. Whenever someone sends you a public key, you store that key in your *public keyring file*. You store your private key in your *private keyring file*.

Never, never, *never* give your secret key to anyone. Protect this private key with as much diligence as you protect the PIN number of your ATM debit card. Anyone who has access to your private key can decrypt any messages that anyone sends to you. In the event that someone does compromise your private key, you can revoke its use. Type **PGP -h** at the DOS prompt for special help on revoking your private key.

Table 11-1 presents a list of commands that you can issue while running PGP. To use these commands, first type **PGP** in the command line (at the DOS prompt), following this text with a dash (actually a hyphen, explain the book techies: -), and then with one of the commands listed in Table 11-1, along with any additional parameters that the command requires, as shown in the following example:

```
PGP -<command>
```

Table 11-1		PGP Commands
Command	*Command Parameters*	*Description*
e	`textfilename userid [userid2, userid3 . . .]`	Encrypts a text file by using the recipient's public key
s	`textfilename [-u userid]`	Signs a text file by using a private key.
sta	`textfilename [-u userid]`	Signs a text file by using a private key so that you can read the output without running PGP.
es	`textfilename userid [-u userid]`	Signs a text file by using your private key and then encrypts the file by using the recipient's public key.
c	`textfilename`	Encrypts a text file by using conventional cryptography.
(n/a)	`encryptedfile [-o outputtextfile]`	Decrypts an encrypted file or checks the digital signature of a signed file to see whether it's a valid signature.
kg		Generates a unique public-key/private-key pair.
ka	`keyfile [keyring]`	Adds key-file contents to your keyring.
kx	`userid keyfile [keyring]`	Gets a key from your keyring.
kv	`[userid] [keyring]`	Views the contents of your public keyring.
ke	`userid [keyring]`	Edits the user ID and password phrase for your private key.
kr	`userid [keyring]`	Removes a key from your public keyring.
kd	`userid`	Permanently revokes your own key with a key compromise certificate. This certificate keeps your key from ever being used again.

(continued)

Table 11-1 (continued)

Command	Command Parameters	Description
m	encryptedfile	Adds this parameter (similar to the DOS and UNIX MORE command) if you're decrypting and want to view contents one page at a time.
p	encryptedfile	Adds this parameter if you're decrypting to recover the name of the original text file.

Creating keys

To get started down the road of secure communications, create your own public-key/private-key pair by using the PGP kg command. Follow these steps (you're prompted after each step; enter all your responses after each prompt):

1. At the DOS prompt, type the following command:

```
PGP -kg
```

After typing this command, you should see something that looks like the screen shown in Figure 11-1.

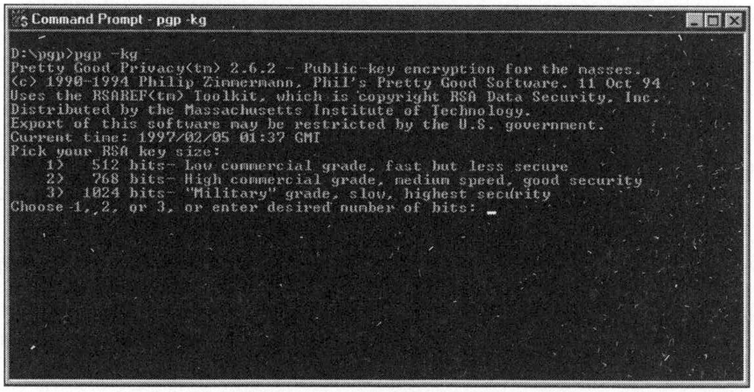

Figure 11-1: Create your own public-key/private-key pair in a DOS shell.

2. After the program prompts you to do so, choose an encryption strength — 512-, 768-, or 1,024-bit — by typing this value at the DOS prompt.

3. **After the program prompts you, enter a user ID to use in accessing your keyrings.**

4. **Enter a pass phrase at the prompt.**

   This pass phrase can be something along the lines of **doodlee doodlee** or anything else that you can remember. Remembering this pass phrase is *very* important. Instead of a single password, you need to enter an entire phrase when decrypting documents.

5. **Generate the random bits by pressing keys on your keyboard.**

   Doing so helps the computer come up with a truly unique (random) number that it uses in creating your keys.

   PGP creates these random bits based on the amount of time that you leave between keystrokes as you press keys on your keyboard. You must continue to press keys until PGP tells you to quit. The number of keys that you must press depends on the encryption strength you choose in Step 2.

You have now successfully created both a public key, which the program stores in the file PUBRING.PGP, and a secret key, which the program stores in the file SECRING.PGP. You can now use these keys to encrypt and decrypt messages.

Encrypting a file

To encrypt a file that you intend to share with someone else, you need to encrypt the file by using that person's public key. After you encrypt the file by using the recipient's public key, only the recipient (the person to whom you're sending the information) can decrypt that file by using his private key. To encrypt a file, type the following at the DOS prompt:

```
pgp -e filename recipientuserid
```

Replace *filename* with the name of the file that you want to encrypt. Replace *recipientuserid* with the user ID of the person to whom you're sending the encrypted file. Make certain that you add the recipient's public key to your public keyring before attempting this process. Running this command produces an encrypted file with the same name as the filename that you enter, but with a .PGP extension. See Table 11-1 for the commands that enable you to add public keys to your keyring file.

Now that you're a PGP encrypting expert, you can use the InterNIC's secure features that we describe in Chapters 5 and 6.

Decrypting an encrypted file

Receiving encrypted files that people encrypt by using your public key isn't much fun unless you can decrypt those files (unless, of course, you're a cryptographer and want to try cracking the RSA Data Security system, on which the whole public key/private key system is built). Decrypting files is simple; for the most part, the process is automatic. At the DOS prompt, type the following line:

```
pgp encryptedfilename [-o outputfilename]
```

PGP expects the encrypted filename to have a .PGP extension. You can also enter a filename for your output file. If you choose not to include an output filename, PGP uses the name of the encrypted file as the output filename (but without the .PGP extension).

The PGP program that we describe in this chapter is, so far, a freeware program. Now, however, Pretty Good Privacy, Inc. offers an entire line of encryption products. Check out the company's Web site at http://www.pgp.com/.

Protecting Your Privacy

Privacy has become one of the most-fought-for, most-talked-about issues on the Internet. Competing forces are trying to tilt the scales of privacy in either direction. On one hand, you have Internet marketers collecting online information as quickly as possible. Certainly, the capability to access demographic and even credit information for the people who access your Internet site is good business sense. Targeting your marketing efforts to specific customers and checking credit approval are only two of the obvious benefits of accessing this kind of personal information about visitors to your site. On the other side of the scale, however, is the individual's need for privacy. This need was certainly evident in the recent LEXIS/NEXIS P-Trac database fiasco. People flooded the folks at LEXIS/NEXIS with calls, requesting that their names and personal information be removed from the P-Trac database.

A matter of money

Privacy also is important in how you spend your money. Digital cash use, which is on the increase because of a growing number of purchases on the Internet, has many people worried about privacy. One of the goals of many proponents of digital cash is that its use on the Internet should have the same anonymity as a cash transaction in the physical world.

But the use of digital money goes far beyond Internet commerce. New technologies such as smart cards, along with the increasing use of debit cards and check cards, are truly increasing the scope of how people transfer money electronically. This issue is certainly more far-reaching and complex than that of the simple encrypted credit-card transaction.

Many issues are important to consider as you delve into the new media world of electronic commerce. As we discuss in Chapter 13, electronic commerce consists of much more than simply selling things on the World Wide Web. Similarly, digital cash involves many more issues than simply paying for items online by using credit cards.

Some online privacy resources

An excellent page on the Internet discusses four aspects of the invasion of privacy: search and seizure, unsolicited e-mail, defamation, and secrecy. Visit attorney Timothy Walton's page at the following URL for more information:

```
http://www.crl.com/@tdwalton/privacy.html
```

If you want to join a discussion of privacy issues on the Internet, we recommend that you check out the following Usenet newsgroup:

```
alt.privacy
```

You can also get involved by participating in the projects sponsored by the Electronic Frontier Foundation (EFF). The Electronic Frontier Foundation describes itself as a "nonprofit civil liberties organization working in the public interest to protect privacy, free expression, and access to public resources and information online, as well as to promote responsibility in new media." You can find the foundation's Web page at the following address:

```
http://www.eff.org/
```

Free speech on the Internet

No discussion of encryption and privacy is complete without at least mentioning free speech on the Internet. Perhaps you've seen the blue ribbons tacked onto thousands of Web pages. These blue ribbons are a means of expressing the authors' support for free speech on the Internet.

Nothing sparked online reaction as did the 1996 attempt by the government to pass the Communications Decency Act. The uproar in the silence of cyberspace was deafening. Web-page backgrounds went black all around the world in protest. In June 1996, a panel of judges in Philadelphia ruled the CDA to be unconstitutional. The United States Supreme Court plans to hear and decide this case in mid-1997. If you purchase this book after that date, you'll definitely want to find out how the case turned out.

To become involved, you can check out what other people are doing at the following URL:

```
http://www.eff.org/blueribbon/
  activism.html
```

The question of free speech on the Internet goes beyond constitutional rights, however, or even the rights of governments to censor information. How free speech is handled on the Internet is also a matter of technology. Using hardware and software to completely censor content is very easy. Your preference may not be to read hateful propaganda while skimming through scientific-newsgroup messages, for example. More and more, the important content becomes hidden amid millions of ads for lower long-distance rates, private access to gigabytes worth of pornography, or promises of millions if you become involved in the latest pyramid scheme.

As the Internet grows, people are deserting traditionally public resources, such as Usenet, for private online resources. You can now find private resources for children, for the aged, for scientists, and for people who are seeking entertainment that remains exclusive and, for the most part, free of unwanted information. We believe that creating new technologies that enable people to have their own safe cyberspace neighborhoods is a great technological solution for people who don't want to be bothered with unwanted information and for parents wanting to protect their children.

Chapter 12

Setting Up an Internet BBS

• •

In This Chapter

▶ Deciding whether to run a BBS on the Internet

▶ Configuring Internet BBS software

▶ Providing simple access to your Internet BBS

• •

A *BBS*, or *bulletin-board system*, is an electronic online service that is accessible via computer and modem, typically at little or no cost. BBSs are available around the world, and each one provides a unique electronic community, a special-interest focus, or a particular company's customer support. Anyone can run a BBS simply by connecting a computer and modem to a phone line and running special BBS software. Even the U.S. government has several BBSs — which proves that anyone can run a BBS.

A BBS differs from the Internet in one important way: the manner in which you access the site. To contact a BBS, you must dial a specific phone number that the administrator of the site provides. To go to your favorite BBS that deals with movie reviews, for example, you must make a modem connection by using the phone number for that site. After you finish with the movie site and want to go to your favorite game BBS, you must disconnect from the movie site and then make another modem connection by using a different phone number. Jumping from one BBS to another really gives your modem a workout.

An Internet BBS is much simpler to use than historical or non-Internet BBS systems. An *Internet BBS* is an electronic online service, accessible via the Internet, that enables users to access BBS-style services, such as discussion groups, file-exchange areas, and e-mail. By connecting to the Internet, you no longer need to connect directly to other BBS systems.

Nobody calls these services BBSs anymore, however; now they're known by a variety of names, depending on the type of services that they offer. HotWired (at http://www.hotwired.com/), for example, is an interactive electronic magazine that resembles a traditional BBS. Even CompuServe and other commercial online services now seem like huge Internet BBSs that also happen to provide Internet access around the globe. The term *Internet BBS* fits as well as anything else, so that term's the one that we use in this chapter.

Note: Software that enables people to work together on a computer network is often known in the corporate world as *groupware*. Little technical difference exists between groupware and a BBS package.

The primary difference is that BBS software must provide a more robust set of capabilities to handle new user login, daily use limits, more sophisticated security mechanisms, and so on. Groupware also implies the presence of features that are not available in traditional BBS software, such as document management, workflow tracking, and other business-oriented productivity tools.

Why Set Up an Internet BBS?

The $10,000 question is: Why set up an Internet BBS? If you already have a World Wide Web site, distribute files through FTP, run an interactive mailing list, distribute information through an e-mail information server, and have a Gopher site to make sure that everyone in the world can access information from you on the Internet, why should you bother with an Internet BBS?

We can offer several good answers to this question, as the following list shows:

✔ **Setting up and maintaining an Internet BBS is simple compared with setting up even the most trivial World Wide Web site.** Internet BBS systems, such as the one we discuss later in this chapter, have been designed for easy and painless installation. The configuration for an Internet BBS is very similar to the security configuration for an FTP server (as discussed in Chapter 10).

✔ **A sophisticated set of interactive tools is available for an Internet BBS.** Typical BBS software provides many of the same communication and information-sharing resources that you find on the Internet. Newsgroup-style conferencing, real-time private chat, complete e-mail support (including person-to-person file exchange), and powerful database-query interfaces are only a few of the resources that BBS systems offer. Even the most technical Internet expert may run and hide at the mere thought of having to provide all these features by using the World Wide Web and other Internet utilities.

✔ **If you run a BBS, you control everything.** You aren't at the mercy of the often-aggravating Internet anarchy (such as the one that controls the Usenet newsgroup hierarchy). If a user of your BBS becomes inappropriate (posting material not in keeping with the content of your BBS), you delete that user by removing his access to your system. If you don't like the content of a certain conference or chat area, simply deny people access to that part of your system. The BBS package gives you control of content, access, and privileges — features that sometimes are elusive, if not downright impossible to create, on the Web.

✔ **The enhanced control and sophisticated communication features of a BBS open the doors to revenue-generating possibilities.** Because you control everything, you can charge for access to your BBS and to any or all of the resources that you provide through the service. Having your own BBS is something like having your own Internet kingdom — you're the ruler.

✔ **You realize savings by using the Internet's communications backbone.** Installing phone lines to enable people to access your system is expensive and requires a great deal of overhead to support your site. Remember that as a dial-up system, the older type of BBS needs a phone line and modem for every person who wants to access the site at the same time. If you have 25 people online checking out your site at the same time, your system requires 25 phone lines and 25 modems. If you make your BBS available via the Internet, however, you don't require cumbersome and expensive duplicate phone lines and modems. The Internet becomes your own private network, connecting those people who are interested in your site to the BBS that you make available on the Net.

You should see what School District #38 in Richmond, British Columbia, has done. This educational system is made up of 22,000 students in kindergarten through grade 12. They've created a very powerful communication system by using an Internet BBS. Stewart Lynch, director of technology and information services in the district, believes that Internet bulletin boards are ideal for schools to consider for instituting an e-mail and online conferencing system. You can see more about the project by visiting the following URL:

```
http://www.sd38.bc.ca/Lynch/
```

Colleges and universities are always looking for ways to expand their enrollment bases. Restrictions in faculty size and on-campus housing, however, greatly limit the capability of schools to expand. Using the schools-without-walls concept, one business approach may be to help a school set up a correspondence curriculum by using a BBS on the Internet as the delivery mechanism.

The user-group BBS

One of the largest groups of users of Internet BBS systems consists of special-interest groups that want to connect their members via the computer. Therefore, the fact that user groups make up the largest number of Web sites announcing access to their BBSs via the Internet should come as no surprise.

You may also want to visit Designlink, a San Francisco-based BBS for photographers, designers, illustrators, and other artists. The BBS provides networking, e-mail services, archives, shareware, and portfolios of artwork. You can access the Designlink Web site at the following address:

```
http://www.designlink.com/DLPages/aboutDL.html
```

One group that is not represented as a BBS on the Internet is local government organizations. Adding access to government organizations' sites via the Internet could create some interesting advantages. Consider approaching local public-service bodies, such as the chamber of commerce and city council, and helping them establish an Internet presence for their BBSs.

Setting Up an Internet BBS

In this chapter, you find everything that you need to know to set up your own Internet BBS by using a software package called FirstClass, by SoftArc, Inc. SoftArc's FirstClass software is both groupware and BBS software — one reason why the corporate-workgroup software market uses this program so widely.

You can visit the SoftArc Web site by going to the following location:

```
http://www.softarc.com/
```

At this site, you find more information about FirstClass and instructions on how to connect to its BBS via the Internet.

Note: FirstClass is soon to provide Internet server programs, including World Wide Web servers and built-in FTP servers. Other Internet BBS and groupware programs are heading in the same direction; Lotus Notes should be Internet-capable soon. For people who use Lotus Notes at work, this single development represents the elimination of the last great barrier to practical telecommuting.

Setting up the server software

If you have the computer and the FirstClass software, you can bring the BBS to life. You start by installing the server software. With the FirstClass system, setting up the server is a two-disk, five-minute operation.

Because the documentation provided with the product is so complete, we provide only a high-level overview of the server setup process itself. Just follow these steps:

1. **License the server.**

   You must know your license information and enter the information after the setup program prompts you for it. You receive this information at the time that you purchase the software.

2. **Configure the server name.**

   You must identify your server. The name that you give to your server is what people will use to access your FirstClass BBS over the Internet.

3. **Set up the modem session.**

   If you anticipate that people will access the BBS via modem connections (the traditional BBS setup), you need to follow the steps for setting up modem sessions.

4. **Set up the network session.**

   Set up this portion of the server if you expect to have people coming into the system via a computer network. You need to set up this portion of the server package so that people can access the BBS via the Internet.

5. **Back up the server.**

   Regular backups are critical in maintaining a BBS on the Internet. Start your backup protocol with a clean server setup.

Now you're ready to start the server system. To launch the server, first make sure that the FirstClass tools system is not active. If the system is operating, shut it down by clicking the small X in the upper-right corner of the FirstClass tools window before attempting to launch the server. After you disable the tools package, launch the server system by double-clicking the FirstClass icon in the folder or window in which the icon appears.

After the system launches, you see a window similar to the one shown in Figure 12-1.

This window, which contains a great deal of information about what is happening with your FirstClass system, remains active as long as you're operating the server. You can use this window to review who is accessing the system, when that person came online, and what method of connection (modem or network) the person used to gain access. A comprehensive archive system built into the FirstClass product stores this information.

FirstClass installs on your system a folder (or, in Windows NT, a subdirectory) called FirstClass Post Office. In this folder, you find all the data related to messages, files, and other important information. Maintaining this folder as it is installed is important. Do not move, rename, change, or delete the folder; doing so could cause serious damage to your BBS, resulting in lost data.

```
   File  Edit  Server  Diagnostics

┌─────────────────────────────────────────────────────────────┐
│                  FirstClass® Server 2.600                     │
├─────────────────────────────────────────────────────────────┤
│ [12/5/95 2:10:57 PM] 1:Hurdler Card 1 Port 1:SupraFax 14;4 - HWHS on:CD HWHS │
│ [12/5/95 2:10:57 PM] 2:Hurdler Card 1 Port 2:Hayes Ultra - HWHS on:CD HWHS   │
│ [12/5/95 2:10:57 PM] 3:Hurdler Card 1 Port 3:Hayes Ultra - HWHS on:CD HWHS   │
│ [12/5/95 2:10:57 PM] 4:Hurdler Card 1 Port 4:Hayes Ultra - HWHS on:CD HWHS   │
│                                                               │
│ Server: ICAN  Site: ICAN_CA  Serial number: 1200477          │
│                                                               │
│ 6 Sessions:                                                   │
│ Session 1 : Modem [Hurdler Card 1 Port 1]        Idle         │
│ Session 2 : Modem [Hurdler Card 1 Port 2]        Idle         │
│ Session 3 : Modem [Hurdler Card 1 Port 3]        Idle         │
│ Session 4 : Modem [Hurdler Card 1 Port 4]        Idle         │
│ 2 Network sessions                                            │
│                                                               │
│ Extra memory usage:  Session: 140K  CLUI: 32K, 616 MaxItems  Gateways: 100 │
│ Load: Sync PrivGroups Gateways                                │
│ [12/5/95 2:11:00 PM] Warning: Gateway 'SoftArcOnline' [34537] has no password. │
│ Stats Routes                                                  │
│ [12/5/95 2:11:01 PM] FirstClass® Server 2.600 started.        │
│ [12/5/95 2:11:02 PM] Init session Error 1054 - Modem returned "ERROR"  Sess 2 │
│ [12/5/95 2:11:06 PM] Init session Error 1034 - No response from modem  Sess 3 │
│ [12/5/95 2:11:06 PM] Init session Error 1034 - No response from modem  Sess 4 │
└─────────────────────────────────────────────────────────────┘
```

Figure 12-1:
Read the
FirstClass
Server
information
window
after
starting the
application.

When you first start your server, the system is empty; you can access no users, conferences, or information files. You must add to the FirstClass system the details that bring your BBS to life.

Administering the system

After you install the software, you need to configure the server to handle information and accounts the way that you want. Again, this process is simple after you get used to the look and feel of the FirstClass system.

To administer the FirstClass server, you must log onto the system as the Administrator. To do so, double-click the FirstClass Administrator icon or folder. A window similar to the one shown in Figure 12-2 appears.

Almost all the functions that you, the Administrator, need to perform are available through this window. You can access this window remotely by using the FirstClass client setup to log on as Administrator. You need to set up the client with the user ID and password for the Administrator. After you do so, you can monitor the system and make changes from anywhere, as long as you can connect to the server.

The capability to access the system remotely is a powerful feature of FirstClass. Remote access enables you to be away from the system and still perform most of the duties that are necessary to keep your system up and running. But remote access also brings up a potential security problem. Make sure that you carefully protect the Administrator's account information.

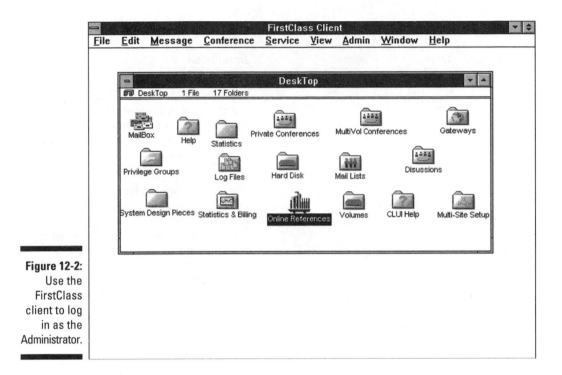

Figure 12-2:
Use the
FirstClass
client to log
in as the
Administrator.

If someone gains access to your server with the Administrator's privileges, that person can change everything about your system — not a pretty prospect for BBSs that have elaborate structures. Like any site on the Internet, a FirstClass BBS requires that you carefully implement and maintain a security strategy.

On the Administrator's desktop are several icons, each of which provides access to the inner workings of the FirstClass system. Table 12-1 describes the icons that you use to manage the FirstClass BBS.

Table 12-1	**Icons for Managing the FirstClass BBS**	
Icon	*Name*	*Description*
MailBox	MailBox	This icon opens the mailbox for the Administrator. In the mailbox, you can find all incoming and outgoing mail sent to or generated by the Administrator.

(continued)

Table 12-1 *(continued)*

Icon	*Name*	*Description*
FirstClass News	FirstClass News	This icon opens a folder that contains general news and system information. You can access this icon after you first launch the system. You can use this option to keep up on what's new with the FirstClass software.
Private Conferences	Private Conferences	In this folder, you store information about FirstClass private conferences, which enable you to deliver information to a controlled base of BBS users. After you set up a private conference, people who want to gain access must know the password to enter. You control access and the information that users share within the conference.
Help	Help	FirstClass comes with a fairly detailed Help window, which provides information on how to operate the various features of the BBS. Double-click this icon to search the various Help files. You can customize and add to the Help files to create your own Help windows for your BBS users.
Log Files	Log Files	This icon opens a directory for the log files kept by the FirstClass system. This directory contains information on who uses your BBS each day. The log files are named by the dates on which they're created. The size of the Log Files folder grows each day you operate the system, because FirstClass creates a new log file each day. To save disk space, you may need to erase files from this directory periodically.
Hard Disk	Hard Disk	This folder gives you access to any storage device available to the FirstClass server system. These devices include the hard drive on your computer, CD-ROMs, and other storage devices. This folder is useful in enabling visitors to your system to access files that you store in various locations on your server.

Icon	*Name*	*Description*
Privilege Groups	Privilege Groups	This icon enables you to set access privileges for users on your system. As the Administrator, you want to ensure that all your users can access information on your system and to prevent them from doing things that they shouldn't.
Statistics & Billing	Statistics & Billing	This icon gives the Administrator access to the section of FirstClass that collects statistics on what each visitor to the site does after coming into the FirstClass system. Using the Statistics folder, you can generate detailed reports about what people do at your site and create bills for information that people access via your system.
Mail Lists	Mail Lists	This folder stores information about the public mailing lists on your FirstClass system. Mailing lists are great tools that enable users of your system to send mail to specific groups of people on the server. This capability is similar to an automated Internet mailing list, described in Chapter 7.

Also included on the Administrator's desktop are icons for gateways, address books, and other features of the FirstClass system that we don't examine in this book. Rest assured that the documentation that comes with the FirstClass product provides details on how you can use these items to augment your FirstClass BBS.

Managing users on the system

When you first launch the FirstClass server, no users are registered on the system. You must either register each user manually or set up the server so that users can register new accounts automatically. Because of the potential number of users who may access your system via the Internet, manual registration is not a viable option. Manual registration is more acceptable for those BBSs in which you want to greatly restrict access to the information that you provide.

Registering users automatically

Auto-registration gives new visitors to your site a window that they can use to set up their own user IDs and passwords. This feature also forces the users to complete detailed information about themselves. To use the auto-registration feature, follow these steps:

1. Choose <u>A</u>dmin⇨System Profile from the Administrator's desktop.

The System Profile dialog box appears, as shown in Figure 12-3.

2. Select the Network Auto-registration check box in the Options area.

After a user connects to your BBS for the first time, she sees the window shown in Figure 12-4.

After a user completes the information window and clicks the Register button, a confirmation window displays the user's ID and the password that she selects. If the information is okay, the user closes the window by choosing System⇨Close from the menu bar and is ready to log into your BBS.

The information that the user enters in the auto-registration window appears in the appropriate sections of the User Listing. You can view the list of users registered to your site by choosing Admin⇨List Users from the Administrator's desktop.

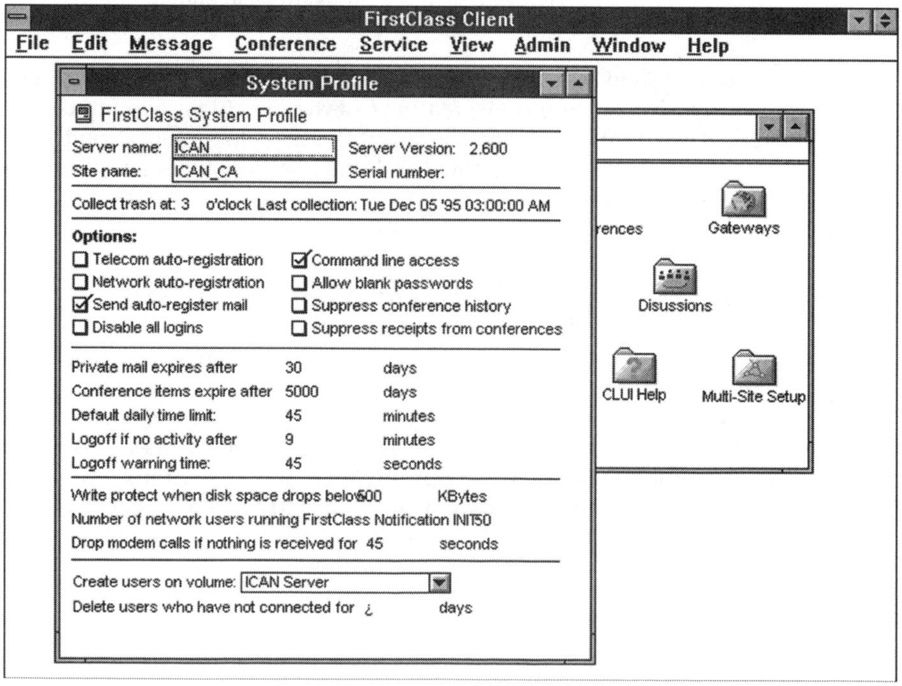

Figure 12-3:
Configure your FirstClass system by using the System Profile dialog box.

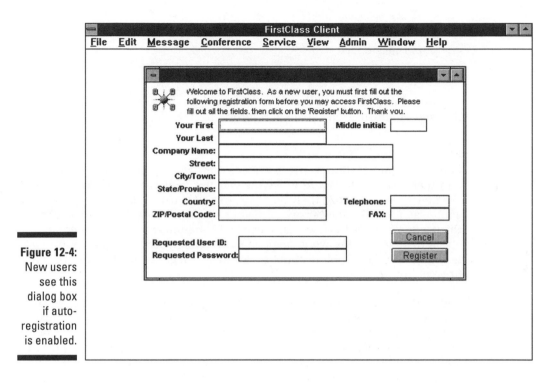

Figure 12-4:
New users
see this
dialog box
if auto-
registration
is enabled.

Have the server notify you after a person auto-registers a new account. If you choose the Send Auto-register Mail option in the System Profile window, you find mail highlighting who's requesting a new account at your site. Be aware that choosing this option could create a great deal of mail activity if many new users who decide to auto-register visit your site.

Viewing user information

You can easily view user information on the FirstClass system. You can open specific user information by double-clicking the user's name in any of the following places:

- ✔ The List Users dialog box (open by choosing Admin⇨List Users)
- ✔ The From, To, or Cc portion of a message
- ✔ A directory list
- ✔ A history list (a log of who's logged into your BBS)
- ✔ The system monitor
- ✔ A "who's online" list
- ✔ The participation list for a chat

  ✔ A chat invitation

  ✔ A permission list

  ✔ A list of subscribers

Just about anywhere you see a user's name, you can double-click it to get the kind of information shown in Figure 12-5.

Changing user information

In the User Information window, you can view and change users' account information (refer to Figure 12-5). You can also view the users' desktops and see how they customize their desktops to better use your site. Doing so is a good way for you to better organize your site. Additionally, you can access the users' résumés to view customized information that the users enter about themselves. Knowing the people accessing your BBS by the information that they make public about themselves is a great way to know how to present your BBS to best serve those who access it.

You can also view the features to which you give your users access. You can change the feature list to modify what each user can access. You can, for example, limit users' chat, conferencing, or downloading features, or a host of other features that are available to all FirstClass BBS users. The items that you select in this section for specific users override the default items that you select for all users who come on the system.

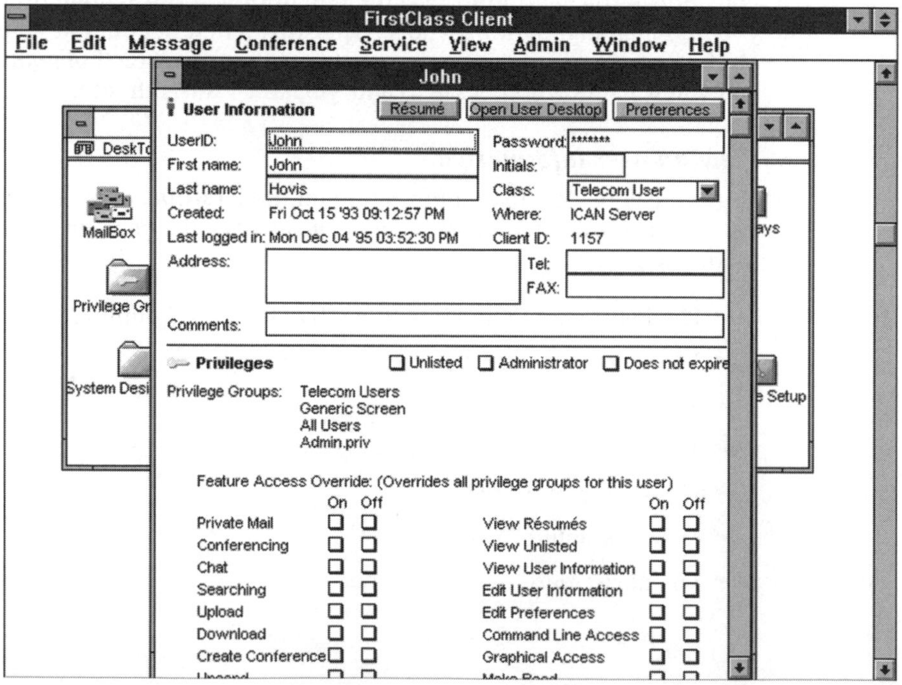

Figure 12-5:
View user information by double-clicking the user's name.

FirstClass gives you as much control as you could possibly want of how users access your site and what they can do there. The capabilities built into this BBS package make administering a site on the Internet much easier than is normally possible by using more conventional protocols to set up a site on the Internet.

Setting up conferences

You may be saying, "I know what a conference is in the real world, but what are you talking about when you mention a BBS conference?" In FirstClass terms, a *conference* is nothing more than a shared mailbox or bulletin board that stores messages about a particular topic.

Conferences are a powerful organizing feature of the FirstClass system. Without conferences, visitors must wade through large volumes of information to find specific items (messages) that pique their interest.

Conferences are much like newsgroups on the Internet; they represent places where visitors to your site can go to view and comment on specific topics of interest.

To make FirstClass conferences more like newsgroups, SoftArc provides an add-on product that enables the conferences that you initiate to connect directly to newsgroups on the Internet. (See Chapter 8 for more information on newsgroups.) By opening a conference folder on your system, visitors to your site can access posts sent to newsgroups on specific topics by people across the Net. This feature of FirstClass acts as a gateway between your BBS and an Internet News server. This newsgroup gateway product also enables visitors to respond to posts (messages sent by other users) to specific newsgroups without using a newsgroup reader client. Just by having the FirstClass client and access to your site, people can connect to their areas of interest without needing to configure additional software or figure out how to access different sites that host different topics.

When you first launch the FirstClass system, only one conference — the News Conference — appears on the system. By default, this conference appears on every user's desktop.

Note: You can change the way your desktop appears by using the Sample Desktop option in the Privilege Group setup.

As a FirstClass Administrator, you're responsible for everything about the conferences on your site. You must plan the structure of the conferences, create the conferences themselves, and define access privileges for the general public. You also must configure the conference options, organize the data that people store there, and determine how to manage the data after it's in the conference. Setting up and maintaining a conference requires a great deal of work. But don't worry; the FirstClass system makes all the work easy.

Creating public and private conferences

To create a conference, you must first determine whether you want the conference to be public or private. Create a public conference if you want all users of the system to be able to view that conference. Set up a private conference if you want only specific groups of people, to whom you give permission, to view this information.

To set up a public conference, simply choose Conference⇨New Conference from the Administrator's desktop. Choosing this option places a New Conference icon on the Administrator's desktop.

If you're going to create several public conferences, create a folder for your conferences (by choosing Conferences⇨New Folder) and then drag and drop the public conferences from the desktop into that folder. This way, you can keep the desktop organized and give visitors to your site an easier path to navigate.

To set up a private conference, follow these steps:

1. **Open the Private Conferences folder on the Administrator's desktop by double-clicking the associated icon.**

2. **Choose Conference⇨New Conference.**

   An icon for the conference appears in the Private Conferences folder (see Figure 12-6).

3. **Give the conference a name by highlighting the conference name below the conference icon and typing the new name there or by choosing File⇨Get Info and then typing the name in the Info dialog box that appears.**

   Give the conference a descriptive name to help the visitors to your site find topics of interest quickly. Close the dialog box by choosing Close from the dialog box's Control menu.

Controlling access to a conference

After you create and name conferences (both public and private), you may want to protect the conferences from accidental deletion by the Administrator. To do so, highlight each conference on the desktop, choose File⇨Get Info from the Administrator's desktop, and select the Protected check box in the Info dialog box that appears. (To make changes in this conference later, deselect the Protected check box.)

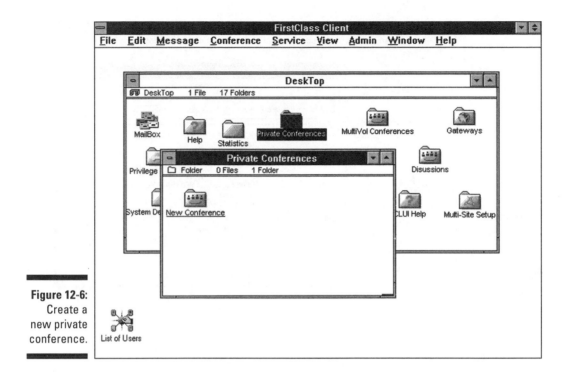

Figure 12-6:
Create a
new private
conference.

Many conferences require specific access control. To add or change access to a specific conference, highlight that conference (by clicking its icon) and then choose Conference⇨Permissions from the Administrator's desktop. The window shown in Figure 12-7 appears.

From this window, you can control who has access to the conference, what information conference attendees can view, what they can do with the information in the conference, and who can make changes in the conference itself. If you're creating private conferences, you also use the window shown in Figure 12-7 to specify who can enter the conferences. By listing the subscribers, you ensure that only those people whom you identify can access the information that you present in the conference.

How you use those conferences at your site depends on your objectives and how you want to control information flow to and from your visitors. As you actually set up conferences, you find many more interesting and powerful capabilities than we can present here.

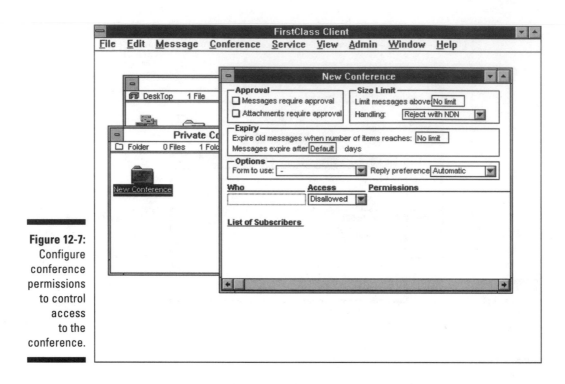

Figure 12-7:
Configure
conference
permissions
to control
access
to the
conference.

Establishing privilege groups

FirstClass is not making a social judgment in using the term *privilege*; that's not what privilege groups are all about. Instead, this powerful tool is simply another way for you, the Administrator, to organize the desktops of visitors to your site. Privilege groups are another control-granting device to help you structure your Internet BBS site to best achieve your objectives.

In the FirstClass system, a *privilege group* is a group of users to whom you give specific capabilities on the system. The program automatically creates several privilege groups after you install the FirstClass server. If you want to control access to commands and conferences for groups of users, use privilege groups.

The privilege groups that automatically appear when you install FirstClass are All Users, Network Users, Telecom Users, Other Sites, Command Line Users, Macintosh Users, Windows Users, and Autoregistered Users. You control what visitors can and can't do by making changes in the privileges you define for these groups and by adding additional custom privilege groups.

By changing a Group Privileges form for a particular group, you change the privileges for the entire group. To open a Group Privileges form, open the Privilege Groups folder on the Administrator's desktop and then double-click the icon for the particular group of interest (see Figure 12-8).

In this window, you can control up to 27 aspects of what visitors to your site can do. This interface is much simpler to work with than the control mechanisms that you use in other client/server systems.

With the Group Privileges form open, you can grant or deny access to various users, helping you structure total access to your BBS site. Optionally, you can view the desktop of a typical member of this privilege group by clicking the Model Desktop button, which you find at the top of the Group Privileges form. The Model Desktop shows you what members of this group see after they log in and enables you to customize their desktops by adding and/or deleting icons.

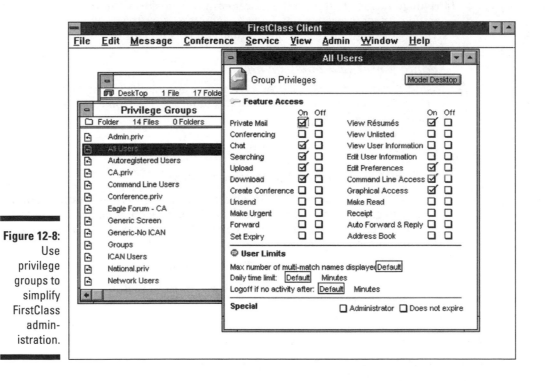

Figure 12-8:
Use privilege groups to simplify FirstClass administration.

Adding a privilege group

To add a privilege group to your BBS site, follow these steps:

1. **Open the Privilege Groups folder on the Administrator's desktop.**

2. **Choose Admin⇨Add⇨Privilege Group.**

   A new Group Privileges form opens. This form looks like the one shown in Figure 12-8 (refer to the preceding section), but without any of the Feature Access check boxes selected.

3. **Change the name of the new Group Privileges form by choosing File⇨Get Info from the FirstClass menu bar.**

4. **Fill out the Group Privileges form to meet your requirements.**

5. **Close the form.**

By following these steps, you add the new privilege group to the list in the Privilege Groups folder on the Administrator's desktop. Before the privileges can take effect, however, you must specify the users to whom you're restricting or granting the privileges that you specify in the new group.

Adding a user to a privilege group

To add a user to a privilege group, you must access the User Information window that we discuss in the section "Managing users on the system," earlier in this chapter.

Follow these steps to add a user to a privilege group:

1. **Open the user's User Information window.**

   You can open this window in several ways, as described in the section "Managing users on the system," earlier in this chapter. Essentially, wherever you see a user name you can double-click that name to open the User Information window.

2. **Scroll down the form to the Privileges section.**

3. **Enter the name of the group that you want to include in the user's privilege list.**

   Enter as many privilege-group names as necessary to define the access that a particular subscriber can have on the BBS.

4. **Close the form after adding the privilege groups.**

Now, whenever the subscriber accesses your site, that user is limited to the set of features that you define in the privilege-group list in the User Information form. Repeat this process for each person you assign to different privilege groups on your BBS site.

Assigning privileges to subscribers is a time-consuming and tedious proposition if thousands of people visit your BBS on a regular basis. To reduce potential administration duties, carefully consider how you want a new subscriber to access your site; then think about the paths that you may want to make available to your more-valuable visitors. As you distinguish casual visitors from power users, add privileges for the users to whom you want to grant more access. By planning a privilege-gaining strategy, you greatly reduce the amount of administration time that you must dedicate to hosting an Internet BBS site.

Privilege groups provide a powerful means of controlling what people can do at your site. This feature is particularly important to site developers who want to make some information available at no charge and provide more detailed data for a fee. FirstClass makes implementing such an access plan easier than do most client/server packages available on the Internet.

Creating a mailing list

Public mailing lists on the FirstClass server enable users on your server to easily send mail to a specified group of people who visit your site.

To set up a mailing list, follow these steps:

1. **Open the Mail Lists folder from the Administrator's desktop.**

2. **Choose Admin⇨Add-Mail List.**

   This action creates a new, empty mailing list.

3. **Choose File⇨Get Info from the FirstClass menu bar.**

4. **Enter the names in the mailing list, just as you would if you were mailing a note to the people whom you want to be the list.**

   Figure 12-9 shows the mailing-list window.

5. **After you finish adding names, close the mailing list.**

Create as many mailing lists as you need to suit your needs and those of your subscribers.

Note: Communicating the purpose and intent of your lists is important. Inform people about what's appropriate or inappropriate material for your list. Fewer things are more aggravating than for a busy person to wade through nonsensical or unwanted e-mail. A large subscriber base creates potential for e-mail abuse of your site by overzealous marketers. By developing a list-use policy and making that policy available to everyone on the system, you can better handle people who may abuse this powerful privilege. Protect your site by holding to these policies. Monitoring your own lists is important.

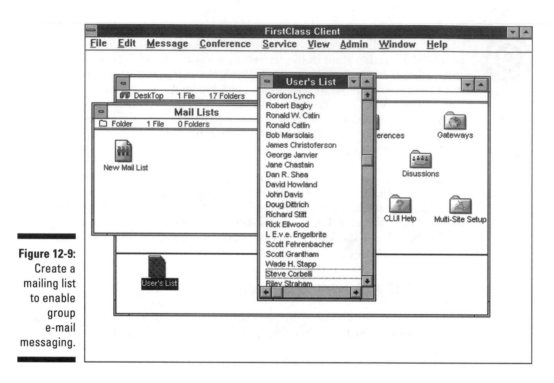

Figure 12-9:
Create a
mailing list
to enable
group
e-mail
messaging.

Setting up your BBS to connect to the Internet

To connect your FirstClass BBS to the Internet, you first need the TCP/IP Protocol option from SoftArc. This product provides the software mechanisms that enable a Macintosh and/or Windows-based client to access your BBS on the Internet.

Installing the protocol license

To install the TCP/IP protocol license, follow these steps:

1. **Shut down the FirstClass server.**

2. **Launch FirstClass Tools by double-clicking the Tools icon or folder.**

3. **On a Windows NT machine, choose Configure⇨Add License; on a Macintosh, choose Configure⇨License Limits.**

4. **On a Windows NT server machine, insert the TCP/IP Network Option license disks, and choose Upgrade; on a Macintosh, insert the TCP/IP Network Option license disk.**

   On the Macintosh, the upgrade finishes immediately, and the disk ejects. Mac users, therefore, can skip Step 5.

5. **Click the OK button.**

6. **Quit FirstClass Tools.**

Specifying the TCP/IP ports

Now you must specify the TCP/IP ports that provide Internet access to your BBS. To do so, follow the steps outlined for each server type in the following paragraphs:

✔ **For a Windows NT server,** you need to change the NETINFO file in the FCPO/SERVER subdirectory. To modify the file, use a text editor such as Notepad or your word-processing program. You need to change the NETINFO file to specify the port from which Internet visitors can access your site. The specific port and syntax of the command that you enter depend on the access method that you use. The FirstClass instruction manual clearly outlines the specific command to enter, depending on your situation.

✔ **For a Macintosh server,** you also need to modify the NETINFO file to call the specific port to which you make Internet connections. Use TeachText or SimpleText (or your favorite editor) to create the NETINFO file. After you create the file, save the file in the folder in which you keep the FirstClass Post Office. As is the case with the Windows NT NETINFO file, the specific port that you call on the Macintosh depends on what type of connection you use with the Internet. Follow the FirstClass documentation to make the appropriate port specifications.

Configuring the BBS

Before you launch your BBS, you may want to check and change your network configuration to accommodate more visitors simultaneously at your site. The FirstClass system comes set up to enable two LAN visitors to access your site at any time, but two users probably are not enough for an Internet site.

Before you raise the number of users to the maximum (100), take into account the fact that you may need additional RAM. Ideally, you should raise the number of visitors to the maximum that you anticipate at your peak operational times. You may need to tweak this number with some trial-and-error settings before determining what figure meets your needs.

To change the number of network sessions, go back into the FirstClass Tools program by launching the program from the desktop and follow these steps:

1. **Choose Tools⇨Configure⇨Network Sessions.**

   The Network Sessions configuration window appears.

2. **Enter the number of network sessions that you want the program to support in the Network Sessions text box.**

3. **On a Windows NT server, click the OK button; on a Macintosh server, click the Configure button.**

4. **Exit FirstClass Tools.**

5. **Restart the server.**

With the network configured and the TCP/IP option installed, your FirstClass BBS is Net-ready.

Distributing the FirstClass Client

To get people to access your Internet BBS site, you must get the FirstClass client onto their computers. One of the best ways to accomplish this goal is to create a Web page with instructions on how to download the FirstClass client and with instructions for the new user to follow to access your Internet BBS site.

If you set up your server to provide automatic registration, anyone who has the client package can log on to your site and create an account for access. The process can be simple and doesn't need to take a great deal of time for your users to complete.

If you took the time to visit some of the sites described in the section "Real-World Internet BBS Examples" earlier in this chapter, you saw this Web/BBS strategy in action. At the SoftArc Web site (at `http://www.softarc.com/`), for example, you find a link to download the client software package based on the type of computer that you use.

The SoftArc Web site also gives the IP address and port number that you must enter in the FirstClass client to contact the SoftArc Internet BBS. Providing this information on your Web site is important so that new users can contact your BBS without difficulty.

Whoa! Ride the Wild Mustang

Mustang, a popular BBS software company, has been building online communities since 1986. If you're running Windows 95/NT, Mustang's Wildcat! Interactive Net Server is the software that you may want to use to create your own online community. You can download an evaluation copy of the Wildcat! software at the following address:

```
http://www.mustang.com/
```

If you read the sections of this chapter that discuss the FirstClass BBS, you have a good idea what to expect from a complete, powerful Internet BBS system. The Wildcat! software includes the following features:

- ✔ Message system
- ✔ File-transfer system
- ✔ Security
- ✔ Polls and questionnaires
- ✔ Teleconferences and chat
- ✔ Wildcat! 5 browser
- ✔ Custom connector
- ✔ Electronic commerce
- ✔ Servers (HTTP, FTP, SMTP, and POP3)

By using the Wildcat! system, you can create an Internet or an intranet site that's accessible from Netscape Navigator, Microsoft Internet Explorer, or Mustang's Wildcat! Navigator. (*Note:* An *intranet* is a local-area network that runs network software, such as a Web server.) The Wildcat! system gives you such interactive functions as custom conferencing, e-mail, chat (both private and group), searching and viewing capabilities, and file uploading and downloading from one of the Wildcat! custom file libraries. This software also enables you to send instant pages to other Wildcat! users.

One interesting feature of Wildcat! that you don't find in many other packages is the capability to build your own custom questionnaires. Figure 12-10 shows one feature that you don't find on just any Web site: a list of who's online.

Sending messages by using the Wildcat! Message System

Companies such as CompuServe and America Online started the idea of forums (places where people could gather electronically and chat). The popularity of the forums on these private networks sparked early interest in Internet programs such as News and IRC (Internet Relat Chat). Wildcat! offers a messaging system that mimics the forums on these services.

In the Wildcat! message system, you can set up conferences in which you configure each conference for Internet e-mail, Usenet news, public messages, and private mail. This system doesn't skimp on features, offering spell checking, quoting (including the text of the message you are responding to), and file attachments, as well as Internet e-mail features such as replying to and forwarding e-mail.

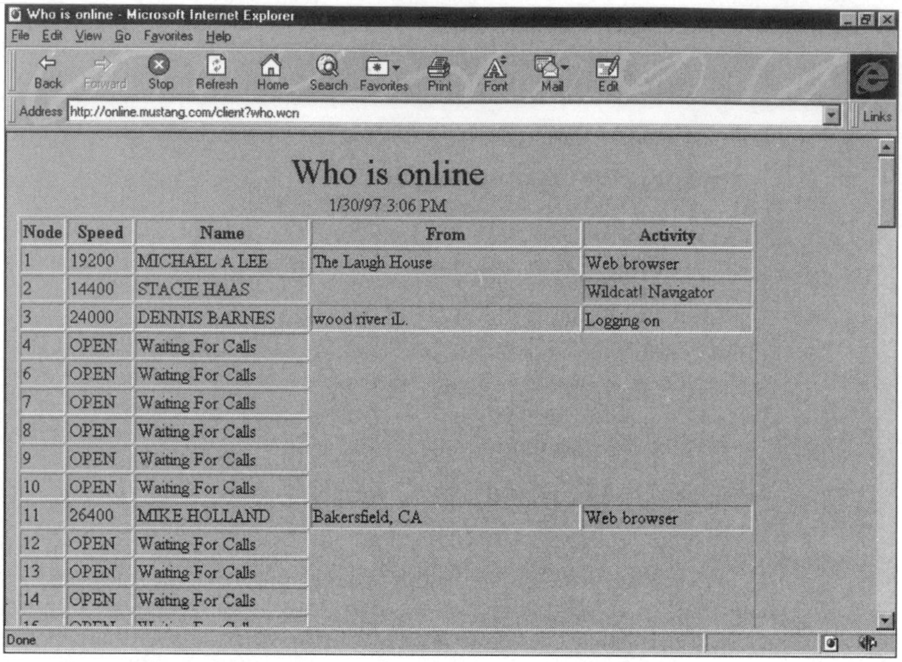
Who is online - Microsoft Internet Explorer
File Edit View Go Favorites Help
Back Forward Stop Refresh Home Search Favorites Print Font Mail Edit
Address http://online.mustang.com/client?who.wcn
Links
Who is online
1/30/97 3:06 PM
Node Speed Name From Activity
1 19200 MICHAEL A LEE The Laugh House Web browser
2 14400 STACIE HAAS Wildcat! Navigator
3 24000 DENNIS BARNES wood river iL. Logging on
4 OPEN Waiting For Calls
6 OPEN Waiting For Calls
7 OPEN Waiting For Calls
8 OPEN Waiting For Calls
9 OPEN Waiting For Calls
10 OPEN Waiting For Calls
11 26400 MIKE HOLLAND Bakersfield, CA Web browser
12 OPEN Waiting For Calls
13 OPEN Waiting For Calls
14 OPEN Waiting For Calls
Done

Figure 12-10: Find out who's online at the Mustang site.

Moving files around

Wildcat!'s file-management system offers a powerful interface. In Figure 12-11, you see that you can search for, upload, and download files. Clicking the Info hypertext link displays information about the file in the bottom frame.

Because this interface is much easier for people to use than FTP is, consider setting up this feature for file transfers within your company, for file transfers between your company and its clients, and for public access to company information.

Part of setting up your own system is the capability to define file areas. You can add hundreds or even thousands of file areas, creating a diverse system.

Another nice feature in Wildcat! is automatic virus scanning, which helps protect your system from the devastation of viruses.

Securing your site

One of the most important parts of any Internet site is security. Customize your site by using the built-in Wildcat! security system, which enables you

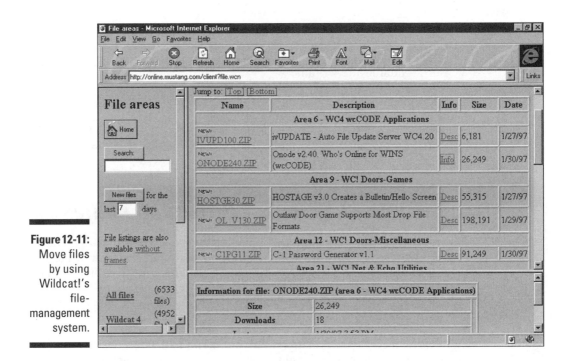

Figure 12-11:
Move files
by using
Wildcat!'s
file-
management
system.

to determine which files, messages, and menu options your users can access. Wildcat!'s security and access profile system uses a *nonhierarchical system*, which means that you can modify a certain group's access without affecting that of other groups. You can use this feature to set up custom intranet systems throughout your company, each with its own access permissions.

Remember, however, that Wildcat! enables people to access your computer and its files. This ease of access is one of the most serious security concerns that you may have with the system.

To help set up security, you can set file permissions. Each file has certain attributes (more commonly known as *properties*) that customize how the world can interact with this file. You can, for example, make the file invisible while someone searches a directory. (The file then becomes a *hidden file*.) Anyone who knows or can guess the name of a hidden file, however, can still access the file's contents. Being hidden is an attribute that provides a limited amount of security, similar to what you get in setting up incoming directories in FTP sites (refer to Chapter 10).

Two more common permissions that you can set are the read and write permissions. You can also set file permissions so that files have any of the following properties:

> ✔ Read-only
> ✔ Write-only
> ✔ Both readable and writable

Set a file's permissions to read-only if you want to provide information that no one can change. Write-only permission enables someone to put files on your computer without giving anyone else permission to read the file. Read and write permissions enable visitors to your site to both read the files that are there and place new files on your site.

Ask me no questions, I'll tell you no lies

A powerful capability that comes with having your own Internet site is that of collecting information about the people who visit your site. You can use this information to tailor your content and advertising for the audience that you attract to the site. Creating questionnaires can also enable you to improve customer service, fix problems with products, and create sellable marketing information.

Whenever you collect information that you intend to sell or give to another party, the ethical course is to tell people about that intent and enable them to remove their information at any time. You should check with an attorney before attempting to collect information for such purposes, to make sure that you're complying with all consumer laws.

Everywhere you go on the Net, someone is trying to collect marketing data from you. Marketing data is one of the hidden gems of the Internet. Collecting quality marketing data is like mining for those hidden gems. The Wildcat! system enables you to build your own questionnaires (the basic marketing collection tool) without any programming knowledge. The built-in Questionnaire interface enables you to gather data, take polls, and accept online orders.

Many people use questionnaires for marketing research and customer support, but scientists (such as sociologists) can also use this feature as a research tool. Unlike the people who answer Web-page questionnaires — the nearly anonymous nature of those people makes research results questionable — the people who visit your Wildcat! site are registered users, so you can make the research results more focused and meaningful.

Talk to me!

The Internet has long been famous for its chat groups. Before the Internet entered the public arena, private networks and bulletin boards provided thousands upon thousands of chat areas. As time went on, these chat areas grew sophisticated, offering special chat areas, privacy, and other features. The Wildcat! teleconferencing system offers a sophisticated chat system. You can set up multiple channels in which users can meet to discuss their business or to chat socially.

Unfortunately, this option is available only if you're using the Wildcat! browser (see the following section). This feature should soon be available for the Netscape and Microsoft browsers. Mustang is working on ActiveX controls and plug-ins now.

Browsing with a Wildcat!

Mustang ships its own Web browser with the Net Server software. You don't need to use the Wildcat! Web browser to use Net Server, but using this browser does give you a richer multimedia experience as well as access to areas (such as chat) that currently aren't available if you use other browsers.

The Wildcat! browser also offers features such as a sophisticated editor for accessing and adding information to the message libraries. Another area that becomes richer and easier to use if you employ the browser is the Wildcat! file system. The browser enables you to search for files and even mark files for downloading easily. The latter capability enables you to choose all the files that you want to retrieve before you start a single downloading session. If you use a different browser, you must wait for each file to download before selecting the next one.

One other nice feature is *multitasking* (the capability to perform several tasks at the same time). While you're still downloading files, you can move on to other functions, such as checking your e-mail messages.

Using all the features

Mustang's software supports several features beyond Web publishing, file transfer, and chat, and you can build a fully functional Internet site by using this product. The following sections briefly discuss using Web servers, FTP servers, and mail servers, as well as setting up your site for electronic commerce.

You can use this program as starter software. You may want to graduate to more-sophisticated software as your site becomes more popular, but until then, this software has everything that you need to get started. Because most Internet servers operate in a similar manner, migrating from the Wildcat! Net Server software to other servers is a simple, straightforward task.

Electronic commerce

The Wildcat! Interactive Net Server includes wcSubscribe, an electronic-commerce gateway for receiving and processing transactions. If you're charging for access to your system, you can use this program to manage your accounts. For detailed information on using Wildcat! for electronic commerce, access the Mustang Web page (at http://www.mustang.com/).

Servers

As most high-end BBS systems do, Net Server offers Internet and direct dial-up capabilities. Along with the access services, you get a full-blown Web server, an FTP server, and both SMTP and POP3 e-mail servers.

Wildcat! could be the software package that gets you started running your own Internet site. It certainly has all the basic components you would expect to find as part of an Internet site and an excellent migration path from Wildcat! to other servers. You can feel safe in knowing that the Wildcat! security system protects your system from someone who may not have the best intentions. If setting up individual servers seems a bit intimidating, we recommend Wildcat! as a good starter package.

Part IV

Site Builder Skills for Today and Tomorrow

The 5th Wave — By Rich Tennant

ORIGINAL VAN-GOGH-OF-THE-MONTH CLUB

"SINCE WE BEGAN ON-LINE SHOPPING, I JUST DON'T KNOW WHERE THE MONEY'S GOING."

In this part . . .

The Internet is changing very quickly, but the change is not a magical one. The Internet is just software and telecommunications services linking computers together. Aside from political change, only two things affect the Internet: new software technology and new computer communications services.

If viewed from this perspective, preparing for the future of the Internet is simple. New computer software enables new Internet services, and faster, more reliable communications technology paves the way for new software. This part analyzes the future of the Internet and suggests ways to prepare for it. The exciting second-wave of the World Wide Web brings us all a few steps closer to the promise of a single, seamless interface for the Internet.

Chapter 13

Electronic Commerce

● ●

In This Chapter

▶ Defining electronic commerce

▶ Getting comfortable with authentication

▶ Feeling secure about World Wide Web security

▶ Getting data from one place to another securely

▶ Cashing in on electronic money

● ●

*E*very Internet site needs the capability to conduct secure and reliable online commerce. More than ever before, people need a clear definition of electronic commerce. Just as commerce involves more than sales, electronic commerce encompasses more than the online sale of goods and services. Commerce, electronic or otherwise, entails the following elements:

- ✔ Marketing
- ✔ Sales
- ✔ Invoicing
- ✔ Purchase orders
- ✔ Payment
- ✔ Delivery of products and services
- ✔ Taxes and tariffs
- ✔ The use of consumable and durable goods

Electronic commerce involves all these components. In this book, for example, we talk about marketing your Internet site. We don't, however, discuss the complicated topic of product marketing, beyond what you can do to market your products by using the latest multimedia software and hardware. Marketing of online products is not always done online, of course; during Super Bowl XXXI, we saw an advertisement for an online product.

Understanding Electronic Commerce

Preparing your site for electronic sales is the focus of most discussions of electronic commerce. Some of the same considerations for safe and reliable sales transactions also prepare your site to handle electronic invoicing, an electronic purchase-order system, electronic funds transfer, and even the reliable and safe delivery of some products and services.

Following are some examples of electronic commerce:

- **Shipping.** If you've ever used (or seen the commercials for) the major shipping companies, you already know that shipping information is online now. Setting up your Internet site to query these information systems automatically and then integrating the shipping information with your billing system is an important step in electronic business.

- **Tax filing.** The way that companies file taxes is changing. The government now requires companies larger than a certain size to file their tax documents electronically. Such a tax-filing system makes perfect sense if the goal is to reduce paper and create a more efficient system, not only for large corporations but also for all companies. Electronic tax filing by all companies is an eventuality, and creating an Internet site that prepares you for it makes sense. You can prepare now for what must surely come, instead of waiting to react to the swift changes that are certain to sweep us all toward these eventualities. It's only a matter of time until all major accounting packages are Internet-ready.

- **Retail.** As stores stock new consumable and durable goods, they update their inventory systems. In the world of global networking, nothing prevents these inventory systems from linking directly to the suppliers or to an automated reorder system.

A key component of most successful forms of electronic commerce is a secure Internet site. After you set up a secure environment, you can establish each area of electronic commerce with little fear that anyone can compromise corporate secrets or misappropriate electronic funds.

After they establish secure environments, not-for-profit organizations can receive electronic donations, product manufacturers can sell directly to consumers, and service companies can collect fees. Creating a secure sales environment isn't difficult — but it can be expensive. To simplify the process, this chapter gives you a solid overview of the technology that you need and explains each step of setting up a secure environment.

The chapter covers no single solution; instead, it gives you the foundation that you need so that you can decide which solution is right for you. The specific product manufacturer or Internet shopping-mall service provider that you choose can give you a great deal of support and guidance (after you write a check). You can expect quality technical support as part of the service or product for which you pay fees to your service provider.

If the thought of spending money to gain security support makes you a little queasy, remember that, if you're generating online sales or contributions to your cause, you're making online money. Making money on the Internet takes money, so dive right in and do it!

Authentication

In Chapter 11, we cover the basics of encryption. As we describe in that chapter, most Internet security measures include the use of public-key cryptography (that is, the use of public and private keys to encrypt and decrypt information). Encryption guarantees privacy. *Authentication,* on the other hand, verifies the identity of the party with whom you communicate. Creating a secure communication link doesn't do much good if you really aren't sure who's at the other end of the link. Without authentication, you have no way of being certain what person or organization is sending an encrypted message, and an impostor could use someone else's computer.

Imagine, for example, the problems that could arise if the U.S. military were to accept and carry out encrypted orders without first verifying that the orders come from the President. Authentication has been part of important military command messages for many years. So you can see that, without authentication, encryption solves only half the security problem of online communication.

Using a digital signature

You accomplish authentication by using a *digital signature* (an electronically encrypted authentication). In the same way that you sign a letter or memo, you can apply a digital signature to an encrypted message.

The term *signature* may be a little confusing. A digital signature is not a graphic picture of your actual written signature; think of it as being more like an electronic watermark.

Public-key encryption works well for the creation of digital signatures for the following reasons:

- ✔ A recipient can decrypt information that you encrypt with a public key only by using the corresponding private key.
- ✔ A recipient can decrypt information that you encrypt with a private key only by using the corresponding public key.

You can digitally sign an encrypted message by using your private key to encrypt a message. Then someone must use your public key to decrypt the message. If the recipient can decrypt the message by using your public key, the message must be from you. The recipient of your message, therefore, establishes the authenticity of your message — establishes that you really sent it — by using your public key. (Refer to Chapter 11 for more information on public and private keys.)

Again, the need for official public-key directories becomes apparent. Here's why. Suppose that you have someone's public key. How do you know where that key came from? Having the Internet industry create an official — and trusted — public-key directory gives users one more level of trust and authentication in using digital signatures. If you can check a public directory to authenticate a public key, you can feel confident that the message you decrypt with a public key is, in fact, from the person whom you believe sent the message. Unfortunately, this trust issue can go only so far. At some point, you must just believe (within reason) that you can trust the public key that you've received.

Authenticating a public key

One way to further authenticate your message is to authenticate the key that you have in your possession. You do so by using a *key certificate* — a digital document that attests to the ownership of a public key by a particular person or organization. *Certificate Authorities* (CA) issue key certificates, and a higher authority in turn authenticates these Certificate Authorities. At the top of the authentication hierarchy (the most trusted people in the world concerning keys) is a private company, entrusted as the keeper of the keys, so to speak. Only after verifying the key certificate for a particular public key can you be reasonably certain that the key belongs to the person or organization that appears to be using that key.

The *Public Key Certificate Standards* (PKCS), the Internet standard that deals with public keys, states that every digital signature must point to a certificate that validates the public key of the signer. This setup enables software (such as Netscape's Navigator and secure e-mail software) to authenticate digital signatures automatically by contacting the appropriate CA and then viewing the corresponding official public-key certificate.

With all this talk about business on the Internet, a great idea may be to start a new Certificate Authority. The assignment and management of key certificates and corresponding public-key directories soon may be critical for all secure Internet communications. Contact RSA Data Security, Inc. (at http://www.rsa.com/) for more information about starting your own CA.

Public-key certificates create confidence in the authenticity of certified public keys. Two or more certificates may link in such a way that the certificates certify the authenticity of the other certificates. This link is known as a *certificate chain*. This chain continues from certifying authority to certifying authority until you reach the company or organization considered most trusted.

To obtain a public-key certificate, you first must generate a public-key pair. (See Chapter 11 for more information on this topic.) Then you must send the public-key part of the key pair to an official CA, along with proof of your identity — a notarized copy of your driver's license, for example. After validating your identity, the CA sends you a key certificate, verifying that you registered the public key and that the CA officially recognizes the key as belonging to you. (The section "Getting a digital ID and public-key certificate," later in this chapter, provides a little more detail on this process.)

The CA maintains your public key in a public-key directory and gives a copy of your key certificate to anyone who requests one. If your private key ever becomes compromised, the CA can add your key certificate to a *Certificate Revocation List* (CRL), which invalidates the previously certified public key.

World Wide Web Security

With its simple graphic interface, the World Wide Web is now the home of the Internet marketplace. Most of the encryption technologies discussed in this chapter focus on making the World Wide Web a secure place to transact business.

A typical World Wide Web sales transaction may proceed something along the following lines:

1. Joe Smith views an online catalog and finds things that he wants to buy.

2. He accesses a secure order form, in which he enters the items that he wants to purchase and his credit-card information.

3. He transmits the order and payment-method information to the secure server, on which a program is set up to verify the payment method.

4. The company notifies Joe Smith that his order is accepted and tells him when to expect the shipment of goods or how to access online goods or services.

This typical transaction involves the following main components:

- ✔ The nonsecure online catalog and the secure World Wide Web form.
- ✔ The secure World Wide Web server.
- ✔ An electronic payment method.

The following sections explore these elements as they relate to secure business transactions on the Web.

The online catalog and the Web order form

Many excellent books can show you how to create online catalogs and Web order forms. Products such as Microsoft's Merchant Server can help you create complete catalogs and secure sales environments. Most of the commercial online-sales products, however, are still fairly expensive. These products normally provide the following elements:

- ✔ **A database** or access to a database in which you store product information.
- ✔ **A dynamic Web catalog-page-creation utility.** Each time someone accesses your online catalog, the utility dynamically creates catalog Web pages. This way, the pages automatically add price changes, catalog changes, and specials based on information that you store in the database.
- ✔ **A credit-card processing system.** These systems handle complete credit-card processing, normally using an additional service that a bank or other credit-card processing service provides.
- ✔ **Digital cash processing.** We cover this feature in greater detail in the section "Electronic money," later in this chapter.

After you establish a secure environment, the information in your Web order form is transmitted securely from the purchaser to your secure Web site. If you're worried about how safe these transactions are, the fact that some banks are now using secure Web pages to enable people to access their bank-account information should reassure you.

For a good example of a securely transmitted form, check out Wells Fargo Bank's On-Line Banking page at `http://www.wellsfargo.com/`. Figure 13-1 shows the bank's site certificate. This certificate is your way of authenticating your connection to the bank. As you can see in the figure, a Certifying Authority issued the site certificate.

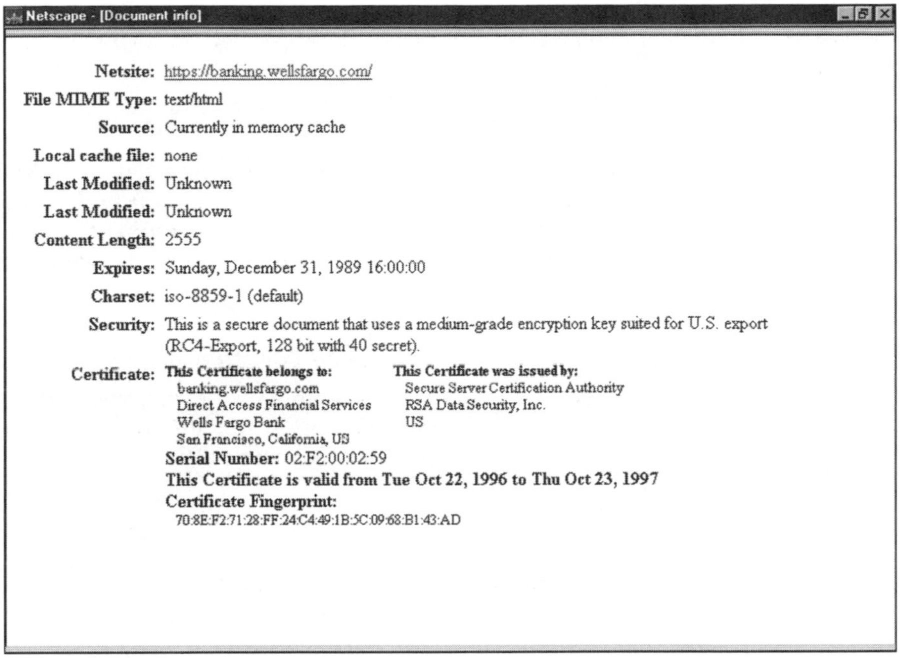

Netscape - [Document info]

Netsite:	https://banking.wellsfargo.com/
File MIME Type:	text/html
Source:	Currently in memory cache
Local cache file:	none
Last Modified:	Unknown
Last Modified:	Unknown
Content Length:	2555
Expires:	Sunday, December 31, 1989 16:00:00
Charset:	iso-8859-1 (default)
Security:	This is a secure document that uses a medium-grade encryption key suited for U.S. export (RC4-Export, 128 bit with 40 secret).

Certificate:

This Certificate belongs to:
banking.wellsfargo.com
Direct Access Financial Services
Wells Fargo Bank
San Francisco, California, US

This Certificate was issued by:
Secure Server Certification Authority
RSA Data Security, Inc.
US

Serial Number: 02:F2:00:02:59
This Certificate is valid from Tue Oct 22, 1996 to Thu Oct 23, 1997
Certificate Fingerprint:
70:8E:F2:71:28:FF:24:C4:49:1B:5C:09:68:B1:43:AD

Figure 13-1:
You can view the site certificates of the servers to which you connect, such as the server of the Wells Fargo On-Line Banking page.

The secure World Wide Web server

Not all Web servers are created equal. Shareware Web servers run on just about all computer platforms but usually don't include any type of encryption capability. Other Web servers, such as Netscape's Commerce Server, provide secure communications by using the Secure Sockets Layer (which we explain in the section "Using the Secure Sockets Layer (SSL)," later in this chapter).

After purchasing and installing a secure Web server, you need to perform some setup functions to activate its security capabilities. Most important, you need a public-key/private-key pair for the server to use. This key pair is known as the server's *digital ID*. Typically, secure Web server software includes utilities that generate a public-key/private-key pair and a certificate request that a CA accepts. (For a background discussion of key pairs, certificates, and CAs, refer to the section "Authentication," earlier in this chapter.) If your secure Web server doesn't provide such a utility, contact the company that sold you the software and ask how to generate these keys.

If you're using a digital ID for authentication, your digital ID incorporates your host name. This way, the URL of a site includes the same host name as the digital ID. Web browsers such as Netscape Navigator automatically verify that the host name matches the one embedded in the digital ID and display a warning if they detect a discrepancy.

For detailed information on how to set up your site to use a digital ID, visit the following Web site:

```
http://www.verisign.com/pr/pr_ns_secure.html
```

If you plan to run a Netscape Commerce Server or a Netscape News Server, you need to obtain a digital ID from VeriSign, which for now is the most trusted Certifying Authority. VeriSign is a private company that manages many of the authentication-management techniques that we describe throughout this chapter.

Getting a digital ID and public-key certificate

If you operate or plan to operate a secure Web server, you should apply to VeriSign for your digital ID. For information specific to your Web server, contact the VeriSign Web page at the following URL:

```
http://www.verisign.com
```

Processing your request for a digital ID takes about a week, so apply for a digital ID before you try to open your Internet shop. Follow these steps to obtain a digital ID:

1. **Install your secure Web server software and name your site.**

2. **Create a Distinguished Name for your Web server.**

   Follow the instructions that come with your Web server to create a *Distinguished Name,* which is the trusted name of your server. This name is the one that you give your server. (Sometimes the domain name of the server is also the Distinguished Name.)

3. **Document your Web server.**

   This documentation includes a letter that identifies the *Webmaster* (the Web administrator) for your site and a "Proof of Right to Use" the Distinguished Name. You find detailed information and the complete text of a sample letter on the VeriSign home page. After you fill out this letter, send the letter with your Proof of Right to Use application.

4. **Based on the Distinguished Name that you choose, generate an RSA key pair (public-key/private-key pair).**

   Your Web server documentation tells you how to perform this procedure.

5. **E-mail your application to VeriSign, requesting your digital ID.**

The appropriate e-mail address for your application appears on the VeriSign home page (at `http://www.verisign.com/`). The VeriSign Web page lists specific e-mail addresses for each type of secure Web server.

6. **After you submit your request, mail a signed authorization letter with your payment arrangement, such as credit-card number or purchase order.**

   Send the letter to the following address:

   VeriSign, Inc.
   2593 Coast Avenue
   Mountain View, CA 94043
   USA

7. **After you receive your digital ID, follow the instructions in your Web server documentation for installing the ID.**

For additional information on obtaining digital IDs and public-key/private-key pairs, contact RSA Data Security, Inc., at the following URL:

`http://www.rsa.com/`

Using the Secure Sockets Layer (SSL)

The *Secure Sockets Layer (SSL)* is the most popular protocol that provides security and encryption for all communications between a client and a server. To provide this security, authentication of the server is a requirement, and authentication of the client is an option. With the client authenticated, the server knows who is communicating with it.

Software developers use the Secure Sockets Layer in writing programs that need to communicate securely at all times. Unlike the security that's built into secure Web servers, public-key encryption programs use SSL for all data communications.

One of the main advantages of the Secure Sockets Layer is the fact that SSL is indeed a layer — in other words, application programs (such as FTP and the World Wide Web) run on top of SSL. SSL negotiates all the security between the client and the server program before an application program exchanges even 1 byte of data, so all the data goes out securely.

The Secure Sockets Layer enables a special type of security known as *channel security*. Channel security provides the following basic features:

✔ **The communication channel that your program uses is always secure.** After the Secure Sockets Layer negotiates the connection by exchanging keys, all transmissions are secure.

> ✔ **You always know to whom you're talking, because the channel (the communication session between two computers) is always authenticated between the client and the server.** This type of authentication is the same that we discuss in the section "Authentication," earlier in this chapter, except that the programs perform this authentication automatically.

> ✔ **The transport protocol (TCP/IP) provides reliability.** You can depend on the fact that messages that you send reach their intended destinations. (Macintosh computers include a message integrity check.)

The Secure Sockets Layer provides a comforting level of security. Using programs that have built-in security is far easier than handling security yourself — and certainly better than having no security at all.

Using Secure Hypertext Transfer Protocol

SSL is not the only protocol available for ensuring security and encryption on the World Wide Web. One alternative is the *Secure Hypertext Transfer Protocol* (S-HTTP), which EIT developed in early 1994. Terisa Systems, a company cofounded by EIT and RSA Data Security, distributes S-HTTP commercially.

An extension of the familiar HTTP protocol, S-HTTP hasn't gained as much popularity as the Netscape SSL approach. Unlike SSL, S-HTTP supports both public-key technology and the traditional shared-secret (password) technology, but its implementation of public-key cryptography is quite different from that of SSL. S-HTTP does not require the client (the person using a Web browser) to have a public key.

The following list describes some of the features of S-HTTP:

> ✔ Capability to authenticate clients

> ✔ Capability to authenticate servers, including support for a hierarchy of site certificates

> ✔ Support for digital signatures to authenticate the messages that you send

> ✔ Support for differing levels of security, based on the needs of the application

> ✔ Secure communications through *corporate firewalls* (computers set up to protect networks from prying pranksters)

On the other hand, the following list describes some of the features and advantages of SSL over S-HTTP:

✔ Ease of implementation (doesn't require any special Web-based programming)

✔ Increased client/server security by hiding the entire communication session, not just the transaction

✔ Better server authentication

✔ More reliable client/server communications, because SSL is part of the underlying communications layer

Both the SSL and S-HTTP technologies offer security for World Wide Web transactions. Which protocol may finally emerge as the dominant technology is uncertain. You need to pay more attention to this issue if S-HTTP becomes the standard; if so, you're going to need to create pages that you design specifically for secure communications.

Electronic payment methods

One of the main reasons for setting up a secure environment for online sales is to collect the money. Boy, *that* term's ready for the scrap heap. Who uses *money* anymore? Electronic financial transactions are quickly replacing hard currency, both online and on the street. You can use your ATM card for just about everything now. Credit-card companies are moving to create *smart cards* with embedded chips to process cash debits.

The Internet presents an entirely new set of challenges involving collecting money from customers. One of the biggest concerns about online sales is the security of credit-card transactions. But as many people argue, this fear is overblown. After all, you risk your credit-card number every time you hand the card to a store clerk or waiter, leave the number with your travel agent, or print your number on some type of mail-in order form. Given current computer security, online transactions — even without security — probably are safer than most of the other credit-card transactions that you make every day.

What makes Internet transactions scary for many people is the apparent anonymity of the transactions. The buyer probably doesn't know the person who's receiving the credit-card information. But you can make the same argument about mail-order transactions. Authentication (as we discuss in the section "Authentication," earlier in this chapter) takes some of the fear out of anonymous electronic transactions.

After the fear is gone, however, the question of how you carry out transactions over the Internet remains.

Credit-card transaction systems

The simplest and most obvious way to transact business over the Internet is to have customers pay for goods and services by providing their credit-card numbers. Many companies are working diligently to make this method the most secure type of transaction that can possibly take place on the Internet. VISA and Microsoft teamed to develop a technology called Secure Transaction Technology (STT) to facilitate secure electronic payment systems.

VISA and Microsoft also extended SSL to create Private Communication Technology (PCT). PCT provides better authentication than Secure Sockets Layer by extending SSL, but it remains 100 percent compatible with the SSL standard.

After you know that you can transmit credit-card information securely, you need to figure out how to handle the rest of the transaction. VeriFone, Inc., a supplier of transaction automation system solutions, offers a suite of products that delivers software products for processing payment transactions over the Internet. The company's products include an electronic wallet for consumers (a little like a debit or ATM card for the Internet), a virtual point-of-sale terminal (or cash register) for merchants, and an Internet gateway (a way to make a payment) for Internet shoppers. These products go beyond simply accepting credit-card transactions; they offer a complete solution for vendors who want to accept online transactions. These solutions can take a transaction from the buyer's order through credit-card approval at the bank.

Verifone's system is not limited to credit cards; the company's software can handle many of the new electronic payment forms that we discuss in the following sections. Check out the company's Web page at the following URL:

```
http://www.verifone.com/
```

Electronic money

Another option for a secure Internet sales environment is the use of electronic-money technology. Because you can't pay for things on the Internet by shoving dollar bills into the floppy-drive slot on the front of your computer, someone needs to create a way to pay for things on the Internet electronically. One method may be plastic money (credit cards). With credit-card transactions, however, you have a certain amount of uncertainty. (Is the card good? Is it going to be good when the transaction goes through? Is someone using the card fraudulently?) The solution for these uncertainties is a relatively new concept known as electronic money, which has some advantages over traditional credit-card sales. Electronic money is normally defined as some type of secure document (digitally signed) that has some value based on the purchase price of the document. This special signed document is transferred over the Internet after you purchase something. The vendor can then convert the document to cash from the company that originally created the document.

Several companies offer secure electronic-money systems for the Internet. One such company is DigiCash, which uses digital signatures to authenticate digital cash. In this system, the user's computer generates a random number, which becomes a note that the user can send by using electronic mail or a World Wide Web form. The vendor receives the note and submits the note to DigiCash, which credits the vendor's account with electronic cash. This electronic cash is a little like a Las Vegas poker chip; the vendor can choose to cash in the notes whenever he wants the real, hard cash.

For those of you who worry about the privacy of your personal finances, a technique called *blinding* keeps the bank from knowing who generates the note. By using blinding, you make these electronic transactions work just like cash transactions; no one can track them.

For more information, see the DigiCash Web site at the following address:

```
http://www.digicash.com/
```

CyberCash is an electronic-transaction-processing company that has a few twists. Unlike other companies, CyberCash doesn't require consumers to have a relationship with CyberCash to use its system. Consumers simply need to download the CyberCash Wallet software, which is available at no charge on the CyberCash Web site. This software creates the link between the consumer, the seller, and their respective financial institutions.

To receive CyberCash from people on the Internet, you set up accounts directly with CyberCash. These accounts are noninterest-bearing holding accounts. You can transfer digital cash into or out of the accounts. CyberCash also enables you to set up financial transactions on an as-needed basis, such as to transfer money from one person to another across the Internet.

For more information, check out the CyberCash Web site at the following URL:

```
http://www.cybercash.com/
```

Other electronic-money systems are likely to emerge. Watch these developments with interest, because the future of privacy in electronic commerce is at stake. All types of companies currently conduct online sales by using combinations of all the technologies that we discuss in this chapter. Visit some of the online malls and shopping networks to see how companies are handling Internet sales today. Search for the term *online malls* in any of the search engines to find online malls and shopping networks.

Note: Some companies charge a fee to accept and process transactions. We don't recommend using such companies if you can avoid doing so. If you consider conducting business with one of these companies, make sure that you read all the fine print in the contract; you may find some real eye-openers.

Chapter 11 goes into some detail about some of the privacy issues related to digital money. What direction the industry may take with regard to digital cash isn't completely clear at this point. The ideal is standardization on a single digital monetary unit and ways to transfer, protect, and spend the digital cash. This type of standardization is unlikely to occur in the short term. For now, you're going to have to put up with many competing standards. Having your money backed by a private company that could go out of business in a volatile emerging marketplace is a little scary, so buyer, beware!

Chapter 14

Promoting Your Internet Site

· ·

In This Chapter

▶ Becoming electronically famous

▶ Marketing with the Web search engines

▶ Using new marketing strategies in cyberspace

· ·

*Y*our Internet site is your connection to the rest of the world. People who ask us about creating a presence on the Internet usually blanch a cool shade of white and then green as we explain that their little business now has a global storefront. "I don't need that much!" is usually the cry. That most businesses and organizations don't really need global attention is true. But in many cases, the idea that your organization doesn't need global access is just a matter of limited thinking. Few people ever really consider the ramifications of an inexpensive global storefront.

Figuring out what to do with simple and inexpensive global access is a big part of considering how to promote your Internet site. We mention "simple and inexpensive" because most people in the world have had global access to everyone else in the world via telephone for many years. The hassles and costs associated with international phone service has kept our borders safe for decades. Alas, the Internet has changed all that. Now, instead of considering how to gain broader access to your clients, constituents, friends, and associates, the question is what you're going to do with that access now that you have it. The situation is a little like that of the dog chasing the car. With the chrome bumper firmly within its jaws, what does the little dog intend to do with its prize? (Stick with public transportation!)

As soon as the World Wide Web first took off, the Internet promotion game was afoot. No one really understood how the game worked, so all who were playing started counting hits on their Web pages to see how many others in the game were dropping by. Counting hits was fun! But it was also totally useless in most cases. (How many times, for example, have you come across little counters on people's personal Web pages?) If you're running an online publication that depends on advertising or subscription-based access, of course, you do care about how many people visit your site. In fact, the bigger the numbers you accumulate, the more advertising or subscription prospects you have. The same can be true if you're using the Internet to sell products directly to the public. In such cases, visitors to your site become like customers in your store or subscribers to your publication. But what about those companies that don't sell directly to the public?

A great majority of Internet sites, whether simple home pages or complete sites with many types of network servers and utilities, are for individuals, companies, and organizations that don't offer products directly to the public. The number of people who visit these sites is less important than is the quality of what a visitor can find there. If you're buying a new modem, for example, you probably just run down to the computer store and surf the shelves, comparing prices, features, brand names, and box colors. After you get the thing home and the installation goes awry is when you want to find the manufacturer's home page. You look on the manufacturer's Web site for upgraded software to match your operating system, installation instructions, and possibly company contact information. In the case of computer hardware manufacturers, we've been pleased to see how much excellent information you can find on their Web sites. But if you have our luck, you have trouble just installing the modem you need to connect to the Internet!

So now you know something about two different types of Internet sites: One depends on the greatest number of people landing on the site, and the other depends on people finding the site if they really need to. You need to promote these two types of Internet sites somewhat differently. We begin in this chapter with some of the basics common to both types of sites, such as getting a listing in the various Internet search engines.

Graduating from Being Known to Being Famous

You can make your Web site known among Web surfers — or you can make your site *famous*. Before you launch any cybermarketing attempt, therefore, take time to ask yourself, "Do I want my site just to be known, or do I actually want it to be famous?" Then answer your own question. To help determine the answer, consider these factors: If your Internet site offers resources that you intend for only a small group of people to use, being known may be quite enough for your purposes. On the other hand, if your goal is to reach as many people as possible on the Internet, you definitely want your site to become famous.

Being famous, of course, always has its price. In the case of a famous Internet site, you must work to keep your site fresh and exciting. As do movie stars, Internet sites must keep taking on new roles to stay in the public eye.

If you want to transcend being known and enter the realm of being famous, try to make your site a cool site. Several pages on the Web offer a "cool site of the day." Getting chosen as a cool site can take you from where you have only hundreds access your Web site to having tens of thousands of visitors. (See the section "Cool Site of the Day," later in this chapter, for more information.)

Becoming infamous on the Internet is much easier than becoming famous per se. Users have coined many new words over the Internet; one of the better ones is *netiquette*, derived from *Net* and *etiquette*. Because the Internet has no rules — only guidelines — you need to become familiar with the netiquette of your area of the Internet, just as you'd need to discover all the different customs and protocols should you move to a new country. Be sensitive to cultural differences on the Internet. Take the time to study the customs and protocols of a particular group of Internet users before using shared Internet resources to promote your Internet site.

Knowing Your Audience

Whether you want your site simply to be known or your goal is to own the hottest site on the Internet, you must know your audience. Not knowing the people for whom you create your site is like trying to paint in the dark. Fortunately, defining Internet audiences is now the subject of research by some of the top marketing agencies in the world. Even Nielsen, famous for its TV ratings, has joined the Internet rating game. Internet users are literally as diverse as the cultures of the world. The studies that advertising companies and organizations such as Nielsen conduct help define who is using the Internet and for what purpose.

On the Internet, the one thing that you can count on is the fact that everything's changing. By *everything*, we mean any and all the following characteristics:

- ✔ **The profile of the average user.** Formerly a young-white-male-dominated market, the Internet has changed over the years so that its demographics include a far more diverse group of people than ever before.

- ✔ **The number of people connected.** The time isn't far in the future when Internet access may become as common as telephone and television use. Actually, the Internet is likely to *be* your telephone and television!

- ✔ **The type of Internet access that people use.** Soon everyone is going to have dedicated, high-speed access to the Internet. Expect conventional modems to become the horse-and-buggy method of connecting to the Internet and cable, fiberoptic, and wireless connections to take their place.

✔ **Hardware technology.** In earlier chapters in this book, you see how connectivity to the Internet through high-speed hardware is changing what the average Internet user can do on the Net. Cable modems, DSL modems, and even ISDN have changed the way people can experience the Internet.

✔ **Software products.** Network programmers are creating many new types of network programs. A mere handful of useful programs once limited people's access to and use of the Internet. But not anymore!

In deciding how to advertise your Internet site, think about the needs, inclinations, and perspectives of the people you expect to visit your site. Identify your site with keywords or phrases to appeal to your audience. But don't forget that smart six-year-olds are likely to wander onto your Internet site once in a while, too. Attractive graphics, alluring animations, and exciting sound effects are what catch the attention of such unexpected visitors — and they're likely to bring your site to their parents' attention, too, if you catch can theirs.

The Little Search Engine That Could

The cliché "If you build it, they will come" may be true for baseball fields — but not for Web pages and other Internet resources. If nobody knows about your presence on the Internet, that's exactly who you can expect to visit your site — nobody. Just as you can advertise your business by putting your phone number in the local Yellow Pages, you can advertise your Internet site in online directories and through search engines. *Search engines* are programs provided as Web pages that enable you to search for key words and phrases found in Web pages indexed by this program. Many types of programs, known as *crawlers* and *spiders,* wander around the Web creating these indexes so that people can navigate through the hundreds of thousands of Web pages on the Internet without getting lost.

One of the most successful types of Internet business has been the World Wide Web search engine. Without search engines, finding what you need on the Internet is a near impossibility. Figuring out how to make the best use of the search engines in promoting your Internet site is of great importance. Search engines are usually the first place everyone starts in visiting the World Wide Web. In fact, most search engines use a customized screen that loads each time users start their Web browser. We suggest configuring your Web browser to load a popular Web search engine, such as Yahoo!, as the default home page. You can set your browser's default home page or start page by using your browser's configuration menu. The search engine, a logical starting place, therefore becomes an "Internet Main Menu" for the average Internet user.

Taking advantage of search engines in promoting your site is the single most important thing you can do in marketing your site. In the following sections, we take a look at some of the different types of search engines, as classified by the following list:

- ✔ Edited lists of sites
- ✔ Web crawlers, spiders, and worms (sounds creepy, doesn't it?)
- ✔ Site-published resource lists

Yippee! Hurray! Yahoo!

One of the most popular types of search engines is the edited list of sites. Yahoo! is a good example of such an edited list. People submit their Web pages and newsgroups for inclusion in the Yahoo! directory. One reason for Yahoo!'s success is that a real, live human being manually visits the submitted resource and determines whether to include it in the directory. Each page is submitted to Yahoo! in a specific category or categories. The person at Yahoo! checking out the resource makes certain that the submitted page is appropriate for the category for which it was submitted. This screening process results in an edited but still very complete list of Internet resources. Having Yahoo! include your Internet site in its directory is very important.

Sometimes you must be persistent in your efforts to get Yahoo! to include your site in its directory. The number of requests for a listing in the Yahoo! directory has resulted in a long waiting list. Our experience is that a certain number of requests simply fall through the cracks. Be patient and don't bombard the folks at Yahoo! with requests. But if your site doesn't appear after a reasonable amount of time, checking to make sure that your site is still in the running for a listing is a good idea.

Submitting your Internet site to Yahoo! is a little trickier than getting a listing with some of the other Web search engines. Because a human reviews each site for Yahoo!, and because the service is free, the Yahoo! folks expect you to do some of the work of figuring out exactly where in their directory to list your resource.

You can enter your Internet site into more than one Yahoo! category. Your first step is to access the main Yahoo! page at the following URL (see Figure 14-1):

```
http://www.yahoo.com
```

Notice in Figure 14-1 that you have several different categories from which to choose. For complete instructions, you can click the link on the main Yahoo! page entitled "How to include your own site." Or you can go directly

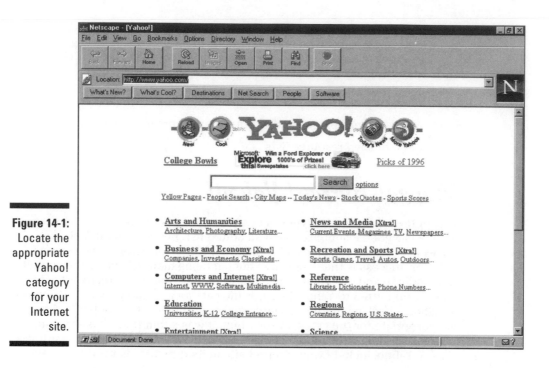

Figure 14-1:
Locate the
appropriate
Yahoo!
category
for your
Internet
site.

to adding your site. Find the category that best fits your Internet site. After you locate the correct category, click the Add URL icon at the top of the Yahoo! page. This action launches a new Yahoo! page containing a form for adding your URL to the Yahoo! directory.

If you choose a category that's too general, you receive a notification to choose a more specific category. If you receive such a notification, select the subcategory that's closest to the topic of your Internet site.

Figure 14-2 shows the Yahoo! Add URL form. Fill out a separate form for each Internet resource you want Yahoo! to list. The two most important items on this form are the *Category* and the *URL* fields. Filling these two fields in correctly is important. After you select a Yahoo! category and click the Add URL icon, the form appears with the category field already filled in with the category of the page you were on at the time you clicked the Add URL icon. If you entered this category in error or weren't in the correct Yahoo! category as you clicked the Add URL icon, you can change the category now by typing in the correct one. (The easiest thing to do, however, is simply to return to the Yahoo! category where you want your resource listed and click the Add URL icon again. That way, you're certain that the category field is filled in correctly.) You must enter the category title exactly, or it is rejected by Yahoo!

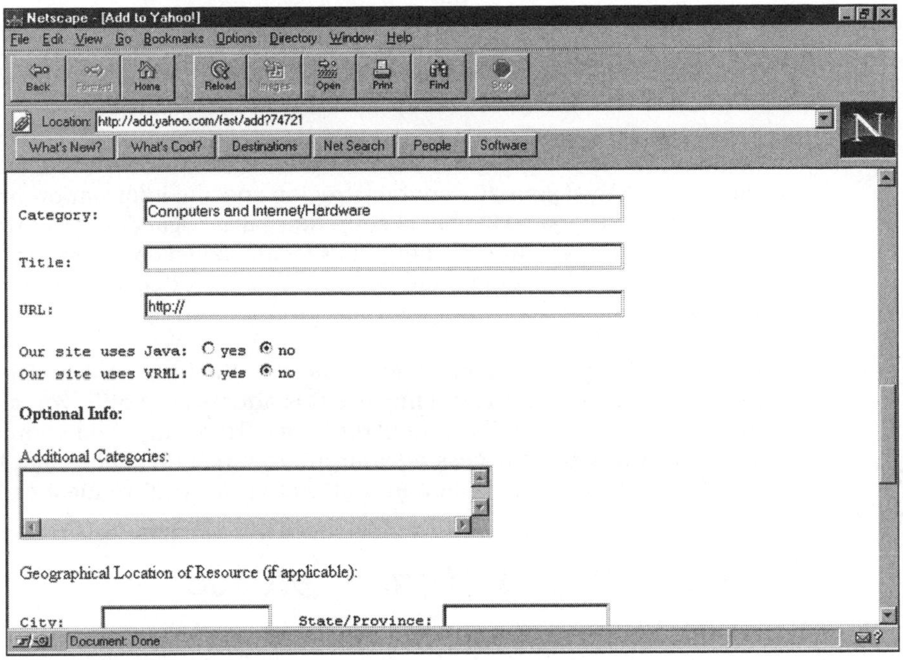

Netscape - [Add to Yahoo!]

File Edit View Go Bookmarks Options Directory Window Help

Back Forward Home Reload Images Open Print Find Stop

Location: http://add.yahoo.com/fast/add?74721

What's New? What's Cool? Destinations Net Search People Software

Category: Computers and Internet/Hardware

Title:

URL: http://

Our site uses Java: ○ yes ⊙ no
Our site uses VRML: ○ yes ⊙ no

Optional Info:

Additional Categories:

Geographical Location of Resource (if applicable):

City: State/Province:

Document: Done

Figure 14-2:
Fill out the
Add URL
form to
have your
Internet
resources
added to
Yahoo!.

In the Add URL form is a place where you can add categories for your site.
To include your page in more than a single category, you really need to have
already browsed through the different Yahoo! categories and made a note of
the page titles of each appropriate category. You then want to finally click
the Add URL icon only after you're on the category page you feel is most
appropriate to your Internet site. That category automatically appears on
the form. Then, in the box provided on the form, enter the additional
category names. Make sure that you enter them exactly as they appear on
the Yahoo! category pages.

Complete the rest of the Add URL form, being careful to enter the URL of
your resource correctly and completely. Remember that an Internet resource can be a Web page, a newsgroup, a mailing list, or many other
possible Internet information types. Don't be confused because the http://
part of your URL is already filled in for you. If your Internet resource is not a
Web page — you have a mailing list, for example — you can delete the
http:// part and enter the correct URL. (You may, for example, need to
enter a mailto: or a news: URL type in place of http://.)

As you enter a Web page URL, you need to note whether your page uses Java
programs, as this information is an important consideration for many
visitors. People who want to access your resources want to know whether

their software can view your site in its entirety. Many people don't use Java-enabled software — and even those who do aren't guaranteed that their programs can correctly run your Java programs. Java is still incompatible with a number of Web browsers.

Entering the location of your Internet site on Yahoo!'s Add URL form is important only if your site contains region-specific information or resources. If, for example, you own a bagel shop that takes local delivery orders from your Web page, you want to note your locale. Bagel connoisseurs in Algiers can then avoid disappointment because you can't deliver hot, fresh bagels to their door.

Finally, add your name and e-mail address to the form so that Yahoo! representatives can contact you. They use this address to notify you after entering your resource into the Yahoo! directory. They may even contact you with questions about accessing your Internet resource, although this situation is rare. Click the Submit button to send your request on its way.

Directory assistance, please

Another type of Internet directory does not rely solely on people submitting their resources for indexing. *Lycos, AltaVista, Infoseek,* and *Inktomi* are examples of search engines that use special programs to search the Internet, looking for Internet resources to index in their directories. These search programs have all sorts of bug-related names, such as *worms* and *spiders.* (We, however, think that these programs would be better named Internet ferrets.) The programs constantly search the Internet for new resources to list.

Such programs primarily search the World Wide Web for new Web pages. Some also search the Usenet newsgroups, indexing newsgroup information. This kind of program has its good aspects and its bad aspects. On the good side, these programs — we henceforth call them *spiders* for simplicity's sake — collect keyword information from hundreds of thousands of Web pages throughout the Internet. Whether someone specifically submits a URL or keeps a low profile on the Web, these Web spiders seek out and locate new Web pages and include those pages in their keyword index. If you're searching on an obscure topic, you have a much better chance of finding what you're looking for by using the search engine of an Internet directory that employs a spider.

The downsides to using a spider-based search engine are that you often receive not only too much information but a lot of out-of-date information as well. Searching on a keyword or phrase may return results numbering in the thousands. Most search engines return their results ranked by *relevance.* In other words, the first results in the list are more likely what you're looking for than are those farther down the list. But such is not always the case, and searching through thousands of results is both time-consuming and tedious.

Domo arigato, Mr. Roboto
Thank you, Mr. Robot

Doing your part to make Internet directories more useful is easy. An important file to have within your Web-publishing directory is a *ROBOTS.TXT* file. Spiders, Web robots, worms, and other wandering Web-indexing engines use this file primarily to exclude directories and files you don't want them to index. You may, for example, create several Web pages as tests that you don't want showing up in searches through Lycos and AltaVista. A ROBOTS.TXT file is a simple text file that you create by using any text editor. You save your completed ROBOTS.TXT file in your Web-publishing root directory (which is the same directory in which your main home page normally resides). The following sample displays a comment line, beginning with a pound sign, that states that it allows any user-agent (crawler, spider, and so on), plus a couple lines specifying directories that we want robots to stay out of. These lines begin with the word Disallow. The following is a sample of a ROBOT.TXT file:

```
# SCIENCE.ORG Robot File
User-agent: *
Disallow: /test
Disallow: /graphics
```

You can find the full specification for creating a ROBOTS.TXT file at http://info.webcrawler.com/mak/projects/robots/norobots.html#format.

One reason that so many results return from these searches is that the searches include Web pages, which were never really meant to be indexed. Suppose, for example, that you want to learn more about Visual Basic, the Microsoft programming language. You perform a search on the words *Visual Basic* — and wind up with thousands of results. You find that these results include listings for everyone who's ever used the words *Visual Basic* in their online résumés as well as anyone who's ever put up a job posting looking for Visual Basic programmers. Often, wading through these inappropriate Web pages to find the specific information you want just isn't worth the trouble.

Expired and broken links also are problems you encounter in using both spider-based directories and hand-entered indexes. Many Internet information resources are time-sensitive or temporary. Many others simply either move, usually by changing service providers, or stop publishing their resources. People searching though these types of indexes for information should consider wearing a hat to keep from pulling out their hair in frustration. Even so, without these types of search engines, finding information on the Internet would be nearly impossible.

Feeding the worms and spiders

Instead of waiting for a spider, worm, or Web robot to find your Internet resource, you can increase your chances of getting indexed by submitting your URL to different search engines. Table 14-1 lists in alphabetical order a few of these search engines, along with their URLs.

Table 14-1	Short List of Internet Search Engines
Internet Search Engine	**URL (Internet Address)**
AltaVista	`http://www.altavista.digital.com`
Excite	`http://www.excite.com`
HotBot	`http://www.hotbot.com`
Infoseek	`http://www.infoseek.com/`
Inktomi	`http://www.inktomi.com/`
Lycos	`http://www.lycos.com/`
WebCrawler	`http://www.webcrawler.com/`
World Wide Yellow Pages	`http://www.yellow.com/`

Each search engine in Table 14-1 includes its own mechanism for enabling you to add your URL to its index or directory. Using your Web browser, go to the Web pages listed in the table and look for the link or button on the page that enables you to add a URL. This process is much simpler than that of submitting your URL to Yahoo!. In most cases, you simply type in the URL of your resource and click a *Submit* button. The search engine takes care of adding your site to its index. It usually sends some sort of spider to index your entire site (all your Web pages).

Submitting your URL the easy way

Hundreds of search engines and directories are on the Internet. We doubt if anyone really knows how many are there. Some guesses put the number of these services at somewhere slightly less than 500. If you just became a little faint at the thought of having to enter your Internet site URL into all those different search engines, however, take heart. Services exist that enable you to automatically enter your URL into many different search engines at once.

One such service, *WebStep Top 100,* estimates that adding a link to 100 different search engines takes a professional about ten hours. The WebStep site lists 100 different directories and search engines, rating each with from one to four stars. You can save time by choosing to add your site only to three- and four-star directories. You can use the WebStep site as a quick access guide to each of the 100 search engines and directories the site lists. But don't expect any real shortcuts. You still must manually enter the information about your resource into each directory's Add URL form. If you're in a hurry, however, and time is more important to you than money, WebStep offers to add your URL to 100 directories for only $95*. WebStep can be contacted at the following URL:

```
http://www.mmgco.com/top100.html
```

!Register-It! is another service that offers a free service that enables you to enter your information once and, by doing so, automatically enter the information into 16 of the top directories and search engines (see Figure 14-3). Of course, !Register-It! also offers a commercial service that enters your site into 100 directories for $39*. You can surf to the !Register-It! site by pointing your Web browser to the following address:

```
http://www.register-it.com/
```

The very first service of its kind, *Submit It!,* offers the same free 16 submissions and offers several other commercial rates for submitting your resource information to up to 300 directories. The service also offers special rates to Webmasters who need to submit URLs for several different companies. Submit It! Pro, a commercial service, for example, advertised rates of around $200 for 10 companies and around $300 dollars for 20 companies*. You can reach the Submit It! site at the following URL:

```
http://www.submitit.com/
```

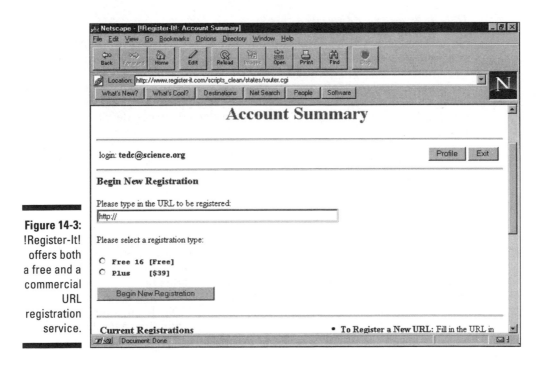

Figure 14-3: !Register-It! offers both a free and a commercial URL registration service.

---

* All prices are subject to change; you need to contact each company for its current rate.

The last service we cover here is *Postmaster*. This service is similar to the others in this section, with a few exceptions. The folks at Postmaster offer to add your site to more than 400 different directories and search engines. They also offer to send your URL to more than 6,500 individuals. This service is aimed mainly at organizations with a bit of cash. The company offers to submit 80 posts, for example, for $6,000*. You can reach the Postmaster site at the following address:

```
http://www.netcreations.com/postmaster
```

Using a service saves you time, whether you choose to take advantage of the free offers or pay a fee to have your site added to many directories. Be aware, too, that some of the search engines to which you submit your URL may offer additional exposure for your Internet site for an additional fee. Some value-added services include posting an announcement on a special page that highlights new submissions; others may post your listing in their directory in a larger and colored font. As many of these registries grow to rival the traditional printed phone books, having your listing stand out from the many other listings becomes a challenge. You must decide for yourself whether the additional exposure these marketing features add is worth the extra money.

Using an online ad agency

Sit back and relax while Internet promotion specialists take your Internet site from obscurity to fame. Traditional ad agencies have only recently become aware of the potential of the Internet. Most agencies don't fully understand how to go about marketing someone's online presence. Several companies, however, have done really well in online marketing. One of these companies, *DoubleClick,* provides a full service ad agency devoted to online promotion.

You can contact DoubleClick at the following URL:

```
http://www.doubleclick.net
```

Aliweb, alakazam!

You need no magic to add your Internet resources into Aliweb's directory. The Aliweb directory uses a different method than Yahoo! or any of the Web spiders to compile its listings. Aliweb builds its index by reading special *index* files on your computer. You (or the person who maintains your Internet site) build these index files, named SITE.IDX. Then, after you register your site with Aliweb, the service visits your site several times a week to read your SITE.IDX file for the most current site information.

---

* All prices are subject to change; you need to contact each company for its current rate.

The following list describes advantages to using a system such as Aliweb:

- ✔ **Resources in Aliweb are always up to date.** (You find few expired or broken links.)

- ✔ **You have complete control over what resources appear in Aliweb.** (No pages appear that you do not specifically enter into the SITE.IDX file.)

- ✔ **Update-to-implementation time is relatively fast.** (Changes you make appear as soon as the Aliweb engine queries your site, which means that the wait before the updates appear may be two or three days maximum — quite speedy compared to that of any other service.)

One requirement to using the Aliweb systems is that your Internet site is available over a dedicated connection. The Aliweb queries come at regular intervals. If the engine can't reach your site several times in a row, Aliweb removes your site's information from its database. This practice helps ensure that the information in the Aliweb database is always current.

The first step in getting your site ready to register with Aliweb is to create a SITE.IDX file. To create this file, you must use a normal text editor or a word processor that can save to text-only (TXT) format. The SITE.IDX file contains *records* — blocks of information that describe your entire Internet site. Each record contains specific *name-value pairs* that describe each resource or *template type*. A name-value pair is a fancy way of saying that for each *name* (what is known in databases as a *field*, or a *column*) you have a *value*. The following table serves as an example. This table is an example extracted from a SITE.IDX file. The names appear in the left column and the values appear on the right.

```
Template-Type:      USER
Title:              Joe P. Macandsun
Handle:             joe@virtualcorporation.com
Email:              joe@virtualcorporation.com
Work-Phone:         800-555-1234
URI:                http://www.virtualcorporation.com/joe/
```

This table is an example of a record that describes a USER. In a SITE.IDX file are records that describe different template types. Your SITE.IDX file always begins with two records, one that describes your Internet site and the other that describes your organization. The following is an example of a typical SITE.IDX file:

```
Template-Type:         SITEINFO
URI:                   /
Host-Name:             SCIENCE.ORG
Admin-Handle:          webmaster@science.org
```

```
Owner-Organization-Name:   SCIENCE.ORG (tm)
Description:               The WWW Server at SCIENCE.ORG
                          Keywords: Research, Science,
                          Technology

Template-Type:            ORGANIZATION
Organization-Name:        SCIENCE.ORG
Organization-Handle:      SCIENCE
Organization-Phone:       619-943-9382
Organization-Fax:         619-944-6888
Organization-Email:       info@science.org
Organization-Postal:      258 Neptune Avenue
City:                     Encinitas
State:                    California
URI:                      http://www.science.org/
Description:              SCIENCE.ORG (tm) is a non-profit
                          science and technology research
                          and development lab.
Keywords:                 Research, Science, Technology
```

Use the preceding two record types to describe your site and organization in as much detail as you want. An important point to keep in mind is that you can't deviate from the template. To describe users, services, and documents, you must use the correct associated template type. The first example in this section demonstrates the template type for users. The two most common template types are SERVICE, which you use to describe an Internet service such as FTP, Finger, or some other service, and DOCUMENT, which you use to describe a document that's available through a service. Examples of documents are Web pages and files available through Gopher or FTP. The following are examples of both the SERVICE and DOCUMENT template types:

```
Template-Type:    SERVICE
Title:            FTP
URI:              ftp://ftp.science.org/
Description:      FTP site for sharing research info
Keywords:         Anonymous, FTP
Admin-Handle:     jasonc@science.org

Template-Type:    DOCUMENT
Title:            ActiveX Source
Admin-Handle:     tedc@science.org
URI:              http://ebola.science.org/ActiveX/
Description:      A source for ActiveX controls
Keywords:         ActiveX, COM, DCOM, Microsoft, WWW, Web
```

Promoting Yourself

Not everyone who wants to promote an Internet site is a business or organization. Some people may want to promote their personal site or possibly tell people how to reach them by e-mail. Most of the search engines and directories listed earlier in this chapter enable you to submit a personal Web page URL.

A hint about getting people to visit your personal Web page is to have an interesting theme. You can content-relate this theme to one of your interests or hobbies. Having a focused content about a specific topic makes placing your page in a directory that much easier and also attracts people who share your interests to your home page. Making the page interactive keeps them coming back. A good example of this is a fun page we created a couple years ago: the Coombs Family Reunion in Cyberspace page (`http://www.science.org/coombs/`). We enabled visitors to this page to leave their own messages and family histories. Pretty soon, we had wonderful messages from distant relatives from all around the world. Most of these people came across our page doing something that most people do at least once — use one of the search engines to search for their name. (Where do you think the idea of the Coombs Family Reunion page came from?) Finding other people with the exact same name can be fun, especially if you get to meet them, as one of the authors of this book did.

The first directory that enables people to enter their home page, e-mail addresses, and favorite URLs was *People On the Net*. We started this directory several years ago because it was a fun idea. You can access the People On the Net directory at the following URL:

```
http://www.science.org/people
```

Soon after we started People On the Net, a really wonderful service called *Four11* started up. Four11 not only provides the most complete listing of people on the Internet, but the service also offers access to all the U.S. telephone directories. If you're looking for someone in the United States, we know of no quicker way to find who you seek than if that person's either listed in the phone book or has an e-mail address registered with Four11. Even Yahoo!, which used to maintain its own listing of people, now uses the Four11 service. The Four11 directory includes the following directories:

- ✔ **E-mail addresses.** This directory is an important one in which to appear.
- ✔ **Telephone.** This list comes straight from the telephone white pages.
- ✔ **Netphone.** Want people to call you on your Internet phone system? Add your name to this list.

✔ **Government.** Here is the contact information for the White House, the U.S. House of Representatives, and the U.S. Senate. If you're not on this list, you didn't get elected.

✔ **Celebrities.** This directory includes lists of celebrity mailing addresses and e-mail addresses. If you're a celebrity actor, model, author, or VIP, make sure that you add yourself to the celebrity directory.

Four11 also offers additional services to paid members. You can maintain a Web page on the Four11 server, create searches that continue searching even while you're offline, and use several other services such as the *iName* service. Get an iName personalized e-mail address for life that redirects e-mail to any e-mail account of your choice. While you're getting yourself set up with an iName, go ahead and register yourself in the Four11 directory so that people can find you online. Entering your name in the directory is free. Simply go to the Four11 home page at the following URL and click the *Add Me* link:

```
http://www.four11.com/
```

The following table lists some of the other places you can add your name and personal profile so that people can find you on the Internet. Figure 14-4 shows the InfoSpace page.

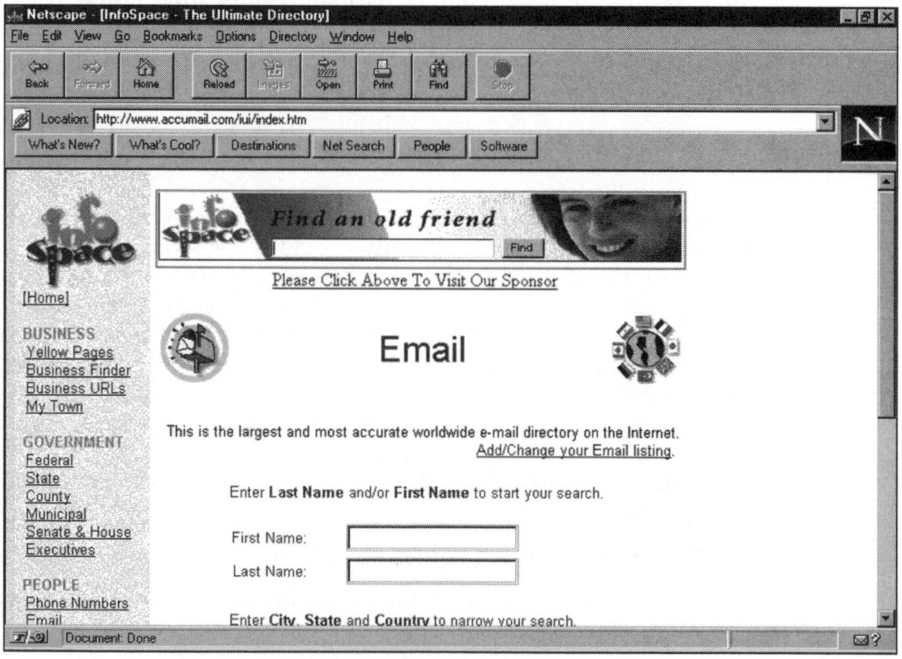

Figure 14-4: InfoSpace is one place to add your name when promoting yourself.

Service	URL
World Wide Profile Registry	`http://www.wizard.com/wwpr.html`
Bigfoot	`http://www.bigfoot.com/`
InfoSpace	`http://www.accumail.com/iui/index.htm`
WhoWhere	`http://www.whowhere.com/`

Cool Site of the Day

If traffic to your site is what you're looking for, your goal is to shoot for a listing in one of the *Cool Sites of the Day* pages. The idea started several years ago with Glen Davis launching the first Cool Site of the Day page. His Internet site was so overrun with people trying to load his page that his Internet Service Provider could barely handle the traffic. Every day, these pages feature a different Web page as a cool site. Thousands of people make a point of finding out just where clicking the link to the Cool Site of the Day takes them.

Becoming the Cool Site of the Day probably means that your site is going to receive visits from tens of thousands of people in a single day. Make sure that your connection, your computer, and your software can handle that many connection attempts. If your site becomes overloaded, replace your Web page with a brief explanation that your site is overloaded with requests and for visitors to try back later. Don't just turn your computer off or shut down your Web server. That upsets people, and they may never return to your site. Another alternative is to find someone with a very fast connection and a powerful computer and ask that person to temporarily host your Web site. Create a simple home page with a link that takes people to the temporary site.

Now several years old, Infinet runs the Cool Site of the Day page (see Figure 14-5). As always, Infinet takes recommendations for the day's cool site. (Recommending your own Web page as the Cool Site of the Day is okay.) To correspond with Infinet or to find out for yourself just what's cool today, go to the following address:

```
http://cool.infi.net
```

A good idea doesn't stay lonely for very long. Just about everyone now has a list of cool links. Netscape Navigator, for example, provides a button for "What's Cool?" as part of the Navigator interface. In case you use a different browser, clicking the What's Cool? button takes you to the following URL:

```
http://home.netscape.com/home/whats-cool.html
```

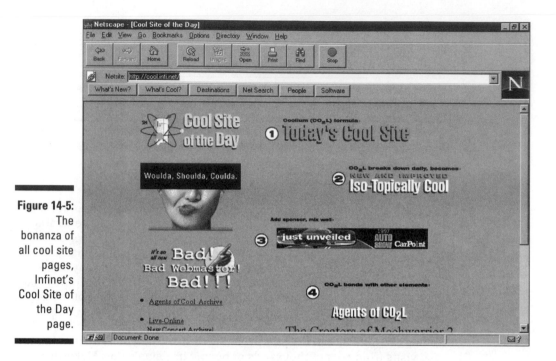

Figure 14-5:
The
bonanza of
all cool site
pages,
Infinet's
Cool Site of
the Day
page.

Yahoo!, the mother of all Internet directories, used to point to Glen Davis'
Cool Site of the Day. That support probably helped make the site as popular
as it is today. Not to be outdone, the Yahoo! main Web page now has its own
"Cool" icon at the top of the page. Clicking the icon takes you to the following address:

```
http://www.yahoo.com/Entertainment/Cool Links
```

If you're going to diligently pursue becoming a cool site in one or more of
the lists of cool sites, you want to make sure that your Web site

✔ Is graphically appealing.

✔ Contains interesting content.

✔ Loads quickly (Go easy on those Java applets!).

Don't be discouraged if no one immediately selects your site. The number of
Web sites is rapidly approaching the one million mark. The companies that
run the lists of cool sites receive a large number of requests every day for
consideration as the cool site. Your persistence and creativity is bound to pay
off eventually. (See Chapters 5 and 6 for tips on creating a great Web page.)

Extra! Extra! Read All about It!

Make your site big news. Newsgroups were among the first popular gathering places on the Internet — so popular, in fact, that the words *newsgroups* and *Internet* were once almost synonymous. A *newsgroup,* by the way, is one of the many discussion areas available on the Internet. Newgroups were originally formed (and are still formed today) to enable users to share information or carry on electronic dialogue about anything and everything. If you tell people in newsgroups that you have an online presence, you automatically increase your visibility.

Certain newsgroups work better than others as places to post announcement of your new Web page. Begin with general newsgroups that were specifically created for posting announcements. One recommendation is the `comp.infosystems` hierarchy of newsgroups, located at the following address:

```
comp.infosystems.www.annouce
```

You can use *newsreaders,* such as the ones that come with either Microsoft's Internet Explorer or Netscape Navigator, to read and post messages to newsgroups. In writing your posting, tell newsgroup readers a little about what to expect after they log onto your Web page. Remember to include your URL. Getting caught up in the description of your site while completely forgetting to tell people how to get there is all too easy.

The following list offers guidelines to keep in mind if you post your site to newsgroups:

- ✔ Post messages to newsgroups with the same topic or focus as the Internet site you're promoting.

- ✔ Read the newsgroup before you post to it. Reading posts that are completely unrelated to the information pertinent to the newsgroup is aggravating.

- ✔ Don't post the same message to hundreds of similar newsgroups.

- ✔ Don't advertise specific items as you would in a magazine or newspaper; save specific product or service information for the people who are interested enough to seek out your online presence.

- ✔ Newsgroups archive their messages, so they erase your posting after a period of time. The more active a newsgroup is, the quicker the messages disappear. Posting to a newsgroup one time doesn't guarantee that your message is around forever.

- ✔ Make certain that your posting and the content of your Internet site appeals to the audience of a particular newsgroup before you post your message with that newsgroup. If you post to `alt.wolves`, for example, don't post a "Humans Against Wolves Home Page" message unless you're looking for a fight.

Chapter 8 contains a complete description of News and how you can use both Usenet News and private newsgroups.

It's a Jungle Out There — How Amazon.com Does It

Whether you're marketing fresh lobster from Maine, tours of the Holy Land, coffee from Hawaii, or rare books from your attic, you can sell your wares on the Internet. You don't need to be a big mall, like the Internet Shopping Network, to be a big success. The Internet is often called the "great equalizer." You have just as much opportunity to sell your products in this electronic village as the bigger guys do. You just need a few tricks up your sleeve.

A wonderful success story began in 1994 when Jeff Bezos founded Amazon.com. This Internet-only bookstore has one of the world's largest selection of books and is the leading bookstore on the World Wide Web. If you're wondering what the Amazon has to do with books, the company is named after the Amazon River, which is more than eight times the size of the next largest river in the world. Amazon.com claims that its catalog of books is more than eight times the size of the largest physical bookstore.

One of the tricks up Amazon.com's sleeve is to partner with Internet site developers. Just about anyone can become a "branch store" for Amazon.com by listing books in a Web page and linking to the Amazon.com site. This partner program benefits Amazon.com by having thousands of Web pages selling their books, and the commissions paid back to the partners is a great incentive to continue selling books through Amazon.com.

Find out about the Amazon.com partner program by going to the Amazon.com home page at the following address:

```
http://www.amazon.com/
```

You can use this same strategy in promoting your own products of services. Create partnerships and pay commissions to people who promote your products. To do so correctly, you need the assistance of a network programmer. The programmer must create a program that tracks how purchasers of your online product land on your Internet site so that you can appropriately credit whoever promotes your product.

Forming partnerships certainly fits with the overall cooperative model of the Internet. Many other business models certainly can find their way successfully onto the Internet. Perhaps your ideas can create the next huge success.

Promoting Your Electronic Mailing Lists

Information is one of the hottest products going on the Internet. After all, aren't we currently in the Information Age? If information is your product, one of your most important considerations is how to distribute what you know.

One great way to distribute information is by creating an *automated mailing list* — which is nothing more than a vehicle that enables people to sign up to receive your information automatically or to participate in e-mail conversations. (See Chapter 7 for complete instructions on how to create an electronic mailing list.) More and more people subscribe to automated mailing lists every day. Some electronic mailing lists, such as the one run by Robert Seidman, have more than 15,000 subscribers.

Follow these significant ways to increase participation in your mailing list:

✔ Post messages in newsgroups about your mailing list. (If you're working with newsgroups, follow any guidelines they have for posting. Newsgroups usually post such guidelines in a newsgroup *FAQ*, which stands for Frequently Asked Question.)

✔ Mention the mailing list on your home page and tell people how to subscribe.

✔ Enter your mailing list in some of the search engines that post mailing list information.

As we mention in the preceding list of suggestions on how to promote your electronic mailing list, placing a link from your home page is one of the best ways to promote your list. You can offer a complete description of the list and provide a `mailto:` URL that enables people to send a *subscribe* e-mail message to your list server.

Entering your mailing list in a search engine doesn't guarantee that people can find your list, but doing so does increase the chances enormously. Yahoo!'s list of mailing lists is the most complete resource of electronic mailing lists on the Internet. You can begin browsing their resources at the following address:

```
http://www.yahoo.com.Computers and Internet/Internet/
            Mailing Lists/
```

Many "lists of lists" are available through the World Wide Web. Yahoo! is only one of the sources. Another significant index of mailing lists can be found at the following URL:

```
http://www.internetdatabase.com/maillist.htm
```

Many people get caught up in advertising their Web pages and forget about promoting all their other Internet resources. Getting people to subscribe to your electronic mailing lists creates an online community centered around your Internet site. Forming this type of community can prove much more valuable than simply trying to get hordes of people to see your Web page.

Remember that e-mail isn't limited to text. Your electronic mailing list can distribute full multimedia files, HTML files, or even sound files. Sending a lot of multimedia can possibly lower your list server's efficiency but certainly makes your mailing list more interesting.

Advertising Your Anonymous FTP Site

Anonymous FTP sites are wonderful places to store and share programs, information files, or other types of electronic information. If you decide to run an anonymous FTP site, you quickly find that advertising the site is simple. *Archie,* started in the late 1980s at McGill University, is a search utility that checks a database containing the filenames of files stored in anonymous FTP and Gopher sites around the world.

Adding your anonymous FTP site to the Archie database is simple. Just find the Archie server nearest you and send an e-mail message to the administrator. If you need help finding the Archie site nearest you, check out the Archie page at Yahoo!.

Figure 14-6 shows a Web-based Archie request form. Using this form, you can search an Archie database for keywords that match the names of files stored in anonymous FTP sites. If you're offering files from your anonymous FTP site, you can see the importance of registering your site in the Archie database.

You can access the NCSA Archie Request Form at the following address:

```
http://hoohoo.ncsa.uiuc.edu/archie.html
```

In addition to Archie, the University of Illinois has put together the Monster FTP Sites List. You may want to contact the university to add your site to the list. You can access the Monster FTP Sites List at NCSA's Web site at the following URL:

```
http://hoohoo.ncsa.uiuc.edu/ftp/
```

Remember to advertise your anonymous FTP site on your Web page. You can create lists of files and documents available in your FTP site with links directly to the file by using an `ftp:` URL. That way, people can download files from your anonymous FTP site by clicking a link in your Web page.

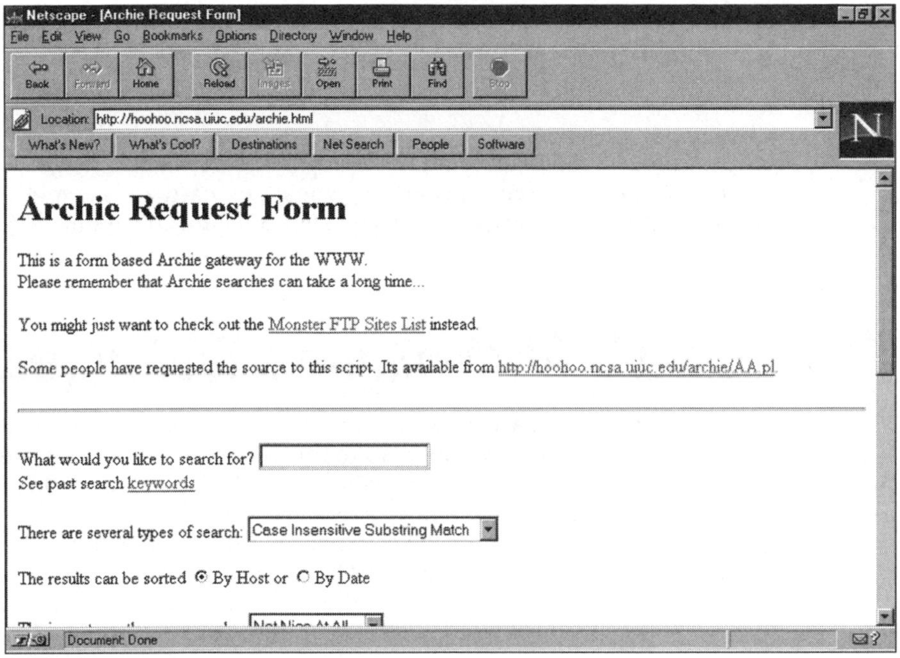

Netscape - [Archie Request Form]

File Edit View Go Bookmarks Options Directory Window Help

Back Forward Home Reload Images Open Print Find Stop

Location: http://hoohoo.ncsa.uiuc.edu/archie.html

What's New? What's Cool? Destinations Net Search People Software

Archie Request Form

This is a form based Archie gateway for the WWW.
Please remember that Archie searches can take a long time...

You might just want to check out the Monster FTP Sites List instead.

Some people have requested the source to this script. Its available from http://hoohoo.ncsa.uiuc.edu/archie/AA.pl.

What would you like to search for?
See past search keywords

There are several types of search: Case Insensitive Substring Match

The results can be sorted ⦿ By Host or ⃝ By Date

Document: Done

Figure 14-6:
You use the Archie Request Form at NCSA to find files stored in anonymous FTP sites.

Sending Electronic Postcards

Postcards don't sound very high-tech, do they? But we include a discussion of electronic postcards in this chapter because they provide a fun and interesting way to announce your Internet resources to friends, clients, and prospects.

Today, most people pay more attention to the information they receive through e-mail than they do to the mountains of paper that the postal service delivers. A nice break from the usual e-mail is an electronic post-card or greeting card. Point your Web browser to the following URL to find out how you can send electronic postcards:

```
http://postcards.www.media.mit.edu/Postcards/
```

To send a postcard, go to the electronic postcard rack at the URL we've listed and pick a card — any card. You find many different categories, including holiday cards, famous art, photographs, bug drawings, science, pictures from outer space, and more.

After you choose a card (actually a graphic), enter the e-mail address to which you want to deliver your card. (You don't actually deliver a card. Instead, you send an e-mail message to the recipient notifying that person that a postcard is waiting.) Finish creating your card by entering a private message and your name. Your card goes out as soon as you click the Submit button.

The recipient, armed with a password, can then use his Web browser to view the card you sent. Even though viewing a postcard takes longer than reading an e-mail message, receiving an electronic postcard adds something special to the communication. Whoever you sent the card to isn't likely forget that you sent it.

Physical World Promotion Techniques

Getting lost in the marketing possibilities offered by your connection to the Internet is easy. But you want also to remember some of the more conventional marketing methods, such as radio, TV, and print magazines. These days, you see URLs at the end of movie trailers, TV shows, TV commercials, and in magazine ads. People now expect to find along with these forms of communication an Internet address that takes them to a site where they can get more information. You must find out how to use the resources around you, whether through word of mouth or corporate letterhead, to promote your Internet site.

Word of mouth

Tell people you're online. You are the best marketer of your information. Gone are the days where you may need to give a lengthy description while waving your arms trying to describe the Internet or the World Wide Web to people. The Internet is now a ubiquitous part of life in North America and parts of Europe and Asia. Tell people that you have an e-mail address, a Web site, and other electronic resources that you provide online.

A side benefit to discussing your online presence with others is the fact that they discover that you keep up with the times and use the resources around you to succeed. Of course, having someone grab a pen (if the person can find one), ready some paper (other than the restaurant napkin), and then write out *h-t-t-p-:-/-/* can prove time-consuming and frustrating; by the time he's written everything down, he may have lost interest. So try combining word-of-mouth advertising with printed materials.

Printed materials

Online advertising hasn't replaced printed advertising yet; printed materials remain one of the most effective ways of telling people that you have an Internet site. Putting the URL of your site on your business card, along with your e-mail address, makes finding and contacting you online fast and simple — no one must struggle to find a pen, paper, and a place to write down your information. In fact, including your e-mail address and URL in all your printed material, such as stationery, advertisements, business cards, newsletters, brochures, and slide presentations, is always appropriate now. The following list provides some additional suggestions for advertising your Internet address:

- Run small advertisements in appropriate media.

- Add your URL and e-mail address to coffee mugs, pens, floating key chains, and other advertising specialty items.

- Add your home page URL to greeting cards. You may be surprised how much closer contact you maintain with distant associates or even family and friends from long, long ago if you keep in touch electronically. Aunt Marsha and Uncle Herb may have e-mail and a home page, too.

The telephone

The telephone remains one of the most important business tools in the world; the Internet hasn't replaced Ma Bell yet. But the problem with the phone is the fact that most people use it only to talk to people during business hours or to leave the ubiquitous voice mail. You need to take advantage of current telephone technology to direct people to your more interactive technologies. Your company's interactive voice response system (you know — the electronic voice that answers the phone) can offer electronic alternatives for customers looking for more information about your products or services. Direct them to your Internet site. You could use a recorded message such as the following example:

> "If you want further information, you can browse our World Wide Web site at [address] or download the most current specifications from our FTP site at [address]. You can also contact the sales department directly through our NetMeeting connection. Connect to [address]."

Millions of people still use the telephone to transact business, provide information, and talk with friends. No reason on Earth exists why you shouldn't take advantage of this old technology to direct people to your exciting online presence.

Chapter 15

The Next Wave

*E*veryone who's interested in the Internet wants to know what's coming next. Perhaps the most significant thing happening with the Internet is a change in the way that people access the network. Recently, WebTV made its debut in the home consumer electronics marketplace. (Check out *WebTV For Dummies* from IDG Books Worldwide, Inc.) The set-top WebTV boxes turn your television set into a Web- and e-mail-enabled communication device. A little slower coming to market are *network computers* (*NC*). Touted as the inexpensive network connection device of the future, the NC is designed more for the business customer than for the home Internet surfer.

Network computers and WebTVs are not the only things on the horizon. High-speed, dedicated connections are becoming more commonplace with DSL digital modems, cable modems, ISDN, and an increase in the number of organizations that are connected via fast telephone connections. New wireless connection options are appearing daily. First came RadioMail, a way to access your e-mail by using a wireless personal digital assistant (PDA). Now e-mail also can go directly to digital wireless telephones — small, wireless Web-access devices that enable you to surf the Net without a physical connection.

Faster hardware, wireless connectivity, and new network software standards are paving the way for the next generation of the Internet, now being called *Internet 2*.

Web Television

We're all members of the TV generation. The "boob tube" has been enter-
tainer, nanny, educator, bearer of news (both good and bad), and all-around
time-killer to the entire Baby Boom and later generations. Now this big part
of our lives can also give us access to the pastime that ranks second to the
TV in killing time: the Internet. This newest way to access the Internet
through your television set involves two components: the WebTV hardware
and software. Two companies' products have primarily pioneered this new
way to access the Internet:

- Sony's WebTV Internet Terminal
- Philips Magnavox WebTV

These two companies, Sony and Philips, provide the hardware — a set-top
box — that turns your television into a virtual Web surfboard. The set-top
box uses a modem to connect between the Internet and your TV (or to the
back of your VCR, if it's connected to the TV).

The following list describes some of the hardware that comes with a WebTV:

- **Set-top box.** This unit is the heart of your WebTV system. The box sits
  on or next to your television set and connects to the TV in a manner
  similar to that of a cable-TV set-top box.

- **Remote control.** This unit is more than your average TV remote. Details
  at 11! (Actually, later in this section.)

- **Built-in modem.** The early models include a 28.8- or 33.6-baud modem.
  Later models undoubtedly will include faster modems.

- **Infrared keyboard.** This wireless keyboard works clear across the
  room without the hassle of having wires strung everywhere. (This item
  is an optional device that makes inputting text much easier than using
  the remote control.)

- **Expansion port.** This port is for hooking up an optional printer. (The
  printer isn't included with the standard unit.)

Among the reasons that WebTV so interests so many people are its cost and
simplicity. Rather than pay a thousand-plus dollars for a computer and then
need to become somewhat of a PC expert to enjoy Internet exploration,
people can now spend just a bit more than $300 and use a TV that they
almost certainly already own, along with a very TV-like remote — items that
almost everyone is comfortable using.

WebTV brings the Internet to your home in ways that a regular PC can't. For
one thing, the set-top box optimizes the screen display for your TV, which
results in high-quality images on your TV, no matter how large a screen you

may own (see Figure 15-1). Your connection is relatively fast, too, even with a modem, because of the special compression technology that the WebTV Network provides — technology that's not available to PC users.

WebTV connects to the Internet by using a regular phone line. Installing a second line, however, probably is a good idea. Otherwise, while you connect to the Internet via your TV, your telephone can't use the line for regular phone calls (the same situation that occurs with the use of any other modem).

But how, exactly, can you surf the Web without a computer? The answer lies in the powerful WebTV remote-control unit, shown in Figure 15-2, as well as in an optional wireless infrared keyboard. The remote control can turn on your television set, act as a mouse for clicking hypertext links, and replace the normal keyboard arrow keys for moving through a Web page. You also use the remote to enter text via an on-screen keyboard. Of course, you can still purchase the optional wireless keyboard to type text, if you prefer. (You need to type text to tell WebTV what Web page you want to load, for example.)

Figure 15-1: Surf the Net on your television by using WebTV.

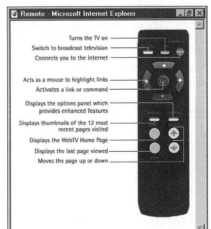

Figure 15-2: This gizmo isn't your parents' remote control.

Before you start using all this great WebTV hardware, however, you need an account with the online service that makes all this Web access possible. Most of the WebTV hardware vendors help you set up your account with WebTV Networks, Inc., the TV-based online service (see Figure 15-3).

Figure 15-3:
The WebTV Web site is your starting point on the Internet whenever you use WebTV.

With your WebTV account, you get an e-mail account and unlimited surf time on the World Wide Web. You simply pay a monthly service fee (currently, less than $20), and you get unlimited access time to your e-mail and Web accounts.

You're probably thinking, "If WebTV's so great, how come everyone isn't rushing out to get the thing?" Well, many people are. But WebTV *does* limit your access to the Internet to only e-mail and the World Wide Web. And as this book certainly points out, the Internet involves a great deal more than just surfing the Web and sending e-mail. If you use only WebTV, you can't create your own Internet site. You can, of course, use different Internet accounts to access other Internet services and run your own Internet site and still use WebTV for your evening Web surfing from the couch.

Another downside of current WebTV is the fact that the devices don't support many of the new features that make the Web exciting, such as Java and ActiveX. WebTV is almost certain to add these features soon (otherwise, WebTV isn't going to be around much longer), but for now, you can forget about them on your TV screen.

Network Computers

If you need the power of a computer, full access to the Internet and all its applications, and still don't want the cost and complexity of a personal computer, you can try the *network computer,* now called simply the *NC.*

Spinning Web pages for WebTV

WebTV is among the first new technologies to access the World Wide Web outside the world of computers. Because television sets display graphics differently from computer monitors, however, Web pages appear differently on TV than they do on your computer.

First, you must understand that people who are viewing your Web pages on a computer sit an average of 18 to 20 inches from their monitors. People who are surfing the Web on their TVs usually sit 10 or more feet away.

The makers of WebTV changed a few of the defaults for their devices, such as the type size and font style that you see on-screen. Conventional computer-based Web browsers use Times New Roman as the default font style, whereas WebTV uses the clean, straight-lined look of a sans-serif font.

Furthermore, the WebTV system now compresses screen size — a minimum 640 pixels across on a computer monitor — to only 560 pixels on your TV screen. This change is important to keep in mind, because WebTV does not support horizontal scrolling. Any text or graphics that extends beyond 560 pixels doesn't appear on a visitor's TV screen. And if you want everything to appear on a single page, without the WebTV visitor's needing to scroll up or down, you must keep the height of your image to fewer than 378 vertical pixels.

Early versions of WebTV don't support some of the features that Web pages commonly use, such as frames, Java, JavaScript and VBScript, and ActiveX controls. If the WebTV system encounters any of these features, it ignores them. If you include these features in your Web page, they either don't show up or don't work as you'd hope. Other features, such as image maps (pictures with "hot spot" areas you can click to navigate to other Web pages), don't always work in WebTV. You need to set up alternative ways for people who use WebTV to reach some specific Web content on your page if you use an image map.

Some television-specific suggestions can help you set up your Web page for maximum appearance on WebTV, as follow:

- Use fat horizontal lines on your page, because thin lines don't appear well on a TV set.

- Use dark background colors, avoiding white and red (because those colors distort).

- Keep your pages simple and graphical. Too much text bores the TV viewer quickly.

If you find these recommendations to be restrictive, consider creating more than one Web-page design. By setting up your Web server to detect what browser type a visitor is using to access your page, you can provide WebTV content only to WebTV viewers. Check out the Web site at http://www.webtv.net for more information on WebTV-specific HTML tags.

Oracle Corporation, long known for its high-end database-management system, was one of the early proponents of a low-cost information appliance. Network Computer, Inc., is the company that now develops this early NC (see Figure 15-4).

Figure 15-4:
The
network
computer
(NC) is a
low-cost
way to
access the
Internet.

You can find out more about Network Computer, Inc., on the company's home page at the following URL:

```
http://www.nc.com/
```

Benefits of NCs

At first, no one was certain that the NC idea would catch on. Following are some of the arguments against NCs that you may hear even today:

- ✔ "Why buy a $500 network computer if I can get the full power of a PC for only $1,000?"
- ✔ "If I'm running off the network, my applications are sure to run slowly."

Network computers are certainly simpler to set up and run, with no application software to install. And you never need to worry about upgrading your software, as you should be able to run the latest version over the Net. Network administrators love network computers because they no longer need to worry about remote administration hassles. The NC boots from the network, completely configuring itself from software stored on network servers.

You often hear that applications running over a network run more slowly than they do on a PC, because instead of storing programs locally (as a PC does on its hard drive), the network computer loads applications from a server over the Internet. This efficiency downside does indeed exist, but the advantages of the NC approach are many (and they far outweigh the disadvantages), as follow:

- ✔ You never need to install another piece of software.

- ✔ Your software never becomes outdated (as long as the server from which you load your software keeps up to date).

- ✔ You don't need to worry about running out of hard disk space while you're loading new software.

- ✔ The owner of the server handles all your backups automatically. (You *do* back up your files, don't you?) The sad fact, however, is that few people back up their files sufficiently. This automatic-backup capability, therefore, is a really nice feature of network computing.

- ✔ A *SmartCard* that plugs into the network computer gives users secure access to the Internet. Every person who uses the network computer has a unique SmartCard that he inserts into the NC.

- ✔ You don't suffer all the configuration hassles that you currently experience if you use someone else's computer to access your Internet account; the SmartCard automatically configures the NC to access your personal account. The card itself is not a computer card, but appears more like a credit card or ATM card.

Thin is better

I doubt whether Jenny Craig had anything to do with the network computer, but network computers *have* entered the world of fat versus thin. Network computers, however, aren't PCs on Slimfast. PCs are known as *fat clients,* which merely means that applications running in a network environment both reside and run locally on the PC. *Thin clients,* on the other hand, are computers such as NCs (and even some PCs) that load programs from the network and run the programs without saving them locally.

As we mentioned in the preceding section (and mention again here), among the advantages of using a thin client are that you never need to install programs, you always load the latest version of the program, and you don't necessarily need to load each part of an application from the same server.

Concerning this last advantage, one part of your application may come from one company, whereas others come from different companies entirely — all via the network. The advantage of this application model is that the individual users can customize their applications to use the features that best meet their own needs. If, say, Ebonics actually becomes a recognized language in school districts throughout the country, vendors can make electronic Ebonics spell checkers available on the network instantly.

The NC OS

Network computers, because they're small and efficient, use small, specially designed operating systems. Two of the big competitors for the NC operating system are JavaOS (the Java operating system) and Microsoft Windows CE (*Consumer Electronics*).

Network computers such as Sun Microsystem's JavaStation use JavaOS (of course). JavaStation (see Figure 15-5) is a complete, powerful thin client, complete with Sun's Web browser, HotJava; administration tools; and DHCP (Dynamic Host Configuration Protocol), which the JavaStation uses for configuring during bootup.

Windows CE, formerly code-named Pegasus, is a 32-bit operating system designed for more than just network computers. Complete with a special version of the Internet Explorer browser, Windows CE runs on many small devices, such as those in the following list:

✔ Hand-held PCs.

✔ Wallet PCs.

✔ Wireless communication devices, such as digital information pagers and cellular smart phones (up-and-coming digital phones that can run programs).

✔ Next-generation entertainment and multimedia devices, including Digital Video Disk (DVD) players .

✔ Internet "Web phones." You can now make telephone calls over the Internet by using several different software packages, a sound card, and a microphone. Phone manufacturers are even creating phones that can communicate over the Internet. Two popular programs are Internet Phone (www.vocaltec.com) and NetMeeting (www.microsoft.com).

Figure 15-5:
JavaStation
uses the
Java
operating
system.

You can't run just any Windows program on Windows CE, however. Someone must write special programs to run in these small-device environments. Expect to wait a while until plenty of useful programs are available for use in this operating system.

If you choose to use a device running Windows CE or JavaOS, you can also expect to wait a while before anyone writes applications that make these devices truly useful tools. Giving up your PC now also means giving up many of your current productivity tools.

Internet Access

No more modems? Before long, the ubiquitous modem screech may be gone forever. New types of connectivity are quickly replacing conventional modems. Yes, modem speeds today are cranking up to 56 Kbps — but what's 56,000 (kilo) bits per second if cable modems can give you transmission speeds in the tens of millions of bits (megabits) per second? Some high-end network devices, such as ATM (Asynchronous Transfer Mode), are facilitating transmission in the billions of bits (gigabits) per second. Downloads that once took hours are now measured in tenths of a second.

@Home

Super-fast dedicated Internet connectivity is now available through your cable-TV connection. Using both fiber optics and cable-TV cables that are already in the ground, @Home (if you had @Home, you'd be there by now) is part of a high-speed network called *HFC* (for hybrid fiber-optic coaxial).

@Home currently is available through only a few cable providers, including TCI, Cox, Comcast, and Intermedia. Visit the @Home Web site at the following address:

```
http://www.athome.net
```

While visiting this site, you can enter your information in a form to find out when cable Internet access is going to be available in your area. We bet you can hardly wait.

Oops, did we say *wait?* You may never need to wait again. According to @Home, a 2MB file that takes more than 9 minutes to download over a 28.8 Kbps phone modem takes fewer than 2 seconds over cable.

To use this service, your computer needs a special modem called a *cable modem*. Instead of connecting to a phone line, your cable modem connects to the same cable that you now use to receive cable-TV programming. By the way, you can still get your favorite cable TV programming at the same time you're using the Internet. The network traffic does not interfere with the TV signal on the cable.

You can get the cable modems from your cable provider. The cable company may even help you install the modem. They cost just about the same as other modems. (They run you around $200.)

@Work

So your Internet connection at home is flying, now that your computer's hooked to the cable that once brought you reruns of "Gilligan's Island." What about that poky Internet connection at work? If you're like us, your company is blessed with a T-1 connection. That type of connection is a little expensive, but hardly anything works like a good T-1 connection to make your hours on the Internet more productive — hardly anything, that is, until you can get cable-modem access to the Internet at work. Most local-area networks operate at a speed of 10MB per second. The @Home and @Work network provides you this access speed directly to the Internet.

If your company provides telecommuting options to its employees, using @Work from home enables you to access a corporate network at the same speed as a directly connected computer.

One important thing to keep in mind: The @Work network is optimized for data, not for video or music. If teleconferencing is part of your telecommuting plans, you may want to check with @Home before signing up.

DirecPC (satellite)

No cable? No problem. DirecPC can bring the Internet to you via satellite at 400 Kbps per second (more than three times faster than ISDN). Yep, once the gateway to pay-per-view boxing and hard-to-get TV programming, the satellite now dishes out Web pages as well.

To get started with DirecPC either at home or at work, make sure that your home or office building has a clear line of sight to the south and is capable of handling a 21-inch satellite dish (about the size of a large pizza box). You also need a Pentium PC and an Internet Service Provider. Sorry, but DirecPC does not support DOS, Macintosh, UNIX, or Windows 3.1 (or earlier). In other words, you must use Windows 95 or Windows NT.

If you order the DirecPC service, you get the dish and everything that goes with it: the software, the cable to connect the 21-inch dish to your computer, and a card that goes into your computer.

Note: You need one free ISA slot for the card. Check the manual for your PC to see whether it supports ISA expansion slots. Many new computers support only PCI expansion slots.

DirecPC is not for the Internet addict. In addition to the normal Internet Service Provider fee, DirecPC charges a basic monthly fee, plus about 80 cents per megabyte of data transferred. So if you download a 7MB file, that transfer costs you about $5.50.

Building Extranets

Caterpillar Corporation has been moving stuff around successfully for a long time. So when the folks at Caterpillar needed to move data, they didn't fool around. Caterpillar is now involved in one of the greatest experiments in Internet commerce ever: the InfoTEST Enhanced Product Realization (or EPR) Manufacturing Extranet. Caterpillar became involved in this experiment to help reduce response time on customer-requested product modifications.

Chapter 13, which discusses electronic commerce, introduces the idea that electronic commerce is more than selling things on the Internet. Linking all the companies within a *commerce chain* (that is, manufacturers, parts vendors, shippers, and distributors), along with their customers, into a single, secure network builds capabilities for increasing service heretofore unknown in the world of commerce.

This type of network, which you create on the Internet but make available only to members of the commerce chain, is called an *extranet*. The EPR Manufacturing Extranet is an example of this type of commerce chain, consisting of companies that are physically located around the globe. The Caterpillar extranet includes more than a dozen companies in its commerce chain.

Creating extranets is not a difficult task. All the technology necessary to make extranet commerce chains, such as those that InfoTEST is creating, is available today. For this type of network to become a commonplace reality, however, a shift must occur in the mental image of how organizations work together. Peter Senge, author of the popular book *The Fifth Discipline* (published by Doubleday), describes the type of cooperation that's necessary if companies want to remain competitive and successful in the near future. People can no longer run companies without feeling as though they're part of a larger system or organism. Each company — and each person in each company — is now an integral part of the much larger commerce chain.

Creating software that enables the simple, secure sharing of information enhances the capability to create such commerce chains. The development of, say, a distributed accounting system — one in which portions of the same accounting system reside in each of the members of the chain — should simplify accounting dramatically.

Imagine a system in which you never wonder where your orders are or whether you're going to get paid. Your accounting system can become integrally tied to the accounting systems of everyone else in the chain. Purchase orders log in on one system at the same time that someone creates them in another system. Invoices, shipping documents, and orders no longer flow between systems or even through a system; they're all part of a single networked, distributed information system. This type of system is the future of commerce. Organizations that create products for this type of system can expect to remain — or become — successful.

For more information about what InfoTEST is doing, point your Web browser to the following URL:

```
http://www.infotest.com/
```

To find out more about the work of Peter Senge, check out the following address:

```
http://learning.mit.edu/
```

Look, Ma, No Wires!

Mobility is one of the attributes of 21st-century people. Everyone's on the move. Cellular phones, new digital PCS phones, Specialized Mobile Radio (SMR), personal digital assistants (PDAs), Global Positioning Systems (GPSs), pagers, message watches, and palm-top computers are only some of the ways in which people stay in touch with one another, know where others are in the world, and remain connected.

Social issues that go beyond the scope of this book drive the need for wireless connectivity. The world now requires nearly instantaneous responses on issues ranging from global politics to global commerce. Knowledge becomes accessible as people carry the means of education around with them, so that lifelong learning becomes daylong learning.

Wireless technology reaches the public in many ways. Many communications satellites go into orbit every year, and a global cellular telephone system is soon to become a reality. But satellites are only one way to deliver wireless technology. Radio technology continues to grow, moving from analog telephony to digital standards for delivering data, such as CDPD (Cellular Digital Packet Data). By using CDPD, you can run standard IP-based network applications via a wireless connection.

Currently, speed is one of the limiting factors in wireless technology. Microwave wireless networks run at 10 Mbps Ethernet speeds but currently can't handle some of the faster 100 Mbps Ethernet speeds that many organizations now use. Radio modems can transmit and receive data at speeds up to 28.8 Kbps — last year's modem speeds. But now, with analog modems running at speeds of 56.6 Kbps, and with the arrival of new technologies such as ADSL and cable modems, 28.8 Kbps seems pretty slow. (*ADSL,* by the way, is a new high-speed modem that can deliver a throughput of greater than 2 Mbps across a phone line.)

Compression technologies, such as those that you use in audio and video compression, must improve so that effective bandwidth on wireless connections can increase. A company called Wireless Connect is creating a client/server architecture that enables you to use standard Internet protocols efficiently across wireless networks. The company has added intelligent compression (its product is called Venturi) to everyday Internet protocols such as HTTP, FTP, and SMTP. This compression/decompression of Internet traffic can increase speeds and lower the load on existing wireless and landline-based circuits.

For more information about Wireless Connect and its work, contact the company at the following URL:

```
http://www.wirelessip.net/
```

Wireless communications not only are here to stay, but they're also quickly becoming important to communications all around the world. Many countries have skipped the implementation of a wired phone system to opt for wireless communications. New technologies enable us to make better use of the wireless frequency spectrum, enabling more and more devices to use these frequencies. With more satellites, more radio receivers, and better communications hardware, wireless technologies continue to grow, becoming a more important part of our everyday lives.

Part V
The Part of Tens

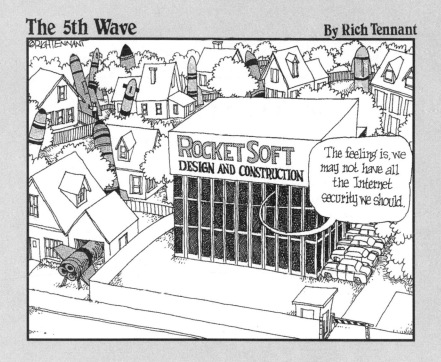

In this part . . .

This part of the book is the most fun. The Part of Tens chapters highlight ten things that we thought you'd like to know about but that didn't fit anywhere else in the book. Among these are ten Internet services you can't live without. Running a killer Internet site means using tools that make it simple. The better your tools are, the better your site becomes. Finally, this part has ten technology add-ons you can add to your site.

Chapter 16

Ten Trends in the Interactive Global Village

*T*he Internet of today is still a confusing environment for many people. The World Wide Web and e-mail — Internet programs that are simple for most people to use — remain a mystery behind the scenes, much like the great of Wizard of Oz. Just about everyone now recognizes the potential of the Internet. Realizing the potential of the Net, however, does not always mean knowing what to do with it. Creating the future of the Internet is transforming the future of communications.

Everyone says that the Internet is a major force of social change, but where's the proof? Endless Internet hype is overwhelming — not to mention annoying. We wanted to know exactly why the Internet is supposed to change everything, so we looked for good examples and convincing reasons. The following sections present a few trends that impress us.

Science on the Internet

The Internet has its roots in the scientific and research communities. Expanded communications and collaboration tools have increased the speed at which information disseminates in these communities. Scientists and science students are realizing truly remarkable advantages from the Internet.

One resource that has been in the news lately is The Visible Human Project, a large set of digital images that displays every detail of human anatomy, 1 millimeter at a time. You can access the project, which includes both male and female anatomy, at the following URL:

```
http://www.nlm.nih.gov/research/visible/visible_human.html
```

To science, The Visible Human Project represents the opportunity to incorporate a precise electronic anatomy model into all kinds of biological research. Now programmers can write new software, giving researchers around the world an interactive biology laboratory in which they can conduct endless experiments. Only the capabilities of the computers and software involved limit the potential of such an interactive biology lab.

Another exciting Internet science project involves astronomy. The Hubble Space Telescope has helped renew interest in astronomy, but its effect is much more significant now because of NASA's use of the Internet. Via NASA's Web site, you can download astrophotographs taken by the Hubble, sometimes within hours of their transmission back to Earth. The NASA Web site is located at the following URL:

```
http://www.nasa.gov/
```

Interactive Shopping

The Internet Shopping Network (at `http://www.internet.net/`) is reporting a significant increase in sales, primarily because of shoppers from outside the United States. This trend makes a great deal of sense, if you think about it. Although many Americans live just around the corner from a physical shopping mall, people in other countries (especially developing ones) don't have this luxury; their shopping options are severely limited. The Internet Shopping Network offers an excellent solution to their problem.

Along with enabling retailers to reach the overseas market, the Internet is proving to be an excellent sales vehicle for retailers that offer unique or specialty items. If a product is hard to find in the real world, the Internet is the place to sell that item. In fact, specialty retailers generated impressive sales even before the Web offered security features. People who wanted to purchase specialty or hard-to-find items were willing to take the chance that a hacker may intercept their credit-card numbers; more often, they found alternative ways to make their payments.

A new technology called digital ID (which we describe in detail in Chapter 11) promises to make Internet shopping as simple as clicking the ad for the product that you want to buy. Expect Web browsers such as Netscape's

Navigator and Microsoft's Internet Explorer to soon supply customers' digital IDs (if they have those IDs) to merchants automatically after those customers decide to make a purchase. This type of setup means that you no longer need to fill out a long form and type your credit-card number each time you make a purchase.

Online Advertising

If you create an Internet site that includes online sales, you're going to be confronted with two specific areas of concern: advertising and selling. Advertising and purchasing are going to become interactive, with sales generated instantly if you place the right ad in front of the consumer at just the right time.

Network agents

In the future, your customers are likely to use personal network agents that can filter out ads that don't interest them. The network agents that are being developed can describe customers' interests and buying habits to automated advertising generators so that these programs can dynamically create ads to appeal to a specific customer. You want to stay abreast of agent technology so that you can make maximal use of this technology to further target your customer base.

Credit checks

The new intelligent advertising-generation programs may have access to credit ratings and the current bank-account balances of the customers who are viewing your advertising. More likely, your Internet commerce site is going to access an Internet credit agency that doesn't reveal confidential information but does track (and score) the purchasing habits of your potential customer.

This type of automatic credit checker may be a little scary to the average consumer, providing personalized and targeted advertising at the expense of consumer privacy. As the developer of an online store, you must weigh the pros and cons of using such a system.

No matter what happens, Internet shopping is certain to have a unifying effect on global society. Currency differences have no meaning on the Internet, and for the first time, the shopping experience is identical no matter where you live.

Access to Government

Another trend that is certain to develop in the future is a set of Internet tools that changes the way in which U.S. citizens interact with their representatives. Through the Internet, voters can inform elected officials of their opinions, as well as track officials' performance through voting records and multimedia political archives. Keeping abreast of government activity can become simple, and real facts about government actions may be available at everyone's convenience.

Ideally, the cumulative effect of these changes is going to be positive. Interactive Internet government presents the possibility of a more accessible governing process that could revolutionize the way that government officials and the governed relate to one another.

Virtual Communities

Another exciting development is the emergence of virtual communities. Entire towns are organizing to establish a presence on the Internet.

Electronic villages

The city of Blacksburg, Virginia, for example, worked in cooperation with Virginia Tech to create the Blacksburg Electronic Village. You can visit this impressive creation at the following address:

```
http://www.bev.net/
```

Clearly, the electronic village has helped bring the people of Blacksburg together, even though they clearly were very "together" to begin with.

Internet coffee shops

Another interesting trend in community development is the emergence of Internet coffee shops. These establishments, which are appearing in all parts of the world, offer Internet access along with a hot cup of java and a friendly atmosphere. Internet coffee shops are a great way to build real-world relationships surrounding the Internet.

The desire to associate and conduct business within our own communities seems to be human nature. Becoming part of the online community can bring about the same sense of camaraderie and, with it, trust, relationships, and business. As in any community, the responsible store owners are the ones who help shape the neighborhood.

Recently, some people have discussed the possible harmful effects of the Internet on cultures — how the Internet may work to water down or homogenize cultures around the world. True, the Internet may influence languages, which have long separated cultures, to grow more similar or possibly even merge into a single global language. But the capability to communicate with people in other cultures, as we now can do through the Internet, can work to maintain diversity by sharing the unique aspects of those cultures with all people who have online access.

We also hear the ridiculous statement that the Internet, in reducing the diversity of the global community, may wipe out the incentive for creativity. We believe quite the opposite: The Internet acts as a place to share diverse ideas, spawning new creativity.

Virtual Workplaces

You may already be one of the millions of Americans who telecommute. If so, you know how significantly telecommuting changes your life. Although you may still be employed by a company, you're empowered to create your own work environment and develop your own work habits. This opportunity can be challenging, but the rewards are well worth the extra initial effort required to get your bearings and develop good telecommuting skills.

The benefit of telecommuting to companies is also significant. Studies have shown that worker productivity increases if management puts effective telecommuting practices into place. Telecommuting has become such a mainstream and important effort that even the State of California's transportation department, CalTrans, is researching ways to implement telecommuting practices in California companies. Recently, the idea of a paperless office has engaged the imaginations of companies everywhere. According to *Wired* magazine, however, the hype about the paperless office is over; now companies are excited about the idea of an officeless office.

As you may expect, the growth of the Internet is adding momentum to the telecommuting movement. One of the barriers to effective Internet telecommuting is the lack of a file-transfer standard for the Internet. Working with other people via the Internet is difficult without a simple way to share computer files, such as spreadsheets and word-processing documents. This situation is bound to change soon, as a new Internet file-transfer service becomes available. Watch our site for more information (at the following address):

```
http://www.science.org/internetsite/
```

Internet Programming

Internet software is no more difficult to build than traditional software is, and anyone who has computer programming experience can build these programs. We've watched Internet programming evolve from laboratory experiment to corporate technology to its current Web-oriented phase, and we see its future in Internet broadcasting. Developments in Internet programming technology are sure to become some of the most important keys to the future of the Internet and to the world that the Net helps create. Many companies have products that make Internet programming simple and fun. Macromedia's Backstage product, for example, helps you create powerful Web-based database applications. Check out the following URL for more information:

```
http://www.macromedia.com/
```

Some other Internet programming technologies, such as Java and ActiveX, have made network-application development a reality for almost any programmer and removed such work from the arcane world of the UNIX gurus. For more information about ActiveX, you can visit the Microsoft home page at the following URL or find more information on the science.org Web site:

```
http://www.microsoft.com/
```

Anyone setting up an Internet site needs to become familiar with Java and find out more about some of the exciting standards that are going to change how software communicates. For more information on Java, point your Web browser to the following address:

```
http://java.sun.com/
```

Chapter 17

Ten Internet Services Your Internet Site Can't Live Without

* *

In This Chapter

▶ Increasing access to your Web page

▶ Making a little money with your Web page

▶ Participating in a Webring community

▶ Spiffing up your Web page by adding some extra services

▶ Delivering goods online

* *

*T*his book covers many details about getting your site online, setting up the software to provide services, marketing your site after you're online, and more. Now is our chance to tell you about some of the services on the Internet that we think you're going to love using, just as we do.

Link Exchange

You've seen banner ads gracing thousands of Web pages. The cost of some of those ads can be astronomical. But what if you could place your banner ad on tens of thousands of Web pages for free? Well, you can do that *almost* for free, through Link Exchange, which is one of the most valuable services on the Internet because the service is a barter arrangement. You agree to place banner ads on your page that the Link Exchange provides, and for every two times someone views the Web page on which you place the ad, your banner ad appears on the Web page of another Link Exchange participant.

The great thing about the way the service works is that the more people who visit your page, the more your ad appears on other people's Web pages. The thing can really snowball. By using Link Exchange, you can easily keep track of how many people visit your pages, how many people click your banner ad to visit your page, and how many times your banner appears on other Web pages. Using Link Exchange is fun and costs you nothing.

Link Exchange gives you a special ID, which tells Link Exchange when some-one loads a banner from your page. Apply for this ID at the following URL:

```
http://www.linkexchange.com/
```

Commonwealth Network

The idea of bartering banner ads, as you do in Link Exchange, is useful and interesting but does not generate any income. Commonwealth Network, on the other hand, actually pays you for running banner ads. Check out the Network's Web site at the following URL:

```
http://commonwealth.riddler.com/
```

Add to your Web page the HTML that you get from Commonwealth to load a new banner ad from Commonwealth Network, and each time someone visits your page Commonwealth records the visit. You get paid each time a unique host visits your page within a 24-hour period. (In other words, if the same host visits five times in a single day, you get paid for one visit; if the same host visits once each day for a week, you get paid for seven visits.)

For each 20,000 paid hits to your Web page, you earn about $150. On high-volume sites, you can earn up to $20,000 a month, and even on lower-volume sites, you sometimes can pay your monthly Internet fee with the money that you earn.

The company that runs the Commonwealth Network, Interactive Imagina-tions, pays royalties monthly. Make sure that you read all the rules before you sign up.

Because of large demand, the Commonwealth Network sometimes closes its membership application. If you're excited about the possibility of having your Web site make money and don't want to wait, consider the Internet Banner Network (at `http://www.banner-net.com/`) This network pays only a third of what Commonwealth pays but is another option.

Webrings Keep Visitors Coming Back

If cyberspace is truly an online community, it could use some community planning. That's exactly what an online organization called Webring is attempting to do: bring organization to some of the content on the World Wide Web. If you use this new organizational structure for Web pages, your site can become part of an Internet community instead of just one more page in someone's directory.

Webring is a ring of Internet sites and Web pages that have a common theme or similar content. If you click a Next or Previous link in one Web page in the ring, you travel to a different page. If you click long enough, you return to the page from which you started.

Instead of managing the links in a ring manually, Webring manages a database of rings on the Webring site at `webring.org`. That way, if someone leaves or joins the ring, no one must change the HTML on any Web pages. The ring and all associated changes are completely managed by Webring.

No limits exist to the size or number of rings that you can form in Webring. You can create your own ring or join an existing ring. Hundreds of rings, on just about any topic that you can imagine, await you.

Visit the Webring site at the following URL:

```
http://www.webring.org
```

Like many services on the Internet, Webring is a free service, supported through sponsorships.

The Amazon.com Associates Program

Wanna buy a book? `Amazon.com` is a huge online bookstore, offering more than a million titles available for purchase online. `Amazon.com` maintains an excellent site that offers descriptions of each book, plus some reviews and even interviews with the authors. What makes the company stand out in our minds isn't so much the fact that it has a successful online bookstore as the fact that it has an interesting business model — one that you can take advantage of.

Just about everyone has a favorite book. Why not try selling that book from your Web page? `Amazon.com` makes this task simple. Instead of setting up everything that you need to become an online bookstore yourself, you can become an `Amazon.com` associate. For every book that you sell through your Web page, you're paid a referral fee. With a catalog of more than a million titles at your disposal, however, you can do more than just recommend your favorite book; you can also promote books that support your industry or special-interest organization. That way, you provide an excellent service to people who visit your Internet site.

To become an `Amazon.com` associate, fill out the application form at the following URL:

```
http://www.amazon.com/exec/obidos/subst/assoc-
    application.html
```

You begin earning referral fees for sales that you generate through your links. Every week, you get an update that tells you what links people clicked, how many people clicked links, how many books were sold through your site, and (the best part) how much money you earned.

VeriFone Moves Money

Three distinct parties are involved in the Internet sales transaction of the future: the merchant, the customer, and the acquirer/processor. The *merchant* is anyone who has an Internet application, such as a Web page, with a catalog of goods or services to sell. The *customer,* who wants to buy something from the vendor's catalog of goods or services, either enters information in a Web form or uses a special electronic wallet. Where else would you keep electronic money other than in an electronic wallet? Then a bank or other processor of credit-card information (known as an *acquirer* or *processor*) processes the transaction. The acquirer/processor with which the vendor has a merchant account debits the credit card and pays the vendor.

We present this scenario so that you can better understand the products that VeriFone offers for completing the entire electronic purchase transaction. This transaction involves the following three products:

- ✔ **vGate.** Banks or providers of merchant credit-card processing use this software.

- ✔ **vPOS.** Internet merchants use this point-of-sale software for selling their products online.

- ✔ **vWallet.** A customer who wants to purchase something online can use this software. The vWallet software can process the transaction by using a variety of methods, including credit cards and smart cards.

For someone who is setting up his own Internet site, the vPOS software is important. Products such as Microsoft's Merchant Server and Oracle's Project Apollo incorporate the vPOS software today, and some version of vPOS is likely to end up on just about every Internet site in the world at some point.

If you're getting into the online sales business, you should know that conventional businesses pay a smaller discount fee on credit-card transactions — around 1.65 percent less than online businesses. Unfortunately for the online businesses, most acquirer/processors consider them to be high-risk, and make them pay fees of between 5 percent and 6 percent.

Extra! Extra! Read All about It!

According to Individual, Inc., the company that runs NewsPage, you have two excellent ways to create a high-traffic Web site. One way is to provide highly relevant, useful information to your Web site's visitors; the other way is to keep updating your information frequently so that people want to visit your site again. NewsPage gives you a hand both in providing the content and keeping it updated automatically. Nothing's better than a Web page that updates itself every day with the latest pertinent information.

To find out how you can become part of NewsPage, point your Web browser to the following URL:

```
http://www.newspage.com/
```

Some people say that no news is good news. We find that adding news to our page increases the number of people who visit our page on a regular basis. Adding such news is also an excellent way to provide meaningful content with a minimal amount of effort.

Keeping Track of Your Guests

So you're not a programmer, and you think that the letters *CGI* mean "Can't get interested"? You can offer visitors to your Web page all sorts of services that require no CGI (Common Gateway Interface) programming whatsoever. One of the features that many people like to add to their Web pages is a guestbook for people to sign.

Think of a guestbook as being something like an answering machine. If people call you on the phone, and no one is home to answer, you'll never know who called. The same is true of your Web page. Sure, your Web server can give you the IP address of everyone who visits your home page, but having that information is not the same as knowing exactly who was there.

You can add this nice implementation of a programming-free guestbook to your Web page. You can find the instructions for using the guestbook on the GuestPAD Web site at the following address:

```
http://www.GuestPAD.com/
```

Testing Your Web Pages

Few things are more laborious and time-consuming than maintaining Web pages. If you have many Web pages, you can spend more time maintaining the pages than you do creating new, interesting content. We found a solution to this problem: Doctor HTML. You can use the program at the Doctor HTML site to test your Web page automatically. You can access Doctor HTML at the following URL:

```
http://www2.imagiware.com/RxHTML/
```

Doctor HTML performs all available tests by default. If you don't want the Doctor's entire bagful of tests, select only the tests that you want it to perform. While choosing which tests you want the Doctor to perform, you can choose the amount of detail that you want Doctor HTML to display in its final report.

Doctor HTML can also test your entire Web site. This test is a fee-based service that first maps your site and then runs tests on each page of the site. Contact the folks at Imagiware, Inc., for more information about this pay service.

Beyond the Simple Counter

PAGECOUNT is a service that Web International offers. If you don't mind having a banner ad on your page, you can receive free counter and Web-statistics services from the company. Most counters merely count the number of people who visit your page. This service gives you all the great statistics that you'd expect from a full-blown Web-statistics package. True, many Web-statistics packages are available. In using those statistics packages, however, you must make sure that your logs are up to date, remember to run the statistics program regularly, and then wait while the program chugs through the numbers. You don't need any of these things if you use PAGECOUNT.

The banner that appears on your page displays the count of accesses. By the way, you can start the count at any number you want (to avoid embarrassment if you're just starting out). Changing the start number doesn't affect your statistics; PAGECOUNT still keeps an accurate count of the true total.

To start using this service, access the PAGECOUNT home page at the following address:

```
http://www.pagecount.com/
```

NetDelivery Service

Electronic online delivery is quickly becoming one of the most exciting businesses on the Internet. By using the publish-and-subscribe model, companies have started offering many types of content delivery on the Internet.

One of the services that we find particularly interesting is NetDelivery. This Colorado-based (actually, Internet-based) Internet company offers a unique service, both to Internet site operators who need to deliver products or information over the Internet and to NetDelivery's customers (who are called *members*).

You can find the NetDelivery Web site at the following address:

```
http://www.netdelivery.com/
```

This service is perfect for you if your Internet site provides content, merchandise, or information services. Your clients don't need to come to your site to fetch their data; you can deliver the information right to their desktops, daily, weekly, or monthly by using the NetDelivery service.

NetDelivery is a young company, and we expect it to eventually have a lot of competition on the Internet. The field of online delivery offers a great deal of opportunity. You may even consider providing this sort of service yourself.

Chapter 18

Ten Technology Add-ons for Your Site

*M*ost Internet sites provide the same old set of server software as part of their Internet presence. You get the Web server, the e-mail server, the FTP server, the list server, and the news server — and then what? After all, you can't just paint your Internet site a different color and give the site a red tile roof to make it look distinctive. The services that you offer are what make your site distinctive. But not all services that you offer are for the sake of visitors to your site. Remember that your Internet site also provides Internet access and services for others in your organization. The first technology add-on that we describe in this chapter, for example, enables people to provide their own services right from their desktops.

The Internet Utopia

Netopia Virtual Office, a Farallon product, is one of the new ways to communicate with people on the Internet or on your local intranet. All you need is a Web browser. In addition to collaboration capabilities, the product enables you to create your own World Wide Web address.

Find more about Netopia software at the following URL:

```
http://www.netopia.com
```

Conferencing

What office doesn't have a conference room? The Internet enables you to conference with many people across the world by using Microsoft's NetMeeting software. The Netopia software works with NetMeeting to provide such services as a shared whiteboard (much like the one you scribble on in your office, except that it's electronic and on the computer), application sharing, and Internet telephony. With these features and the inherent power of Netopia's screen sharing, messaging, and simple file sharing, you could hardly ask for a more powerful office tool.

Using the Voice Chat feature is simple, but you must have a compatible sound card and microphone. (We find that using a high-quality microphone helps the quality of the conversation.)

To have two-way, telephonelike conversations, you need a special full-duplex sound card. *Full-duplex* communications enable people at both ends of the conversation to speak and listen at the same time (as they can on a telephone).

A quieter type of chat — text chat — is available. This option enables two people to communicate by typing text. You enter the text and then transmit it to the other party every time you press the Enter key or click the Send button. After your text appears on-screen, your name appears before the text.

Digital Camera

A picture may be worth a thousand words, but today, pictures are measured in bytes. Almost all the major camera manufacturers are coming out with digital cameras. Depending on how much you want to spend, you can get digital pictures that rival the finest film. Whether you have a high or low budget, you can find a digital camera that captures images without the hassles of film and development (and, ultimately, scanning the developed print into your computer).

One of the highest-quality, most-affordable digital cameras is the Dakota DCC-9500. To find out more about this cool digital camera, call 800-52-FOCUS and tell the people who answer that you just read about the Dakota in this book.

We like this camera because it comes with a motorized zoom feature, automatic focus, a built-in flash, and a PC-card memory-expansion slot. If you expect to take a significant number of pictures, you can purchase memory-expansion modules to increase the camera's memory capacity.

Flatbed Scanner

Scanners have been around for years and now come in all shapes and sizes. Little photo scanners can scan 4×6-inch color photographs; Paperport scanners take up little room on your desk and can quickly scan black-and-white documents. The flatbed scanner, however, is still the most versatile and useful of all the scanner types.

Most flatbed scanners can scan larger document sizes (11×14 inches) than can other scanners and have higher scanning resolutions. The other advantage of flatbed scanners is that, if you're going to do a great deal of scanning, you can purchase automatic sheet feeders for the devices. This addition can make scanning multiple-page documents a snap.

Stereo Mixer and Microphone

Sound is becoming a common technology on the Internet. Simple text and graphics are being replaced by an audio-media type that is just as important as visual media (as radio has shown us). People now use more than one technology to present sound over networks. Many people still use historical means of providing sound by capturing sounds in a sound file and then publishing the file (the same way that they publish any other file type) for others to download and hear.

The quality of the sound recording is directly proportional to the resulting file size: The better the quality of the recording, the larger the file's size. Users frown on large file sizes because of their long download times, however, so few people consider sound quality to be important.

Then someone introduced a second technology into the sound publishing arena: *MIDI*. MIDI's special files do not really contain sound. Instead, MIDI is a special control protocol that musical instruments use to record and play back sound. Most sound cards today have the capability to record and play back MIDI sounds. The advantage of this technology is that MIDI files tend to be very small. Thus MIDI background music across the Internet became not only possible, but MIDI brought the first really useful sounds to the Internet.

But MIDI does have one a huge limitation. MIDI limits you to sounds that your sound card can generate. You may not, therefore, hear the same sounds that you record but, instead, a reasonable facsimile. You also can't hear sounds (such as voices) that a MIDI-compatible instrument can't create.

An even newer technology than MIDI now enables you to hear sound files that previously were too large to reasonably download and play. This technology, available for both audio and video, is called *streaming*. A file of any type that you stream across the network "plays" (or processes) while the file continues to download. So instead of waiting for an entire file to download and write to a file on your machine before you can listen to its sounds, you can now begin listening nearly immediately, as the data transfers from the source to your computer.

Purchasing a higher-quality microphone is a good investment if you're provikqng audio content from your site. In the same way that professionally produced graphics give your site a quality look and feel, professional-sounding audio also leaves a good impression of your organization. Upgrading your microphone is a small price to pay for quality.

An additional piece of equipment that can add to the quality of your sound recording is a mixer. A *mixer* is a piece of sound equipment that recording studios and live performers use to better control the sound coming from musical instruments and microphones. Mixers can have many features. The basic mixer has a place to plug in one or more microphones or musical instruments and has some sort of output plug. At a minimum, you should look for a mixer with two microphone inputs and a stereo output.

You can use mixers with added features to enhance the quality of sounds you send to your sound card. A basic mixer that we use, a Radio Shack SSM-100 stereo sound mixer, also includes an equalizer. This feature enables you to boost certain frequencies while reducing the signal of other, less-desirable, frequencies. This inexpensive mixer also features fader controls that enable you to fade from one channel into the next. This control is useful for disc-jockey-type use of the mixer.

Internet Broadcasting

Internet audio broadcasting is becoming an important new wave in entertainment. With the equipment that we recommend in the preceding section and additional music inputs, such as a CD player, you can create your own Internet audio-broadcasting channel.

No laws currently govern the use of the Internet as a broadcast medium. Our hope is that people use this powerful capability to broadcast globally for little or no money. Don't let the big companies that are already in the conventional broadcast markets become the companies that end up controlling this medium as well. Make certain, however, that you comply with any licensing requirements before you embark on an Internet-broadcasting career.

Network Fax Servers

Fax has become a household word. Almost every business now has a fax machine; most modems are now fax/modems; and many people have fax machines at home, in their cars, and built into their cellular phones. Networks and the Internet have taken fax technology, which was already a great idea, and made it even better.

FaxBack, Inc., a spinoff of Intel, offers network fax solutions. You can find the company's Web page at the following URL:

```
http://www.faxback.com/
```

Some people believe that Internet documnet delivery may one day do away with the need for fax machines. This belief may or may not be accurate. In any event, the fax machine isn't going away soon — fax-machine use still far outweighs personal-computer use. The interesting thing is that fax server technology now enables pople who have no computer to view the contents of the World Wide Web. Fax-on-demand systems, which are becoming popular for corporate delivery of public information, can also deliver fax Web pages on demand. You use a touch-tone phone to select the Web page that you want, and the page comes directly to your fax machine.

Internet fax servers

Fax technology has had one major drawback, in that it's long been tied to the conventional phone system. Every fax that you send gets billed at the normal phone charge. International business phone charges have decreased, because information has been condensed into a fax that's often transmitted in less than a minute's time. Still, sending a fax requires making an international long-distance phone call.

Systems called Internet fax servers route faxes across the Internet, rather than through the public phone system. Any computer that you connect to the Internet can send a fax anywhere in the world through a fax server. The fax server in the remote location can deliver the fax via the network or dial a local phone number and then deliver the fax to a conventional fax machine.

Network delivery of fax documents enables a wide range of add-on capabilities, such as these:

- Fax mailboxes
- Storing and forwarding of fax documents
- Document-type conversion
- Encrypted (secure) delivery
- Registered delivery and document tracking

The savings in fax delivery alone are enough to make this Internet-site technology one of the most useful imaginable.

Network Modems

If your company has an investment in several computers that connect on a network, you can probably find a way to improve the cost-effectiveness of your computer system. Several of the computers on the network, for example, probably have modems, either internally or via serial attachments to external modems. Each computer that has a modem then connects to an external phone line — one that probably doesn't go through the company's phone system.

But your network can easily support a single modem that you connect not to a computer, but to the network itself. With such a setup, any computer on the network can access to the modem, which itself connects to a single phone line.

We tested the Shiva NetModem E and found the device to be an effective network tool — one that we recommend to anyone who has a network and modems. We calculate that you can save about $1,120 the first year — you don't need to purchase a modem for every computer on the network, and you realize annual savings from running a single phone line. (You can buy two network computers for that amount of money.) You not only save money by going this route, but also overcome future limitations and costs.

For more information, contact Shiva at the following URL:

```
http://www.shiva.com/
```

Citrix WinServer

Throughout this book, we discuss fat and skinny clients, and explain how applications that take advantage of skinny clients are more efficient and easier to maintain than those that require fat clients.

A program called Citrix WinServer (or WinFrame Server), based on Windows NT, enables you to run almost any Windows program within a skinny client. Imagine running a large accounting program — not simply a Web front end for an accounting program, but the actual accounting program — from within a Web browser. WinServer enables you to provide client/server and your old legacy software remotely through a Web browser.

If you need to run applications from your Web browser, Internet Explorer automatically loads the appropriate ActiveX control; Netscape Navigator requires you to load and install the Citrix plug-in to do so.

The exciting part is that you don't need to wait for your application to load across the network before you run the application. By using the Citrix ICA technology, you transfer only keyboard commands, mouse movements, and display data across the network. In other words, you see the display information as the server sends it, and you can respond to the data by using your own keyboard and mouse.

By using remote node functionality (capability to connect to a remote server), based on the Windows NT Remote Access Server system, WinFrame Server delivers access to all network applications and network resources across a dial-up connection as though the remote node were directly connected to the network. You can set up applications to run remotely or locally on your machine. You can quickly switch between remote and local applications by using a hot key.

The WinFrame Server supports remote access from thousands of remote clients. This capability enables your company to set up a powerful telecommuting system, as well as to support traveling executives, sales-people, and support people.

```
http://www.citrix.com/
```

PointCast I-Server

PointCast was one of the first (and best) Internet information services. The PointCast service uses a publish-and-subscribe model, making PointCast an extremely useful news service. By using publish-and-subscribe, you no longer need to go surfing around looking for information. Instead, you can download news, weather information (with maps), several magazines, market information, and more right to your desktop. Even if you aren't running the PointCast client application, you can use the PointCast screen saver, which continually displays updated news.

The PointCast I-Server is an excellent add-on to your Internet site.

Setting up and maintaining I-Server is easy. The server works closely with the Windows NT Internet Information Server. One of the setup procedures configures your Internet Information Web server to use two of the special administrative I-Server directories.

For more information about the PointCast I-Server, go to the following Web site:

```
http://www.pointcast.com/
```

Macromedia Flash

In the first edition of this book, we called Macromedia Director an important piece of software for creating a multimedia Web site. Macromedia now has a new product that's similar to Director, yet much simpler. Macromedia Flash enables you to create powerful interactive Shockwave multimedia content. Shockwave is the Macromedia player that enables viewers to view content in a Web page. Shockwave content includes animations, graphics, and special interactive objects that do your bidding whenever someone clicks those objects in a Web page.

You may think that something this fancy in your Web page may take a long time to load over a slow modem connection, but it doesn't. By using special vector technology that keeps your files small, and because your files stream over the Internet, your animations begin playing immediately. And the Shockwave Flash client is free to anyone who wants to view the Flash content in your Web pages.

For more information contact the Macromedia home page, check out the following URL:

```
http://www.macromedia.com/
```

Appendix

About the CD-ROM

● ●

*T*he *Setting Up An Internet Site For Dummies* CD-ROM contains some of the software that we feature in this book. The CD also contains additional tools that you, as a site builder, may find valuable. You find software for both Windows 95 and Macintosh on the CD. The CD also comes with a table of contents in the form of an HTML document.

CD-ROM and software compilation copyright © 1997 IDG Books Worldwide, Inc. All rights reserved. Individual programs are copyrighted by their respective owners and may require separate licensing. This CD-ROM may not be distributed without prior written permission from the publishers. The IDG Books Worldwide logo, ---- For Dummies, ...For Dummies, Dummies Man, and Software for the Rest of Us! are trademarks under exclusive license to IDG Books Worldwide, Inc., from International Data Group, Inc.

System Requirements

Make sure that your Apple Macintosh or compatible meets the following system requirements for using this CD:

- ✔ A computer with a 68030, 68040, or PowerPC processor.

- ✔ System software Version 7.1 or higher (System 7.5 is recommended).

- ✔ A CD-ROM drive — double-speed (2x) or faster.

- ✔ At least 4MB of free RAM for most programs. (*Free RAM* is the amount of memory available to the Mac if no other programs are running. You can check your available memory by clicking the Apple menu in the Finder and choosing About This Macintosh.) In some cases, turning on virtual memory helps if you're a little short of memory, but some demos may run erratically.

- ✔ A monitor capable of displaying at least 256 colors or grayscale.

- ✔ A modem with a speed of at least 14,400 bps.

- ✔ At least 200MB of hard drive space available to install all the software from this CD. (You need less space if you don't install every program.)

PC users should meet the following system requirements for using this CD:

- ✔ Windows 3.x (that is, 3.1 or 3.11), Windows 95, or Windows NT installed on your computer.
- ✔ If you're running Windows 3.x: a 386sx or faster processor with *at least* 8MB of total RAM.
- ✔ If you're running Windows 95 or Windows NT: a 486 or faster processor with *at least* 8MB of total RAM.
- ✔ At least 200MB of hard drive space available to install all the software from this CD. (You need less space if you don't install every program.)
- ✔ A CD-ROM drive — double-speed (2x) or faster.
- ✔ A sound card with speakers.
- ✔ A monitor capable of displaying at least 256 colors or grayscale.
- ✔ A modem with a speed of at least 14,400 bps.

If you need more information on PC or Windows basics, check out *PCs For Dummies,* 4th Edition, by Dan Gookin; *Windows 95 For Dummies,* 2nd Edition, by Andy Rathbone; or *Windows 3.11 For Dummies,* 3rd Edition, by Andy Rathbone (all published by IDG Books Worldwide, Inc.).

Installation Instructions

Use your Web browser to open the file INDEX.HTM to view the CD-ROM's table of contents.

In Windows 95, you can navigate directly to the software that you want to install from the CD-ROM by clicking the directory links in the table of contents. If you click the LISTSERV Lite hyperlink, for example, your Web browser shows you the contents of the LISTSERV directory.

If you double-click the 95 folder icon shown in the LISTSERV directory, Windows 95 opens the folder and displays its contents. You can now double-click the SETUP.EXE icon to install the software on your computer.

You can also use the Windows 95 Explorer to access the contents of the CD just as you can any other CD. Just open the drive and view its files and folders as you do any other CD.

We designed the *Setting Up An Internet Site For Dummies* CD-ROM to work on either a Macintosh or a Windows 95 computer. If you use the CD-ROM on a Macintosh, you can't access the Windows 95 files, and if you use the CD-ROM on a Windows 95 computer, you can't access the Macintosh files.

If you insert the *Setting Up An Internet Site For Dummies* CD-ROM into a Macintosh computer, the Finder automatically opens the Setting Up a 'Net Site folder. You can view the CD-ROM table of contents HTML document by double-clicking INDEX.HTM in the Finder.

The CD-ROM table of contents gives you an overview of the folders and files available in the Macintosh version of the CD, but because of differences in how Macintosh Web browsers navigate the CD, you can't go right to the Macintosh software by using your Web browser. Instead, you must go back to the Finder to access the contents of the CD.

If you find software on the CD-ROM that you want to install, return to the Macintosh Finder. Navigate to the CD-ROM folder that contains the software you want to install, just as you'd navigate to any other folder on your Macintosh by using the Finder.

In addition to software for the Macintosh and Windows 95, the *Setting Up An Internet Site For Dummies* CD-ROM contains copies of Web pages that the nonprofit research and development laboratory `science.org` created. These pages list resources for Web site builders. Scroll to the bottom of the table of contents HTML document to see links to the site builder resource pages.

We hope that you enjoy the book and CD-ROM and that your site-building projects are a success!

Installing Support Software

Before you can use this CD, you need to have a Web browser installed. You use your Web browser to access the list of files on the CD.

To install a Web browser you need to download a version from the Internet or purchase a browser at a local software store. As most folks normally use Web browsers to download software, you need to use a file transfer program to download the browser itself — Fetch, if you're using a Macintosh, or FTP, if you're using a PC. You can access the Netscape FTP site and find several versions of Netscape Navigator in the /PUB/NAVIGATOR directory. Follow these steps:

1. **Access the Netscape FTP site by using an FTP client program and connect to** `ftp.netscape.com`.

2. **Change the directory to /PUB/NAVIGATOR.**

3. **Select a version of Navigator by choosing a directory that displays the browser version number that you want to download.**

4. **Change directories to the directory containing the version you want and then download the file that you find in that directory.**

5. Use the Run utility in Windows to run the program you download, and Netscape Navigator installs on your hard drive.

You can now use Netscape Navigator to access the INDEX.HTML file that you find on the CD.

What You Find

The following sections describe the software that you find on the book's CD-ROM and tell you on which computer systems these programs can run.

Software for PCs running Microsoft Windows

CyberMailer Pro, by Insanely Great Software (CBRMAILR directory): A simple utility for sending e-mail to lists of recipients.

LISTSERV Lite, by L-Soft (LISTSERV directory): A free, limited version of the classic electronic mailing list server program, ported to Windows 95/NT.

Internet Watch Dog, by Netwin LTD (NETWIN directory): An automated Internet services monitor.

SLMail, by Seattle Lab (SLMAIL directory): A full e-mail server program for Windows 95/NT.

WildCat! Interactive Net Server, by Mustang Software (WILDCAT directory): A complete Internet/intranet BBS solution.

WFTPD, by Alun Jones/Texas Imperial Software (WFTPD directory): An FTP server for Windows 95/NT.

Software for Apple Macintosh and compatible computers

Adobe **PageMill 1.0 Tryout** (PageMill 1.0 Tryout folder): Version 1.0 of the popular Mac Web page creation program. (Optionally, you can download the new PageMill 2.0 Tryout from Adobe.)

Bare Bones Software's **BBEdit Lite 4.0** (BBEdit Lite 4.0 extractor): A handy freeware text editor useful for HTML. A demo of the commercially available BBEdit 4.0 is also available on the CD.

Stairways Software's **NetPresenz 4.1**: A useful FTP server program for Macintosh. (Formerly named "FTPd.")

Software for both Apple Macintosh and Microsoft Windows systems

Claris **Home Page 2.0 Trial** (CLARIS directory [Windows] or Claris Home Page 2.0 Trial [Mac]): A solid Web page creation tool for both Macintosh and Windows. This trial version is fully functional for 30-days.

Pegasus Mail by David Harris (PEGASUS directory [Windows] or Pegasus Mail self-extractor [Mac]): A friendly and very popular e-mail client program for Windows and Macintosh.

FirstClass by SoftArc, Inc. (SOFTARC directory [Windows] or FirstClass Evaluation Folder [Mac]): A BBS package for Windows or Macintosh.

If You've Got Problems (Of the CD Kind)

The programs we include on the CD should install without problems. If you have problems installing any of the programs, we suggest that you visit the Web page of the software creator first. On the CD, you find links to all the Web pages. If you visit the software creator's Web page, you can normally find a list of system requirements. Make sure that your computer meets these requirements.

If you're running several programs at the same time, try shutting down all other programs and reinstalling the software. Running too many programs at the same time may consume all available memory. If you regularly run many programs at the same time, you may want to consider adding additional RAM (Memory) to your computer. Contact your local computer store for more information on adding additional memory to your computer.

If you still have trouble with installing the items from the CD, please call the IDG Books Worldwide Customer Service phone number: 800-762-2974 (or outside the U.S.: 317-596-5261).

Index

(continued)

(continued)

• O •

• P •

Notes

Notes

Notes

Notes

IDG BOOKS WORLDWIDE, INC.
END-USER LICENSE AGREEMENT

4. **Restrictions on Use of Individual Programs.** You must follow the individual requirements and restrictions detailed for each individual program in the Appendix of this Book. These limitations are contained in the individual license agreements recorded on the disk(s)/CD-ROM. These restrictions may include a requirement that after using the program for the period of time specified in its text, the user must pay a registration fee or discontinue use. By opening the Software packet(s), you will be agreeing to abide by the licenses and restrictions for these individual programs. None of the material on this disk(s) or listed in this Book may ever be distributed, in original or modified form, for commercial purposes.

5. **Limited Warranty.**

   (a) IDGB warrants that the Software and disk(s)/CD-ROM are free from defects in materials and workmanship under normal use for a period of sixty (60) days from the date of purchase of this Book. If IDGB receives notification within the warranty period of defects in materials or workmanship, IDGB will replace the defective disk(s)/CD-ROM.

   (b) IDGB AND THE AUTHORS OF THE BOOK DISCLAIM ALL OTHER WARRANTIES, EXPRESS OR IMPLIED, INCLUDING WITHOUT LIMITATION IMPLIED WARRANTIES OF MERCHANTABILITY AND FITNESS FOR A PARTICULAR PURPOSE, WITH RESPECT TO THE SOFTWARE, THE PROGRAMS, THE SOURCE CODE CONTAINED THEREIN, AND/OR THE TECHNIQUES DESCRIBED IN THIS BOOK. IDGB DOES NOT WARRANT THAT THE FUNCTIONS CONTAINED IN THE SOFTWARE WILL MEET YOUR REQUIREMENTS OR THAT THE OPERATION OF THE SOFTWARE WILL BE ERROR FREE.

   (c) This limited warranty gives you specific legal rights, and you may have other rights which vary from jurisdiction to jurisdiction.

6. **Remedies.**

   (a) IDGB's entire liability and your exclusive remedy for defects in materials and workmanship shall be limited to replacement of the Software, which may be returned to IDGB with a copy of your receipt at the following address: Disk Fulfillment Department, Attn: Setting Up An Internet Site For Dummies, IDG Books Worldwide, Inc., 7260 Shadeland Station, Ste. 100, Indianapolis, IN 46256, or call 1-800-762-2974. Please allow 3–4 weeks for delivery. This Limited Warranty is void if failure of the Software has resulted from accident, abuse, or misapplication. Any replacement Software will be warranted for the remainder of the original warranty period or thirty (30) days, whichever is longer.

(b) In no event shall IDGB or the author be liable for any damages whatsoever (including without limitation damages for loss of business profits, business interruption, loss of business information, or any other pecuniary loss) arising from the use of or inability to use the Book or the Software, even if IDGB has been advised of the possibility of such damages.

(c) Because some jurisdictions do not allow the exclusion or limitation of liability for consequential or incidental damages, the above limitation or exclusion may not apply to you.

7. **U.S. Government Restricted Rights.** Use, duplication, or disclosure of the Software by the U.S. Government is subject to restrictions stated in paragraph (c) (1) (ii) of the Rights in Technical Data and Computer Software clause of DFARS 252.227-7013, and in subparagraphs (a) through (d) of the Commercial Computer— Restricted Rights clause at FAR 52.227-19, and in similar clauses in the NASA FAR supplement, when applicable.

8. **General.** This Agreement constitutes the entire understanding of the parties and revokes and supersedes all prior agreements, oral or written, between them and may not be modified or amended except in a writing signed by both parties hereto which specifically refers to this Agreement. This Agreement shall take precedence over any other documents that may be in conflict herewith. If any one or more provisions contained in this Agreement are held by any court or tribunal to be invalid, illegal, or otherwise unenforceable, each and every other provision shall remain in full force and effect.

Installation Instructions

Use your Web browser to open the file INDEX.HTM to view the CD-ROM's table of contents.

In Windows 95, you can navigate directly to the software that you want to install from the CD-ROM by clicking the directory links in the table of contents. If you click the LISTSERV Lite hyperlink, for example, your Web browser shows you the contents of the LISTSERV directory.

If you double-click the 95 folder icon shown in the LISTSERV directory, Windows 95 opens the folder and displays its contents. You can now double-click the SETUP.EXE icon to install the software on your computer.

You can also use the Windows 95 Explorer to access the contents of the CD just as you can any other CD. Just open the drive and view its files and folders as you do any other CD.

We designed the *Setting Up An Internet Site For Dummies* CD-ROM to work on either a Macintosh or a Windows 95 computer. If you use the CD-ROM on a Macintosh, you can't access the Windows 95 files, and if you use the CD-ROM on a Windows 95 computer, you can't access the Macintosh files.

If you insert the *Setting Up An Internet Site For Dummies* CD-ROM into a Macintosh computer, the Finder automatically opens the Setting Up a 'Net Site folder. You can view the CD-ROM table of contents HTML document by double-clicking INDEX.HTM in the Finder.

The CD-ROM table of contents gives you an overview of the folders and files available in the Macintosh version of the CD, but because of differences in how Macintosh Web browsers navigate the CD, you can't go right to the Macintosh software by using your Web browser. Instead, you must go back to the Finder to access the contents of the CD.

If you find software on the CD-ROM that you want to install, return to the Macintosh Finder. Navigate to the CD-ROM folder that contains the software you want to install, just as you'd navigate to any other folder on your Macintosh by using the Finder.

In addition to software for the Macintosh and Windows 95, the *Setting Up An Internet Site For Dummies* CD-ROM contains copies of Web pages that the nonprofit research and development laboratory science.org created. These pages list resources for Web site builders. Scroll to the bottom of the table of contents HTML document to see links to the site builder resource pages.

We hope that you enjoy the book and CD-ROM and that your site-building projects are a success!